DATA TRAILS

CONTENTS & CREDITS

First Printing by Catalyst Game Labs, an imprint of InMediaRes Productions, LLC
PMB 202 • 303 -91st Ave. NE, E-502
Lake Stevens, WA 98258

Find us online:
info@shadowruntabletop.com
(*Shadowrun* questions)
http://www.shadowruntabletop.com
(Catalyst *Shadowrun* website)
http://www.shadowrun.com
(official *Shadowrun Universe* website)
http://www.catalystgamelabs.com
(Catalyst website)
http://shop.catalystgamelabs.com
(Catalyst/Shadowrun orders)

INTRODUCTION

Lots of classic adventure stories talk about fantastic realms, weird kingdoms full of wonders and hidden dangers, where one of the prime risks of being entranced by the sights around you is that you'll be too distracted to notice the death about to lunge out of the shadows.

One of the great things about the Sixth World is that everyone carries around such a realm right in their pocket.

The Matrix is the vast, wild, and wooly frontier, an infinite land of secrets, oddities, and sensations that will make you forget that none of it is physically real. This being the Sixth World, it is also full of things that can kill you.

The great attraction of the Matrix, of course, is that every great secret in the world has been on it at some point. Most, if not all of those secrets are still there, buried deep in the vast anomaly known as the Resonance realms. The power and the information the Matrix contains makes it attractive to shadowrunners, who are always willing to risk a little brain fry if it means obtaining a small piece of power and a few nuyen to help them live unfettered for one more day.

Data Trails offers expanded information and rules for using the Matrix in *Shadowrun*, providing new options for existing characters, new ways to create Matrix-based characters, and a whole lot of information and tools to make the Matrix- based parts of your games even more entertaining. Specifically, here's what you'll find:

The World in Your Pocket provides an overview of how the Matrix is used in the current *Shadowrun* setting and information on how different groups of people are responding to the new design.

True Hackers, Lusers, and Dirtballs is a glimpse into hacker culture—what motivates them, how they deal with each other, the different ways they can help on a Shadowrun, and some of the organizations and tribes that bring them together.

On the Bleeding Edge offers new qualities for characters with a Matrix emphasis.

Born to Hack presents decker- and technomancer-based life modules for use with the Life Module Character Creation system outlined in *Run Faster*.

Killer Apps and Razor Forms presents new programs and complex forms for the denizens of the Matrix.

The Guts of the Matrix offers new gear, including new cyberdecks and ways to customize your commlink.

The All-Seeing GOD contains a briefing on the hard-hitting security forces of the new Matrix, with outlines of some of the differences between security at various megacorporations and sample security NPCs.

The Perfect Host offers more details on the immersive world of hosts in the Matrix, with detailed examples of several host archetypes.

Deeper and Deeper sets up deep Matrix runs for players, giving them the chance to bring the whole team into untamed areas where they can pit their wits against feral data.

Principles of Insanity covers the bizarre fringes of the Matrix—artificial intelligences, e-ghosts, dissonant technomancers, and more. It also discusses using AIs as player characters.

Mastering the Matrix offers advice on different ways to integrate Matrix work into *Shadowrun* campaigns, along with plot hooks to get you going.

Nothing could ever cover everything there is to know about the Matrix, but with the essentials in this book, you'll be ready for some of the wildest, strangest campaigns the Sixth World has to offer.

DATA TRAILS CREDITS

Writing: Jason Andrew, Raymond Croteau, Olivier Gagnon, Jason M. Hardy, Aaron Pavao, Scott Schletz, Dylan Stangel, CZ Wright

Editing: Jason M. Hardy, Andrew Marshall

Proofing/Playtesting: Thomas Baatz, Forrest Bedke, Brooke Chang, Bruce Ford, Joanna Fournes, Eugen Fournes, Grant Gajdosik, Sandy Gamboa, Mason Hart, Pete Houtekier, Alex Kadar, David Dashifen Kees, Holly Lausmann, Keith Menzies, Jeff "Plotnikon" Plotnikoff, Jimmy Reckitt, Carl Schelin, Frank Sjodin, Jacki Unger, Jeremy Weyand

Art Direction: Brent Evans

Cover Art: Mark Poole

Art: Piotr Arendzikowski, Gordon Bennetto, Joel Biske, Victor Perez Corbella, Laura Diaz Cubas, Igor Fiorentini, Benjamin Giletti, Katy Grierson, Phil Hilliker, David Hovey, Kgor Kieryluk, Victor Manuel Leza Moreno, Mauro Peroni, Kristen Plescow, Rob Ruffolo, Marc Sintes, David Sondered, Eric Williams, Erich Vasburg

Cover Layout: Matt "Wrath" Heerdt

Iconography: Nigel Sade

Interior Layout: Matt "Wrath" Heerdt

Shadowrun Line Developer: Jason M. Hardy

GOD SPEAKS

Lurker's heart pounded. He crouched within a clump of kelp on the bottom of the ocean floor and yanked with trembling fingers on the chain that locked him into the host. He knew the intrusion countermeasures were nearby, but he couldn't see them. The pressure gauge on his wetsuit pointed toward the red, indicating Grid Overwatch Division knew his location. He should have been kicked out of the host, bleeding from biofeedback damage. He should have been dueling IC to the death. Instead he was hiding. Anchored to the bottom of the ocean, crushed by his phobia of being underwater. This had been a straightforward job. What the frag had gone sideways?

The meat-world view of the inside of a van shrank away and blinked out at the same time the crisp, clean, vibrant lines of virtual reality shot forward to encompass the hackers. The host, a massive yacht, drifted on unseen waves before them. The stamp on the hull displayed the logo of the corp whose exploration division would soon be missing one file, provided all went well.

The rigger, serving as mastermind for the evening, patched the two hackers and the rest of the team into a tac-

tical network. Numbers flared and faded out in their shared view: "3, 2, 1, Go!"

With a flick of his wrist, the elf threw a pair of red marks that looked like a rubber-stamp of the word "Approved" on the host and slipped in. Once inside, he gasped; his persona, along with everything else here, floated. *Some drekhead built this place with an underwater theme.* He scowled as he surveyed the surroundings and took deep breaths, trying to calm his increasing panic. The already deep lines on his face creased more, and he ran a hand through his pale hair in aggravation.

Next to him, a young human slipped into the host and nodded to himself. A scuba wetsuit zipped up from his feet to his head, corralling his mop of shaggy dark red hair. His perpetual grin disappeared behind a snorkel and regulator.

"Hey, suit up before someone sees you," the young man said to the elf.

The elf started. "Right," he said, and a replacement icon in scuba gear folded over his persona as if swiped over him by an invisible hand. "Sorry," he muttered. *Underwater,* he thought to himself. *Why did it have to be underwater?*

Water—or the digital appearance of water—was everywhere. Colorful schools of fish darted past drone submersibles, snorkelers swam slowly by, and a cluster of nattering

BY C2 VVRIGHT

merfolk passed through an arch of coral with the words "Archangel's Cathedral" spelled out in bright anemone. Lights and music pouring out of the arch identified it as the local social media hangout. Past the din, wide disks of beige coral covered an expanse of sea floor, and giant fronds of kelp stretched up out of sight.

"Come on," the elf said. "Let's find the cameras."

The two swam forward into the green water. The younger one said, "You know, I hate to say it, but—"

"Then don't say it," the elf snapped. "You might call yourself 'Kid,' but you don't have to act like one."

"What I was saying," the Kid said, unconcerned, "is that this seems pretty straightforward. Clear the team in meatspace: cameras, locks, alarms. The team gets in by the servers and plugs in a tap. We jump in, grab the paydata, and we all get the hell out of here. Okay, we're talking about AA-corporation's property here, but it's pretty straightforward."

The elf scowled and called up his agent program. A thinner duplicate of the decker, nearly skeletal in his fine suit, dark glasses, and trench coat, gathered into focus from the surrounding data.

Agent Birdwatcher said, "What may I do for you, Lurker?" The elf winced at the name.

"Hey, I've heard of you!" the Kid said.

"Keep me apprised on the communications coming in and out of Security," Lurker said. "Notify me if there's trouble."

The agent gave a curt nod and disappeared. Lurker spared the Kid a glance. "It's not by choice. That's the problem with names. People remember them." He spotted a submarine nearby and nodded toward it. "Let's go."

"Nothing wrong with people remembering who you are," the Kid said with a grin.

Lurker shook his head. "You're a hell of a lot safer if no one can find you."

"Suit yourself," the Kid said. "I think it's better if they know what's coming. Maybe it'll make them think twice before messing with you."

They swam toward the submarine, and Lurker checked his gear. The dial on his pressure gauge indicated their slowly rising overwatch score. If the dial reached the red, the Grid Overwatch Division, or GOD, would bring the hammer down, ejecting them from the Matrix. Law enforcement would pick up their dumpshock-addled meat bodies moments later. The watch on his wrist showed the real time their team would follow in meat space. This *was* a straightforward job, though thinking as much rankled him.

camera controls, was the first target. They spotted some patrol IC in the form of anglerfish, hideous with their giant lower jaw, spines, and rows of long teeth. Instead of bioluminescence glowing off the dorsal spine that hung in front of their faces, a searchlight shone slowly back and forth. The fish drifted past, taking no notice of a couple of personas running silent. The men boarded the submarine.

They sat in the seats at the control console. Lurker pulled up the feed from the cameras with the team in meat space. The Kid waved his hand across a control panel, and the map of the facility glowed into view, complete with icons representing the team members' positions, cameras, locked doors, and anticipated security routes. Lurker set his hand down on the map display and pulled it free like a sheet of film. He threw it forward into the air and it clung to space, visible to them both.

Rooster, the team's covert ops specialist, was on point. His icon crept down the hallway. The Kid stuck his finger into a view screen and made a spinning motion. The image swirled like a tiny tornado, clinging to his finger as he pulled it away. It stretched out a few centimeters and then snapped back from his hand onto the screen, settling into a two-minute loop of empty hallway. Rooster led the team past, unseen and unrecorded.

Lurker turned a key a quarter-turn to the left, and the accompanying maglock on the door ahead of the team shone green.

"Hold," Lurker sent over the network. A guard meandered into camera view on the other side of the door. His head swung back and forth in a cursory scan, and he exited the room. "Go," Lurker said.

The last runner's boot disappeared inside the room, and the door closed with a soft "shush" just as the guard rounded the corner and wandered into the hall. The Kid snapped his fingers over the view screen and it returned to normal recording. They watched the guard stroll past on the feed.

For minutes they leapfrogged looping cameras, unlocking doors, and keeping automatic alarms silent as the team moved deeper into the facility. Two of them working in the Matrix made the job go much faster.

"We're getting a little warm," Lurker said, showing the Kid their overwatch score displayed on the dial of the pressure gauge.

"I got it covered," the Kid said. He stared at the gauge for a moment and the dial moved backward, easing the heat.

"Good work," the elf said. They watched the team approach a pair of heavy doors. "Last one," he murmured. Three stamps of approval, and the door lock was his. The lock shone the green light of entry, and the team disappeared into the server room. There was nothing to do but wait for the team to connect the dataline tap to the proper server.

They exited the submarine and hid in a nearby cluster of coral. A figure in scuba gear swam their direction.

"Spider," Lurker whispered, pointing out the figure.

The figure switched on a flashlight, and several anglerfish joined him as he scanned the submarine. Beams of light the hackers sat motionless. After a few moments the flashlight beam switched off, and the security spider swam away into the dark. The anglerfish drifted off aimlessly.

Lurker let out a breath. His eyes swept the area and noticed a new feature. A massive trench had appeared in the sea floor. A huge cloud of bubbles rose out of it, and he found himself beginning to hyperventilate. He took advantage of the distraction to still his breathing. *Pull it together!*

Jagged, broken masts rose from the trench, followed by the ruined shell of an immense eighteenth-century man-of-war. The shipwreck shouldn't have held together for all its damage, but there it was, looming before them.

"There's the archive. That's where we'll find our payday," the Kid said. Together they swam into the wreck.

Thin shafts of grainy light warbled through the holes in the structure, providing the thinnest of illumination, but when they found the target it was as visible as if hit with a spotlight. A wooden chest bound in shining metal gleamed at the base of a short ladder in the belly of the vessel. Lurker pulled a set of long picks out of a wrap attached to his belt and started work on the lock.

Agent Birdwatcher materialized. "Chatter indicates Security is aware of your presence," it said.

"Frag," Lurker said. The top of the chest swung open, revealing a fat paper file bound with a chunky lock. A muffled "thunk" sound spun them around in time to see a creature—with the head and front legs of a lion and the body of a large fish—flail back from the recoil of a blunderbuss roughly as large as it was. A bola of anchors and chains spun past Lurker's head, and he dove for cover.

"Crack that file!" Lurker ordered Agent Birdwatcher. Lurker's arm waved in a downward sweep toward the sea lion. Two cannonballs catapulted out of nowhere toward the creature; one connected, momentarily smashing its tail but otherwise doing no damage.

"Get him, Spike!" the Kid shouted, and a dog materialized in mid-leap at a wave of his hand. The beagle, which appeared to have abnormally large teeth, dove at the sea lion and took a large chunk out of its side.

The creature fired again, narrowly missing Lurker. With a grunt, the elf leapt up and brandished a short sword glistening with blue binary code. Lurker landed, and the sword sunk into the sea lion's back. It exploded into data streams that quickly dissolved into the surrounding water.

A fleshy tentacle smacked into and around Agent Birdwatcher's neck. Lurker swore and shut down the agent program. He typically wasn't seen and was unaccustomed to fending off intrusion countermeasures; he didn't need to defend his 'deck on two fronts. Birdwatcher faded into nothingness, and Lurker found and removed the marks the attack left.

The Kid's hand made a twisting motion toward the approaching creature, a dark green humanoid with black eyes and tentacles covering the space where its nose and mouth should have been. It twisted like a sponge being wrung-out, and when it returned to normal, its formerly beefy body sagged, emaciated under the effects of the technomancer's Resonance.

Lurker dove toward the lock on the file, but a tentacle wrapped itself around his leg, yanking him backward. Close examination revealed two sucker marks on his suit. "Shit!" he swore, and then scrubbed them both off.

The Kid rolled his hands together, and Spike dug in the ground at the Kid's feet. Blue threads gathered themselves into a ball, growing thicker and denser with their actions. The Kid hurled the ball at the tentacled creature, and it flew over and bounced just short, kicking up sand and debris from the sea floor into a cloud of noise around the creature, completely obscuring it within. Blood trickled from the Kid's nose.

Another sea lion dropped into their midst, aiming its blunderbuss at Lurker. With a muffled boom, the bola's chain slammed into his legs, wrapping itself around them with its momentum. Panic seized Lurker's throat as the anchors locked him to the sea floor. *It's not real, fragger! Keep it together*, the more rational part of his brain screamed. His lizard brain, though, was having trouble listening.

Wide-eyed, he flailed the short sword at the sea lion, but it easily dodged the shot.

Spike barked wildly at the sea lion; each bark materialized into a small pulse of electricity. The pulses multiplied, striking the sea lion and obscuring it from view. A two-meter-long shark darted out of nowhere and head-butted Spike in the side. The dog exploded in a burst of data streams and pixels. The pulses surrounding the sea lion disappeared, and it aimed its blunderbuss at the Kid.

The tentacled creature and the cloud surrounding it disappeared, and a strange humming sound preceded the appearance of a thin, pale-green humanoid in the tentacled creature's place. It had long, black, straggly hair, webbed, bone-like fingers, and it peered at the scene through yellow, glowing eyes. It pointed at Lurker, and a thin stream of pink stretched out from his persona into the gloom.

"Frag! I'm being traced," the elf said. He fought to keep his voice steady as the water pressure steadily increased. The anchor wasn't dragging him further underwater, but it felt that way. "Get the hell out of here and warn the others!" He found and scrubbed away the tracer's marks.

"I can't leave you in here," the Kid shot back, dodging a bola from the blunderbuss. He brought his fist down on the file's lock and it shattered.

"Do it! Take the file and get the hell out of here. I'll be right behind you!"

"Shit," the Kid said, and his persona disappeared with the file.

The bull shark launched through the space the Kid had occupied just a moment before. It pulled up short, then wheeled on Lurker. The elf dropped into a crouch, and the shark flew by overhead. Lurker took the opportunity to run. The anchor attached to his legs didn't restrict his him motion on the host, but without breaking the chain, he'd never be able to jack out. He dove into a cluster of kelp to hide.

He checked on the team. Through the network he could see footage of the team shooting their way out of the facility. The Kid's glasses caught a shot of the rigger's face contorting in horror as he heard the news that they'd been made. That camera view swerved sharply to the right, to the van door opening on a pack of figures in full security armor, automatic weapons trained toward the camera, flashpaks and a searchlight from a nearby armored truck nearly blinding the view altogether. There was shouting, a struggle, and both feed windows blinked out.

His pressure gauge needle pointed to the red. What more was there to do than wait? *Isn't that how you've stayed alive so long, coward?* His mouth twisted with disgust and sudden rage.

The IC had disappeared, no doubt searching the nearby area for him. The kelp's constant gentle swaying froze. Lurker's heart felt as though it stopped, too. The only movement was a shower of fine dust particles drifting down through the water, glimmering in the sunlight that shone in dappled lines on the ocean floor. As it drifted toward the ground, a section of dust in the middle seemed to fill an invisible mold. It took the dimensions of a human shape and slowly coalesced into a discernible form. A man stood there. He wore a pale fedora, black tie in a fine, gleaming fabric, and a crisp, double-breasted suit. A pocket square poked out from his breast pocket. His eyes fell unerringly on Lurker amidst the kelp, and his mouth broadened into a smile.

The man lowered himself to look Lurker in the eyes.

"You're coming with us. Don't worry about your meat. We've got it in a safe place." The man tore the chain in two as if it were no stronger than paper.

Lurker leapt out of the Matrix and back into his body. A heavy weight struck him on the head, and everything went black.

The decker had trouble distinguishing whether he was in virtual reality or meatspace. Maybe the seams of his dream were too hastily stitched onto the data entering his brain? But when the light hit his eyes, the pain that bloomed in his head gave him his answer. His hands were bound at his sides on some kind of bed. The man standing a couple of yards away looked as crisp and neat as his persona had in VR.

"You're awake," he said, "Good. Let's get on with this." He straightened his tie. "I trust you know who we are?" He waited for a moment. When Lurker said nothing, he continued. "This is a safe room under the jurisdiction of the Corporate Court. I work for the Grid Overwatch Division."

Lurker's stomach heaved. The whole universe spun around him.

"Allow me to be forthcoming. You're very good at what you do. We are very good at what we do, which is why you're here and not dead in the trash compactor." A brief smile flashed across his face. He lowered himself into a squatting position and ran a hand over the elf's hair. "Our terms are exceedingly simple: Work for us," his voice was nearly a whisper, "and we won't brick your brain."

THE WORLD IN YOUR POCKET

Andy Murano, draped in the kimono-clad samurai Matrix persona of his dad's Sensei, stood frozen in awe at the virtual world spread out before him.

He was normally limited to PubGrid access on his Meta Link, but dad had bought a new Sensei and had the one-month trial activated. He'd come out of his first trip raving about the corporate grid and starting to work out how he could adjust the budget to get permanent access.

Andy had only been on two grids in his twelve years of life. He always had the PubGrid and got to visit Seattle's Emerald City grid on a school field trip last year. He'd come home much like his father had, with a desire to get access to a better grid, but his dad crushed the idea with an iron fist. "Money's tight, and you'll just waste your time virtuexploring. The Public grid is good enough for you," he'd said. Andy made a short retort before his dad's cyberhand cocked back to his shoulder, backhand ready to meet backtalk.

But now was his opportunity to see something greater. Dad had crashed after an eighteen-hour stint of virtuexploring and would be out for hours. Andy had spent an hour trying to get his crappy trodes to link up with the fancy Sensei and eventually took the risk of pulling dad's trodes off his head. He didn't stir at all while Andy pulled the leads through his father's matted nest of dirty hair.

His body was in his closet with his favorite Seattle Screamers cap pushing down the ill-fitting leads into place on his head. His mind was in paradise.

Sprawling in every direction was a collage of strange sights that had Andy's virtual head darting back and forth in an effort to see everything all at once. He was holding his virtual breath, which could go on forever, but Andy felt another rush of heady exhilaration as he took in the exotic scents of Renraku's virtual realm. He couldn't even identify most of what he was seeing, but all of it was wonderful. A breeze brought a slight chill to his virtual skin. Walking the streets of Purity would have made him pull his coat in tighter, but here it was perfectly pleasant, as if a moment before he were just a touch too

warm and the stir of air was just what he needed. When the breeze stopped, he felt like the temperature was perfect.

He stood and took in the sensations for what seemed like forever before he realized he was wasting time, though no time spent here seemed like a waste to him. He just had so much to see. The whole world stretched out around him, one amazing sight after another.

He spotted a neat-looking little village full of small brick buildings and thought himself in that direction. Movement was amazing, a single jump over all intermediate places. He spotted other personas all over the virtual landscape and marveled at the variety.

An instant before his feet touched the ground the virtual world was suddenly stripped from him and replaced with sharp pain like a knife in his skull and a dull aching emptiness. He felt his physical self being pulled up, becoming weightless, and then bouncing off something soft, into something hard, and settling thankfully back onto the softness. He could hear sound that might have been words but they were sliced to ribbons by the knife in his head. He felt another wicked crack of pain, this one on the outside of his head, that helped him realize he was back in the real world and on the receiving end of a metal hand upside the head.

The blow cleared his ears enough to pick up the verbal snippets, "ever touch it again" and "eating paste forever," adding more clues to his situation. It seemed to take forever to finally fully grasp that he was back in his room, his father had woken and found him in the closet, and that the glory of Okoku was gone, a void in his life left in its place.

Andy glared through tears at the hazy light streaming in from the other room. Dad was probably back on Okoku, living a life the man didn't deserve in Andy's mind.

Thoughts and plans Andy had never considered began to grow in the back of his mind. Today, tomorrow, or, dare he be away so long, a week from now, he would get back to Okoku. He might have to trade his dad's life for the keys to the kingdom. It would be worth it.

OUR NEW
(VIRTUAL) REALITY

- We've had a little bit of time to get used to this new Matrix structure, so I think it's high time we get some insight from both those who've been wrestling with the new code and those living in the real world.

  We'll start with a little point-counterpoint, followed up with some solid opinion pieces, then a piece of corporate propaganda I found, trailed by a blurb on the methods we use to access the Matrix, and finishing up with a little informative grid guide for those without the means to take a look in advance.

  Comments are on, but keep in mind these are real people with real thoughts, not runners corrupted by the truth. These people are out in the world and using the Matrix for "normal" things. Not to sound like a hypocrite (though I have indeed been one quite often—such is the cost of raising a child), but it's not all about hacking. I feel the need to make sure even those visiting with just a 'link understand the virtual world around them.

- Bull

A NEWER, SAFER WORLD

BY DANIELLE DE LA MAR

Since the earliest tests in the city of Bogotá and on the Zurich-Orbital platform, the new Matrix protocols have proven themselves time and time again to create a safer, more secure, more reliable, better-connected, easier-to-access Matrix. The efforts and cooperation shown by the member corporations of the Corporate Court, heads of nations around the world, and individuals too numerous to name have ushered in a new era of Matrix safety unseen since the invention of ASIST technology. The new architects have taken the best aspects of each previous generation of Matrix technology, integrated them through extensive testing, called in hand-picked experts to test the integrity of the systems, and brought about the "Orichalcum Age" of life with the Matrix.

After years of abuse by hackers and grotesque manipulations by technomancers, emergent species, and AIs, our Matrix had been corrupted to an unimaginable extent. This twisted environment was a playground for social malcontents with little to no regard for the safety of the billions of legitimate users around the world. Hackers not only aggressively used but also freely distributed their programs, allowing anyone in the world with the desire to damage the very source code of the Matrix, often unwittingly, free rein in the virtual environment. Now, through a combination of incorruptible base-coding secured in the datavaults of Z-O, constant monitoring by the Grid Overwatch Division (GOD), and upgraded access tracking, the new Matrix protects authorized users from the abuses of virtual terrorists. Our new Matrix provides users with the safest place to do business, relax, connect with friends, and play all the Miracle Shooter™ they want.

When we look at the fears of the average citizen when asked about the Matrix, security is their chief concern nine times out of ten. The old system left everyone feeling vulnerable to hackers at every turn. The sudden shift to a wireless world was an economic boon, but the short-term money left the megacorporations focused on short-term gain, while they neglected to adequately preserve security. The rise of the commlink, an inconspicuous yet powerful processing system, allowed hackers to abuse the device and bend it to their nefarious ends. That is no longer the case. The new structure limits command acceptance from commlinks, keeping everyone protected from their abuse by hackers. This limitation is the smallest of the security features the new Matrix offers. At the other end, and truly one of the greatest features of our new Matrix, is the constant and precise monitoring of every corner of the grids by GOD and their duly authorized representatives. The grids are a great placid sea where the agents of GOD monitor every ripple created by unauthorized activity. A poetic expression, but the best way to describe the current environment without delving into several terabytes of technical data.

All the safety and security in the world means nothing if the system isn't available to you when you need it. Thanks to the cooperative efforts of the corporations involved, the new Matrix is the most reliable worldwide network to date. The last generation of wireless Matrix was built within a combination of the little boxes on the arms of everyone and the big boxes housed within the offices of the world's corporations and countries. It was a brilliant move to create a Matrix that was not based on a single or even a thousand machines, but instead on billions. Our Matrix takes that evolutionary baby step and moves us from *homo neanderthalensis* to *homo sapiens* with a Matrix that simply exists. If every device in the city of Seattle were to suddenly cease functioning, the Emerald City Grid would still be there for citizens around the world. Just look to Boston. Though the city is still under quarantine from the viral encephalitis outbreak and communication is still restricted, the Boston Hub is still up and running for others to do business on and connect through.

Remember the days of long-distance telecomm calls? Neither do 88 percent of other users on the Matrix. That relic of a wired era has long been gone, but for decades we've connected to LTGs and RTGs to get where we needed to be. The new Matrix doesn't care if you're in Cairo, Kansas, or Kandahar—the public grids are everywhere. Staying connected is easier than ever before with this free-to-use, globe-spanning marvel of modern ingenuity and coding acumen. If the basic Pub-Grid is too mundane or your work requires a little more style and panache, all the major metroplexes and most nations have created Regional grids accessible from their physical space, and each of the Big Ten megacorporations has its own globe-spanning grid above the public grid. Whether you're scraping by on the edge of the Aurora Warrens, exploring the deepest jungles of Amazonia, or working from a posh corner office in the Aztechnology Pyramid, some grid—probably more than one—is there for you.

Even better, the grids are not just available, they are easy to access and use. Over the last decade, the virtual world has become as much a part of the physical world as the ground we stand on. Advertising, street signs, virtual visitors, virtual offices, and VirtuArt all fill our world beyond its normal physical capacity. With public grid overlays and universal access, we can reimagine a world without the graffiti of the anarchistic youth; we can cover the scars created by criminal shadowrunners and their errant gunfire; and we can maintain connections to PANICBUTTON, DocWagon, and local law enforcement no matter where we are.

Our place in Matrix history will certainly be viewed as a renaissance of good judgment and level-headed, security-conscious decision-making. Citizens of the world will be safer and more comfortable in the new Matrix thanks to the efforts of the CC and all its members.

SAFE FOR WHOM?

BY MILES COURT

I'm no hacker; let's just get that straight from the get-go. This is not some, "Woe is me! I shouldn't get my neurons melted while I'm breaking the law because I'm not hurting anyone with my victimless crime" bulldrek.

Break the law, suffer the consequences. There's a price for everything, omae, and if you're out performing illegal activities on the Matrix you can't hide behind the virtuakeyboard and cry foul.

Now that I have everyone's attention, I'd like to get to the point. Our new Matrix, billed as the safest design since the advent of ASIST, is piling up a body count in the past year that surpasses the murder rate of Tenochtitlan. I've read the reports that play it down and use graphs and pie charts to make it look like everything has to do with how they categorize deaths, but the straight numbers don't lie. Current year-to-date total of murder victims in Tenochtitlan, as of 04/31/2076: 221. Year-to-date total of deaths of individuals suffering lethal biofeedback while utilizing ASIST immersive technology as of 04/31/2076: 372. How can that be called safe?

It shouldn't be. But that's how it's described by the megacorporation-controlled mass murderers that they ironically refer to as GOD. This new design is killer, and it's designed that way for one reason and one reason only: because the powers-that-be can't let anything get out of control. *Anything*! Follow the rules, don't buck the system, and you'll be fine. Step out of line and they'll melt your brain and leave you a drooling simpleton.

Why do they come down on hackers, or any other anomaly for that matter, like a sledgehammer on a macadamia? Because they need to exert control over the creature they've created. All this access, all this global connection, wasn't part of their plan. Yeah, they wanted a Matrix they could control and they're doing that, but they didn't want a Matrix that was everywhere. How do you keep the workers in Africa uneducated and digging up diamonds for a pittance when a cheap commlink in the wrong hands could create a revolt like we haven't seen since the Awakening? They've got a creation that they don't truly know how to control. Consider the unimaginable horrors that must be inside the Boston quarantine—just how bad did it get for them to block it off from the rest of the Matrix?

Wake up, people! Look beyond the shiny new grid layout and the "safety" provided by GOD. It's a Matrix that is the first step back toward total social control by the megacorps. They've laid this tool out for us and sold everyone on its amazing features, but once they get us all in, you'll start to see the changes. More restrictions, less access, "harmful" data redacted or destroyed mid-sending, and artificial barriers created around "dangerous" places will be just a beginning before the megas are back in control of all the information flowing around the world.

⦿ Separate from this original post, this same angry gentleman posted some interesting data compilations. He had a string of rants with them, but I'll give it to you raw and let his single rant stand for his views. Note the timeline for comparisons—ten years in the left column, two years in the right.

⦿ Bull

● I put some thought into who I should ask and where I should pull data from to give us a good rundown, and I did a little skulking with an eye open for strong (and well-supported) opinions. A lot of folks have mentioned similarities to the old, pre-wireless system. I saw complaints from former script-kiddies who can't let their programs do all the hacking for them spamming forums around the world. I got a solid feeling that the sheeple are quite happy to know that GOD is looking out for them. I heard the newest generation of hackers and coders talking about how superior their Matrix was to the old one. It was the phrase "their Matrix" that really pissed me off. My point here is that one view isn't going to cover the Matrix. In order to avoid the same old drivel from the JackPoint hacking crew, I picked my favorite Matrix philosophers from several sites and waved a credstick under their noses to give me their views on the new Matrix.

Here's the paid advertisements and opinions of a few folks out there. I made sure to tell them the money was for the honest truth, not what they thought I wanted to hear. Some are motivated by a desire to get posting status on JP, but they best understand that isn't done by kissing my hoop. I want sharks in the JackPoint tank, not guppies. I pulled together a little compilation from my four main categories of Matrix gripers; Geezers, Generation Wi-fi, Grid-Iron Gang, and Sheeple.

● Bull

GEEZERS

I got about the same opinion about this "new" Matrix as you, Bull. There's a reason they called it wire "less" when they screwed it up the first time. Now they bring back the "cyberdeck" and think they've made a step in the right direction. If I was able to go pull the old CTY-300 out of the closet and snap a clip on a wire and get access the real way, I'd be happy. Yes, the airwaves aren't full of kids, creepers, and agents on a mission like they were, but that doesn't make this new incarnation better. Just a little less annoying.

I'll give them some cred for slipping the grids back into reality, or at least validity. They managed to bring a little order to the chaos. Whoopty-do. Problem is, anyone, anywhere, can still press the power button and slide into the virtual realm from anywhere in the physical. No connection between meatspace and the virtual just means the virtual terrorists need to do their work from farther away. Just wait until the next wave of Matrix miscreants rolls in from the no man's land of the NAN, the cesspool of the Barrens, or the mess of metahumanity that is the ACHE. All they need to do is scam a little better service and keep an eye on their wake. Make too many waves and they'll need to duck and run, but even if they do get slammed, they just need some meat haulers around to move them before the GOD-squad shows up.

ASIST-RELATED DEATHS		
Reported by	(2064-2073)	(2074-2075)
Federal governments	1,216	2,395
Ares (includes KE)	978	1,894
Lone Star	1,182	1,696
NeoNET	941	1,376
AA-rated Megacorps	561	998
DocWagon	750	997
CrashCart	436	672
Mitsuhama	521	504
Saeder-Krupp	422	384
Shiawase	361	308
Evo	298	306
Renraku	214	234
Wuxing	168	203
Aztechnology	152	190
Horizon	154	142
Total:	8,354	12,299

New sense of false security, same waiting game until it goes sideways.

Angry old guy rant over now. And don't you dare edit that out.

As for how I see this new Matrix, it works and it pulls at some nostalgic heartstrings. The separation by grid is a throwback to earlier times, but anyone with an ounce of free spirit can see the back-step it made. Maybe that was good. Maybe opening the floodgates of the Matrix with the first wireless initiative was a mistake, but it was a mistake made by megacorporations who had enough control over their citizenry that when the world walked up to the brink of destruction, the corporate wageslaves still went to work. The wild places still went crazy, but that was fine with the megas as long as it didn't hit their bottom line. It's this kind of thinking that is really the only weakness that we will ever be able to use to bring them down. Their hubris had them believing they had control, and they let the Matrix free from its wired cage. The next decade taught them the error of their ways, and now they're backtracking. I just hope everyone out there realizes this is probably just the first step. The Matrix grew too wild for too long, and now the megas are going to prune it back to a nice manageable neighborhood lawn. The grids and new host designs are just the start. I'm an old dog, and it's way too late for me to start learning new 'trix, so I'll leave it to the young pups to conquer this new beast.

Just remember, as it was, it will always be; it's all about control with the illusion of freedom.

MISSION ACCOMPLISHED

AN 459

357

Danielle De La Mar

CONGRATULATIONS ON CREATING A BETTER TOMORROW...

GENERATION WI-FI

I'll introduce myself first. My nom de la rue is Tsk. Pronounce it however you want until you meet me and know me. I'm a child of the wireless Matrix, and by that not only do I mean I grew up and spent my formative years learning on that gloriously free system, but I'm also a technomancer. Ooo, scary, run away now; ignore her words, she's trying to trick you; beware the code, it will corrupt you; yada-yada-yada. I understood the old system, and much to the chagrin of many I understand the new one too. In fact, I might understand this one even better, but I'll stick to the topic at hand and save that speech for another place.

I'll start by saying that we must have been doing something right. We had a world wide web of 'links creating our Matrix. We were connected. We were free. And now—well, now we're all separated again. Not only separated but catalogued as well. While our last Matrix was made by our collective processing power, the 'links, terms, devices, nexi, RFID tags, and everything else, this new one is not. It just *is*. Wipe out most every piece of electronics in a fifty-klick radius and guess what happens to the "de la Mar" 'trix? Nothing. Still there, with all your data intact. Everything is backed up everywhere. Sure, there are still dead spots—wireless signals don't send themselves, so if something isn't doing that work, you're not online—but the redundancy is unparalleled. Or, as the case may be, superbly paralleled.

Back to the point, though. What does this all mean to us? It means that this Matrix is a new frontier. A new place to explore. A new way to encounter dangers that we aren't expecting. Yes, GOD watches over all of us on this new Matrix, but why? I admit hackers are sometimes disruptive to the norm of life, but they are a minuscule fraction of the world's population. They don't do that much, no matter what line of drek the corps have been feeding the world. As for technos, they're a minuscule fraction of that fraction and to tell the truth, GOD doesn't really pay much attention to us. For all the fear and scariness that the press puts out there, I've done plenty of my Matrix mojo without scrubbing my trail and GOD hasn't bothered to kick me, or even look into my lack of Matrix tact.

AIs are a different story, though. Their kind, well, they seem to get extra-special attention from GOD. Maybe it's because of this whole CFD scare and some of the rumors about what it really is, but most of the AIs I know spend a whole lot of time on the run. Whether they're ducking GOD, a demiGOD, or just a corporate snatch team, they're public grid enemy number one!

Got off task again, but that's good info to know and hopefully helps shift some opinions on who the bad guys are. The new Matrix for those who grew up with the last one is and isn't much different, depending on what you used it for. Everyday users find the new Matrix similar to the old as long as they have a decent grid subscription. They connect a little differently and now have a grid access they use regularly, but it looks much the same to them in terms of sculpting. It's similar enough that occasionally the old terms get applied to the new structure, but what can you expect? A node was a node for a decade, and now we need to split the term and don't even use the original. Confusion occurs at times, but most people know what you're talking about from the context. One big difference for everyday users are those who can't afford local, national, or corporate grid access and have to settle for the Public grid. They access the Matrix from what basically looks like the basement, with every other grid sitting above them. That serves as an unsubtle reminder of their place in the social pecking order of the new Matrix. From the other side, if you have your subscription from a megacorp, you look down on everyone else, including the other megas, because that's just how megas are—each one thinks they're the best and makes sure their citizens understand that as well.

The big change for those of us raised on the wireless Matrix is the change to coding. My generation was the generation of the script-kiddie. If you could write code or get your hands on some pre-written code, you (or an agent program) could function as a hacker. A great hacker, no, but good enough to get yourself in trouble or out of it in a pinch. It wasn't about skills on the fly, it was about having solid code ready to fling out at a moment's notice.

Those days are gone, and they might be gone for good. The post-'75 Matrix is all about variable code, or what folks call code cultivation. I'm a techno, so I don't know exactly what that means or how it works, but the basic idea is that the code is always changing how it reacts to other code. Seems like the opposite of what anyone would want from computing code, but it works and this new Matrix has left the script-kiddie coders in the past.

That concept certainly pissed off the script-kids, but it made the Matrix a place for professionals again. The sculpting isn't much different, but the need for a deck and some serious on-the-fly coding skills changed the game. Then there's GOD looking over your shoulder. I know I said I don't worry about it with my techno skills, but I know how it works. At least I know that the more illegal actions a hacker performs, things that violate the basic rules of the Matrix, the more disruptions they create. A few here and there, no biggie, but they keep adding up. If they hit the disruption threshold set up by GOD, well, then it's game over. And GOD, mainly through the Big 10 that run the show on the orbital, has done a great job of keeping the new cyberdecks rare and in the right hands. The fact that they tend to fry the hardware along with the wetware when they come adds to this scarcity.

Damn, I get distracted easy. Okay, Matrix for the modern day from those who grew up with the last one. I see it as safer, but safer in that Stepford Wives, creeps-

ville kind of way. They've sorted the system out, kept the number of rabble down and in line, and made sure everyone has access. For those of us already used to that, our Matrix was always wireless, worldwide, and free. it's the small changes that have made the biggest difference: the role of the grids, nodes now being hosts and devices, and the sheer vastness of its operations. They say the Matrix doesn't have distance like the real world, but it does, it's just different—and for us, that's a big difference.

GRID-IRON GANG

Hey Bull, I hope you can follow this. I might have gotten a little side-tracked here and there, but I tried to just let the thoughts flow. Hope your circle gets what they need from this. Thanks for the ¥, I'll use it wisely.

This Matrix is smooth, vast, easy, creepy, cliquish, fast, sleek, and a zillion other words I'd need to use gizoogle to look up. I can't read code and I can't write programs, and I'm definitely not a techno. All I am is a smart kid with a little more money than others and a great desire to explore the strange new world without having to go much further than my back porch or hit up the darker side of town without worrying about some ganger flat-lining me or making me his slitch. It would be better to actually get to hop on a plane and head over to Africa, but I'm happy to zip over, with a quick stop in the empties, and visit new people and places.

Man, I love the empties. The vast nothingness of the PubGrid in the boondocks. Riding on the empty airwaves. It's a great place to just sit and think or to hook up with some pals and chat or to just get away from the spam and slam of the local grids. No one drops their advertising in the middle of farm country.

Back to Africa. So lively, so different. And Asia—man I love Neo-Tokyo. And HONG KONG!!! Never been in real life and I can't do much more than chat and see the sights while I'm there, but just to have a globe of exploration with this much depth, variety, and dare I say, safety, is a kid's dream. When I need to research a paper, I don't head over to the library, I head for the source. Need to know what the latest political upheaval is in the NAN? I don't look it up, I go exploring. I take a jaunt to their area of the PubGrid, but mostly I look for others like me. Others who spend their time just chilling on the PubGrid, simslumming as some call it. But really just looking for a place to get away, a chance to make a break for the wide open. We feel safe behind the anonymity of our avatars and protected knowing that GOD is watching out for us. Maybe not specifically for me, but I know they're out there. I've seen them— hell, almost everyone I know has seen them. They aren't hiding, and when they rain down some virtu-holy retribution, they don't keep it quiet. They're loud, blatant, and want everyone around to know when they're on the case. I think it's part of their plan. Be seen, don't be bashful about doing your job, and make examples of the people who get caught in your crosshairs.

GOD even watches out for me in the Barrens. They may all be stuck on the PG, but the stories I get from locals, the experiences I can have from just a virtual viewpoint are great, and it's good to know there are eyes watching the scene. Gang fights where all you see are ducking and diving avatars with the occasional deck-jockey popping on to scrub 'links are awesome, and the worst I'm gonna get is a little headache if the deck-jockey goes too wide on the code-slashing. Maybe I'll need to buy a new 'link, but I'll keep my wetware intact. And on the other side, I love seeing the trenchcoats drop in, whip up the old tommyguns, and shred some ganger deckjockey. Is that a little sadistic? Maybe, but it keeps my virtual streets safe and applies some classic true Darwinian philosophy: It's not the strong who survive, it's those who adapt the best.

We are a generation built for adaptation. I've had three Matrix variations in my life. Yeah, I might have only watched some *Snuggly Bears* episodes on the pre-Crash 'trix, but it was there. I grew up with the wide wireless world growing wilder and wilder. Fear at every turn that my time in the Matrix was going to leave me a gibbering husk because some AI/techno/e-ghost/wackhacker/unknown Crash remnant whatever was out spamming and slamming local airwaves and frying everything in sight. Freedom is great, but it's chaos without rules. I'll take the stricter de la Mar Matrix over the anarchy of wireless "freedom" any day.

SHEEPLE

There are few things in my day more satisfying than seeing the demiGODs in action. I love to see those Red Ninja pop in, lay waste to some criminal hacker (who a moment before was hiding) and then clean up the scene and be off on their way. Not everyone gets to witness this, but I spend my virtual time within the friendly scenes of Okoku, the Renraku grid, keeping an eye on the GridGuide host. It's a frequent target by deviants trying to scam a ride, cover their trails, make a quick getaway, or just stop the system to slow the response of local law enforcement, and therefore a frequent place to see our Renraku demiGODs pop in for a little cleanup work. We have plenty of our own security—our IC is top-notch—but a Track and Dump, knowing that it's our personnel who are going to have to go deal with the criminals who are probably hiding on someone else's property, just isn't as satisfying. We could lose good Renraku citizens—or worse, they could end up convalescing for months and never be the same again. Better that the hands of GOD come down and bring justice across the grids.

Speaking of the grids, what a great idea. Everyone in their own space, not cluttering up the entire Matrix with Aneki-knows-what. I know that when I'm within the Renraku grid, I'm among family. I can let down my guard and just enjoy my virtual entertainment and social life. Work as well, but we can all admit we relish the time we can spend as our alter egos on *Red Samurai Run*, *RenRak'n the Night*, and *In My Sights*. I've played a little *Miracle Shooter*, but who wants to go spend time on the other grids where you have to worry about not only your opponents but whatever other deviants are hanging around.

Especially the PubGrid! National and city grids aren't too bad, but GOD has a lot of space to watch over on the PubGrid and anyone, absolutely anyone, can get access. Criminals, predators, hackers, runners, any nation's citizens, and Aneki-knows-who could be hiding behind that bland persona. I know most hackers hide or are easy to tell from their super-sculpted avatars, but what about those lazy slumming Ares kids with daddy's money and no sense of discipline? Or that NeoNET rabble with their Transys-Avalon gear and complete lack of common sense or decency? Whole place gives me the creeps. At least I can visit a few of our Japanese cousins and feel safe. Yeah, they're not perfect, but at least they understand the concept of honor.

Though I should mention Horizon. I like their grid, and I have a secondary subscription for it. Great entertainment locations and relatively peaceful, thanks to their corporate philosophy. Good to know not all American corps are just out to blow up their neighbors or pillage their own people. Though General Saito did bring some proper order to CalFree for a bit, leaving behind a fine influence.

The Aztechnology grid has merits. It's great for vacationing, with plenty of hosts sculpted like sunny vacation spots with premium virtu-hol (which I think might have a little BTL coding in it, but who's complaining). Their sensory input feeds are second to none.

Since I'm giving grid opinions at this point, I might as well mention Saeder-Krupp. S-K's grid feels safe—almost too safe. Reminds me a little too much of a time in their national past where our countries were allies, if you get my drift. Draconian is appropriate and kind of expected, but overall it feels a little cold to me most of the time. I can't offer much firsthand experience about the Evo grid, since I've never been there. "Weird" is the description I've heard. People say it's very unnatural; "alter-natural" was the term they used. Expected with their reputation, but I haven't been yet so I'll hold judgment until I visit it for myself.

Overall, I think Danielle de la Mar led the charge in the right direction. I'd never want to go back to a wired Matrix, but I'd take that over the wireless chaos that the de la Mar 'trix has repaired. We live in a fine time to experience the new Matrix and all the wonders it has for us to access.

- And that's just four of the views out there. Next up is a little clip from an Ares Instructional piece that I lifted. It's nothing fancy, just another little bit of what we are up against in the way of public opinion.
- Bull

THE NEW MAP
OF THE MATRIX

AN EDUCATIONAL EXPLANATION
OF MATRIX ARCHITECTURE

Good morning, boys and girls. Welcome to the Introduction to Global Matrix Architecture discussion. I understand you have all been interacting with the Matrix for years now, and most of you probably feel as if you understand it far better than I, but this discussion is intended to introduce you to the greater aspects of the Matrix, outside of the Ares Global Grid. Please enter any questions you might have as we go along into the question queue, and I will get to them as they best fit.

Let us begin.

The Ares Global Grid is not the Matrix. In fact, despite all its vastness, it is only a small part of the Matrix. It is the safe place where you, the young citizens of Ares, can work, play, and learn in safety. Most of you remember the chaos of the post-Crash wireless Matrix and the dangers that arose from this vast network of uncontrolled computing. The Emergence of electrokinetics, the massive spike in artificial intelligence population, and most recently, the horrors of cognitive fragmentation disorder caused by the massive code corruption created by EKs, AIs, and soulless hackers.

From the chaos, the great Danielle de la Mar, along with the top technical minds here at Ares with assistance from the other member corporations of the Corporate Court, reshaped the wireless Matrix. Together, we reined in the wildness of the Wireless Matrix Initiative and began bringing order to the electronic maelstrom.

The Ares Global Grid is one of eleven authorized global grids. There is one for each of the ten member corporations of the Corporate Court, including us, and one public grid that is administered by the Corporate Court itself. These eleven grids form the ground and sky of the modern Matrix.

The public grid, or PubGrid, is the ground. Some think of it as the universal connector for everything, but it is no larger than our grid. It is simply laid out on a different plane on the Matrix, not sharing its virtual space with others. The PubGrid is free to access for anyone with a wireless capable device. I see the question has been asked about the difference between this and the WMI Matrix, and I can understand the confusion. The PubGrid is almost as wild and dangerous as the old WMI system, but the difference is its separation from the rest of the grids and even from its own hosts, along with the presence and monitoring by the Corporate Court's Grid Overwatch Division, or GOD.

The global grids for the ten members of the Corporate Court share the sky of the Matrix. From every point in any global grid, a user can see all of the other grids and request access. From the PubGrid, the corporate grids are above. From the corporate grids, the PubGrid is the base of the horizon and all the other corporate grids are spread evenly just above the horizon line.

Local and national grids are only accessible from within their own virtual vicinity of the Matrix. While the Matrix isn't tied to a specific physical location, it reflects the concept of distance in relation to devices within the physical world. This then determines the general location of a local or national grid. From a grid-to-grid viewpoint, local and national grids are always at the far left of, and slightly below, the corporate global grids when they are available. This available selection of grids varies and is administered and modified by your host grid (the one you are currently accessing), your 'link (based on the settings built in by its manufacturer), and any changes you make to your own preferences within manufacturer limits.

Here on the Ares Global Grid, you have been protected and watched over by the demiGODs of Ares. Each global grid has its own demiGODs who all answer to the CC's GOD. On the PubGrid, only GOD comes to your aid, and the vastness of the PubGrid and the lack of character of many of its users keep them busy. Their response to unauthorized code manipulations is prompt and unforgiving. Use of the public grid by those with Ares Global Grid access is not recommended and should be avoided unless no other communication avenues are available.

Local and national grids are acceptable alternatives and are where you will find many hosts unique to their parent cities or countries. Ares authorizes access to the global grids of our fellow corporations on many occasions but warns that protection for Ares citizens is only guaranteed on the Ares Global Grid. Accessing any host from a global grid other than the Ares Global Grid invalidates your corporate citizenship protections and leaves you within the jurisdiction of the grid provider.

Exploration of the various grids is expected from the inquisitive and inspired minds of the youth of Ares. Though this is expected, we also expect those same minds to remember the law. Just as we respect the laws put in place by our own executives, we must respect the laws put in place by those with authority over the other grids and hosts of the Matrix.

Once you are out in the virtual world, you'll see things in much the same way you do here in Detroit, with the exception of the available hosts. Hosts pay to be accessible from all grids, though some pay even more to be exclusive and limit access from certain grids, especially the PubGrid.

Thank you for listening, and make sure to keep the personal safety and security features on your commlink active at all times. Things in the Matrix work at the speed of thought, and that means danger comes faster than a blink. Be vigilant and be ready.

* Next up is a quick piece from a lovely young woman who prefers the instructional to the exploratory. BMQ got a healthy number of life lessons on the WMI Matrix and settled down after the changeover. She's spending a lot more time snooping quietly and gathering data, so she wanted a chance to do a little write-up for JP. Nothing world-breaking, but sometimes it's just nice to know a computer tech who can string interesting sentences together instead of relating everything to their latest "ground-breaking" code.
* Bull

HOW DO WE USE IT

POSTED BY: BMQ

There are a lot of different ways to access and use the Matrix, some far superior to others. Opinions vary, so I'll go with the overall consensus and give you a run-down in no particular order, though I will offer some color commentary along the way. A ten-nuyen Soy-bucks card awaits the person who can ID my setup. PM me at BIBLIOMATRIXQUEEN.

ACCESS

Matrix 101 is using the standard everyday commlink. Whether you're scraping along with your Meta Link or impressing the executives with the latest custom-shelled Caliban, this is the basic doorway to the Matrix for the bulk of the planet. Your commlink acts as a status symbol among the corporate masses and as a warning in the shadows. Among the corps, the better the commlink, the more likely the individual is someone of power, as the high-end machines are not cheap, and the latest doesn't stay the latest for long. On the shadowy side of the streets, the better the commlink, the more paranoid the runner—and usually the more successful. Rookies often keep their trusted Emperor or Sensei, or stick to the Meta Link because they know it or it's all they can afford. When you see a runner with an Elite, Ikon, Avalon, or Caliban, you know they're not wearing it to show off their wealth. They've got it running whatever they can to prevent hackers from turning their lives upside down. They've also lived in the shadows long enough to afford it and know that surviving in the shadows is a privilege, not a right. They've earned their Matrix safety.

* For all you genius street toughs out there who come up with the ingenious plan of stuffing your Meta Link components into a discarded Caliban shell—don't bother. No one falls for it, the coding is just too obvious. Same goes vice-versa. Don't bother to try and slum it with a disguised Avalon.
* Kane

* Don't be so discouraging, you grump. Just remember that the cover is only as good as the code. If you want to hide what kind of 'link you're rocking, make sure your hacker custom-tweaks the persona to fit your needs. The standard options on the 'links are pretty universal, and they all reflect the processing power of the 'link.
* /dev/grrl

Though rare, there are still people who use an old-fashioned desktop terminal to access the Matrix. Whether they're anachronistic or nostalgic, or too stubborn to move into the current decade, they get their latest screamsheets from the comfort of their own home or a local library that has a few for public use. The biggest difference—and I'll say disadvantage—between a dataterm and a commlink is its lack of mobility, but people who use these aren't concerned about being mobile for their Matrix needs. Another point to consider is that the dataterm determines your persona when you go full VR, and they're usually pretty basic. Expect them to carry some kind of tag from the location you're borrowing them from if they're public. Personal dataterms have a wide variety of icon selections just like commlinks. The last point to consider is their access. Because they aren't mobile, they have limitations in the places they get a solid connection to and will always be registered to a global, local, or national grid.

* Quite a few folks think these things are great for a little anonymous access, but with the number of cameras and other surveillance devices around, they can track you back to a location with a very small amount of legwork.
* Bull

Now what about those Matrix cowboys? The ones that use their cyberdecks in order to access the Matrix everyday? They're dead. If you're confused, look at it this way: No one but GODs, demiGODs, and a select few are supposed to own cyberdecks. These are not mass-produced, cookie-cutter devices you go and pick up on your way home. They are highly restricted Matrix machetes designed for one thing and one thing only: breaking the rules that were so carefully put into place by the corporate masters. Anyone using a cyberdeck who doesn't belong to one of those narrow groups is a dead man decking. At some point someone is going to catch up to them and fry them for fragging up the system. There are only a small range of cyberdeck producers, all tightly controlled by the Corporate Court and its member megas. Decks create avatars that look just like their commlink-created counterparts, though several custom programs allow cyberdeck avatars to change appearance rapidly.

MATRIX BASICS

Each corporation that produces a commlink is targeting a specific sector of the population. Even though they are infinitely customizable with the right skills, software, tools, and hardware, they come with a basic suite of features tailored to attract a specific audience. The Basic Persona is the generic Matrix representation of users who don't do much to customize their avatar. The Base Theme represents the easiest modifications to make to the basic room of the device.

Model (Rating)	Basic Persona	Base Theme	Device Icon
Meta Link (1)	Plain metahuman	Cube structures	Cube with metahuman icons on each face
Renraku Aguchi (1)	Kimono-clad peasant	Paper house	Small paper house
Sony Angel (1)	Angels	Cloud heaven	Ornate heavenly gates
Transys Arthur (1)	Knight	Medieval home	Small stone home
Sony Emporer (2)	Robed figure	Imperial palace	Ornate doorway
Leviathan Technical LT-2100 (2)	Merfolk	Underwater home	Bubble-shaped house
Microtronica Azteca Raptor (2)	Hawkman	Small forest	Birds nest
Xiao Technologies XT-2G (2)	Plain figure	Nightclub	Neon sign
Common Denominator Element (2)	Elemental humanoid	Home themed by element	Swirl of all the elements
Renraku Sensei (3)	Kimono-clad samurai	Dojo (training house)	Ornate paper structure
MCT-3500 (3)	Plain figure	Empty cube	Cube-shaped MCT logo
Matrix Systems GridGopher(3)	Humanoid rodent	Gopher hole	Hole in a dirt mound
Erika Elite (4)	Fashion model	Dining room	Crystal key in a fancy lock
FTL Quark (4)	Spaceman	Atomic nucleus	Swirling atom
Hermes Ikon (5)	Business person	Office	Office building
Novatech NetNinja (5)	Ninja	Rice paper home	Spinning shuriken
Transys Avalon (6)	Monarch	Castle	Castle
PULSE Wave (6)	Personal icon from data gathered by the device	User's home space	An oscillating wave
Fairlight Caliban (7)	Completely black humanoid	Island	Boat in a storm
Fuchi Cyber-X7 (7)	Crystalline warrior	Crystal house	Crystal shard

PERCEPTION

The devices we use to provide us access to the Matrix are only part of the process. How we perceive the Matrix is equally as important, and the devices we use make all the difference. While the value of access devices can be argued from several angles, there is a definite ranking system for the devices we use to perceive the virtual world. Worst to best, here you go.

KEYBOARD WITH FLATSCREEN OR TRIDEO

The bottom of the line, most basic method of input and perception is the old-fashioned keyboard and a flatscreen monitor or trideo set. While the trideo at least offers a 3-D view, a flatscreen leaves Matrix movers with a narrow input of the reality of the Matrix. It's slow and not exactly easy to use, but it's completely safe. There's zero risk of anything harmful coming from the Matrix but also zero chance of doing anything other than ordering your next pair of Zoé shades. Trideo at least gives you access to some of the Matrix games, but trying to play with a keyboard is pretty lame. To get beyond the most basic Matrix games, you need the next step up.

> Last month a hacker by the name of Deetz made a run on Z-O from a custom set of dataterminals in his doss running with a flatscreen. He made some serious breakthroughs and would have been dumped by GOD

several times over, but he ran a redundancy trick on the terms. He thought he had it made until his door got kicked in. Safe isn't always safe.

» Glitch

GLOVES, GLASS, AND HEADPHONES

To experience the true potential of the Matrix, users need to embrace its mobility and freedom, which means they need some primary sensory input to help them get started. This is where augmented reality (AR) really starts to make a difference, and where the first taste of virtual reality (VR) begins.

Matrix beginners need three things (as referenced in my header): gloves, glass, and headphones. In order to interact with AR on the move, users need something better than a keyboard and touchscreen. AR gloves are step number one, as they let a user "touch" the virtual world around them. They come in every style imaginable, and users often own several pairs, especially in places where weather and work might call for a change on a daily basis. Winter gloves, disposable latex medical gloves, leather work gloves, diving gloves, dress gloves—the list goes on and on. Even specialized gloves like shock gloves can have an AR access feature added. The gloves allow selections and typing to occur in AR as long as the user has the next piece of the puzzle. Well, they actually can still select things in AR without the next piece, but they'll be relying on blind luck to make what they want to happen, happen, since they can't see what they're pointing at.

Part two is glass. Although modern surgery and gene manipulation have made corrective lenses (both glasses and contacts) largeley unnecessary, these items are more common today than at any point in metahuman history. They aren't correcting vision now, they're enhancing it. Glasses, contacts, goggles, helmet visors, facemasks, monocles, cybereyes, and a myriad other, even more interesting devices serve as windows to the Matrix. AROs, devices, messages, advertisements, and anything else you can imagine being seen by the eye (and even some stuff you can't) fill the virtual world around the denizens of the Sixth World. These pieces of glass (or whatever) reveal these wonders.

While the eyes perceive the Matrix through the glass, headphones let the ears hear the virtual world. Advertisements, music, messages, warnings, news, and tons of other virtual vibes can add a second sense of connection to the virtual world. Headphones aren't just limited to those big bulky retro models. Earbuds, cyberears, helmets, hats, and headbands get audio accessories all the time.

This trio of devices gives the user a more immersive experience and lets them see, hear, and interact with the Matrix in a more fluid and natural way. Casual Matrix users and the average corporate wageslave are usually quite happy just getting this level of contact with the Matrix. But the virtual world has so much more to offer.

TRODES

Seeing and hearing over a distance have been around since the earliest vidphones, but the modern world offers the next step. Electrode and ultrasound nets (trode nets, or just trodes for short) are the doorway to the virtual world. While they can function and offer some similar options to other virtual sensory devices, their true value comes when you open the virtual doorway and let them take you full VR. Trodes are the beginner's key to truly feeling the power of the alternate world of the Matrix.

Worn on the head, trodes send signals straight to the brain that can augment or overwrite the normal messages the brain gets from the real world. The majority of people use trodes to deliver the primary sensory information about the Matrix to their brain when they decide to open the door to VR. This means the trodes translate the Matrix to visual, auditory, and tactile signals, overwriting what the brain would get from the user's eyes, ears, and tactile nerves. With a sim module on the user's commlink, cyberdeck, or dataterminal, they can also smell and taste the virtual world. Simply put, trodes make you feel like your Matrix persona.

AR is a little different. Trodes can act as a DNI (direct neural interface) connection running from your mind straight to your devices, including the glasses and headphones you're using to interact. You think it, it happens. No typing out messages, just think them and send. Want to hear a different song? Think it. The trodes take the place of the gloves or keyboards for input and access while playing in AR. If there's a sim module involved, the user can also feel, smell, and taste the Matrix in AR. These senses blend with the real world for interesting results. The sensitivity settings can be set between the access device and the trodes to determine how much of each sense (touch, smell, and taste) comes from virtual vs. physical reality. Users in high-pollution areas often overwrite the smell of the air with something more pleasant; dieters will flavor their low-cal soypaste into something more exotic; and even a chilly and rainy day can be made to feel like a warm day on the beach. Most trodes have safety measures to prevent users from freezing to death but place few other limitations on what virtual sensations are allowed. Similar safety features are also in place for visual or auditory information while in AR in order to avoid a user "walking" around in the Matrix instead of the real world.

» It doesn't take much to override the safety features and make a user blind or deaf, so this is one of the best features to use to mess with trode users. Some creativity with the smell and taste feeds can have the user vomiting in a heartbeat or just nauseated enough to make a run for the bathroom.

» Netcat

- It's true. I made a few too many comments about prego-nose to 'Cat, and she tweaked the smell feed on my DNI to show me what it was like. Nasty.
- Slamm-0!

DATAJACK

A datajack is like a wedding ring for the Matrix. This shows you're serious about your relationship with the Matrix and you don't want anyone to come between you and your latest V-feeds. It's got all the same DNI connectivity of trodes but is a whole lot harder to take away. Datajack users also have the option of plugging straight into devices for some direct control and access via a little cord they spool into the 'jack. In the corporate world, datajacks are almost as common as eyeballs—that's to say, everyone has them. Most corps offer an incentive program for workers to get a datajack to increase productivity. That's if the parental incentive to get your child wired with a datajack to help in their education and safety didn't already get them jacked up.

- And finally, we've got a little splatter piece on the major grids. This guy is pretty vague, so add your thoughts freely.
- Bull

GRIDS

We can't talk about the Matrix and not discuss the grids. Each grid could be written about endlessly, and some (if not all) are still in a state of change, trying to adjust to the new Matrix and grab the most market share. A few basics for each as they stand now should be enough to get even the saddest nature lover plugged in and looking for some virtual real estate to explore.

GLOBAL

ARES GLOBAL GRID

As one of the earliest supporters of the new Matrix, Ares got a prime name pick, selecting the name Ares Global Grid. Matrix users see this grid as a medieval castle with the Ares logo proudly waving on flags above the walls.

- Don't forget the cannons and ballistas.
- Sticks

Their grid themes everything with medieval overtones. The ground is a plain of green fields, unpaved roads with wagon ruts, forests in the distance, and most hosts near the ground have a stone foundation rendered beneath them.

- Ares has small "forts" spread around the grid where users can pop in for a little Matrix combat. Users step in, grab a virtual weapon from the medieval weapons rack, and go to town against each other. It's not real Matrix combat, but it allows Ares to check out prospects who have solid mental agility.
- Stone

- Way to host open auditions for your demiGODs and KE deckers. Ares, I applaud you.
- Kane

AZGRID

There is no mistaking the hulking virtual ziggurat that is the AzGrid. The green behemoth sports virtual carvings of Aztec idols on each side, built within the stepped structure of the Aztec icon.

Stepping onto the grid transports users to a pseudo-history of Aztechnology's creation. Aztec accents highlight everything in this virtual realm. The ground looks like the ancient Aztec cities in their prime with hosts adding ziggurats to the landscape. The edges of the cities look like rainforests and mountains but cannot be reached, simply holding their place in the distance no matter how Matrix users move toward them.

- Be careful here. Hacker gangs have taken to using this grid as a bloodsport training ground of sorts. Along with the young hotshots, AZT lets their corporate deckers tool around and practice their dirty work on troublemakers.
- Picador

- And their definition of troublemakers is loose.
- Butch

ETERNAL HORIZON

To access the Horizon grid, one must simply reach for the setting sun. In the sky of the public grid, the seven-pointed half-sunburst has a 3D cast to its jutting points that make it almost look like a weapon. From all the other grids, where the icons shift to the horizon, it looks very much like a setting sun.

Crossing onto the Eternal Horizon is like stepping into a perpetual vacation. The folks at Horizon have designed their grid to take on the cast of the California coast at sunset. A single long stretch of coastline goes on forever, with beachfront shops on one side and the waters of the Pacific lapping up onto the beach on the other. Out in the water are boats of varying design. Yachts, catamarans, sailboats, speedboats, and even rafts float on the water before the eternally setting sun. The shops and ships are the hosts of the grid as one might guess, but a lot of people spend their time just sitting on the beach enjoying the sunset.

- Or hopping in a hut for some simsex, BTL-code, or any of the other debauchery one would expect on a grid from the biggest source of simporn on the Matrix.
- KidCode

- Sometimes letting in new people is really annoying, but sometimes they drop nuggets of amazing value. This is the latter. Horizon has a great PR rep and fronts for more famous people than any other corp. Those famous folks make lots and lots of poor decisions in regards to their self-media collection, and Horizon happily protects them from the worst of their choices by spreading the rest for free publicity and a steady stream of black funds.
- Pistons

EVOGRID

Along with NeoNET, Evo had significant pull in the management and manufacture of the new Matrix. Their unique perspective on life shaded not only their choice of grid icons, but also the internal layout of their grid. EvoGrid does not have a single symbol on the virtual plane. Instead their icon is a revolving Vitruvian Man with limbs that change with each rotation to show the many variations of metahumanity.

- Matrix rumor says that certain combinations of limbs and features allow possible access to special sections of their grid.
- Snopes

On the grid the theme of evolution and variation continues. Evo's grid has one of the most finite appearances of the globals once you get on, but the appearance is deceiving. EvoGrid consists of twelve distinct surfaces arranged like the inside planes of a dodecahedron, each with their own theme that changes daily. The spatial deception comes when users try to walk from one plane to another and never reach an edge. The hosts on the grid gain accents to reflect the plane on which they are currently located. This changes, just like the identity of the planes.

- Some host owners are paying extra to Evo to be on a specific themed plane that better accents their business.
- Glitch

MCT GLOBENET

The MCT cube is not the most remarkable icon in the virtual realm of the Matrix. The letters M, C, and T are blocked and angled on a revolving cube. Mitsuhama obviously doesn't feel they need more than that, and they're probably right as they usually have the highest grid population count of any of the megas at a given moment. They're focused on being global, not glitzy.

- They were the first to make their grid fully global and earned a lot of users for that. Finding out just what they had to do to accomplish that feat might make for some useful paydata.
- Slamm-0!

Once on MCT GlobeNet, users are greeted with a pleasant and serene Japanese mountain village. Homes and shops with traditional rice-paper walls line the streets, with each door leading to a different host. The focal point of the entire village is a traditional-style pagoda towering over the smaller structures. The pagoda is the location for all the premier-level hosts as well as most of MCT's own hosts.

- While the "premier" concept may sound like a money-making ploy, the right to have your host accessed at the pagoda is based on your reputation with the Japanese Imperial State, not on paying Mitsuhama.
- Glitch

NEONETWORK

No one doubts that NeoNET is the strongest force behind the new Matrix. Their grid appears as their iconic star in the Matrix. Due to their influence in so many areas of the new Matrix, the star is usually larger than every other grid's icon.

- It's a pissing contest on other networks, too, where the NeoNET grid logo will be smaller, only slightly but somehow perceptible, or even blocked by sculpted features that move with the user and keep it mostly out of sight.
- Icarus

Once on the NeoNETwork, users get a sprawling cityscape with connected hosts filling the city's skyscrapers. It's often overwhelming to those who are unfamiliar, but regular users quickly adjust thanks to Neo, the informative agent that all NeoNET subscribers get access to.

- Neo is a nosy little fragger. He pops in at some very inopportune moments, so be careful.
- /dev/grrl

- That's part of his programming. If the grid detects any sleazy activity, Neo pops around as an early reminder to behave yourself—and as a sort of targeting system for NeoNET's demiGODs.
- Netcat
- Slick. Leave it to the progenitors to have some extra security tricks already.
- /dev/grrl

RENRAKU OKOKU

While MCT has a pagoda inside their grid, Renraku's red pagoda is the doorway to their global grid. Revolving in the sky or on the horizon, the doorway to the realms of Renraku is always welcoming. As part of the Renraku rebranding and as a great way to increase their market share of global grid subscribers, the Okoku grants "Explorer Visas" to anyone who wants to visit their grid. The Explorer Visa allows visitors access to the grid but does not allow access to any of the hosts on their grid. Okoku is also available for a free one-month full trial to anyone who purchases a Renraku-brand commlink.

- Great way to get on with a throwaway. Recon, spying, or even just slumming or virtua-cheating are popular with the Renraku free trial.
- Glitch

Renraku has themed their grid to reflect their new brand philosophy. Seeking to be the brand of "Home and Heart," Renraku has sculpted Okoku to resemble idealized versions of villages around the world. The grass huts of Polynesia flow seamlessly into the perfect slice of small town Americana, which glides into the Provençal countryside, and on and on through villages from all corners of the Earth. Hosts are obviously the shops, homes, and attractions, with a smooth blend of the local flavor thanks to the owners' desires to keep the theme.

- Even feels kind of homey all the time with a little borderline hot-sim emoticode.
- Netcat
- Over the whole grid? That's a lot of computing power.
- /dev/grrl
- Renraku awoke arguably the largest AI ever. They aren't short on codejuice.
- Netcat

SAEDER-KRUPP ÜBERWELT

The SK grid is accessed through one of the most interesting icons on the Matrix. The megacorporation originally went with the traditional logo, but as others made their grid access points a statement, S-K followed suit. From the public grid Matrix, users look up to see a massive silver dragon flying over an Earth the diameter of its torso. The dragon's claws sweep over the planet as it spins and its eyes scan the surface as if watching over the whole world. The icon changes slightly when viewed from the other grids as the dragon lands and its wings furl up over the globe resting in front of the majestic-looking creature. It's interesting to note that the dragon is not Lofwyr.

- The older generation can recognize the dragon. Though some features are softened to add a more benevolent look, the dragon is Dunkelzahn.
- The Smiling Bandit

Going inside the ÜberWelt is like getting shrunk down and landing on that Earth. The sky holds a ghostly visage of the dragon peering down over a world much like our own. The theme is Berlin, circa 1990, complete with fresh scars of a torn-down wall. The hosts sit inside the buildings lining the streets. The only non-historical piece is the S-K headquarters building that always sits in the distance representing the main S-K host as well as several hundred other corporate-sponsored hosts.

- Quite a few Matrix gangs are pulling on some even older German imagery. S-K runs a tight ship and stamps out anything they find but the gangs aren't slowing. Not sure who's trying to rile the dragon with this, but they're doing a good job.
- Snopes

SHIAWASE CENTRAL

It has been three-quarters of a century since the Shiawase Decision, which made Shiawase the first megacorporation, and they remain a household name. They're not known for the latest tech, the biggest guns, or the hottest formulae. Instead, they have built their megacorporate empire on something everyone needs: power. Shiawase is the second-largest producer of energy in the solar system, behind only the sun itself (and they harvest so much solar energy that some managers have joked that the sun is one of their best employees). While their name is known by all, it is their logo they let represent their grid on the Matrix.

Once on Shiawase Central, users are treated to an inside look at where their energy comes from through idealized imagery. Perfect windmills line a vast beachfront with wave turbines rolling perfectly with the incoming waves. Nuclear cooling towers rise over a field of shining solar panels with steaming geothermal generators and hydroelectric dams in the distance. Hosts on the Shiawase grid glow bright with the abundant energy provided by all of Shiawase's power sources.

- Shiawase runs all their power control hosts from their grid so a lot of side ops lead here. It's a tough nut to crack, so stay smart. Get on, get it done, get off. Don't linger on those hosts; they scan by the nanosecond.
- Slamm-0!

WUXING WORLDWIDE

The five-petaled lotus has symbolized many different things through the ages, but today the first thought is always Wuxing, Inc. While the corporate logo is a stylized side view of the famous flower, the Wuxing Worldwide grid is accessed through the spinning metallic lotus.

Inside the grid of the AAA shipping magnate one would expect a theme of the sea, but instead the masters of Wuxing have sought a calm and mystical place to lay over the world. Draped in the mystic elements of feng shui, wujen, Daoism, qigong, and dozens of smaller, less-well-known traditions, the entire grid looks to be laid out across a Chinese countryside with small parks, temples, and gardens dotting the never-ending landscape. Hosts blend beautifully into the serene countryside and allow all Wuxing Worldwide subscribers a chance to visit the peaceful plane.

- The peace is precious to Wuxing. Company deckers patrol their grid, stamping down those who bring chaos to the orderly world of Wuxing.
- /dev/grrl

- Beware the Wuxing quintuplet personas. They're abundant and frequently used by the Wuxing deckers, posers looking to get attention, or the little ones themselves.
- Pistons

- Well, four of them maybe ...
- Clockwork

NATIONAL GRIDS

ALOHANET (HAWAI'I)

Access icon: A smoking volcanic mountain with a lei around it

As the nation is spread over a chain of volcanic islands, their national grid reflects this in its design. Since AlohaNET is a national grid located in the vast emptiness of the Pacific on the PubGrib, many users jump to it as a stopover or point of reference when PubGrid wandering. The island chain of the grid is similar to the actual nation, but the spans of water between are filled with a mix of virtual wildlife and advertising as denizens of the island nation try to lure visitors to the physical islands instead of just tripping by virtually.

- Watch out for the hosts or personas near Nihoa Seamount. It's in the middle of "water," but it's the home of the Sea Dragon and she's got some technical assets in the area. Usually ships, but a few hosts are accessible in the area.
- Frosty

- Great virtual meet spot. On a relatively inexpensive grid but with plenty of virtual open space.
- Kia

AMC NATIONET (AMC)

Access icon: A polar bear that walks in place and occasionally rears up and roars

One would think the people of the Algonquin Manitou Council would want their virtual reality to be an escape from their physical reality, but their national grid is not the case. Snowy fields as far as the eye can see greet users who hop over to the AMC NatioNet. Native structures and touches accent the virtual world here and provide bits of culture and history for users through imbedded informational AROs all over the grid.

- Though a national grid, AMC NatioNet has a lot of no-access zones around the country. It's not a restriction issue as far as I can tell, but a lack of hardware and bandwidth that keeps it blank.
- Glitch

- What about the PubGrid in those areas?
- /dev/grrl

- As available and shoddy as it is everywhere else.
- Slamm-0!

CALFREENETWORK (CFS)

Access icon: The CFS national flag

When stepping onto the grid of the California Free State, one would expect to be wowed by the many wonders of the Bear Republic. Sadly, the CFS has yet to really flesh out the plan for their grid, thanks to way too many internal political issues. Right now, the best you get is a sunny sky as far as the eye can see.

- There's a lot of work in the CalFree on every angle on the Matrix grid issue. National and local politicians, corps, and even international forces are pushing and pulling all over the state trying to gain leverage on opponents so that they can get control of the grid.
- Mika

- Rumors have Hestaby with a claw in this issue, but that could just be the residual waves from a plot she put in motion before she got kicked to the curb.
- Frosty

- She got bitch-slapped before the big local and national grid issues were even a thing. If there's a stink of Hestaby in the jobs here, it's fresh.
- KidCode

- She lost her place before the public knew about the grid issue. And she's a great dragon. Foresight's pretty much 20/20, too.
- Frosty

CASNET

Access icon: The nation with the CAS flag overlaid

Despite claims to the contrary made by politicians and famous southern figureheads over the past 100+ years, the theme architecture of the CASnet shows that the old CSA was never far from the hearts of those in the CAS. Users walk through the streets, fields, and roads of America in the mid-1800s. The grid's sculpting even adds local accents to users by state. When accessing CASnet in Georgia your persona will suddenly talk with a soft Georgian drawl, while in the mountains of Tennessee you get a solid mountain twang. The designers have just enough sensitivity to make sure no slaves ever appear.

- The accent thing is annoying and a little creepy. I'm not a big fan of having my mental voice overwritten—or more accurately, the coding needed to do that.
- Bull

- I don't like the accent because it reminds me of all the metaracist trash I dealt with growing up.
- Mr. Bonds

- Maybe that's the point.
- Kane

- So are we talking Humanis influence in the grid plan, or HN?
- Pistons

- Humanis on paper, but we can be pretty sure where the funding comes from.
- Clockwork

- HN?
- KidCode

- Hit me private. I'd rather not draw them over if they have agents regularly searching for mentions of their name.
- Bull

DAKOTANET (SIOUX)

Access icon: A pair of crossed tomahawks, one classic, one modern

The best way to describe the DakotaNet is simply nondescript. Its theme is non-existent, and the sculpting is about on par with that of the PubGrid. Vast and open with hosts and personas left to their owners' design choices, it makes for an eclectic mix on a plain background.

- Boring by design. Anything too extravagant sticks out and draws attention.
- Plan 9

PAGPÁGTZELZÌL "FOREST OF WISDOM" (SALISH-SHIDHE COUNCIL)

Access icon: A rotating trio of redwoods

When it comes to tribes of the NAN with a reputation on the Matrix, the Salish are not the first group to come to mind. This reputation may be changing soon, as they've jumped into the new grid with both feet. Speaking of both feet, when accessing their national grid users are entreated to walk within the temperate rainforests of the Pacific Northwest. The sculpting is extensive and quite distracting to those unaccustomed to their grid, but natives find it to be a beautiful escape to nature even when accessing it from the heart of a city.

- I think the Salish are up to something. No one goes to this kind of sculpting efforts for nothing. From a virtual metaphor stance, they are the massive forest surrounding the Emerald City. Whether that forest is dark and scary or full of e-deer and virtua-rabbits is up to the grid's controllers, and they change that up on a regular basis.
- Mika

- Can't a nation actually want to treat people to the world the way it should be to hopefully promote them to want to preserve that world in real space?
- OrkCE0

- No.
- Sticks

- No!!!!
- Clockwork

- Not in this century. Or any other for that matter.
- Frosty

- No. But it's cute you think that way.
- Sounder

- I left four. The others I deleted.
- Glitch

PUEBNET (PCC)

Access icon: A dreamcatcher with idols from all the tribes of the PCC

The Pueblo Corporate Council is considered one of the most forward-thinking of the Native American Nations. This status led everyone to expect their Matrix to be the most extensive and elaborate, but the PCC decided instead to make their most universally accessible technological aspect a throwback to the early days of the tribes of the PCC. The grid varies slightly by region, with touches designed to fit the historical inhabitants of each region. Areas where many tribes settled are a mix, with accents from each tribe sometimes touching the same place.

- The accents are quick identifiers as to which local Matrix gang you're going to get assaulted by. They're all over the PuebNet, and most of us in the know have hunches they are a bit better funded than they should be.
- Mika

- Hacker gangs being subsidized by corps to test out products (while doing some damage to rivals) are becoming more and more common in the new Matrix. With the strict laws about cyberdecks and how frequently GOD fries them, it should be obvious when a group of gangers are blasting away all over the grids. But news is only news in detection range.
- Snopes

SOLNET (AZTLAN)

Access icon: A spinning Aztec calendar stone

Aztlan's national grid functions much like their national government: as a puppet for Aztechnology. It's like a mini AZT grid, and they even share the same demi-GOD personas. An important point to know about SolNet is that only Aztlan citizens have full access. Guests on the grid have limited access to the hosts on the Azzie home grid.

- That whole same personas thing is a great cover to use the same deckers on both grids. Don't expect a grid hop here to slow pursuers of the government nature.
- Glitch

- As if a grid hop would stop anyone who works for Aztechnology.
- Slamm-0!

TÍRTELENET (TÍR TAIRNGIRE)

Access icon: The rotating flag of Tír Tairngire

The Tír national grid might as well be the corporate grid for Telestrian Industries. The elven megacorp isn't an AAA (yet), but they're starting to get a little practice with running their own grid by providing the nation of Tír Tairngire a national grid at no cost to the government. While the Emerald City grid of Seattle to their north has green overtones, TírTelenet uses a rich purple and sculpts everything with rounded edges for a curvy and smooth-looking visual experience.

- Telestrian has been getting a lot of time in front of the CC lately. Whether they're addressing reports of harmful biofeedback use by unauthorized Telestrian deckers or

bargaining for a seat on the orbital is a matter of much speculation.
- Thorn

- I'd assume both. My guess is that TI is using the decker actions as a way to get in front of the CC more often. How else do reports like that make it out of a grid they control?
- Bull

UCAS ONLINE

Access icon: The UCAS flag in the shape of the UCAS waving on a flagpole

When accessing UCAS Online, users walk within the ideal small town of a Norman Rockwell-inspired America. The entire grid carries strong pro-UCAS overtones with flags flying on houses, businesses, and flagpoles. The grid gains minor thematic additions with decorations increased between July 1 and 4 and on October 15. Depending on what state you are accessing the grid from, there are also some other bits of local flair, such as state flags and famous buildings with virtual tags providing a little history for the curious.

- All the touches aren't old time. President Dunkelzahn gets some decorations here and there. Actually, the Dunkie spots have been being used by someone to spread the word. Graffiti stating "The Heart Lives" has been popping up.
- Sticks

- The past comes seeking growth in the future.
- Man-of-Many-Names

- What does that mean? Hit me private if you can't reveal it here.
- KidCode

- Thanks for fueling the kids' imaginations, Many-Names.
- Bull

LOCAL CITY GRIDS

CHITOWN (CHICAGO)

Access icon: The Sears Tower at the center of the city's skyline from Lake Michigan

With the massive corporate and governmental efforts going into reclaiming/rebuilding Chicago, it was not a huge surprise to see a local grid suddenly become an opportunity on the horizon. ChiTown is currently operated through a jury-rigged network of out-of-date hardware. The infrastructure contract, along with every other aspect of the new Matrix in Chicago, is up for grabs, and every corp around is trying to snag that lucrative piece of control in their game of Chicago-rebuilding chess. The current theme is a cross between the gangster era of the roaring '20s and the height of the southside Core.

- Shadows in Chicago are hot across the board. Land grabs, territorial disputes, demo work, wetwork, intel ops, data steals—you name the run, they've got an op for you.
- Kia

- Problem with Chicago right now is picking sides. There are a lot of players, and locals definitely have their favorites. If you decide to pull a few jobs and back MCT for the Matrix, you may lose half your contacts who are really hoping to see Ares back in town, or who want to pull in a homeless NeoNET.
- Hard Exit

- That's not the problem. That's the benefit! Let the corps keep pouring in the money.
- KidCode

- Until they decide the bottom line is in jeopardy and they pull out completely, leaving a vacuum for forces worse than them.
- Red Anya

EMERALD CITY (SEATTLE)

Access icon: The Space Needle surrounded by a translucent globe with the word "Seattle" spinning at the equator

Long known as the Emerald City for its greenery and history, Seattle's grid plays on this history. A sky of green and crystalline green accents to everything make sure users know where they are at all times.

- Seattle is actually one of the least-sculpted of cities. Accents and some shapes, but nothing crazy. That may change in the near future. The new trend is all about defining grids through restructuring their identity to limit hackers to their home cities and keep them on their toes when they wander too far from home.
- Bull

- Seattle has many transient hackers and a decent balance of megacorporate powers, so the redefining of the grid isn't a top priority, because it would take a ton of effort.
- Hannibelle
- It's coming. Trust me.
- Bull

- "Trust me," tagline of the world's least trustworthy individuals since the invention of language.
- Clockwork

HUB GRID (BOSTON)

Access icon: An 18th-century schooner flying the flag of Boston

A walk along the cobblestone streets of 18th-century Boston was a pleasant trip back in time before the quarantine. The streets are still there, but now they are eerily empty, a shadow of the local grid that is now blocked off from its own residents. Others sometimes visit to see for themselves, but rumors have begun of e-ghosts and worse stalking the streets.

- Stay away. There are points where the jamming thins or hits a little harmonic dissonance and weakens. What comes to visit is quite unpleasant.
- Snopes

- Hey Snopes, what you got going down over there you don't want the rest of us to stumble on? E-ghost stories are for scared little script-kiddies.
- KidCode

- You've been warned.
- Snopes

NYCNET (MANHATTAN)

Access icon: The Manhattan skyline at night

The Manhattan Development Consortium saw the new grids as a great way to define their city as the pinnacle of technological advancement by sculpting a grid that matches the city nearly identically. The virtual accents of the Matrix blend seamlessly with their physical surroundings, often creating a virtual vertigo as users can't tell what is real and what is not.

- This place is hacking hell. Everyone thought the new layover was going to make tracking and hacking great until they realized that it blends the physical into the Matrix and wreaks havoc on the brain trying to separate the two.
- Hannibelle

- Not that I like seeing others suffer, but I do rather enjoy seeing some security R&D money go to the Matrix and not to more machine guns pointing at me.
- Ma'Fan

TRUE HACKERS, LUSERS & DIRTBALLS

Slamm-0! wasn't small, but the ork towered over him anyway. Some of that had to do with the fact that Slamm-0! was sitting on the floor, leaning against grey wall of a laboratory basement, embroiled in AROs only he could see. He wasn't in full VR, but he might as well have been, because the outside world occupied the barest sliver of his attention. Which explained the ork's imposing posture—it was likely that he had been trying to get Slamm-0!'s attention for some time, to no avail.

"Time's not long," the ork said,

"Not short, either, assuming you consider time as infinite," Slamm-0! said without looking up. "Something that is infinite cannot properly be considered to have any sort of length. Of course, there are those who do not view time as infinite, but see definitive beginning and end points of space time, in which case time would not be infinite, and would in fact by very long indeed."

"You were supposed to be done two minutes ago."

"I was. But I didn't like how I was done. So I'm getting done better.

"Keeping on schedule is better."

Slamm-0! sighed. "It may be an artist's lot to be misunderstood by philistines, but that don't mean we need to cater to them.

The ork was about to speak again, but Slamm-0! waved his hands and cleared all the AROs.

"It's done," he said. "The *right* way."

The ork shook his head and walked ahead while Slamm-0! scrambled to his feet.

"There's a camera on the ceiling to your left," he said. "And another one on the other side of the hall, about five meters away from you. They can't see you. Or at least, that was supposed to be the plan."

The ork stopped glared at him. "Still is the plan."

Slamm-0! shook his head. "No, the plan is better! Because now they can see us, but they don't care! Instead of me erasing the footage, they see our faces, and recognize that we're people whose footage is to be erased at the moment it's captured!"

"Doesn't seem like much of a difference to me," the ork said as he turned and continued down the hall.

"Remember that thing I said about philistines? You're not seeing the big picture. If we're just blanked out, we don't exist. But if it sees us and erases us ourselves, we can still be part of the system, in a good way. We can set off certain triggers. I could make the camera, once it recognized me, put up an ARO that said 'Hi Slamm-0!'And no one monitoring the camera would see a thing."

The ork grunted. They approached the second camera, which was in front of a heavy metal door with no visible knobs.

"Now, if I were good at this, instead of programming it to say 'Hi' to me, I could make it decide to send a message through the system to unlock this door for me once it saw me."

The ork looked at the door. "Didn't happen."

"Of course it didn't! I couldn't have it opening the door as soon as I walked in! That would leave it gaping while we were walking the halls! But what if I told it to wait for a certain pose, while I was wearing a certain shirt?"

He unzipped his armor vest and pulled it open proudly to reveal the rock band t-shirt underneath.

The door clunked heavily then slowly opened.

"Now that's doing it *right*," Slamm-0! said.

THE SOURCE OF FASCINATION

POSTED BY: SLAMM-0!

Don't hate us because we're beautiful.

One of the things you have to understand about hackers is we're bemused, impressed, and irritated at the attention hacker culture gets from the world at large. We see how we're portrayed on trid crime shows, we listen to brickbrains like Danielle de la Mar talk about us, and we hear people tell stories about hackers who swept in and zeroed out everyone's accounts at Zurich-Orbital Gemeinschaft bank in seconds (never happened, of course, but it makes a good story), and part of us is like, "Yeah, you *should* be talking about us, because we're fuckin' *awesome*," but then another part of us is all "You are so wrong, you are *so* wrong, hell, have you even *touched* a commlink in your *life*?" and then another part of us is like "Can't you all just shut up and leave us alone in peace?"

That last one is the reason people think we're all anti-social and crap. But we're not, not really. We just find

the rest of you boring, is all. Don't take this personally. It's just that you all spend a lot of time talking. And sitting. And talking and sitting. And drinking some. Then talking some more. And sitting.

To be clear, I have nothing against talking, sitting, and drinking, and I regularly engage in all three activities. But I can do those things while doing other things, and if I'm doing other things, then I can be talking about those things, instead of—and this is the thing people do that truly drives us insane—talking about *talking*. Talking about *doing* is way more interesting, and actually *doing* stuff is even better. We like the stuff we do, we think it's wiz, and we're totally into it. So when you start talking about us, we get it. This stuff is cool! Everyone should be getting off on it! But then you keep talking about it, and keep talking, and sometimes you get to the boring parts, like who's jockeying to fund a new startup, or the political implications of a new blah blah blah. We don't *care*. We just want to *do stuff*. So that's when we get aggravated and annoyed, and we wish you would leave us alone. People see us as fickle or inconsistent, but we're not. We're okay with you talking about us when you focus on the interesting parts, not so much when you're boring. Simple, right?

So let's focus on just what these interesting parts are.

ELEGANT AND INSANELY GREAT

It's time to get specific. I mentioned that hackers like doing cool stuff—but what kind of stuff, and what makes it cool? I got your answers right here.

WHAT HACKING IS AND ISN'T

There's a perception out there that hacking is all about breaking into other people's stuff. Sure, that's part of what we do, but only a small part. Hacking is the desire to make things happen, to tinker around with the essential building blocks of machinery, see how they work, and find ways to make them work better. This whole concept of people having their own electronic devices got traction a century ago with hobbyists, people who sat in garages and tinkered with primitive circuits and programs on paper tape to see what they

could make happen. Some of them eventually became billionaires, but others of them just kept playing and tinkering, because it wasn't about coming up with the next big thing. It was about doing cool stuff.

> In fact, the annals of hackerdom contain a number of people who made something cool because they wanted to, watched it explode into a consumer phenomenon, then backed away slowly and said "Nah," then returned to their garages. They had no interest in running a huge business. They just wanted to make things they liked. To quote one of these guys: "I'm not an entrepreneur. I'm not a CEO. I'm a nerdy computer programmer ... If I ever accidentally make something that seems to gain traction, I'll probably abandon it immediately." That's a pretty common hacker mindset.
> Glitch

Historically speaking, the "cool stuff" I'm talking about touches everything you do on the Matrix. Commlinks' ancient predecessor, the personal computer; electronic networking; wireless communication; cloud-based file structures; sprawl-wide digital traffic management; ASIST technology; full-on, deep-dive VR runs; augmented reality—you get the picture, right? All these things are hacks, where people looked at the tools that were available and what they were doing, and had that great thought: "I can make this better."

Now, the vast majority of hackers is not going to make something that is universally adopted. And we're fine with it. We want to make something that makes our life cooler, and if other people adopt it, that's great. For my part, I could fill up hundreds of pages of text with different hacks I've made, but most of them are pretty technical, like program optimizations, or coding to make grid hopping faster, or optimization for my persona renderer, or things like that. (That's another reason we sometimes have trouble with the rest of you. I want to talk about high-Q optical whispering-gallery microresonators with my fellow hackers, I can just plunge in. With the rest of you, I have to stop and explain what I'm talking about, even though it's a fairly basic concept. We just don't have a lot of patience for that sort of thing.)

But let me tell you about one of the simple things I did at home for little Jack's potty training. If you've ever been around a kid, you know they're not exactly subtle about when it's time to crap. They squat, they get red in the face, that sort of thing. Problem is, they also sometimes go and hide, so you don't always notice them doing it, and it's important to get them to the toilet quick so they make the right connections. We've got cameras all over the house (including wired ones in places that any asshole who might try to break in would never suspect—understand?), so I got footage of Junior doing his thing a few times, then I programmed an algorithm into the home net so that the cameras would keep an eye on Jack. When he started making motions that seemed to indicate crunch time was coming, it would send us an alert. When I started I had an accuracy rate of seventy-three percent; a few iterations got it to a rock-solid ninety-seven. So that was great. But then I thought, hey, this is still involving work from me. Still have to get up, track down the kid, and bring him to the john. So I told the system to not just alert me, but send some programming to Jack's Bust-a-Move drone (of *course* he has a Bust-a-Move doll. I swear they issue them to kids at birth) telling it to play Christy Daae's "Satin Strut" and walk toward the crapper. He loves the doll, and he really loves the song, so as soon as it plays, he follows that thing anywhere. So he gets to the john, and I'd meet him, and business would get done. Before long, I didn't need to show up—the doll and the kid took care of things on their own.

- I know a guy who has full food service anytime he's within one hundred kilometers of his home. Food preparation is automated, drones load it up, fly it out, and bring it to wherever he is. He says he saves over two thousand nuyen a year since he doesn't order takeout.
- Glitch

- This is all cute, but how about stuff that's useful on the job? Here's what I'm working on: We all know how fond hackers are of ejecting magazines from guns; I'm working on a program that will automatically slap a mark on anyone who wirelessly ejects a magazine. If it came from a legitimate source, fine, they won't care I got a mark on them, I'll delete it soon, no harm done. But for enemies, it'll be a quick way to get a leg up on them. I'm working out a few kinks, but I'll let you know when it's ready.
- Bull

- People will have a counter to that within forty-eight hours of it getting into the wild.
- Glitch

- I'll have a fun two days, then.
- Bull

HACKER SLANG

We all know the importance of slinging the lingo to show you belong and you know what you're talking about. Here are a few terms to know when you're talking to hackers. Just remember not to sling them around with abandon—nothing makes you look more like a noob than overusing slang, or worse, using it wrong. Also, note this is only a small sample of the vast amounts of slang out there. Over the past century, we've had time to develop plenty of jargon.

Bletcherous: *adj.* Aesthetically unappealing, ugly. Almost always used for code or objects, not people.

Creeping Featuritis: *n.* The disease that causes feature after feature to be added to a piece of software, ostensibly improving it and making it more useful but in reality making it more bloated, cumbersome, and inefficient.

Cuspy: *adj.* A program that is well-written and functions smoothly. Significant praise, but still not s good as elegant.

Dirtball: *n.* A small, struggling, outsider group.

Elegant: *adj.* Powerful, cleanly designed, and efficient. Extremely high praise.

Insanely Great: *adj.* Something so wonderfully elegant it threatens your ability to deal rationally with pedestrian reality.

Kluge: *n.* or *v.* A clumsy piece of software or hardware that is rickety, a teetering blend of disparate, poorly combined parts. Or the act of making such a piece of gear.

Luser: *n.* A user who is a loser. According to many hackers, what most non-hackers are.

StudlyCaps: *n.* What the "C" in that word is. A popular feature of hacker words that are multiple terms smashed together.

TrueHacker: *n.* An exemplar of all that a hacker should be—clever, hard-working, dedicated to elegant code.

z: The letter you use to indicate something distributed illegally or in the way the original creator doesn't like (e.g., warez, tridz, BTLz).

HACKING AND BREAKING INTO THINGS

I've established that hacking is not just about breaking into things and doing illicit things, but that doesn't mean it's not about those things. When we take hackers' general curiosity and willingness to poke around and see how things work and combine it with a general disregard for societal and political rules, we can see how breaking into places they're not supposed to be would become a normal part of a hacker's activities. And if I left it that way, it would all seem like nice, innocent fun. Hackers didn't mean any harm when they broke in and erased your entire accounts receivable database! They were just experimenting with what they could do! That would, of course, be a total lie.

As much as hackers like to pretend we're a distinct society, we tend to be motivated by most of the same things that motivate the rest of you. And two of those things—competitiveness and ego—play a pretty large role in our illegal exploits. Yeah, some kid will tell you she just wanted to break into Ghostwalker's commlink to see if she could do it, and that's not entirely false, but it's not entirely true either. She may have wanted to see if she could, but the reason *behind* that reason was to prove her superiority. That 'link is protected by the best security that obscenely large piles of money can buy, and if she cracks it, then she beat them—"them" being whoever programmed the security. You beat someone like that, you walk with a little extra pepper in your stride for a good long time.

That means that a lot of the time we're not just out there exploring—we're showing just how badass we are

and establishing our place in the global hacker ranks. Which may be unofficial but are still tracked in the mind of every good hacker out there.

> So have any of our local hackers ever hit the top of the list?
> Chainmaker

> The three of us who are in charge now? No. We all have our distractions or weaknesses. I've got a temper, Glitch has a sense of fussy perfectionism, and Slamm-0! has his innate Slamm-0!-ness. But we all stand in the shadow of the man who absolutely was number one.
> Bull

> I suppose I may rank higher, but I've never played the game the same as everyone else.
> Puck

What this means for all of you who work with hackers is that you need to always, *always* take their ego into account. The most disciplined hacker in the world is still capable of getting pulled into a pissing contest with someone who crosses them in just the wrong way. Be ready to either put up with some delays or pull your hacker back to their senses to make sure the job gets done.

WHAT HACKING ISN'T

Since my list of "what hacking is" is so broad, this category is pretty small. Are you using your electronic devices exactly as they were when they came out of the packaging? Do you have zero desire to poke under the shell of the graphical OS and see what fun you can have with command lines? Then you're not hacking. And that's okay. That's why hackers put a lot of time into the cool things you buy, so that you don't have to monkey around with them if you don't want to.

But there's one main thing to discuss here that hacking isn't: easy. First, to get a really good solution or program takes time. I really love my Jack-potty-training solution, but if you asked me what would have taken more time and effort, programming the whole thing or just keeping an eye on the kid and making sure he made it to the john, and I'd have to respond with a solid "I don't know." I had more fun doing the programming, but that doesn't mean it's efficient.

The breaking-and-entering part of hacking has never been easy, but the new Matrix has made it harder. In the old Matrix, you were bobbing and weaving in the crowds, trying to let the mass chaos and confusion of the surroundings overcome any efforts to find you. In the new Matrix, everything is designed to make you stick out, and the eyes on the virtual street are more attentive and skilled than ever. They also are ruthless about how they crack down—the polite first warning is largely a thing of the past. You have to be smart, precise, and willing to stay on the move to keep anyone from drawing a bead in you. That makes it stressful, but it also means your work can be done quickly, keeping you in the flow of your overall team mission. It's a rush, pitting your skills and guts against other devices, hackers, and the all-seeing GOD in real time while bullets are flying around you. Easy? No. Awesome? Yeah. If you're me.

> ◉ It may not need to be said, but Slamm-0! embodies the swagger that is an important part of hacker culture. He'll probably cover that later.
> ◉ Bull

THE PURITY OF THE HACK

For TrueHackers (putting words together and using studly caps in the middle of words is a big hacker thing), doing cool stuff is nice, but it's not the only thing. There is an aesthetic value to hacking, where solutions that are clean and simple are valued more than ones that are over complicated and awkward. This latter option is often tempting, because it can be the quickest. Let's take the example of getting a vehicle and two airborne drones to work together with minimal input from the rigger or anyone else. You'll sometimes see claims of out-of-the box compatibility between the systems of vehicles and drones, but unless the gear is all from the same manufacturer, those claims are usually a lie. The systems are built for conventional users, who are going to use each vehicle or drone in isolation, not for those of us who know the benefits of coordination. You can turn on their syncing options, but they're hideously bletcherous.

Now, you can always try to kluge together a quick solution. There are patches you can find sitting around the Matrix that will at least take steps to making the things understand each other's language. There will be some lag in their communications, and pretty much the only thing they'll be saying to each other is "here I am," but at least they're talking.

The kluge is the lowest form of functional fix. It's like stapling together a bunch of fabric scraps you found in the garbage and calling it a blanket. It's ugly, it may be fragile. But it'll work for a time.

If you want something better than a kluge, you want to be cuspy. A possible cuspy solution here would be to use the code for the programs controlling one vehicle, copy it, and re-write it for the other items. If you can pull that off, you don't need a patch doing translation for you anymore. Not only is everything able to understand each other, but they're all speaking the same language, and the code backbones they're built around are the same. That gives you lots of possibilities for how these vehicles can interact. When they're on autopilot, their decision-making process is going to be similar, so they can anticipate each other more easily, the same way twins can often anticipate each other's actions. You have a better, smoother, more free-flowing network now. Your solution is good. But it is not yet elegant.

> ◉ Note that what Slamm-0! says about this being one solution for improving the network, not the only one. One of the great things about hacking is how many routes there are to the same basic destination. In our time leading JackPoint, Bull, Slamm-0!, and I have made a lot of security updates, re-worked some networking standards, and performed other maintenance tasks. In all these tasks, they have come up with ways of doing things that I would never have thought about. Some of them are better than what I have done; some of them, in my opinion, are worse. But they all reveal different ways of thinking that I find fascinating.
> ◉ Glitch

> ◉ I know this is a generalization, but in my experience technomancers are way less tolerant of kluge-y code than deckers. We don't just use the code; we feel it, we live in it. When it's messy, it's like living next to a pig farm—it's offensive and annoying.
> ◉ Netcat

The problem with this solution is that it's going to have the same bugs and weirdnesses that the source code has (which is a frequent annoyance to hackers, and a reason we hate to use other people's gear, because it's either suited to them and not us, or because, heaven help us all, it uses factory-specification code. Blech). If you want a truly elegant solution, you either need to go through some concerted bug-squashing effort or write some new code from the ground up, which is my preferred approach.

- It's true. He never buys any device that makes it from the store to our home with any original code still installed.
- Netcat

When you design from the ground up, you are only limited by your imagination and your skill. So for some of us, yeah, no limits. Want a bunch of pre-programmed choreographed maneuvers in there? Go for it. Want them to change their relative positions immediately based on any damage they have experienced and where it came from? You can do that. Want their responses and tactics to vary based on the faces their imaging software can pick out of a crowd? You totally should do that!

Of course, elegance is not just a matter of piling on features. There are plenty of devices out there with creeping featuritis, piling feature onto feature until you have some nightmare software that is trying to do ten thing sat once. The important thing is *how* you get these features to work together, how the software follows its decision tree, and so on. There's no technically precise way to describe what elegant code is—you have to experience it. But once you see it (assuming you know what to look for) and feel how it moves through its operations, you know.

At the very top of the aesthetic pyramid you have perfect code, as well as several long and annoying debates about whether perfect code is a desirable goal. There's a pretty thick stream in hacker culture that says that worrying too much about perfection keeps things from happening, and having things happen is better than not. We all know kluges aren't great, but they're functional, which is more than you can say for the would-be perfect code sitting uncompiled on some hacker's commlink. It would be great to come up with something perfect, something that is streamlined, bug-free, completely functional, adaptable, and whatever other nice words you want to come up with. But none of us have seen that in our lifetimes, and we don't expect to. We don't want to spend our wheels too much chasing after elusive perfection—but we want to know it's out there, as a distant possibility. Maybe someday, fueled by triple-strength soykaf and a drekload of Womp-Snappers, after thirty-six straight hours of coding, your mind will transcend your body and its physical limits, shake off the limitations of our meatworld-based way of thinking, and understand the ways of code as if native to it, designing something of perfect and pure beauty that will leave all how gaze upon it gasping in admiration.

Until that moment, elegance will do.

HACKERS AND EVERYBODY ELSE

As you probably got from the beginning of this piece, hackers don't always get along with the rest of society. The combined fear and awe mainstream society seems to hold us in doesn't help much, and neither do the many ridiculous depictions of hackers in the media. Like the graphical user interfaces they apparently think we use (where can I get that progress bar that shows me how much longer until I've cracked Ares' prototype database?). And then there's that small matter I mentioned earlier where sometimes, no offense, you all are really, really boring. It makes me crazy how you people often say how boring baseball is, but at least something happens there regularly—pitches in the game today come every fifteen seconds or so. In your small talk, by contrast, absolutely nothing happens for sentence after sentence after sentence, for conversations that can go for fifteen minutes, half an hour, or more. How you have patience for that but not for watching Kale Barson hurl a 160 kph cut fastball that gets people jumping out of the batter's box before it veers left for a strike is beyond me. But I'm getting off topic.

To help you deal with the hackers in your life, whether in your home or on your team, here are some common hacker characteristics you should know about.

HACKERS HAVE A BIAS FOR DOING

Hackers are famous for our all-night hacking binges, for coding for days on end, for skipping sleep to do our thing. Why is it? Because we like to do our thing! More broadly, we just like doing. My affection for watching sports puts me in the minority of the hacking community, who would generally rather participate in something than do something (in my defense, every time I watch a game I'm gathering stats, reviewing work by others, and developing new ways to analyze stats, so I'm hardly watching passively). The things we do for leisure (besides hacking) tend to be more individual than team oriented. Martial arts is a popular pastime, and there is an outdoorsy strain among some hackers. Games—computer and otherwise—are also popular, since they're leisure activities that keep our brain engaged. We're certainly not above engaging in some partying and drinking, if only because it gives us a way to blow off steam. And if we drink enough, our tolerance for talking increases.

- Hackers aren't big at quiet contemplation, but that doesn't mean they don't think about the larger picture. They just prefer to get the big picture by continually poking and prodding at the pieces of it until they assemble the complete whole, rather than stepping back and pondering it from a distance.
- Sounder

HACKERS DON'T THINK HIGHLY OF RULES

Okay, earlier I tried to push back against the idea that hacking is all about illegal activities, but here I'm going to reinforce it a little. If you talk to hackers about their first time hacking something, they'll probably tell you they were breaking some sort of a rule or another. Maybe it was their parents' rules about how to treat the new commlink they just got. Or their schools's rules about using school devices and networks. Or, if you grew up on the street like me, the first experience you had with any electronic device was after lifting it from some sucker who wasn't watching it carefully enough. The point is, most of the time when people started hacking, it was in the face of someone telling them not to do it. But they did it anyway, and they got a result they liked.

That's not something that builds a healthy respect for the rules, and it's the kind of experience that gets reinforced several times throughout a hacker's life. Our role models are people who broke the rules, did things differently, and brought the world to them. That's who we're trying to be, and we're not going to let silly rules of etiquette or even professional conduct keep us from doing our thing. One of the things the trids get kind of right when showing hackers is that no matter what setting they're in, they tend to look different and buck whatever the dominant trend is. What they get wrong is the idea that we're all fat slobs in t-shirts. Some of us are; many of us are not. But we're not going to wear a tie just because everyone else is, and we're not going to be uncomfortable simply because some designer thinks we should be. We're going to wear clothes that feel good if we happen to be in them for twenty-four or forty-eight hours straight, but most of us have figured out how to do that without looking like we just got out of bed.

> ● It's a tricky balance. We don't want society to think we care how we look, but we also like to look cool. We just act like we're looking cool sheerly for our own enjoyment, but that's only partially true.
> ● Netcat

This general lack of rules means our hackles get raised really easily when someone tries to impose rules on us. Any of you out there who have tried to lead a team with a hacker on it know what I'm talking about. You run through planning, outline everyone's roles, and everyone nods but the hacker. The hacker gives you a long list of everything wrong with your plan, including stuff that's part of the hacker's responsibilities and stuff that isn't. Sometimes the hacker doesn't know shit about what they're talking about, but they talk about it anyway because having someone else make a plan for them doesn't feel right.

Luckily, most people who are team leaders have some experience with people, and they know how to manage hackers. You don't force a plan on them, you ask them how they want to accomplish their part of it. Most of the time they'll give you an answer close to what you would have wanted in the first place, and they'll accept any modifications if you introduce them in a way that makes it seem like their idea.

> ● This sounds complicated, but it's easy if you've worked with the person and know what they like. "So we'll have a rooftop entry. Hey, what was that thing you did to the sensors on the job three months ago? <wait for answer> Think you could pull that off again? Wiz!"
> ● Chainmaker

> ● In other words, let their ego take them where you want to go. Hackers are not the only runners for whom that is appropriate.
> ● Fianchetto

HACKERS ARE NOT FOND OF FORMAL SCHEDULES

Want to seriously piss off a hacker? Give them a formal schedule they should follow. I'm not talking about deadlines—everyone has to deal with them, and they're fine. I'm talking about assigning a ten-hour workday, or checking in to make sure they are doing an assigned task when you think they should be doing. We don't like that. We function best when we are interested and engaged, and that does not always come on a predictable schedule.

We're not idiots or children, though. We know some things need to be done by a particular time. And we know deadlines have to exist. The point is, give us a deadline without a schedule of how you want us to get there, and we'll get there. Say we need to work a particular shift each day, and you'll monitor us while we do? Then we'll brick your commlink long before any actual work gets done.

HACKERS THINK THEY ARE EGALITARIAN

One of the prime tenets of hackerdom is who a person is doesn't matter, it's what they do. Hackers say they are willing to accept anyone regardless of their background as long as they can code. Your gender, sexual orientation, race, metatype, ethnicity, and country of origin don't matter if you can deliver the goods. Conversely, they don't think rank or social status are worth a damn. If you did something cool, great—then you're worth something (assuming it wasn't too long ago, and assuming you didn't immediately lock your cool thing away where no one could touch it). Did you inherit a position from your parents, or gain it through your exceptional hoop-kissing abilities? Then we will give you exactly as much respect as you have earned, no matter what it says on your business card.

The other part of our egalitarian nature is we support openness and sharing. That's why so many of us have trouble letting go of the old Matrix. Somehow, we got a network that met many of the ideals we'd been espousing for a century (well, I personally have not been espousing them for that long, since I'm not that old. Bull is). It was open, it was broad-based, pretty much anyone could tinker with it, and a lot of code was shared. Then the corps realized how un-corporate the whole thing was, and they took it away.

But while the corps aren't sharing anymore, we still are. Caches of open source code are still around, and you can find plenty of hosts where like-minded people swap stories and tips. And what is not shared, we're willing to steal, like we did with cyberdecks.

If you want to be a TrueHacker, don't tie up whatever you develop with trademarks and copyrights and drek. Open it up, make it affordable and exciting to use, and the revenue will come. If you have to play all sorts of legal games to make your money as a hacker, maybe you should just put down the cyberdeck and go to law school already.

HACKERS ARE NOT AS EGALITARIAN AS THEY THINK

And now we get to a darker side of hacker culture. Earlier in the century, some people noticed a funny thing. Hackers kept talking about how good code could come from anyone and anywhere, but when you looked at the rosters and (especially) the leadership of the major technology companies, you found they all fit a certain profile. There were a whole lot more people who looked like each other than those who didn't. So what was the problem? Were these other people simply incapable of generating good code? If hackers claimed to have diversity as a virtue, why weren't they associating with a more diverse group of people.

There was a lot of hemming and hawing over this issue, and a whole bunch of excuses. It's not our fault! It's the schools not teaching coding to people at a young enough age (never mind that a lot of us didn't get into hacking from stuff we learned in class, but from stuff we read when we were supposed to be paying attention in class)! We just don't get many applicants from other backgrounds (that couldn't have anything to do with you hiring almost exclusively through personal networks, could it?)! It's not our fault girls and other people can't keep up (not a great argument to make when you are trying to sound egalitarian)! It's your fault for pointing it out, everything was fine until you pointed the imbalance out (um ... what?)!

A lot of these arguments were not strong, but they carried the day for a while because another aspect of hacker culture, the lack of respect for the rules. The people pointing out the lack of diversity in hacker culture felt like outsiders were coming in and trying to impose rules on them, and they reacted the way you'd expect. They rebelled, they made snide remarks, they got their hackles up, and they resisted for all they were worth.

Until the day came when they realized they were being foolish, that if they really wanted the hacker community to be as strong and open as they claimed, they would break down the barriers keeping people out (and stop pretending those barriers didn't exist). They set out to be more open and inclusive, for real.

Ha ha! Just kidding. People don't do that. What happened was, the world itself kept getting more diverse, and all sorts of hackers, both inside corporations and outside, understood that if they really wanted to know what the best hackers were doing, they were either going to have to reach out to a broader range of people or be left behind. So they looked at ways at opening hacker society to more diversity, only to realize they didn't have much of an idea how to do that.

Some of the issue was that hackers are humans (and metahumans), containing the full range of weaknesses of metahumanity. We are prone to blind spots, and the whole thing about blind spots is you don't know you have them. So a lot of us thought we were taking everyone seriously and treating them equally, but we had this bad tendency when a female came up and described the hot new program she wanted to design, we'd nod our heads and say, "Uh huh, well, maybe after you get a few year's experience of coding under your belt, sweetie," but if a guy came up with the exact same proposal, delivered in the exact same language even, we'd be all like "Holy crap, I wish I had a million nuyen so I could invest it in this guy's idea."

Keep in mind this is other hackers I'm talking about. Not me, of course.

- From the collected sayings of Slamm-0!: "Could you change Jack? I'm busy with brilliant coding." Said approximately five thousand times in the past two years.
- Netcat

- Hey, that's just because I'm uniquely brilliant. It has nothing to do with me being a guy and you not being one.
- Slamm-0!

The point is, while challenges have appeared (including the inevitable people who pop up and are all, "We're changing our hallowed tradition of coding, why can't it be like it always was? Why can't things always stay the same for decades on end?") the fact that people have become pretty intentional about progress being made has meant that actual progress has happened, and the range of hackerdom are filled with any and all types of people. But sometimes vestiges of old attitudes and snobbery rise to the surface, so be ready to brush them off. If you're a troll, be ready to confront people expressing doubt about your abilities for pretty much your entire life. And don't expect this to just drain away from society. Remember, we live in the Sixth World, where people can believe firmly in equality and diversity until someone pays them enough to overcome their convictions. Everything else is for sale, why not tolerance?

HACKING AND SHADOWRUNNING

Now that we have the basics of of hackerdom down, let's see how that works out in the field. You probably have a hacker on your team, and if you don't you're going to have to deal with one sooner or later. They're going to be taking a share of whatever you are paid, so you might as well get the most out of them. Here are some tips for feeding and caring for your hacker in the wild.

REMEMBER THEIR BIAS FOR ACTION

If you're going to have a long planning meeting where you map out everything you're going to do on the run, be prepared for your hacker's attention to wander. They might proclaim their boredom, introduce distractions, and otherwise derail what you are trying to do. The worst thing you can do is let it work. We all know that planning needs to happen, and like I said before, we're

not children. We're not skipping important things just because someone can't sit still. So give your hacker a way to actively be involved in the planning. Have them find maps or building blueprints, or look into your target's background, or whatever. Don't insist that they log off of the Matrix while you plan—that's like asking your street sammie to turn off his cyberarm during a fight. Don't think their continual Matrix use is a distraction. Think of it as an asset.

KEEP IT QUIET

Noise is a major pain in the hoop. It's the great equalizer—a mediocre hacker in an ideal, low-noise position can beat out a drek-hot one who's far from his target and in the middle of a spam zone. Take noise reduction and your position seriously. When you're hacker tells you they need a better position, find a way to get it. Unless you have to go through a Zero Zone or something. Then tell your hacker to get a grip on reality and get their fragging job done where they are.

- I don't think people use the air enough. We've got three dimensions—use them. Between magic and tech, there are a number of ways to get aloft, and that can often get people out of some ground-level noise. Just remember the trade off—there's less cover in the skies.
- 2XL

STAY IMAGINATIVE

One of the biggest keys for effectively using your hacker on a run is to remember that most of the time, unless you're running out in the Sahara or something, there are a million things around you that are hackable. Commlinks, cameras, and wireless weapons are the things most people think about, but it doesn't have to stop there. Vehicles, building cleaning systems, lighting systems, ventilation systems, even things like plumbing systems tend to have some Matrix element to them. Your hacker can play a role in making the environment you need for a successful run. Whether they are providing a distraction, raising the temperature in a room so that heat sensors won't notice you, or repurposing drones to bash down doors or something, hackers have a lot to offer besides grabbing paydata and dumping gun ammo. And it's not just in the legwork stage—in combat they have plenty of things they can do to sow chaos and confusion in the battle, and to make attacks or obstacles come out from odd and unexpected directions.

But don't take my word for it. People of JackPoint, let me hear you! What are some things your hacker can do to make your job easier?

- One of the small perks some corps are offering these days is a Dronista, and automated coffee cart that roams office hallways serving up hot, steaming soykaf to the employees. It registers things like arrival time and beverage preferences so that it can anticipate who will want what when, serving it up before people have to order. That's great for them. And for us too, because the arrival and departure habits of hundreds of corporate employees are recorded in its databases. Downloading info from this thing can be really helpful, but it's also so big that you can make a dummy version, slip in a dwarf or small human, and ride them smoothly around the office. Just don't count on them being there for too long—the corps are going to get wise to what we're doing with doom enough, then they'll just go back to making everyone pour their own damn soykaf.
- Sunshine

- Nobody knows everyone in their corp, or even everyone on their floor. So if they get a note from someone they don't know, a lot of the time they won't question it. The trick is to start out with some nice, neutral messages to establish the identity of a fake employee. Don't start out with a message like "Top secret meeting in lunchroom B, stat!" Even the dumbest corp drone is going to see through that pretty quickly. Instead, find out when pretzel day or some other event is happening, then have your fake employee send around notes saying "Hey, remember, free pretzels in the lobby today!" Do a few things like that, and people will start to love the guy. Then, when the time is right and you're sneaking into the office (if you have to do it during work hours, which, in our three-shift world, is quite common), blast out a message from your fake ID about a critical meeting in the conference room, or free ice cream downstairs, or whatever, and watch the people scurry. Works like a charm.
- 0rkCE0

- If you haven't messed with corp AR on a run, you need to. Corporate AR overlays are a little weird—they want to make the place look nice and desirable without looking so nice that the workers will be distracted from what they are doing. That means you won't find a lot of, like, tiki-themed offices or anything. You'll just find a lot of wood grain and marble graphics with simple, classy lettering. These become part of the whole visual background of the place. It isn't that the people don't notice it—if they did, this wouldn't be as fun—but they just assume that it's always going to be there. If you want, you can go for the radical reinvention, putting in a jungle of monkeys or something, which amuses and disorients people for a while, but it can be more effective to tweak what's there. Move the ARO pointing to the cafeteria five meters farther down the hall. Make a few AROs just vanish, so that people used to doing things like turning left at the third ARO get messed up. The delays and confusion you can cause through little tweaks like this are totally fun. If you're not hacking AR as you infiltrate, you're missing out.
- /dev/grrl

HANGING WITH OURSELVES

I started out this whole thing saying how fascinating people find hackers, and how part of us is all "Yeah, you *should* be interested in us." Because we think the stuff we are doing is really cool. So naturally, when we are looking for people to hang with in our downtime (and banging out code during thirty-six-hour binges counts as downtime), we hang with like-minded people.

But when it comes to other hackers, the trick is not all of us are completely like-minded. We all like hacking, but that does not mean we all approach it from the same ways or have the same end goals. We may all like banging out code, but what we want to do with that code can be very different. Right, Puck?

• Right. Some of us want to blast through the horrific pain and limitations of what we call the world and find a better mode of existence. Others of us want to play with remote-controlled toys and watch grown-ups chase little balls around a field.
• Puck

That means that what we do is gravitate toward hacker groups (and their equivalent, technomancer tribes) to find support, share ideas, and embark on projects that we can work on together. Maybe that's releasing private pictures on every corp CEO's commlink, maybe it's finding specs on Ares' latest battlesuit being designed for next season's Desert Wars, or maybe it's trying to destroy the world to bring about Ragnarok and the twilight of the gods. Different strokes.

• Technomancer tribes are equivalent to hacker groups? Only if hacker groups have been harassed, hunted, and had to band together to share tips and techniques for avoiding the people who want to pick into their brains. Has that happened? No. So your equivalence, sweetie, sucks.
• Netcat

Anyway, here are a number of hacker and technomancer groups out there that you can join, or that might cause trouble for you, or might be a useful resource, or whatever.

CHOSON RING

Members: 150
Strictures: Activity, Loyalty, Secrecy
Resources/Dues: Luxury. With an online casino and several examples in the latest in VR and BTL sex, and Choson Ring pretty much has a license to print money. Which they sometimes do, as a sideline.
Description: Every organized crime outfit in the world has long known the importance of having a virtual component—along with good Matrix security. The Choson Seoulpa Ring, though, has been in the leading edge of Matrix crime for years, and they continue to exist as an entirely virtual entity. The ring does not have any official facilities, though any of its higher-ranking members' luxury homes can serve as impromptu meeting locations. But why bother with the meat world when they have such wonderful Matrix facilities? The ring runs the Anieyo Casino, which is a mammoth deluxe virtual gaming site. Any kind of gaming you're interested in can happen there, from obvious things such as card games to slots, to sports betting, to the sort of activities lots of governments and corporations frown on. Wanna lay odds on the number of bodies that will turn up in the Barrens Thursday morning? You can do that. How about betting on the outcome of a hot trial? Sure, that's available too.

• That's no big thing—people just guessing about current events. Why would any government or anything care?
• Chainmaker

• Because governments had too much experience with people making certain bets, then going out to influence the outcome.
• Kay St. Irregular

While you're in the back rooms, be sure to check out the Choson Ring's selection of BTLs. Snuff films, porn, virtual drugs—you name it, they've got it. If you think you have a complete understanding of the full extent of metahuman depravity, examine their holdings. You will find whole new appalling ways people have of getting themselves off at the expense of others.

• Let me just jump in before the speculation or list-making begins and say this: No.
• Glitch

The business is lucrative and the customer traffic is high, but the Choson Ring deals with a particular challenge that has kept other organized crime outfits from diving fully into the virtual world. When things are going well, organized crime outfits can keep violence to a minimum, but they still rely on the *threat* of violence to keep things moving smoothly. One reason they are able to maintain the peace is because would rather comply with them rather than cross them, and the reason they do that is fear. The challenge, then, is how do you instill that fear in people when your organization is virtual, and you can't round up your gang to pay a visit to the people who are causing you trouble? Matrix attacks, forced reboots, device bricking, and bio-feedback are all tools a virtual gang has at its disposal, but what do you do about the person who crosses you and then disconnects entirely? How do you put the hurt on them?

This leads to some significant tasks for the Choson Ring's Matrix personnel. Naturally, they have a lot to do maintaining the casino host, bringing in new programming, and making sure customers behave themselves, but they can't just focus on that. They have to keep a very careful eye on critical people such as suppliers, bribed law-enforcement personnel, and high-value customers, just in case anything goes wrong with them. They are required to be expert trackers, able to give the physical location of any person at a moment's notice (which means yeah, if you go to the Anieyo and make waves, you're going to be noticed and someone is going to try to track you. So behave yourself). They've gotta be skilled in Matrix assault, but they also need to have a database of hired muscle they can send to almost anywhere in the world at short notice. Keeping that database accurate and up-to-date is important, if not glamorous. Calling on help that betrayed you in the past, or is actually dead, is not a good way to maintain your reputation in the ring.

- Slamm-0! is right that maintaining the database is not glamorous, but think about the end result—an accurate database of reliable, skilled muscle. There is plenty of value there.
- Thorn

- Just remember that they are reliable for the Choson Ring, not necessarily anyone else. Keep that in mind when you think about how to present yourself.
- Kia

The Choson Ring will take on skilled, loyal hackers, but this is not a position you latch onto for fun and prestige. There are no dues, because joining the ring is all about sweat equity. You're supposed to earn your keep. If you sign up, you need to be working on ring projects. And it should go without saying that you need to not talk about what you are doing or who your associates are, and you should never double-cross them. Organized crime has never desired a reputation for mercy.

THE COOPERATIVE

Members: 10

Strictures: Dues, Privacy

Resources/Dues: Middle. Dues are 600 nuyen per month and are used to bolster security and secrecy for all group members. This includes online measures (improving their abilities, enhancing the Resonance Library, registering sprites) as well as offline ones (including funding safehouses and hiring shadowrunners).

Description: One of the longest-standing technomancer groups in existence, this group formed shortly after the Emergence, before most people had any idea what technomancers were. The three original members—Cortex, Wizbyte, and Slashdot—helped each other understand what was happening to them. Since that point, they have been very active in any matters involving technomancers, including exploring and exposing the corporate machinations surrounding technomancer experimentation. This did not put them on good terms with MCT and NeoNET, and the mutual grudge between those corps and the Cooperative continues to this day.

The original trio was very cautious about expansion, only allowing people they fully trust into their inner circle. Many people, including technomancers, have worked with the Cooperative in different circumstances over the the years, and it usually takes multiple such exposures before the Cooperative will invite a new member in. Most of the time, of course, the invitation does not happen at all. By 2072 the group had expanded up to seven members; in the intervening years they have only grown to ten.

That growth is the result of four additions, not three, as the group lost a member in 2074. One of their members, Engram, traveled to Las Vegas to participate in the anti-Horizon demonstrations taking place there. Of course, members of the Cooperative do not just travel someplace to wave AR signs and chant slogans. Engram was right in the middle of the Strip when technomancers launched their assault on Horizon (and any other nearby corp) holdings there, and as a result she was one of the first people killed in what became known as the Technomancer Massacre.

The Cooperative is not going to forget what happened in Vegas, but they are also not foolish enough to believe that ten people, no matter how powerful they might be at manipulating the Matrix, are going to bring down a megacorporation. They also know that it's very possible someone in Horizon discovered Engram's identity and traced her back to the Cooperative, as Horizon is not without hacking talent of its own. That means a substantial part of what they have been doing in recent years is playing defense, covering their tracks and identities as much as possible to keep anyone, including Horizon and corporations that still might be interested in technomancer testing, from finding them.

Playing nothing but defense is not in their nature, though. They see opportunity in the CFD situation to bring some pain to one of their old nemeses, NeoNET, and they are anxious to find any evidence of their involvement in the events that led to the CFD virus. If you find anything interesting in your travels, make a copy if you can—the Cooperative may pay you handsomely for it.

That's a lot to keep them busy, but they are not going to forget about Horizon. They understand that the key is not for them to take on Horizon single-handedly—they're pretty much a dirtball when compared to a mega. Their job is to find the right ally (or allies) who will do their dirty work for them. The Megacorporate Revision presents them a good opportunity. Double-A corps who were passed over for AAA status in favor of Horizon have long resented the megacorp, and the possibility that they might actually be downgraded is infuriating to them. They don't need much of an excuse to start bringing the pain to Horizon, so the Cooperative is going to do all they can to provide excuses. Faking memos from Horizon executives targeting certain AAs for downgraded status, exposing security vulnerabilities in certain Horizon holdings (especially in port areas, which have become hotspots in the rising conflict), and leaking information about the domestic and travel habits of Horizon board members are all part of their activities, and all things they might bring outsiders in to help with. If you throw in with them, just remember: Horizon may be the "nice" megacorp, but they've already proven quite willing to get blood on their hands when the Consensus tells them they should. Or when they get mad enough.

Naturally, the Cooperative requires members, or anyone who knows about them, to keep things on the down-low. They are unforgiving about this. Any bit

of sloppiness, any speech out of turn, anything that might reveal anything useful about the Cooperative to outsiders is enough to get you kicked out. They have been careful enough about who they admit that to this point it has not been an issue.

- It hasn't been an issue for members. They've cracked down on a few associates who have not been careful with what they know. Usually they empty bank accounts and steal identities rather than out-and-out kill people, but they make exceptions.
- Pistons

CRACKER UNDERGROUND

Members: 10,000+ total, 2,500 or so active
Strictures: Privacy, Don't be a dick
Resources/Dues: Low. There are no formal dues, though members make contributions to maintain the group's host. Beyond the host, they really don't have any collective resources.

Description: There was a time in the not-so-distant past that the Cracker Underground felt like a piece of the Matrix as a whole. The attitudes that ran throughout this private network—openness, sharing, freedom, all that jazz—were common throughout the Matrix. Maybe the Cracker Underground took it a little farther than anyone else, what with the rampant sharing of cracked tridz and warez and the streams of live sporting events without a subscription and without the express written permission of anyone everywhere—but it felt like maybe the rest of the world would get there, if we gave them enough time.

Now? No. Danielle de la Mar led the Matrix to a new, unfortunate condition, with the enthusiastic support of the megacorps. Freedom and openness don't even register with most people when they talk about the Matrix. Instead, they talk about "safety" and "security." Are neo-anarchist groups facing considerably more censorship and difficulty getting any messages out? Are hacker havens tracked down and snuffed out with alarming rapidity? Have law enforcement officers been able to send people selling pirated copies of *Water Margin 3* into private penitentiaries for ten-year sentences? The answers are yes, yes, and unbelievably yes.

This means that the Cracker Underground is more essential than ever. It's not just about watching trids for free or not paying for hot shooter games; it's about carrying the torch of an ideal, the concept that information should be free, that knowledge should be shared, and that the Matrix is the greatest tool ever invented for spreading the wealth of the world around and evening up some of the imbalances.

Committing crimes is nothing new to the Cracker Underground, even in the days of the old Matrix, but the stakes have gotten much higher. Monitoring is much more strict, penalties are stiffer, and public support is dramatically less. People don't see the Cracker Underground as freedom fighters; they see them as a menace, undermining the safety of their shiny new Matrix.

One benefit of the new Matrix is that members of the Cracker Underground quickly figured out how to build their own host, providing a decent amount of privacy and security. A lot of time in the past few years has been dedicated to bulking that host up, and it's pretty good, especially on the defensive end. Many users would like the offensive capabilities to be bulked up as well, but privacy was foremost on their minds.

The privacy is taken seriously. The requirements are simple—if you allow someone to trace you to the Cracker Underground host, then you are out, never to return. If you are at all uncertain about whether you're being followed or tracked, stay away.

The only other requirement to be a member of this community is simple: Don't be a dick. Add to the community, don't subtract from it. Show some respect for your fellow hackers. Live up to the hacker ideal of appreciating good work, no matter who it comes from. There are plenty of stupid games going on elsewhere in the Matrix—leave them out of the Underground.

In case it was not clear from the above, I'm a long-time Underground member and a firm supporter of its ideals. Yeah, there are lots of games and trids and BTLs there, but there are secret dossiers on corp shadow activities, details on illicit government activities, information on good reagent hunting grounds, and more. The seeds of the revolution are here, and we will continue to do our part to prepare the soil.

ELECTRIC KNIGHTS

Members: 35 or so
Strictures: Loyalty
Resources/Dues: Low. Members give thirty percent of any proceeds from their activities to the gang.
Description: The go-gangers of the Matrix, the Electric Knights take down targets for the thrill of it. Financial gain is nice and all, but not really what they are about. In some ways they're like toddlers (and I don't mean that in a bad way, necessarily), in that they are really interested in dumping things out and seeing how they roll, or throwing paint on the wall to see what kind of patterns it makes.

Sorry—the destructive power of toddlers is high in my mind for some reason.

Anyway, the Electric Knights are creative but destructive. You admire the guts and cleverness that they put into their results, but you sometimes worry about the pain they cause. And you really worry if whatever they've decided to do occurs wherever you're working.

The Electric Knights first made their name when they crashed Seattle's Gridlink system, resulting in an epic traffic jam that people still talk about. They didn't stop there, though. In subsequent years, they hacked the trid display at a Deirdre concert in Tarislar to spell out the words "Trog Power!"; hacked a navigational satellite and sent a handful of shipping boats hundreds of kilometers off course; made thousands of commlinks emit their ringtones at top volume all at once during a Kenneth Brackhaven speech; and, perhaps most noticeably, redirected several trucks carrying livestock to Downtown Seattle and then opened them all at once, sending cows and pigs roaming through the streets.

As you might guess, these guys are widely viewed as a public menace. No one will publicly admit that they like them. In private, though, their antics generate a lot of snickers.

Of course, the life of a Matrix gang member isn't all about pranks. There's routine stuff, like identity theft, pirating trids and BTLs, and others activities that are lower profile than the big hacks but do a better job of generating some actual revenue. Gang members donate thirty percent of what they earn back to the gang. They are not overly motivated to work hard to earn a lot of cash for the gang—if they wanted to work hard at earning nuyen, they probably would have chosen a different lifestyle. They usually do just enough to keep the basement of an abandoned high-rise they are reputed to use as their hideout from falling apart. Then they go back to playing shooter games and planning pranks.

As you probably noticed from the description of their activities, the gang is very Pacific Northwest-focused, likely based in Seattle (some say Tacoma). Their activities have stretched as far south as San Francisco, and there are some odd Matrix occurrences up in Anchorage that have been blamed on them. Still, Seattle and Tarislar receive the vast majority of their attention.

There is not a whole lot of underlying code or dogma to talk about with the Electric Knights. Despite their name, they couldn't care less for chivalry or related notions. Like most of their other activities, they chose the name because they thought it was cool. Nothing more.

Membership stays pretty low, partly because the Electric Knights don't build trust with others that easily, partly because the gang lifestyle isn't lucrative enough to attract a wide range of people. They get a few hangers-on and wannabes coming their way every year, and most of these get turned away. They'll take non-hackers in as members if they think they provide a skillset that is useful to them, like physical protection, but most bruisers aren't interested in spending their days with a bunch of kids zoned out in VR all day. Of the thirty-five or so current members, maybe five are non-hackers. They are reputed to have a technomancer or two in their ranks, but by most accounts these are newly Emerged people still trying to feel their way around their skills.

The Electric Knights don't have enough resources to be mobile, and they don't want the victims of their pranks to track them down, so secrecy is big to them. That means loyalty is big too. They'll forgive a gang member being sloppy—they all are, sometimes—but squealing is unforgivable. You spill secrets to a non-gang member, you can expect information to be circulated to every gang in Seattle that you've done something or other to piss them out. The Knights will then wait for others to do their hunting for them.

> ◉ Like a lot of prank-based gangs, the Electric Knights want people to know what they've done, so they have a distinct signature. Look out for a small icon of a knight riding a bolt of lightning—they send it out just before things go down. If you see it, batten down the hatches, or just get out of Dodge.
> ◉ Pistons

> ◉ They like pranks, are pretty good at them, and usually need cash. If you need a big Matrix distraction, you could do a lot worse than hiring these guys. The trick is finding them. Work through other gangs. They can usually tell you how to run into a member of the Electric Knights, though they can't guarantee the encounter will go well.
> ◉ Haze

KIVANET

Members: 150
Strictures: Attendance, Limited Membership (NAN citizens),
Resources/Dues: Luxury, no dues. The network maintains several hosts, including one built around a Resonance well.
Description: Plenty of people feel there is an element of mysticism or even magic to technomancy, and nowhere do they feel that stronger than in KivaNet. But what more would you expect from a network started on the advice of a bunch of shamans? The main idea behind KivaNet, as far as I understand it, is to take stewardship over the Matrix, particularly the "living parts" (read: Resonance) in the same way that some shamanic elements have taken stewardship of the physical land. Fully sponsored by the Pueblo Corporate Council, the members of this organization are well taken care of, with deluxe headquarters in Santa Fe and satellite offices in Salt Lake

City, Phoenix, and Las Vegas. Members are not paid, but they can stay at the headquarters, with plenty of food provided to them (in fact, they are required to check I'm at one of the physical locations at least once per year or be put on probationary status). They are encouraged to spent their time reaching out to the Resonance, interacting with it gently in an effort to better understand it, then record their thoughts for posterity. Submersion journeys are also highly encouraged—though if that's going to happen, people need the real-world experience to help them grow. That means hanging out at KivaNet headquarters is nice, but it can't be a full-time job.

Technomancers were (and still are) a distinct minority in the group, but they are growing as the PCC finds more technomancers and the organization attracts more members thanks to the glowing word-of-mouth from its members. Of the 150 current members, about forty are technomancers; most of those are technoshamans.

While the basic goals of researching the Resonance and supporting technomancers are clear, the underlying goals—that is to say, the reasons so much money should be spent on those goals—are unclear. With the whole concept of the Resonance realms containing copies of every electronic thing ever, better understanding of the realms is increasingly important, especially from an espionage point of view. Those with a more optimistic view of human nature (there are still a few of them left. Mostly in zoos) say that the PCC is looking for better integration with the realms, a more holistic approach so that we can treat it better than we have the physical and astral realms, which we have polluted in hundreds of ways. The counter of that is that we clearly have already filled the Resonance realms with billions of pieces of our own garbage (if we didn't create them in the first place), so trying to free them from our influence is an impossible task.

> ◉ Doesn't all this sound too noble for a megacorporation—which is what the PCC is? They don't want to better understand the Resonance to protect it, they want to harness it. He who controls the resonance will control the Matrix, or at least that's what they think. This network sounds nice but is dangerous as hell.
> ◉ Clockwork

THE RAVENS

Members: 17
Strictures: Loyalty
Resources/Dues: Middle. Dues are 150 nuyen per month. The Ravens have a private host that is networked with the PCC's KivaNet, and they receive significant Matrix resources from them. They also have use of KivaNet offices in Santa Fe, Phoenix, Salt Lake City, and Las Vegas
Description: Every large group in the world needs its more militant arm, and that's what the Ravens are to KivaNet. While the larger membership seeks to under-

stand and preserve the Resonance realms, the Ravens exact vengeance against those who they feel are mistreating the realms.

That's a difficult, perhaps impossible job. The realms are flooded with billions of pieces of new data each day. While some might see all of that as a form of pollution, the Ravens don't see it that way. The realms are bastions of information, so putting more information there—or, as some theorists would have it, shaping the information that already exists there—is not pollution, but an appropriate use of the territory.

There are some uses, though, that cross the line. Dissonance is an obvious one. The Ravens are harsh on anyone who attempts to introduce or build dissonance pools, dealing with them on a Matrix level while sending physical teams after them if they feel it's necessary.

They also are opposed to efforts to build up walls or partitions in parts of the realms, securing certain stores of data in virtual fortresses. To some corps, building such fortresses is the only way to deal with the security concerns the realms present, but the Ravens will not stand for it. If anyone tries to build structures into the realms that limit access and transit, the Ravens will attempt to break it down. Assuming, of course, they know about it. The realms are vast, so knowing everything people are attempting to do in them is impossible. The realms, though, also appear to be somewhat searchable. Not in our terms, of course. You can just get to the realms, pull up some window, punch in a few words, and be directed to the file you're looking for. It's not that easy. But those with experience in the realms tell me that there is a certain bizarre, underlying logic to the place, and if you are able to attune yourself to it, you can find data stores that otherwise would have taken years or eons to find. Others say that this attunement is in people's heads, and that the only times people are able to find things faster than they expected is due to sheer dumb luck.

If this attunement exists, though, the Ravens have it. I've heard reports from a lot of corp-connected people of small, secure, out-the-way sites being developed in the realms, only to have the Ravens swoop in from out of nowhere and break things down. Whatever sources they have in the realms, whatever tools they are using, are obviously pretty good.

As you might expect, the Ravens are strict in who they accept and demand full loyalty from their members. As far as I know all of the members are Aboriginal Americans; I don't know if all of them also have NAN SINs (or any SINs) at all, for that matter. All of the members are technomancers, and all of them are very skilled. If you are not a techno and not good at what you do, you have no chance of being considered for membership. Once you're in, your full loyalty is expected. Expulsion is the least of the punishments you can expect; all I can say is I don't know anyone walking around who claims to be an ex-Raven.

> Here's the issue—technomancers use Resonance as a sort of intermediary between the Matrix and our minds. So it flows right into our brains. If you can control it, you can do bad things to people's heads, meaning that if there are ex-Ravens still alive, they're likely wide-eyed and gaping in a psych ward somewhere.
> Netcat

REALITY HACKERS

Members: 30
Strictures: Loyalty, Secrecy
Resources/Dues: Middle. Members give twenty percent of any proceeds they get from gang missions back to the gang. They are reputedly based in Puyallup, but whether they have a single facility, multiple facilities, or they regularly move from place to place is unknown. Based on reports of meeting with members physically and the condition of the devices they use, they seem to have decent means.

Description: While the Electric Knights are big and showy, the Reality Hackers and stealthy. The Electric Knights worry about branding what they do and rubbing the fact that they pulled off certain pranks in people's faces; the Reality Hackers figure pulling off the impossible is its own reward. There are merits to each approach, but I'll tell you this from the teams I've worked with—if we need a little Matrix assistance on the side (which should never be the case when I'm on board, but never mind), nine times out of ten I'd go with the Reality Hackers.

> People who are a little more creative about how big-and-loud techniques can be worked into their repertoire would probably shift that ratio.
> Puck

The secrecy of the Reality Hackers means that it's tricky to make a long list of the jobs they have pulled off. Did they get a tap into a large transfer between Wuxing and Brackhaven Investments and break off a piece of the transfer for themselves? Did they scrub information about their members and allies from Shiawase MFID databases? Did they infiltrate a Charisma Associates private host, alter a marketing report about a new one-seater 'copter, then make a bundle short-selling stock when the project tanked, despite the optimistic report? Did they mess with Boston Massacre's smarlinks, comms, and other data streams, costing them a playoff game against the Seattle Screamers while providing a nice bonus to people who bet on the Screamers? The answer to all of those is "maybe."

Note most of those scenarios listed above have some associated financial gain. The Reality Hackers are much more fiscally conscious than a lot of other Matrix gangs. They want to have the latest gear and good medical care,

so they make sure regular nuyen flow into gang coffers, wherever those may be.

The need for medical care comes from the fact that the Reality Hackers are known to be good in any kind of fighting, Matrix or otherwise. They have long been at the cutting edge of integrating Matrix tactics with physical combat, from hacking cyberware to shaping surrounding AR into disorienting patterns to making anything Matrix connected and capable of movement into a potential asset.

Given their skills and their mercenary tendencies, the Reality Hackers may be available for lending Matrix support or providing crucial information. The trick is finding them, as they do not advertise. If you want the support of the Reality Hackers, work every underground Matrix concept you have. And be sure you don't have the stink of The Man on you, because they'll smell it in a heartbeat.

- ◉ So to find them, I'd need to know someone who had long experience with Matrix hacking, a certain disrespect for authority, and a knowledge of a lot of the players in the hacking world. Slamm-0!, would you be interested in taking a meeting?
- ◉ Marcos

- ◉ You also should be smart enough to send messages like that privately, instead of posting them on any sort of forum that lots of eyes can see.
- ◉ Slamm-0!

I have no useful advice on how to join the Reality Hackers. Their need for skilled hackers who know how to acquit themselves well in a fight would seem to narrow their potential field of members, but I know of a few people matching that description in the Seattle area who have never had any indication that the Reality Hackers are reaching out to them in any way. They apparently will recruit whom they will, and there is no reliable way to force their hand.

TECHNICOLOR STREAMS

Members: 50
Strictures: Dues
Resources/Dues: High. Dues are 300 nuyen per month. Members are recognized at Tailspin, Technicolor Wings, and Technicolor Streams locations across the globe.
Description: The Technicolor Wings empire continues to grow as they find new ways to address some of the organization's growing pains. In the earlier part of the decade, the smuggling organization opened up their Tailspin clubs. Continuing their cover as a legitimate shipping organization, TW used the chain ostensibly as a place where their gearheads and flight jockeys could swap tales and relax. An additional function of the chain was recruiting people, using the casual atmosphere to get a feel for newcomers and see what they might be able to offer as members.

Trouble was, word started getting out about that purpose, and people started seeing Tailspin customer information as a way of tracking down TW members and their teams. The need for Matrix security was strong from the start, and it only increased with the new Matrix. TW got some insider status with the new protocols—they provide a service many corps view as useful, after all, and they are a corp themselves—but they also know that the authorities might have an easier time of sneaking a peek into their databases whenever they think it might be useful. Technicolor Wings accelerated their recruiting of skilled hackers (including dealers and technomancers), and they gathered the best of their recruits into an elite hacking corps known as Technicolor Dreams.

While they were initially tasked with increasing security at Tailspin locations, Technicolor Dreams have taken on many more tasks. Hacking can play a vital role in smuggling operations, and TS has become a go-to consultant for TW members looking for advice on crossing tough borders. When they need more than advice, they go ahead and take a TS member with them.

Since so much of TW business involves crossing international and extraterritorial boundaries, TS has also developed a significant expertise on international and corporate law. That doesn't mean they're lawyers who can represent you or anything—it just means they can help you know what is required and what isn't when doing a border crossing. And they can provide advice on how to weasel around those requirements. They also, of course, have a considerable knowledge of the latest developments in national hosts, so if you need information on that subject, they're the ones to turn to.

Thee other subject area where they have considerable expertise is Matrix security, particularly when it comes to defense. Soon after the chain opened, Tailspin gained a reputation for hosting fights, as wannabe shadowrunners were a little over-anxious to prove themselves by challenging whoever they could (one of the benefits of TS or TW membership is access to members-only areas of Tailspin locations, separating you from the wannabes). That same attitude has extended to TW hosts, as people get the bright idea that they can impress the organization by breaking into their hosts. Pile them on top of the corps looking for dirt on Tailspin customers and TW personnel, and you get regular hack attempts. TS hackers have a lot of work on their hands, but they don't want to have to spend their time acting as security spiders. They work hard to design systems that are automated but effective, and their knowledge of automated Matrix security techniques is bleeding edge.

THE WALKING PEOPLE

Members: 60
Strictures: Activity, Dues
Resources/Dues: Squatter. Dues are 50 nuyen per year. The group has a single private host and no physical locations.

Description: This is a group bound and determined to survive every iteration of the Matrix that comes their way. They once were an otaku tribe called the "Routers." They were scattered and changed by the events of Crash 2.0, and following the Emergence of technomancers they banded together to support those among their membership who gained these new abilities.

While life is not exactly safe for technomancers, some of the initial panic has lessened, and the activities of the Walking People have broadened. They have adopted more deckers into their numbers—technomancers used to be about half of their numbers, but now that is down to about a third. They also have a new Matrix to deal with, so some of the emphasis has shifted from helping technomancers survive the world to helping everyone survive GOD.

While they are scattered, most of the members are based in Europe, making them one of the best collectives of Matrix knowledge on the continent—even though they are not collected in any physical sense.

As the group has grown and matured, they have taken on a distinctly neo-anarchist flavor. They've looked at this new, centrally controlled Matrix and found it lacking in almost every respect. The question, then, is what to do about it. Random vandalism to corporate hosts is fun, but has no real long-term effect. Sixty people paying a minimum of dues is not enough to take on a local alderman, let alone a megacorporation, so if they are going to have any effect, they have to be smart and careful.

Fortunately for them, near the center of the continent where most of them are based is the Berlin sprawl. If neo-anarchists are going to have a worldwide impact, it's going to start in Berlin, and the Walking People are going to be there to help. Lately, they've taken to specializing in building hosts from the foundation of the Matrix for small organizations, giving them a foothold in the virtual world. As a result, the Walking People have become very skilled at deep runs. It's a dangerous strategy, one that's likely to cost them a few members, so they are recruiting new members to help them build strength as well as replace potential losses. They can't recruit openly, but they are also not as reclusive as some of the other groups on this list. Ask around to the people likely to know neo-anarchists, and you are likely to find the start of a trail that, before long, will end in one of the Walking People.

If you're thinking about joining the Walking People, remember that this is not the type of group you join so you can use the members' clubhouse or anything. They have a decent host but no physical facilities, and they are not looking for people who are just going to hang out. If you are going to sign up, you need to be active in group activities. Learn about foundations, go on deep runs, help groups in Berlin protect their information, that sort of thing. If you spend a year not doing anything for the cause, you're likely to find your membership suddenly expired.

> ● They are mostly in Europe but not exclusively. I have made good use of them in my time in Bogotá, though I won't say exactly where the members that helped me were working from.
> ● Aufheben

GROUP RESOURCES

The group resource categories correspond to Lifestyle levels (p. 369, *SR5*) and indicate generally what the group has at its disposal. Here are some more specific definitions of each category.

Luxury: The group has a dedicated headquarters that is fully and nicely furnished. It is the sort of place that might attract visitors wishing to simply bask in the ambiance. The central location has a Hardware facility, while the satellite locations have a Hardware shop. They also have other sites for members, including housing that provides a Middle lifestyle. Ratings of hosts in this category should be between 8 and 10.

High: The group has a central headquarters, though not as fancy or high-profile as those in the Luxury class. There are also smaller satellite offices. All locations have a Hardware shop. The central location may provide Middle lifestyle housing, but the satellite locations do not. Ratings of hosts for groups in this category generally should be from 6 to 9.

Middle: Groups in this category have a single location that includes a Hardware shop. They do not have any housing for members. Their hosts generally are rated between 4 and 8

Low: Any central locations these groups have are sparse and lightly furnished, if at all. Hosts generally are rated from 3 to 6. The location contains a Hardware kit.

Squatter: Without a real place to call home, the organization has no tools, shops, or facilities for common use, and they certainly cannot provide any housing. Hosts generally range from Rating 1 to 5

Street: This group has nothing besides the individual talents of its members—and maybe a host between Rating 1 and 3.

ON THE BLEEDING EDGE

Maybe you're looking to build the ultimate decker, or a crushing technomancer. Or maybe you're building a hacker who is going to overcome troubles on their way to greatness. Or maybe you're building a character who is a mixed bag of skills and weaknesses, like the rest of us. Whatever the case may be, here are Matrix-oriented qualities to help make that fully fleshed-out Matrix surfer!

And they're not just for deckers and technomancers—there are qualities here that could be used by just about any character.

POSITIVE QUALITIES

DATA ANOMALY

COST: 3 KARMA

An incessant code tinkerer, you know very effective ways to hide your icon, making it look like nothing more than a piece of errant code. You gain +2 dice when resisting a Matrix Perception test while running silent. Unfortunately, whatever it is you're doing to hide yourself has one little flaw—sprites, those mysterious creatures of the Matrix, can spot you instantly, exactly as if you weren't running silent at all.

FADE TO BLACK

COST: 7 KARMA

When the opposition starts getting marks on you, you know the hurt isn't far behind. That feeling of the noose tightening around your neck, the race to get them before they get you ... well, you hate that drek. So much so that you have developed your vanishing act technique. When making a Complex Action to perform the Erase Mark action, if you succeed in erasing all marks on you, you may then immediately perform a Hide action as part of the same Complex Action you just took.

GO BIG OR GO HOME

COST: 6 KARMA

You don't have time to mess around. When you strike, you strike to kill. Whenever you attempt to place three marks on a target using a single Brute Force or Hack on the Fly action, you suffer a penalty of –6 instead of the usual –10. Now, go get 'em, Tiger.

GOLDEN SCREWDRIVER

COST: 8 KARMA

It happens to everyone: You meet more hacking opposition that you expected, and your shit gets bricked. Maybe it's your deck. Maybe it's your cybereyes. They just love to brick cybereyes, don't they? Well, null persp, chummer, 'cause been there, done that. You are so used to fixing Matrix damage that you hardly think about it anymore. Every hit you get on your Hardware + Logic test reduces 1 box of Matrix Damage *and* reduces the time to do so by half—you do not have to allocate your hits to one or the other.

I C U

COST: 6 KARMA

In the shadows, everyone always runs silent, right? To you, what gives them away is the obviousness of the lack of activity. You're so used to this, you know exactly what to look for. So long as you have visual sight on a target that is running silent, or carrying silent-running devices, you get +2 to your Matrix Perception to spot their hidden icon(s).

NINJA VANISH

COST: 5 KARMA

Even the best sometimes get clipped. Maybe you're in a host, holding off some IC, but there are just too damn many of them. Maybe you're in the middle of a firefight and the enemy hacker is getting the best of you, and you're moments away from having your deck reformatted, when suddenly, the Matrix glitches. A little localized reset saves your bacon. Just like that. What are the odds, neh? Maybe GOD is on your side? That can't be—you must just be that good.

As a Free Action, the character can spend 1 point of Edge to remove all marks a single opponent has on him. Note that in cases where other targets were sharing marks with your target, such as IC in a host, the others also lose their marks.

ONLINE FAME

COST: 4 KARMA

Congratulations, you're famous! Well, sort of. You are only famous as a Matrix persona. Maybe you're a famous blogger, an online gaming hero, or a cyberpunk roleplaying-game freelance author (be still your beating heart). People know your icon and your signature, but even your most ardent fan wouldn't recognize you if they passed you in the street on a brightly lit day. Further, none would actually believe you if you tried to tell them (quite the opposite, in fact). You gain +2 dice to your Social tests and +2 dice to your Social Limit when interacting with someone who knows you, but only when you interact with them via the Matrix. Characters who see your icon are able to identify you with a successful Intuition + Logic (2) Test.

Any character who is able to see both your icon and your physical self is thrown into a conflict. Either they will believe you are truly *him*, or they will refuse to believe and think you are trying to impersonate, erm, yourself.

If they believe you, your bonus becomes +3 on Social Tests and Social Limit toward your ecstatic fan, which now applies to all interactions, not just Matrix ones.

However, if they do not believe you, you suffer -4 to all Social interactions. In addition, the character may outright attack you or call the police to report you.

To determine a character's reaction, the gamemaster may roll a single D6. On a roll of 5 or 6, the character believes you. On any other roll, the character does not.

OTAKU TO TECHOMANCER

COST: 10 KARMA

You were an otaku, a child of the Matrix, bending the Matrix to the will of your mind alone, before it was cool to do so. Most of your kind, assuming they even survived this long, did not emerge as technomancers. But for you, lightning struck twice—you went from otaku to

technomancer. Having known your abilities for longer than just about anyone else alive, dealing with these strange powers is second nature to you. You gain +2 dice when resisting Fading from any source.

PAIN IS GAIN

COST: 5 KARMA

Virtual reality—especially hot sim—can be addictive. But what people don't understand is how exhilarating slicing through the Matrix really is. Not just the simsense feedback. No. To you, it's the thrill of the fight. You never feel more alive than that moment when searing white-hot pain hits you between the eyes as the IC tries to fry you. It's the knowledge that your life is on the line as you redline it, all at the speed of thought, that gets you juiced up.

The character gains +2 to their current Initiative Score on any turn she suffers Biofeedback damage (Stun or Physical). This extra score comes into effect at the same time damage is incurred and lasts only for the current Combat Turn. The character may only gain 2 points of Initiative per Combat Turn in this way, no matter how many times they get slapped around.

PRIME DATAHAVEN MEMBERSHIP

COST: 7 KARMA

JackPoint, the Nexus, the Helix—legendary sites of information-sharing among the shadowrunner elite. Access to these sites is invitation-only, and guess what—you've been invited! You'll be a probationary member for a while, but that's still not bad. You pretty much gain access to most of the information you might ever want, you're just not necessarily privy to the administrative secrets of the haven and some of the more sensitive posts. These sites all operate on a give-to-be-given, information-should-be-free mentality. You will be expected to feed the dataHaven with regular posts sharing your expertise and detailing some of the things you encounter, though it is accepted as a mark of professionalism to censor your information so as to not include names or details that might lead to identification of the specific players involved.

When choosing this quality, pick one of these famous datahavens. It will act as a Group Contact (p. 176, *Run Faster*). The Group Contact is considered to have a Loyalty of 3 and Connection of 5.

PROFILER

COST: 3 KARMA

If you know someone well, you can often guess their actions. Simple enough in theory, and something that you have mastered. Given enough information about someone, you are able to get into their head and know what buttons to push and how to manipulate them. With an appropriate dossier on a person and one hour to study it, you gain a modifier to your dice pool and your Social Limit on all Social Tests involving that person, equal to the net hits on a Matrix Search test (maximum +3).

An appropriate dossier can be gathered via a Matrix Search test. The threshold is always at least 3, but depending on the individual may be as high as 6 (gamemaster's discretion). The information required is always Obscure (–2 modifier) and may be On Another Grid (further –2 modifier, gamemaster's discretion).

The downside to the character's ability to profile others so well is an inability to react smoothly when unprepared. The character suffers –1 to their Social Limit in any and all situations where they could not prepare.

QUICK CONFIG

COST: 5 KARMA

Maybe you're just nova-hot at moving your fingers around, or maybe your mind is highly organized. Whatever the case, reconfiguring your deck is something you do with freakish rapidity. Whenever you reconfigure your deck (p. 228, SR5), you can make two changes with a single Free Action. So, you may switch two programs for two others, or you can swap two pairs of cyberdeck attributes. You can also swap one program and one attribute pair. Note that a single attribute can only be swapped once, so there is still a limit to how much the new config can achieve.

Example: Trix has the Quick Config quality and is currently running a Novatech Navigator with Attack 6, Sleaze 5, Data Processing 4, and Firewall 3 (6/5/4/3). She could use a Free Action to reconfigure her deck and swap Attack and Sleaze and then Data Processing and Firewall to end up with 5/6/3/4). What she could not do is swap Attack and Sleaze and then Sleaze with Firewall (5/3/4/6).

NEGATIVE QUALITIES

CODE OF HONOR: LIKE A BOSS

REQUIREMENT: MINIMUM HACKING SKILL OF 3 OR TECHNOMANCER
BONUS: 15 KARMA

Bricking someone's gear, that's easy. There's no *finesse* to it. Anyone can throw junk code around. A true hacker though—a true master of the skill, a true devotee of the lifestyle—will show perfection in his actions. A character with this quality will not use any action that would cause Matrix Damage, such as Spike or Brute Force (the character is allowed, however, to set Data Bomb traps). Instead, the character must find other means of defeating his enemy, such as using Hack on the Fly to gain marks to Edit or Reformat Matrix items, or perhaps just Jamming Signals. The character will lose 1 point of Karma per target that he willingly causes direct Matrix Damage to (aside from Data Bombs).

CURIOSITY KILLED THE CAT

REQUIREMENT: MINIMUM HACKING SKILL OF 3
BONUS: 7 KARMA

Oooh, an encrypted file ... you just *know* the data in it must be juicy! Let's just take a quick peek, okay?

The character has an unrelenting compulsion to grab protected data, crack it, and see what's in it. Whenever the character encounters protected files (see the Edit File action, p. 239, *SR5*), he must succeed in a Composure (3) Test or attempt to Crack the File. The character is allowed to attempt to check if the file has a Data Bomb on it, and if so, to disarm it. However, the character cannot move on with his life until the file has been cracked and downloaded (he can read it later). Even if the character is in the middle of a host with IC trying to kill him and enemy hackers slinging at him, he will stop what he is doing and attempt to get that file.

But wait, it's not all bad! You get +2 dice to all Crack File tests.

DATA LIBERATOR

BONUS: 12 KARMA

Some would say you're fighting the good fight. Others would sneer that you won't last long in this business. And yet many more would kill you on sight for what you've done.

The character is compelled to give away for free any gained paydata, intelligence, or secret from any mission they perform. The character simply disseminates the data to news outlets, screamsheets, shadowrunner data boards, etc. To anyone who will listen, really.

If the character was specifically hired to collect data, they may still chose to deliver the data to the buyer as normal, accepting or refusing the fee (player's discretion). However, they will then immediately disseminate the data widely.

The character is likely to make friends as well as enemies fairly quickly doing this. Consider it playing a character on the "difficult" setting.

DECAYING DISSONANCE

REQUIREMENT: TECHNOMANCERS ONLY
BONUS: 25 KARMA

It's hard to tell when it started. Yesterday? A month ago? Or was it always inside you, and you just never noticed? But recently, it has grown. Sometimes, it's the dissociative thoughts. Mr. Johnson is talking about robbing a data bank, and all you can think about is a longshoreman in an orange jacket. Focusing is hard. Sometimes it's your makeup. Lipstick on the eyelids, eyeliner around the lips. But mostly, mostly, it's the Matrix. Everything about it is starting to feel wrong. What others call data, you call broken thoughts masquerading as information. It's put together wrong. It feels so, so much better when you put it the way it ought to be ...

A character with the Decaying Dissonance quality has been infected with Dissonance. This is not a well-understood thing. It's not exactly a mental illness. It's not a virus. It's a state of being, something that changes in one's core. The character is starting to think that what others call clean and orderly feels wrong, very wrong. They want to see things put together all differently. They want to deconstruct everything, mix the pieces, and put it back in a way that makes sense only to them, and maybe others like them.

This quality manifests in several ways. Whenever the character is in a stressful situation (such as combat), the character's communications become nonsensical. To restore order to his thoughts, the character must take a Simple Action and succeed in a Composure (2) Test. Success means the character can communicate normally for the rest of the combat. Failure means any attempts to communicate result in gibberish, though the character can understand what others say.

Outside of combat, the character can easily get distracted. This is off-putting to people speaking to him, resulting in a –1 die penalty to all Social Tests. It also affects his ability to remember things. Any glitch on a Memory Test counts as a critical glitch.

Lastly, and perhaps most importantly of all, the technomancer has problems with the way the Matrix is around him, particularly while in hosts. When in a host,

the character must pass a Composure (3) Test or start randomly using Edit File on data around him. Data affected in this way becomes gibberish, unreadable to anyone.

This quality can be bought off, but only as part of a Submersion. Eliminating this quality replaces the normally chosen echo. Note that the quality must be paid off with the regular Karma cost, on top of any Karma expenditure associated to the Submersion.

ELECTRONIC WITNESS

BONUS: 5 KARMA

The character is part of a movement of people who constantly record everything around them. Always. All the time. The idea is that something interesting may eventually happen. Maybe it's not something you'd immediately notice as interesting, but if you archive it, maybe you'll spot something useful later. And you believe that, if everyone did the same as you, the world would be a much better place. And hey, you can sell your recordings too, so that's always good.

With this quality, the character must acquire gear to record video and sound and wear it at all time (cybereyes and cyberears would be perfect, but sensors can otherwise be mounted in gear). This gear must always be on. The character will *never* turn off wireless functionality on their gear. If the character takes the Day Job quality, then they meet the conditions of the job simply by *being*, as they then sell the recordings to specialized data brokers and make their money this way. If they opt not to take Day Job, then the character can do what they wish with the recordings.

In any situation where the character cannot record or turns off wifi on his gear, then they feel especially agitated, suffering a –1 dice pool penalty to all actions.

FARADAY HIMSELF

BONUS: 7 KARMA

Maybe it's your diet. Too much iron in it? Maybe it's your cyberware, causing interference. Whatever it is, you are a bit of a problem. Whenever you are near, the static on the line goes up. Anyone within ten meters of you (including yourself) suffers +2 Noise. This noise can be reduced in the normal way and is cumulative with whatever noise penalties would normally apply. It is worth noting that anyone outside of the ten meters who is attempting to connect to you (including attempts to hack you) do not suffer this extra noise penalty.

LATEST AND GREATEST

BONUS: 5 KARMA

The character just loves her tech. Really, really loves it. That is, until something better comes along. After all, the problem with getting things is that you get something you *used* to want, right? The character has an unstoppable desire to upgrade her gear. Every month, she must upgrade or buy a more expensive version of one of her most commonly used pieces of gear. For example, a hacker would seek to upgrade her deck or commlink. A street samurai would get a better, more expensive assault rifle, or, of course, cyber upgrades—such as the next highest rating of cybereyes with more accessories in it. Magic-users would want higher-rating focus or lodge. If all else fails, moving up to the next Lifestyle bracket is always an option.

The character must spend at least sixty percent of her earnings on these upgrades. It is possible to earmark earnings for a specific purchase down the road if she's saving up for a particularly shiny new toy, but this money is unavailable to the character until then.

LEEEEEEROY JENKINS

BONUS: 20 KARMA

Planning is not your strong suit. Following other people's plans is not your strong suit. Rushing in swinging with both fists is the only plan you ever need.

The character must succeed in a Composure (3) Test to resist attacking any identified threat immediately. This attack can be conducted using any Combat skills, any Direct or Indirect Damage spell, drones that can be directed to attack the target, or assaults against the target's persona or gear using any Matrix or Resonance action that causes Matrix, Stun, or Physical damage.

The character doesn't care if the odds are against him, the attack is downright suicidal or just plain stupid: they will attack. Crucially, they will also not bother sharing their attack plan (such as it is) with their teammates.

The character can, however, recognize they are in a losing situation and back out of the fight, but only after a minimum of 2 Combat Turns have passed.

If the character roars his or her name as a Free Action right before the first blow is struck, they gain +1 die to their first attack. Good luck.

NERDRAGE

BONUS: 8 KARMA

This character is a little more comfortable with machines than other individuals. Whenever the character fails a Social Test—whether he initiated it, or was the target of one—the character takes it extremely personally and feels deeply humiliated about the encounter. They subsequently build bitter feelings against the individual (if it was a group of people, the bitterness targets the formal or nominal leader of the group). Distracted by their shame and rage, the character starts suffering a –2 dice penalty to all Social

Tests. However, the character can remove this penalty by getting back at the target character by gaining 1 mark on their commlink and performing an Edit File action on it to deface it. The character does not need to perform this themselves—anyone doing this on their behalf is a-okay with them.

The character must "get back" at all characters that humiliated them before losing the dice penalty. If the character is able to confirm the target is now dead (such as by putting a bullet in their head themselves), then that works too.

This quality can be bought off following the normal rules at any time, the character having learned to let it go a little better.

PRANK WARRIOR

BONUS: 15 KARMA

The character has an ongoing prank war with another hacker, but the proportions are a little bit out of hand. What started out as a joke is now as funny as a serial killer with clown makeup. The other hacker will randomly track you down and mess with you and your team, even (especially) in dangerous situations. The hacker will never *quite* go all the way—just enough to make you sweat rather profusely. For example, the hacker may randomly fire off a few Data Spikes at your gear, enough to half-brick it, or contact security of the facility you are invading and tip them off that someone is infiltrating, but without actually giving them your exact position or identity. They may hack your cybereyes to make you see things that aren't there, and so on. Don't think turning off your wifi is going to help—that will just make the hacker escalate his offensive, while crippling yourself.

This quality should come into play at least once per play session.

WANTED BY GOD

**REQUIREMENT: MINIMUM HACKING
   SKILL OF 3. CANNOT BE
   TECHNOMANCER
BONUS: 12 KARMA**

Chummer, I don't know what you've done, but you attracted the wrong kind of attention. You have somehow made it on GOD's Most Wanted list. In case you're wondering, that's not good.

You will suffer convergence when your Overwatch Score hits 30, instead of the normal 40. On top of that, seeing as you are a High Value Target, a High Treat Response squad from the authorities of whatever grid you just got kicked out of will always come bearing down on you. They may or may not be out to take you alive—guess you'll find that out when they come for you.

BORN TO HACK

If you didn't have a list of places to go to when bad drek went down, you could count the number of weeks you were likely to survive on one hand.

Jackie had three different spots to lie low between home and the open-air food market near Touristville—a sparsely populated Cuban restaurant, a former repair shop where some older people of the neighborhood gathered to play chess and checkers, and a rickety clinic run by a cranky old ork. They were spaced well enough that if gunfire broke out on the streets or some gang members started throwing unnerving looks in her direction, she could get to a spot in a block or two and generally stay out of trouble. Yeah, if the gunfire got too hot too fast, she might have to duck behind a broken wall before she could get somewhere more sheltered, but that only happened occasionally.

Today, though, everything was going wrong. A big, roided-out human spotted her from a block away, and she could see a combined hunger and mindless rage in his eyes that told her to stay far away. She crossed the street to get away from him, but he crossed too; she took a left away from her normal route, and he followed. She walked quicker, moving toward a dwarf and a human who seemed to know Roid Boy and not like him. The two of them started yelling at him as soon as he appeared, and he started yelling back, then a few others nearby heard the voices and popped into the streets, and they were the type of people you couldn't just walk by because when their blood was up. They started asking questions to which there were no right answers, and their fists would get real punchy real fast.

Jackie was left with one option, an alley to her left. She didn't know what was down it, which made it a horrible risk, but at present she was way more willing to deal with an uncertain unknown than the sure-thing shitstorm that was about to erupt all around her.

Roid Boy yelled something when she ducked out of view, and she had no desire to hear what it was. This was a rare alley where both buildings near the entrance were intact; one was a burned-out storefront, the other was an apartment building that was falling apart in every respect but still had some residents. Behind the apartment building was an empty lot, but in back of the store was some other old commercial building, with a back door open and a light shining out.

She looked at the door, but four gangers running into the other end of the alley made up her mind for her. She ran for the door, hoping that whatever was behind it didn't suck.

There were stairs going down, then another door. The door was unmarked.

She looked up the stairs, worried that Roid Boy might enter the frame at any moment, then knocked on the door.

A voice came from inside. "Hack it or go away."

She panicked, and she started yelling and hoped what came out made sense.

"I can't, I don't know what you mean, I can't open the door, but there are people out here that are about to throw down and I don't want to be out here and I can't open the door and there are no places for me to go, please, please, please just open it!"

Some muttered voices exchanged words inside, then feet stomped to the door. Mechanisms whirred, the door opened, and an old man with patchy grey hair stood on the other side.

"I've had days like that myself," he said. "Get in here. If you don't know how to hack, you should. Any advantage in a cold world."

She walked in to a room of gear, tools, and chips, random and scattered and all, to her eyes, beautiful. It was a small room, seven meters by seven meters, but it might as well have been a whole new universe.

PATHS TO HACKERDOM

This chapter provides different modules to use with the Life Modules system described on p. 65 of *Run Faster*. They are all focused on building hacker and technomancer characters, so use them to make an awesome Matrix jockey!

NATIONALITIES

The dream some hackers have of developing a Hacker Nation has not yet to come to pass, and thus there is no one nationality that is particularly suited to being a hacker. That means no new modules in this section.

FORMATIVE YEARS

The following modules fit into the Formative Years section of the Life Module system. As with all other modules in this section in *Run Faster*, they cost 40 Karma.

EARLY EMERGENCE

You emerged as a technomancer at a young age, and interacting with the streams of data flowing around you was a normal part of your childhood. You are very comfortable with swimming through rivers of information.

Attributes	Intuition +1
Skills	Compiling +1, Decompiling +1, Software +1, Interest Knowledge: [Matrix-related] +4, Interest Knowledge: [Technical] +4

PART OF THE MACHINE

You grew up among people who work on electronics and other machines. Your living area was always full of spare parts and dissembled devices, and you grew comfortable with them. You also had plenty of time to see how these things worked and how they could be put together.

Attributes	Logic +1
Skills	Computer +1, Hardware +1, Software +1, Interest Knowledge: [Hobby] +4, Interest Knowledge: [Technical] +4

TEEN YEARS

Now here are some modules that characters might experience in the ever-exciting teen years. Like the other modules in *Run Faster*, they cost 50 Karma.

HACKER CLUB

You didn't get traditional schooling, but you were able to find a group of people who shared your interest in manipulating electronic devices, and hanging with them gave you a very specialized but deep education. You also gained some knowledge of tricks that other people don't know.

Attributes	Logic +1, Intuition +1
Qualities	Data Anomaly (3)
Skills	Computer +2, Hacking +1, Hardware +1, Electronic Warfare +1, Interest Knowledge: [Matrix-related] +1, Interest Knowledge: [Technical] +1

TECHNOMANCER BOARDING SCHOOL

As the Sixth World continues to adjust to the Emergence of technomancers, clever entrepreneurs have recognized that there is a demand for places that can help technomancers gain the knowledge they need to use their abilities well—while also keeping them nice and isolated from the rest of the world. If some of them can be recognized as especially talented and funneled into corporate jobs, that's okay, too.

Attributes	Charisma +1, Resonance +1
Skills	Compiling +1, Decompiling +1, Electronic Warfare +1. Hacking +1, Registering +1, Software +1, Interest Knowledge: [Matrix-related]+1, Interest Knowledge: [Technical] +1

FURTHER EDUCATION

For hackers, many of the education paths they may follow are already covered in *Run Faster*, such as Computer Science programs at many universities. Since most kinds of educational facilities are covered in that book, no more Life Modules are added in this area.

REAL LIFE

Nothing like a little real-life experience to give a hacker a taste of how it's really done. The Hacker/Decker sub-category in the Corporate Life Module would be appropriate for hackers, as would the Shadow Work (Decker) option, but here are a few more. As is the case with *Run Faster*, each module here costs 100 Karma.

ESCAPED TECHNOMANCER

The corps have been very curious to see just how technomancer abilities work, to the point of bringing many in as "guests" and performing research on them. Which occasionally involves digging into their brain. You were caught up in such a program, but you were one of the lucky ones—you made your escape. The harrowing experience taught you a number of things, but also left a deep desire for vengeance.

Attributes	Intuition +1, Willpower +1
Qualities	Guts (10), Pain Is Gain (5), Vendetta (7)
Skills	Compiling +2, Con +1, Decompiling +2, Hacking +2, Registering +2, Sneaking +1, Software +2, Survival +1, Interest Knowledge: [Matrix-related] +2, Professional Knowledge: [Tech corporations] +3

HACKER ASSASSIN

You spent some time as a professional hacker, and you were not just breaking into secure hosts. You were there to bring the hurt to people who had it coming (at least according to your superiors), and you didn't just let them off with a warning, or even a bricked device. You made them feel it. You developed a ruthless side, but also some significant skills.

Attributes	Logic +1, Willpower +1
Qualities	Go Big or Go Home (6)
Skills	Cybercombat +3, Electronics skill group +2, Electronic Warfare +1, Hacking +1, Interest Knowledge: [Matrix-related] +2, Street Knowledge: [Tech corporations] +3

HACKER HOBBYIST

Your favorite downtime activity is getting together with other like-minded people, deconstructing machines and lines of code and figuring out how they work. You live and breathe this stuff, and you can work on it in your sleep. Which is good, because sometimes, after those twenty-four-hour hackathons, you're a little sleep deprived.

Attributes	Logic +1, Intuition +1
Qualities	Golden Screwdriver (8)
Skills	[Any] Mechanic +1, Computer +2, Cybercombat +2, Electronic Warfare +2, Etiquette +1, Hacking +2, Hardware +2, Software +2, Interest Knowledge: [Matrix-related] +2, Street Knowledge: [Tech corporations] +3

HIGH-PROFILE HACK

At some point, you scaled one of the Matrix's Mount Everests and performed a legendary hack. Maybe you engraved your initials on the virtual vault door at Zurich-Orbital Gemeinschaft Bank, or maybe you inserted a copy of *1001 Fart Jokes* into Ehran the Scribe's library, or some other act of daring. While the authorities have not been able to pin anything on you, your exploits have made you a known quantity in the hacking world and beyond—both for better and for ill. One of the benefits, though, is that you have access to some people who would not have been available to you otherwise.

Attributes	Charisma +1, Intuition +1
Qualities	Online Fame (4), Prime Datahaven Membership (7)
Skills	Computer +2, Cybercombat +2, Electronic Warfare +2, Hacking +2, Leadership +2, Interest Knowledge: [Matrix-related] +2, Interest Knowledge: Secure Matrix Locations +5

IT ACE

You spent some time working as an IT troubleshooter—maybe for a corp, maybe for the Mob, maybe for the government—and you dealt with a deluge of requests coming in at all times. You learned how to think on your feet, be nimble, and adapt to circumstances. Those qualities now serve you well on the streets.

Attributes	Logic +1, Intuition +1
Qualities	Overclocker (5), Quick Config (4)
Skills	Computer +2, Cybercombat +2, Electronic Warfare +1, Etiquette +2, Hacking +2, Hardware +2, Software +2, Interest Knowledge: [Matrix-related] +2, Professional Knowledge: [Tech corporations] +3

MATRIX GHOST

There are a lot of reasons to remain unseen in the Matrix. Sometimes it's because you're tasked with acting as Matrix security, watching would-be troublemakers from unseen locations; sometimes it's because you're one of those would-be troublemakers, trying to hide from the people attempting to track you down. And sometimes it's because there can be a lot of interesting things to do on the Matrix when no one knows you're around. Whatever the case, you spent some of your adult years in work or a hobby that helped you move around the Matrix—and a little bit of the meat world—without being noticed. Knowing all the tricks also lets you track people who are trying to do what you do so well.

Attributes	Agility +1, Intuition +1
Qualities	I C U (6), Ninja Vanish (5)
Skills	Computer +2, Con +1, Cybercombat +2, Electronic Warfare +1, Hacking +2, Hardware +2, Sneaking +2, Interest Knowledge: [Matrix security] +2, Professional Knowledge: [Tech corporations] +3

OTAKU TIME

You spent part of your life as an otaku, a child of the Matrix. Crash 2.0 left you adrift, but your connection to the Matrix never fully disappeared, and you Emerged as a technomancer. Happily, some of your skills from the otaku days translated into your current life.

Attributes	Logic +1, Intuition +1
Qualities	Otaku to Technomancer (10)
Skills	Compiling +2, Decompiling +1, Cybercombat +1, Electronic Warfare +1, Software +2, Hacking +1, Tasking skill group +2, Interest Knowledge: [Matrix-related] +2, Street Knowledge: [Tech corporations] +3

KILLER APPS & RAZOR FORMS

Deckmaster prepared his cyberdeck carefully. He had been a past master of the Matrix, a virtuoso of working programs. He had wielded IC picks of white-hot titanium and progs of hellfire. IC melted away from him like a tropical heatwave. Demand for his services had been huge.

Then came the changes in the Matrix. The new security waves. The different grids. GOD ascendant. Suddenly, having a hot 'link and a fistful of sweet apps didn't cut it any longer. The posers with their talk of IC Pick Art and strict study of the source and changes came back to power. Those things just ate away at Deckmaster's partying time.

Then the cash ran out. It always did, but this time there were no more gigs. No more shadowrunners searching for him. No more paydata falling out of the databases like manna from heaven. He'd had to scrimp, save, wheel, deal, steal, and otherwise fight for his survival in the shadows.

Then luck came, an extraction gone wrong, a dead decker. A loose cyberdeck filled with wonderful warez. Deckmaster, loving his new street name, would finally be back on top, demanding top nuyen. A few paydata scores, some new datamonger contacts, a new rep. He stroked the Microdeck Summit and smiled. All would be his again. Getting the deck to work with him had been hard, requiring specialized tools, research, and more than one bribe to hardware experts to find out why it was temperamental. The hardware restrictions had only recognized the old owner. But a bit of brute force had fixed that. Hopefully he'd be able to afford a new cyberdeck soon—the case on this one was cracked, and the design was boring anyway. Even in mint condition, this thing wouldn't look good at the clubs.

Deckmaster dove once again full bore into the Matrix, full-on hot-simsense style, the only way to fly. His new persona was chromed to a high finish, changing away like a pinball machine and glistening with gold lights. He chose a random place and slammed the picks into place, chipping the IC away. It took more effort and adjustments of the progs to work right, but he was more than willing to do what it took. It sure beat life eating unflavored, unheated nutrisoy. Knowledge would grant him power once again, and this place, Damballa Investi-

gations and Investments (whatever they might be), was just the start.

He idled around, downloading everything that looked even remotely interesting. Let the datamonger sort through it—that's what he's for, after all. Soon, however, he felt like he was being watched. He shifted his perception around, spotting the icon of a strikingly handsome man in a black chrome suit who started to talk when Deckmaster spotted him.

"Chummer, you came to the wrong neighborhood," the persona said, his violet eyes sparkling coldly. Deckmaster had only moments before he saw the mouth open impossibly wide and flames shot out, sending shockwaves of brain-destroying code down the connection.

CYBER SOLUTIONS BY CYBERPROGRAMS

POSTED BY: GLITCH

I had originally tapped Slamm-0! to write here, but first I got something about artistic coding in the modern Matrix, then I got something that compared the cyberprograms of today to the sport of cricket. I decided it would be best to write this on my own.

- Hey now, cricket is a wonderful sport.
- Goat Foot

Hardware and software have to go hand-in-hand to allow people like us to make our mark on the Matrix, and that is as true today as ever. Making hosts bend to our very will is not easy, thanks to all that has been done to hedge in the liberty that was the old Matrix with new security and restrictions. The Matrix is now designed to make everyone good little victims for the megas' benefits. While the new protocols have changed a lot, information is still power, and it still demonstrates a tangible urge to be free, as the cost of passing data around gets cheaper every day.

So with Slamm-0! falling down on the job, it falls to me to give everyone a quick overview of all the pro-

grams that affect shadowrunners. I'll start with the lowest common denominator: commlinks and their apps.

Actually, there isn't anything "low" about commlinks, especially from an information-gathering or profit point of view. A large number of people practically live with their commlinks (and those with implanted models actually do so), and they typically run the entire PAN of their owners. Add to that shopping patterns, bank records, personal pleasure habits, social networking, and so on, and you've got a poorly secured smorgasbord of data for someone doing legwork. And the apps people use just make it easier, as most of them are designed to prop up the consumerist sentiments and activities of which the corps are so fond. There are so many apps, some with a culture of their very own growing around them, that no one can track them all. Some apps are even status symbols in their own right, as important to users as the brand of 'link they're running, while others can be troubling for us. The major one that everyone is worried about is the classic PANICBUTTON!™, an enhanced emergency calling system that makes priority calls that are monitored by 911, 999, and 112 operators (and all the other numbers there are in the world), as well as priority service from various emergency companies. For a monthly fee, you only have to push a button for nearly immediate response, with only a virtual molly-guard to prevent accidental calls.

> • Part of the contract is that the user shares GPS locations, access to audio and video recording from all devices in the customer's PAN, and a direct dump of relevant data to the BUTTONPUSHER!™ covering a period from a day before the button is pushed all the way until two weeks after the company informs the person that they will stop monitoring them. All at a modest monthly fee. Oh, and that's just the large print.
> • Hannibelle

There are, of course, billions of absorbing little games out there, played by regular corp drones and shadowrunners alike. They can have a useful function—AR games that allow a person to keep an eye on what they're doing, sort of, while preventing boredom from eating away at them can maintain focus on those long stakeouts. I

don't use them while on the job, but in my downtime I'm fond of Spirit Popper. I'm not looking for new people to play with, though, so no invites please.

Legal cyberprograms come next. They're common and ubiquitous, but still potentially useful. They serve more as a reminder that cyberdecks are designed and used for utility and maintenance of grids and hosts rather than outright hacking. The majority of people using cyberdecks are computer techs slaving away far and below security spiders and combat deckers that fill the shadows and bad 'trid shows. While smaller in variety, there are a lot of huge brand-name programs doing similar jobs. They, like cyberdecks, are specialist tools that require extensive skills that border on artistry.

Illegal cyberprograms—the things most of us here are interested in—are the things that make datatheft and combat hacking possible. Sure, most of them are combat programs (spirits, far too many attack programs!), but a good number are utilities that expand the variety of options available to deckers attempting to get by with their wits and onboard software. A small number, designed by the shadow market, even incorporate ideas from commlink apps.

In the end, though, it isn't about what tools deckers have as much as how they use them. Skill, more than ever, matters on the battlefields of the Matrix.

> • And thank Ghost for that! We actually got some of the damn kids off my lawn!
> • Bull

GAME INFORMATION
COMMLINK APPS

Simple little programs, apps are useless for hacking against other devices or hosts. They usually only enhance a user's augmented reality or virtual reality experience, with a few minor options for support programs. A commlink can run as many apps as half its Device Rating, rounded up.

AR Games: Typically casual games that are displayed in augmented reality, allowing a user to enjoy them as a pastime while also still somewhat paying attention to reality. The number on the market is huge, with some older flatscreen and trid games being modified to run on commlinks.

Diagnostics: An ongoing self-evaluation system that monitors all the devices in a user's PAN, giving constant vital statistics on their behavior. Popular with computer-literate and interested users who enjoy trying to squeeze every last bit of usefulness out of devices, they are also popular in keeping people aware of attacks against their PAN in a manner similar to a biomonitor.

P2.1: A dramatic update to the old P2.0 system put into place by Horizon, this social networking app monitors and supports all other social networks that a person might use, incorporating it all into a dramatic web of information. It also generates a P-Score that is a major piece of status in a lot of virtual places and within Horizon as a whole.

Theme Music: An algorithm that constantly monitors the owner of the PAN in all their interactions with devices. Taking this data, it attempts to determine the emotional state of the person and generates a playlist of songs to better support said user, either enhancing the feelings or dampening them. Essentially the mood ring of the Sixth World.

Ticker: A series of commlink apps that provide an information feed from a specified source, the vast majority being legitimate, such as stock markets and news organizations. Some shadow services also use these apps to give details on other shadowrunners, fixers, Mr. Johnsons, police response times, and current payment rates for a variety of services and bribes. Ticker reduces the time for subject-related Matrix Searches in half. Obviously, there are a great many topics out there that don't generate enough traffic to merit an information feed—for example, you can't subscribe to a feed with up-to-the-minute news about Medieval Europe when Mr. Johnson sends you after a weird-looking cup and expect results to come flooding in.

COMMON CYBERPROGRAMS

Originally developed to legally work with networks, hosts, and grids, some of these programs are quite useful for deckers if they have a little bit of imagination.

Bootstrap: An IT expert's tool of choice when working with boot code of a device. Corrupted by many hackers, Bootstrap allows for hidden commands to be input into the device after the next reboot. Popular options include announcing the location of the device when it connects to the Matrix, adjusting the processing of the device so that the default device attributes are the choice of the user, annoying the user with constant demands for ownership permissions, and making a record of every action on the device. This cyberprogram allows for a variety of tasks to be set up in the boot record by way of a Format Device action rather than just setting the device up to no longer function.

Search: When loaded, this cyberprogram tailors the cyberdeck's search algorithms to match the specific iconography of the host, making the decker's Matrix Search results more likely to contain the paydata he's looking for. This is quite popular with Mr. Johnsons, who often provide copies with pre-loaded search requirements that are programmed to self-destruct after use, so that they can only be run once. The program provides 2 extra dice on a Matrix Search action when looking for specific data on a host that contains that data. There is no bonus is if the decker is searching for something that originates from outside the host.

Shredder: Designed to assist in erasing files and all their redundant back-up options that might be around inside a host and grid that the host inhabits, Shredder adds 2 to a cyberdeck's Data Processing attribute for the purpose of deleting a file with the Edit File action. It functions by entering a large amount of random junk data into designated files, overwriting them repeatedly to help deter attempts at recovering them. A nice security option that is legal for users to use. Recovering a file that has been Shredded (or destroyed by a Data Bomb, for that matter) requires constant access to the host or grid the file was originally on, and a Computer (File Recovery) + Logic [Mental] (18, 1 week) Extended Test, which explains why offline back-ups are quite popular.

HACKING CYBERPROGRAMS

Illegal, horrible pieces of code designed to work in antisocial methods against the legal and proper users of the Matrix, its various grids and hosts, and the wholesome and honest protectors in GOD. But enough about the positive things about these programs ...

Cat's Paw: A low-offensive attack program that distracts the user instead of damaging the device he is using, Cat's Paw is useful to prevent a user from performing Matrix actions while not bricking the device they may be using. This program fills the AR display or VR experience with annoying errors, spam pop-ups and pop-unders, or other distracting garbage. On a successful Data Spike action (p. 239, *SR5*), instead of doing damage, the program generates a negative dice pool modifier equal to two plus the number of marks the user has on his target. Marks added or removed after using Cat's Paw will also modify the penalty accordingly.

Cloudless: Not comfortable with your data stored only in the Matrix's cloud? This program uses legacy code from previous incarnations of the Matrix to place data in physical media and physical media only. In addition to saving a file, it allows the user to use a successful Edit File action to move a file off the Matrix into the memory of a single designated device. This test is an Opposed Test, using the normal rules for Edit File (p. 239, *SR5*). The Public grid has a dice pool of 6, local grids a dice pool of 8, and global grids a dice pool of 10 for the purposes of this test.

Crash: One thing deckers have learned about the new Matrix protocols is that the ability to force devices to reboot can be very beneficial. Crash is there to help deckers who want to do this. When running, it attempts to fill a targeted device with an exceptional amount of reboot-worthy errors, adding 2 to the Data Processing attribute of a deck running this program when it attempts a Reboot Device action (p. 242, SR5).

Detonator: With delicate monitoring, this cyberprogram is able to determine how often a file is accessed, and it sets a data bomb to go off after it has been affected a set number of times. To use this program, a decker attempts a Set Data Bomb action; if successful, they can then select how many actions can be executed with the file before the bomb goes off. They can also choose whether the Data Bomb does Matrix damage or just deletes the file. Similar to a Data Bomb, a Detonator can be detected with a Matrix Perception Test and defused with a Disarm Data Bomb action. Notoriously difficult to spot, Detonator-enabled data bombs are considered to have a Device Rating of 3 and a Sleaze attribute equal to [Remaining actions before detonation - 1] for the purposes of opposing Matrix Perception tests. This program costs twice as much as normal hacking cyberprograms, meaning it costs 500 nuyen.

Evaluate: With constant updates from a series of Black BBS that specialize in monitoring paydata auctions, this program calculates how much a certain amount of paydata *might* be worth, in order to allow the decker to only take an amount that would limit the amount of heat they would generate in stealing a little extra while on the job.

Fly on a Wall: Haven't you always wanted to be the fly on a wall, in order to see the look on the faces of people when the final tally of their lives comes up? Well, GOD tends to prevent long-term surveillance by unauthorized personnel, but this program helps rebalance the scales. While this program is running, and the decker is performing no actions other than Matrix Perception tests, the Overwatch Score only increases by 1D6 per half-hour (rolled in secret by the gamemaster as normal). The program requires a Hide action in order to activate properly, and it does not assist in any way in preventing any other icon from noticing the decker.

Hitchhiker: There are some special parts of the Matrix where you can take others with you--and where you definitely don't want to be alone. Grab this program to take your non-hacker friends to foundations and UV hosts.

Nuke-from-Orbit: A hugely powerful file destruction program that requires frequent updates as adjustments in file recovery technology continue to progress. This upgraded and outright illegal program is designed to ensure that no one will ever be able to recover a file that it destroys. If used to delete a file (the Edit File action should be used), this program ensures that no one will ever be able to recover the file from the Matrix A brutal and decidedly unsubtle cyberprogram, any Overwatch Score generated from the Opposed Test is doubled. Offline back-ups and the Resonance realms are the only options for getting the file back. Nuke-From-Orbit has an Availability Rating of 12F

Paintjob: Resprays and textures a persona's icon, assisting in erasing or knocking off marks as it does so, ensuring the decker is able to trust in the fact that his cyberdeck is not being affected by outsiders. This program adds 2 to the Attack attribute for the purpose of making Erase Mark tests.

Smoke-and-Mirrors: Adds significant amounts of misleading location information in order to keep the decker from being located IRL. This program increases the cyberdeck's Sleaze attribute between 1 and 5 (user's choice) with an equivalent amount of noise added to any tests performed with the deck. The noise also affects Trace Icon tests performed against the deck using the program. This program has no effect against convergence (p. 231, SR5), as GOD and all the demiGODs cannot be distracted by so simple a trick.

Swerve: Just as deckers have seen the benefits of forcing other devices to reboot, they have seen a need to keep their devices safe from those efforts. Swerve adds redundant code to the OS of the cyberdeck and any connected devices in the decker's PAN, making it easier for the devices to resist crash attacks. This program adds 1 to the Firewall attribute of a device for the purpose of resisting Reboot Device attempts.

Tantrum: This program overlays cold simsense sensations on top of a Data Spike action, hitting the target with a quick and disgusting sensation if even a single box of Matrix Damage is scored. The program is effective against all technomancers, as well as cold sim or hot sim deckers, but it does nothing to users working in the Matrix in AR, any form of IC, and agents. The program does no damage from the Data Spike; instead, the targeted user experiences Nausea (p. 409, SR5) for three Combat Turns due to the sensory input. Popular options this program uses to make targets feel queasy include the smell of a dirty diaper or the feeling of being punched in the junk.

Tarball: A powerful but inaccurate combat program based on the old tar-based IC used for decades, Tarball adds 2 to the Attack attribute and 1 to the dice pool of Crash Program attempts (both of these bonuses only apply to Crash Program attempts), but its broader-based attack affects a random program rather than a chosen one.

COMPLEX FORMS

Always being researched, developed, manipulated, and perfected by technomancers, Complex forms continue to twist and crack the very concepts of what is "reality" in the Matrix, warping it even further than the already-twisted electronic world where the only boundaries are virtual reality and imagination.

SPECULATIVE DATA GATHERING

Vacuuming up paydata that isn't related specifically to a job is, mostly, an outright act of greed. There might be other mitigating factors to take into consideration, but doing it just for the extra few nuyen to go on the credstick is just how it goes. Doing so, however, means that the runner team is heading deeper down the "cold-hearted bastard" end of things (p. 376, SR5). This should affect the monetary end of things when all is said and done, as the runners pawn the paydata through a regular fixer or a specialized fence known as a datamonger. Note that this will likely also adjust the Karma payout at the end of the gig, which may or may not annoy the rest of the team.

Of course, the opposite is also true. The decker can adjust or outright erase files that will give them no monetary reward but will make them feel better about themselves, as well as trying to strike a blow against the corporations that rule the Sixth World. Corrupting information such as onerous loan records, forged blackmail, or even minor things like traffic tickets can edge the decker towards the "good feelings" portion of shadowrunning.

Those actions—stealing extra data or erasing it—raise the risk of increasing a decker's Notoriety (p. 372, SR5) as those actions will increase the amount of heat put onto deckers in general, and the run performed in particular, as well as running the risk of pissing off the Mr. Johnson.

In the end, everything has a price. What is yours, and what will it be paid in?

DEREZZ

Target: Persona • **Duration:** I • **FV:** L + 2

A stiletto or ice pick as opposed to the typical superheated sledgehammers, the Resonance energy from this form slides into the cracks and holes in the target's armor and strips it away slightly. Make a Software + Resonance [Level] v. Willpower + Firewall test, doing 1 box of Matrix damage per net hit, and dropping the target's Firewall attribute by 1 until the device has rebooted. Additional successful Derezz attacks do not stack the Firewall adjustment, even if they are from two separate technomancers.

FAQ

Target: Device • **Duration:** P • **FV:** L

Scanning the very darkest depths of the Matrix to find out exactly what has been going on with the device they physically have or the host they are current inside of, the technomancer is able to delve into the very deepest questions to find out the true purpose of it. Make an immediate Computer + Intuition [Level] Test with Level / 2 (rounded up) dice added to the pool from the com-

plex form. Gamemasters should provide information to the player based on the number of hits this test generates, with truly obscure or long-forgotten bytes of information requiring 6 hits.

IC TRAY

Target: Host • **Duration:** I • **FV:** L – 2

This form scans the host the technomancer is currently residing in and displays a list of the IC it is currently equipped to deploy, up to the number of hits scored on an Opposed Software + Resonance [Level] vs. Host Rating + Sleaze Test.

REDUNDANCY

Target: Device • **Duration:** S • **FV:** L + 0

This form works with Resonance threads to better allow for secondary and tertiary connections, making the device slightly tougher for a limited amount of time. Redundancy grants additional, temporary boxes to the Matrix Damage Track to one device, giving a number of boxes equal to the hits acquired on a Simple Software + Resonance [Level] Test.

MISREAD MARKS

Target: IC • **Duration:** P • **FV:** L + 2

A nasty little thing that will manipulate how IC perceives the Matrix, and who exactly is friend or foe. Temporarily tricks a targeted IC into thinking your marks are its intended targets, similar to the way someone might mistakenly attack a magic-user's illusion. This lasts for for a number of actions (including Simple or Complex, but not Free) equal to the hits scored on a Simple Software + Resonance [Level] Test. If you have multiple marks in the same host, the mark that is attacked is selected randomly.

ECHOES

Submersion, while an intensive process, can provide a number of rewards. Echoes are the most widely known of these quasi-mystical powers, potentially manipulating the mind and body of the technomancer.

FFF: The Fight-or-Flight Filter echo adjusts the technomancer's basic instincts for combat situations, making them far more efficient than that of a normal metahuman, while also muting the nagging portions of the brain that insist on feeling injuries. The technomancer receives all the benefits, but also all the difficulties, of a pain editor (p. 460, *SR5*) without needing to have the cultured bioware made for them and the surgery to get it implanted. A technomancer must have already submerged at least once prior to taking this echo.

Mathemagics: Adjusting the logic centers of the brain, this echo allows a dramatically large increase in

STYLES OF NOISE

While having the identical effect in the rules, the sources and methods of noise in the world are vastly different things. Static zones have little to no wireless connections, making them areas that limit the amount of connections, and bandwidth, available for the Matrix. Spam zones are the exact opposite, having multiple levels of access, but overburdened by so much traffic that bandwidth is overwhelmed and unable to flow properly. Dead zones, of course, are where nothing is happening, Matrix-wise.

These zones affect the shadowrunners in different ways. Dead zones annoy them with the inability to get even a single bar of connection, while spam zones annoy them by constantly flooding every bit of their perception with advertisements for consumeristic garbage. Creating or enhancing those zones is fairly subtle—after all, if you're not expecting the best wireless service in an area, do you complain about how it really isn't working one day? Or perhaps people just shrug because the spam is particularly thick today—maybe some great new cat video got posted that everyone needs to watch.

If someone uses the wrong type of Noise in an area, however, things get quite less subtle very, very quickly. After all, if there are no people in the area who can see into augmented reality, why would a spam zone suddenly pop up that can be seen by anyone with even the most basic commlink? In the other direction, a spam zone being flooded with static and a lack of ability to get out those advertisements is going to slot off a corporation or two—they don't like people messing with revenue-generators. It's a basic rule of shadowrunning—don't do things that call too much attention to yourself.

the math processing potential of the technomancer. This allows the technomancer to have the ability to perform simple math operations with perfectly accurate results, increasing the Mental Limit for math-intensive actions, such as encryption and decryption, by 2.

MMRI: Known as the Man-Machine Resonance Interface, this echo subtly manipulates the Resonance coming off the technomancer, allowing them to better jump into drones and rigger-modified devices. This provides the same effects as a control rig (p. 452, *SR5*), without the free datajack and datacable. This can be taken up to three times, each increasing the effective rating of the control rig by one.

Quiet: Where this runner goes, tendrils of Matrix connectivity continue to follow along, allowing everyone to benefit from the majesty of the Matrix. Technomancers with the Quiet echo reduce the Noise of their area by 2 (p. 230, *SR5*) for a radius around the hacker of 10 meters per point of Resonance attribute. This echo can be activated or deactivated at will with a Free Action.

Resonance Riding: A strange twist of the Matrix follows the technomancer even through secondary means of connection, giving them the ability to perform some Resonance actions while jacked into the Matrix through a commlink or cyberdeck. While going through this secondary system, the technomancer cannot use their Living Persona or benefit from any of the Living Persona's attributes, or perform the Compile Sprite, Register Sprite, or Thread Complex Form actions. All other Resonance actions are available.

Resonance Scream: Through sheer force of will, the technomancer is able to flood their area with spam messages, annoying the hell out of everyone and increasing the noise of the area by 2 for a radius around the hacker of 10 meters per Resonance attribute, affecting everyone (including the technomancer) therein as if they were inside of a spam zone. This can be turned on and off with a Free Action, which is handy because spam rage is a major issue.

Skinlink: You gain the ability to forge a direct connection with any device you can physically touch. Two technomancers with this echo can mentally communicate simply by touching.

Sleepwaker: The technomancer gains the ability to subconsciously perceive minor events happening around their body while working with the Matrix in VR. This allows them to choose to perform Perception-related Free Actions in the Matrix or the real world.

THE GUTS OF THE MATRIX

You already know that the Matrix is a consensual hallucination created to make it quick and easy to use the colossal ocean of data and information and computing power that has been created by metahumanity. You're aware that you can plug in and get 3D graphical representations of everything from the history of the Qin Dynasty to conspiracy theories about President Dunkelzahn's assassination to the latest street drug prices to simsense escort services to the complete works of Shakespeare spontaneously generated by a near-infinite number of virtual monkeys.

But what is the Matrix, exactly? Where is it? Can someone accidentally unplug it? You've got questions, we've got answers, and they are, in reverse order: no, everywhere, and it goes like this.

THE MATRIX IS IN YOUR POCKET

In fact, the Matrix *is* your pocket, or it could be. But let's not get ahead of ourselves.

Way back in the history of the Matrix, all the way back to Echo Mirage, the Matrix was run on mainframes—giant computers. The Matrix ran pretty much entirely inside these mainframes, and your cyberdeck interpreted the connections between mainframes for you.

Nowadays, we've made computers so compact and efficient that we literally have them in our lingerie (which is useful for things like washing instructions, storing mood music, and earning *Tres Chic Intimates Collection™* reward points). When all those computers work together, you get the biggest, baddest, most mother-fragginest Matrix the world has ever seen.

WHAT THAT MEANS

When everything is the Matrix, you can use anything to get into the Matrix. The commlink is what every shadowrunner will want for their own personal Matrix use, but there's so much more. Need to access the Matrix in the morning and your commlink's at the cleaners? No problem, with a few mods and a Hardware test, you can be surfing the Matrix on your toaster.

For the discerning hacker, there's the cyberdeck. Some hackers say you're only as good as your deck; most of those hackers are dead, but there's some truth to it. Whether you're looking for a new deck or to spice up your old one, you've opened the book to the right chapter, chummer.

When you're bored with commlinks and cyberdecks, start hacking in Insanity Mode. The last section of this chapter is all about how to take common household items and make Matrix magic, for fun or because you're stranded in an electronically locked shipping container with nothing but a troll and a pet robot, and you need to open the doors before you sink too deep into the strait you've just been dropped into. When life gives you lemons, make jury-rigged electronics!

COMMLINKS

Commlinks are still the dominant telecommunications and entertainment devices of the Sixth World, so let's take a quick look at the vital things that make this utility knife of a device what it is.

FORM FACTOR

The form factor of a commlink is the physical shape of the device. The standard form factor for a commlink is a small, flat, rectangular object about fifteen centimeters or so long. Commlinks are also available in non-standard form factors at a slight premium. The most popular non-standard form factors include articles of clothing, pens, glasses, pocket and wrist watches, purses, hats (fedoras are in fashion for both genders), canes, knives, and small pistols.

If you want a commlink in a non-standard form factor, add 2 to the commlink's Availability and 20 percent to its cost. If you want to integrate a commlink into a weapon, add 4 to the commlink's Availability and 50 percent to its cost—it's a bit trickier to install a commlink into a weapon in such a way that it won't be damaged by normal use. In either case, you still have to cover the cost of the form factor separately, if applicable.

For examples of some non-standard form factors, check out the following!

COMMLINK FORM FACTOR

FORM	AVAIL	COST
Non-standard Form Factor	+2	+20%
Weapon Form Factor	+4R	+50%

EVOTECH HIMITSU

This lunchbox-sized commlink appears to be a generic, uninteresting, low-level consumer commlink. In fact, it contains a secret compartment that can hold items no larger than a pistol or a cigar box. The compartment is shielded with its own built-in Faraday cage, and the commlink has a stealth module integrated into the board, giving it Sleaze 5.

MCT BLUE DEFENDER

This commlink comes standard as a wristband that is, as you'd expect, blue. Designed for legitimate sale to security forces and off-the-books distribution to shadowrunners and criminals worldwide, this stylish bracelet protects your devices from evil hackers with a stronger-than-average Firewall.

NIXDORF SEKRETÄR

Are you constantly confused and lost? Does your file directory look like your commlink was the sole victim of the Crash 3.0? Worry no more, because the Nixdorf Sekretar has your back. It has a built-in Rating 3 agent that will organize your calendar, your files, your work, and (with the Liebesekretär upgrade) your love life.*

*Liebesekretär package includes automatic match making, date scheduling, concierge service, and rating system. No guarantee is implied in this service. Some terms and conditions apply. Always use protection.

COMMLINK DONGLES

A dongle is a small device that attaches to a commlink's universal data port and gives it extra functionality. Unless you've got a teeny little commlink, a dongle barely increases the size of the whole thing. A commlink can only use one dongle at a time.

ATTACK DONGLE

This dongle doesn't actually attack people, though that would be cool. It gives the commlink an Attack rating equal to its rating, providing some on-the-fly, quick attack resources. DemiGODs love corporate employees to use these, as they can provide more time for them to track down and punish intruders.

CABLE TAP

This shady dongle has a small split ring that can be wrapped around a data cable, giving your commlink a direct connection to the devices on either side of the cable it's clipped to.

COMMLINKS

COMMLINK	DEVICE RATING	DATA PROC.	FIREWALL	AVAIL	COST
EvoTech Himitsu	2	1	2	8R	11,000¥
MCT Blue Defender	3	1	5	7	2,000¥
Nixdorf Sekretär	4	6	2	5	4,000¥
w/ Liebesekretär				+1	+2,000¥

STEALTH DONGLE

A stealth dongle gives the commlink a Sleaze rating based on the rating of the dongle, for those who want their quick actions to be more subtle, less brutal.

STUN DONGLE

This dongle turns your commlink into a stun gun, though one that requires contact with the target to operate. It is a popular choice of civilians who want inconspicuous protection and a convenient carrying case. It packs three charges in its slim form factor.

RECEIVER

Just plug this dongle into your commlink and you get Noise Reduction 2 for your commlink and all slaved devices! Great for spam zones!

COMMLINK DONGLES

DONGLE	AVAIL	COST
Attack dongle (Rating 1-6)	[Rating x 2]R	(Rating)2 x 3,000¥
Cable tap	8R	500¥
Stealth dongle (Rating 1-6)	[Rating x 2]R	(Rating)2 x 3,000¥
Stun dongle	6R	600¥
Receiver	3	400¥

CYBERDECKS

The cyberdeck is the decker's bread and butter. And knife. And plate. And toaster. Really, it's the entire kitchen. There are lots of cyberdecks on page 439 of SR5, but we know you're hungry for more.

FORM FACTOR

The standard cyberdeck form factor is a smooth, flat, elongated rectangle about twenty-five centimeters long, with plenty of display space for touch controls. Like commlinks, cyberdecks can also fit into non-standard form factors, following the same rules and costs for commlink form factors (p. 60).

CYBERDECK FORM FACTOR

FORM	AVAIL	COST
Non-standard Form Factor	+3	+20%
Weapon Form Factor	+6R	+50%

STANDARD DECKS

For more information about cyberdecks, see **Cyberdecks**, p. 227, SR5.

RADIO SHACK PCD-500

This little wonder is the perfect model for the aspiring young cybersecurity specialist. Bulk discount for educational institutions—contact a sales representative for details. Are you going to squeeze a lot of power out of it? No. But it's like the Radio Shack motto says: "Radio Shack: Better than nothing, most of the time!"

LITTLE HORNET

This compact cyberdeck is made in Chicago under the UCAS ghoul employment program, and we pass the savings right on to you! It's high end goes to pretty good heights, but watch out where you put those low-end attributes. Lots of Little Hornet owners also invest in a Configurator program (p. 245, SR5).

MICROTRÓNICA AZTECA 300

Sold as an upgrade to the 200 model, the Microtrónica Azteca 300 is little more than the 200 with a smaller cooling system and an extra quaternion quantum buffer. Even so, you can't dismiss the extra power the new configuration gives the 300, with some benchmarks outperforming similarly rated decks.

XIAO MPG-1

The MPG-1 is designed by our friends at the Midwest Pirate's Guild with one deadly purpose: smash everything in your way before it can hit back. Lots of IC was harmed in the making of this deck.

SHIAWASE CYBER-4

The first product of Shiawase's reboot of the Fuchi Cyber line, the Cyber-5, was a deck that had high praise but low sales figures, criticized for being out of reach

CLUBS

CLUB	ACCURACY	REACH	DAMAGE	AP	AVAIL	COST
Stun dongle	4	—	8S(e)	−5	6R	600¥

of the larger cybersecurity market. The Cyber-4 was introduced as a low-price, high-performance cyberdeck, undercutting the price point of the CIY-720 while outperforming the more popular cyberdeck in some areas. This model will save you a lot of money, but leave you with one glaring vulnerability. Tread carefully.

FAIRLIGHT PALADIN

An incredible feat of human ingenuity, the Fairlight Paladin is a masterpiece of cyberdeck design and engineering. The Paladin is considered a "pinnacle achievement" by execs and engineers at NeoNET's Fairlight division. Fairlight has sold only five of the decks in the world and report that they are filling orders for another twelve. Some say that the deck costs more to manufacture than the million-plus asking price, making the top-end cyberdeck more of a territorial marker in the industry than a product intended for sale.

SPECIALTY DECKS

Specialty cyberdecks are built with a specific purpose in mind. You can't swap a specialty deck's attributes when you reconfigure, only its programs. On the plus side, they're a bit cheaper than standard decks.

MCT TRAINEE

A spider's got to start somewhere, and Mitsuhama starts theirs with cybercombat training decks. These decks have built-in Biofeedback Filter programs to keep the trainees (relatively) safe. Though if you take one into the wilds of the Matrix, you'd better be ready for the demiGODs to get creative in the ways they cause you pain.

C-K ANALYST

The Cantor-Kurosawa Analyst is what every investigative journalist needs to poke around without being noticed, find the plain truth, package it up, and broadcast it in microseconds. The built-in high-def camera and recording suite, complemented by the hardwired Edit

CYBERDECKS

DECK	DEVICE RATING	ATT. ARRAY	PROGRAMS	AVAIL	COST
Radio Shack PCD-500	1	2 2 1 1	1	2	21,000¥
Little Hornet	2	5 4 1 1	2	5R	89,700¥
Microtrónica Azteca 300	3	7 5 3 1	3	9R	200,000¥
Xiao MPG-1	4	8 5 4 3	3	13R	302,000¥
Shiawase Cyber-4	4	8 6 4 2	3	12R	331,000¥
Fairlight Paladin	6	9 9 8 8	6	20R	1,050,000¥

SPECIALTY CYBERDECKS

DECK	DEVICE RATING	A S D F	PROGRAMS	AVAIL	COST
MCT Trainee	1	2 1 1 2	1	3R	17,250¥
C-K Analyst	2	1 5 4 3	1	5R	83,800¥
Aztechnology Emissary	3	2 3 3 8	1	8R	168,000¥
Yak Killer	3	7 6 2 3	2	13R	194,000¥
Ring of Light Special	4	8 1 2 6	3	10R	242,000¥
Ares Echo Unlimited	5	9 6 4 5	3	15R	395,900¥

program, will make you look like a million nuyen as you tell it like it is to the world.

AZTECHNOLOGY EMISSARY

For the courier on the go, this deck is designed to carry and protect files. It's also handy for protecting slaved devices and your own wetware. Just don't make the mistake of many a medieval noble who wandered out from behind their walls to engage the enemy. Being strong on defense is not the same as being skilled in attack.

YAK KILLER

This powerful but somewhat fragile deck isn't exactly an official product of the Reality Hackers gang of Seattle. Their unusual configuration isn't exactly licensed, the proceeds don't exactly go to the gang, and having one won't exactly make you the gang's best friend, but it's a popular model among up-and-coming deck-trippers.

RING OF LIGHT SPECIAL

If you haven't heard of the trid show, *Ring of Light,* welcome back to civilization from your cave-dwelling sabbatical. The decks used by the virtual fighters in this digital cage match are now for sale to the public, and are required for *RoL*-sanctioned local events and feeder leagues. They're about as stealthy as a troll riding a rhino through a library, but stealth makes for bad trid.

ARES ECHO UNLIMITED

This deck puts the "special" in special forces. It is ruggedized for hard combat missions with security contractors like Hard Corps and Wolverine, along with a number of government and civilian security organizations.

CYBERDECK MODULES

A cyberdeck module is a prefabricated component that extends the capabilities of your deck. Each cyberdeck has one module slot inside its case. Inserting, removing, or swapping modules requires a Hardware + Logic [Mental] (1) Test and about half a minute of time (10 Combat Turns).

Modules aren't as robust as your average deck and are vulnerable to Matrix damage. If your deck is ever bricked, any module in it becomes a useless hunk of slag, even if you repair the deck.

HARDENING

The hardening module acts as a shield between your deck and incoming damage. It has a Matrix Condition Monitor with five boxes, and it takes damage before your deck does. These boxes cannot be repaired.

INDUCTION RECEIVER

When you have this module installed, your deck can tap into data cables and hardlines on contact. By placing your

CYBERDECK MODULES

MODULES	AVAILABILITY	COST
Hardening	3R	1,500¥
Induction Receiver	10R	1,200¥
Multidimensional Coprocessor	7R	1,400¥
Overwatch Mask	9F	4,200¥
Program Carrier	2	900¥
Self-Destruct	12F	200¥
Vectored Signal Filter	3	800¥

cyberdeck directly onto the cable, it becomes directly connected to the devices on either side of the cable.

MULTIDIMENSIONAL COPROCESSOR

This tongue-twister of a module speeds up Matrix signals and commands, granting the deck's operator an additional +1D6 to Matrix Initiative (remember that you can never roll more than 5D6 worth of initiative dice).

OVERWATCH MASK

This handy module confuses GOD's watchful eye by pretending it's part of the Matrix enforcement system. The Matrix doesn't converge on a deck with this mod until its Overwatch Score reaches 4 more than normal (making it 44 in normal conditions).

PROGRAM CARRIER

This module holds a program that your deck can run permanently. You pick the program and we lock it in at manufacture, which means you can't change it, but hey, it's an extra program. Price includes the program cost.

SELF-DESTRUCT

This module is 98 percent explosive material by weight. When your deck detects a specific pre-determined condition (chosen by you), the module explodes, turning your cyberdeck into a fragmentation grenade—see p. 435, *SR5* for all the mayhem that causes. The deck, of course, is completely unrecoverable, meaning maybe don't put one of these into a Fairlight Paladin.

VECTORED SIGNAL FILTER

By adding a dedicated signal filter to your deck, this module gives you Noise Reduction 2.

ODD MODS

If you want to modify a device to increase its built-in ratings, or give it a new function, you've come to the right place. All you need is the Hardware skill, some Hardware tools (a kit will suffice), and some electronic parts. You'll also need some time.

To start the process, pick a device and a modification you want (there's a list of modifications below). Then make sure you have the electronic parts you need. Then you just need to roll some dice and bam! You'll have a modified device. Or a mess.

ELECTRONIC PARTS

We say "parts," but what we really mean is all of the doo-dads and what-nots you're going to need to make your modification. This sort of thing includes integrated circuits, disposable solder packets, ceramic nano-sheets, quantum transducers, optical switches, yadda, yadda, yadda—it's easier to just say "parts" and be done with it.

As you can see, there are a lot of expensive little fiddly-bits needed to make Sixth-World electronics work. To make things simpler for *Shadowrun,* we call the amount of parts required to make one modification a **pack** of parts.

There are a couple of ways to get parts packs, the two most common being to just go out and buy them or to scrounge them by cannibalizing otherwise perfectly good devices.

ELECTRONIC COMPONENT PACKS

Electronic packs are sold over the counter at your friendly local electronics store—buy in bulk for your best deals. You can also get packs when buying tools. Your standard Hardware shop (p. 443, *SR5*) comes with two packs when you acquire it, and will need restocking when you use it up. A Hardware facility (also p. 443,

SR5) has enough spare parts to make up ten electronic component packs when you buy it.

SCROUNGING FOR ELECTRONIC COMPONENTS

It's a lot cheaper to cannibalize other devices for parts. Stripping down an otherwise useful device for parts requires a Hardware toolkit and about ten minutes. Make a Hardware + Logic [target's Device Rating] Test, with modifiers from the Device Stripping Modifiers table. Every hit from this test gets you one quarter of a pack of parts. You can keep the change, as it were, keeping a fraction of a pack and saving it to add to future scavenging results.

ELECTRONIC PARTS

PACK	AVAIL	COST
Single Pack	—	250¥
Five-Pack	—	1,000¥

DEVICE STRIPPING MODIFIERS

CONDITION	DICE POOL MOD
Device is...	
... a commlink or cyberdeck	+4
... cyberware	+0
... another type of device	–4
Each box of Matrix damage	–1

MAKING THE MODIFICATION

If you don't have enough packs of parts to make your modification, the whole process is a no-go. You can't make something out of nothing. If you don't have enough parts, start looking for devices you can cannibalize, and you should be set. Or just go to the store.

Making the modification to a device is a Hardware + Logic [Mental] (15, 15 minutes) Extended Test. You take a –4 dice pool modifier if you don't have any Hardware tools, and the modifiers for working conditions and working from memory (p. 146, SR5) apply.

DEVICE MODIFICATIONS

Here's a list of mods you can perform on a device. This isn't an exhaustive list—if you want to try something that isn't written here, check with your gamemaster to see if you can do it. There are no additional costs for the mods beyond the cost for the parts and for any kits or facilities used. Unless otherwise noted, a device can only have one modification.

Add a Matrix Attribute: You can add a rating that a device doesn't have, specifically Attack or Sleaze. When you perform this mod, the rating starts at 1. You can't add a Matrix attribute to a device that already has that attribute. Remember that all devices have Data Processing and Firewall, even if that information is not listed in their gear entry. The Increase a Matrix Attribute modification can later be added to this modification. The number of parts packs needed for this modification equals the (Device Rating x 2) of the object being modified.

Add a Module: You can hardwire a cyberdeck module into a device. You need the module you want to add to the device. Most devices can only have one module, although cyberdecks can have two—one in the normal module slot, and the one you hardwire in. Hardwired modules follow the same rules as normal modules (p. 64). This requires two packs of parts.

Increase a Matrix Attribute: You can increase a single Matrix attribute by one point, but the cost in packs of parts is equal to the new attribute rating x 2. This modification takes a lot out of the device's other components, causing two permanent and irreparable boxes of Matrix damage to the device.

Modify a Matrix Attribute: You can use this to increase one Matrix attribute and decrease a different Matrix attribute, each by one point. This also works on the attribute array of a cyberdeck. This requires four sets of parts.

Persona Firmware: With two packs of parts, you can add the ability to run a persona to a device. If the device already has this capability, you can't add it again.

THE ALL-SEEING EYE OF GOD

Time moved weird in the Matrix under the best of circumstances, but it was even weirder when Groovetooth was sneaking. Each step felt like it took a full minute, but when she'd check the time, only seconds had passed. She checked repeatedly and got the same result each time, which helped convince her that maybe she could stop. She had more time than she anticipated.

She was slowly making her way through a lovely indoor greenhouse. It was full of ferns, tremendous ferns, ferns of a greater variety and size than she had ever seen in her life. They were thick and lush, easy to hide under and in. Maybe too easy. If she ducked into the thick of it, off the brick path winding through the plants, she would be harder to see, but who knew what was waiting on the ground?

She'd know, dammit. She sent out a clutch of agents in the form of snakes to investigate the ground just to her left. Any hidden sensors would be, you know, hidden, but she needed to at least look for them and hope she got a good scan, in case something came along.

Groovetooth's persona was even smaller than her real life body. It was barely more than a meter tall, in the form of her namesake mouse, with black stripes running down the brown fur on her back. She had programmed the persona very carefully to look dignified and thoughtful—none of that typical mouse whisker-twitching for her. She walked on her hind legs, continuing to step carefully. Her destination, a fountain at the end of the greenhouse, was maybe 75 meters away, but at her pace it felt like 75 kilometers.

Then a report came back from one of the snakes. Activity in the fountain. She had it transmit a feed to her, and she didn't like what she was seeing. Water was flowing toward the center of the pool at the base of the fountain, moving up into a column, taking a vaguely humanoid shape. There was no way this could be good. Chances were that some of her activity had been noticed.

Time to hide. She checked the scan of the ground to her left. It seemed clean. Meanwhile, the watery form was slushing forward through the water toward the edge of the pool.

She plunged into the ferns, disturbing as few leaves as possible. She went behind one plant, ducked, and looked around.

The plant was tall enough but too thin. Her fur could be seen in gaps between the leaves. No good. And she could hear sloshing water approaching.

She plunged deeper, still didn't feel concealed, and went deeper still. Only to realize that she was in farther than she had checked. In too far, as it turned out.

A loud splintering sound caused her to look up. The glass ceiling of the greenhouse was splintering, a spiderweb of cracks moving quickly through it. Then large chunks of glass fell, letting in beams of bright yellow light through to the ground. They were accompanied by a strange choir of voices, high and harmonious but with an edge of hysteria and chaos.

She looked around, desperately seeing if there was a clear path through the multiplying beams of light. She didn't see a great path, but there was absolutely no way she could stay here.

Because GOD was coming.

FEAR AND TREMBLING

POSTED BY: PISTONS
Look, the new Matrix is rough. Should you be worried? Yeah. Cautious? Of course. Scared?

Never.

If you're scared, sell your cyberdeck to someone who can really use it. Because if you run the Matrix with fear, you run it with a time bomb strapped to your chest.

The GODs and demiGODs are tough, merciless, and really good at what they do. But so are the Ancients, the Red Samurai, and plenty of other people we encounter on the street. We don't back down. We get good.

Now that you've had your pep talk, let's look at how our opponents work in the Matrix so you can know what's waiting for you.

AVOIDING THE WATCHFUL EYE OF GOD

I chose the title of this section really carefully, because as much as we can worry about the ways the GODs and demiGODs can hurt us, the thing we really need

to worry about is how they see us. Perception is where they spend a lot of their effort, because they know how important it is to see threats as early as possible.

The crack security people of the Matrix are good at a lot of things, but seeing is perhaps their most underrated quality, because let's face it, it's not glamorous. But Matrix perception is about more than just having good rendering software and checking out all the icons that come into view. It's knowing how to sort through information coming your way and find what's truly important. There was a brief time when hackers thought they could confuse security by flooding hosts with dozens of RFID chips running silent, but once they figured out that demiGODs knew enough to design their scans to screen for icons that were running silent and were not RFID chips, the days of that trick were numbered. That's the part of Matrix security that too many people overlook—it's not about just looking at reality, it's knowing how to define reality so that what you want to see comes to the fore.

Knowing the emphasis security places on perception makes it all the more important to adopt the infiltration techniques that work in the meatworld. Most importantly, look like you belong. If you're going into a crowded host, for example, why run silent? That's a great way to call attention to yourself, oddly enough. Just let your icons move with the crowd of others, and make sure your actions are so smooth that they don't call attention to you. Conversely, are you going to a host predicated on secrecy? Like, say, you decided to run into MI-5 because you're tired of breathing? Then run silent. Spies are slipping in and out of those places all the time, so the demiGODs won't be automatically alerted to another silent icon.

Another pointer that trips people up: Remember that while the Matrix is rendered in three dimensions to help us understand it, distance is an illusion. Especially if you're in a host. You may think you're on the other side of the host from security, but that's not real protection. That distance can be closed in a heartbeat. So don't think about staying as far as possible from security; think about hiding your actions however you can. Ideally, you should be surrounding yourself with other activities to keep security confused about what's really going on.

While not being noticed is great, it's only part of the game, since you're not going into hosts just to pass

through. There's something you want to get done, and you need to do it as effectively as possible. The best advice I can give you is that a good hacker is like a good fencer. When you first engage an opponent, pay careful attention to how they come at you. They'll attack, you'll counter (or vice versa), and then you'll have a chance to see how they adjust. This is critical. You're going to start to learn their tendencies when you see how they come back at you. If you've been around the block a few times, there are certain patterns of attacks and counters that you'll get used to. Ideally, you'll know how to respond to catch them off guard. Because you don't have a lot of time to dick around.

Just as one of the goals in fencing is to get your opponent to overcommit and reveal a vulnerability, the main goal in Matrix jousting is to get your opponent to weaken their firewall. Sometimes this isn't a concern. You may run into some idiot rookie fresh out of spider training who is so weak you can just blow out of the water even if they've got the strongest firewall they know how to mount, but you shouldn't count on that. Usually what you'll need to do is absorb a few attacks, convince your opponent that they really need to come after you if they want to do some damage, absorb their best shot, then lay into them. All the while remembering that if you're in this kind of combat, reinforcements are undoubtedly on the way, so you don't have much time.

That brings me to another characteristic of this Matrix: Don't get married to anything. Backdoors are great, defensive structures are nice, but if you are going to do anything illicit in this Matrix, you need to get in and get out quick. I can and will give you tips for dealing with the demiGODs you might encounter, but in the end the best tip is this: Get out before they get your scent.

THE PANTHEON OF THE MATRIX

As you might expect, each corporation brings a slightly different slant to their demiGOD operations. Knowing their habits is important, as it can give you a few critical extra seconds in the early stages of a hack (which, according to a lot of people running in the new Matrix, should also be the *only* stage of your hack). Remember,

though, that the megas don't allow mere grunts into the ranks of their demiGODs. These people are skilled, smart, and flexible. You may think you have a good initial approach—and that might indeed be the case—but once the demiGODs get wind of you, you'd be surprised how quickly they can adjust from "Follow standard protocol" to "Squash that motherfragger *now*." Anyone's habits can be used as a weapon against them, which can help you against the demiGODs but also hurt you. The demiGODs know this principle too, and they are trained to alter their habits when it will make the difference between defeat and victory in a fight.

That said, here are some of the tendencies to be aware of in each of the Big Ten.

ARES

Ares has the military bred in their bone, and that mindset just does not shake easily. That means their demiGOD operations are set up like a military platoon tasked with guarding a fortress. Border patrols, regular checkpoints, asking random strangers for papers—if you've seen military security doing it in a war trid, it's happening in an Ares host.

They are very sophisticated in how they plan their patrol routes. In their major hosts, these are adjusted daily, based on analysis of traffic and activity (in less-significant hosts, this adjustment happens weekly or even monthly). Having the patrol define a nice, regular route like a square or oval is far less important than making sure the patrols are where they need to be at the times their algorithms identify as optimal.

There are two useful data touchpoints here; one more valuable than the other. Cracking an Ares host and downloading the patrol routes is useful, but only for a little bit. Soon enough, that information is going to be obsolete, so don't steal it until you're ready to use it. Far more valuable are the algorithms themselves, the equations they use to help them decide where people are going to be when. If you have the algorithms, you can figure out the next day's patrol patterns based on an analysis of the traffic on any given day (which is something any reasonably competent hacker should be able to find). Better yet, you can influence that algorithm, sending traffic to a host in ways that will shape the next day's patrol in a way that is favorable to your plans.

This is nice, but don't overestimate the advantage this gives you. Remember, perceiving throughout an entire host is not a difficult thing, so you can never assume that an icon that does not appear to be near you isn't staring you down. But it's also true that the more icons you can place between yourself and a demiGOD, the more trouble they are going to have seeing what you are up to. Does it put the odds in your favor? Not by a long shot. But if you wanted good odds of survival, you'd be on their side, punching endless numbers into a vast database or something. All we can ask is to make the odds slightly less horrible.

In combat, Ares demiGODs strictly adhere to the hit hard, hit fast school of thought. They want intruders hurt in a way that will keep them from thinking about coming back. They absolutely love slugfests, so don't get into one with them. Lots of fighters before you have tried rope-a-dope on a bigger, stronger opponent—don't hesitate to keep moving to wear down their concentration, if not their physical stamina. The more you can stay out of a straight-up fight, the more anxious they'll be, and as we all know, anxious people are prone to mistakes.

- In the meatworld, Ares security can't just sling around bullets whenever they feel like it, because there's too much of a chance of striking something they really don't want a bullet to hit. That concern's a lot smaller in the Matrix. Missed attacks are not as damaging to the surroundings of a host as is, say, a poor grenade toss in the meatworld, and even if it is, a host is easier to repair. This means Ares demiGODs are free to get trigger happy if they want. And they usually want.
- Netcat

AZTECHNOLOGY

I know what you're expecting. We know how Aztechnology works—they're going to be all about frying your brain to a crisp, then serving it to their high priests on a silver platter garnished with lettuce. But that's because you're thinking about the Aztechnology we shadowrunners know and loathe. There's that other Big A, the one the public loves, the friendly face attached to the best PR firm in the world. This other side of them means two things. First, they're the target of a whole lot of attacks besides the ones we throw at them. From gang vandalism to the activities of punks just seeing what they can get away with, there is plenty of petty crap going on in Aztechnology hosts, just because they're so big and prominent. If they leveled the hammer on everyone doing shit to them, they'd lose a whole lot of the goodwill they'd worked so hard to build up.

The second thing to remember is they understand that PR is a powerful weapon, and they're sure as hell going to use it. You can't understand Aztechnology's approach to Matrix defense unless you understand the role PR plays with it.

They've spent a lot of time looking at the issue of how the pubic will react to their security procedures, and that has informed their approach. When it comes to low-level vandalism, for example, they've found that harsh crackdowns are counter-productive. Forcibly ejecting someone who put a graffiti tag in a host builds resentment in the coveted youth demographic, while also making you look uninviting and harsh. So Aztechnology adopted a series of softer responses. Sometimes when a tag pops up, Aztechnology designers build up a new piece of virtual art around it that incorporates (but also overwhelms) the original tag. People enjoy these pieces so much that there is no real outcry when they are erased after a day or two. Other times they will trace the tagger, then put their own graffiti in the tagger's PAN—something that says "You're it," or something similar. This turns the act of tagging into a game, while also sending the not-so-subtle message that the tagger can be easily found, if Aztechnology is so inclined.

The end result of this is that people appreciate the good-natured responses while also understanding that if Aztechnology is not going to make a big deal out of petty vandalism, then petty vandalism isn't going to be much fun. Forbidden fruit is always sweeter.

While looking all easygoing and fun, the Aztechnology demiGODs are of course gathering as much data on the infiltrators as possible. They may trace them, they may follow them on the next visit, but one way or another, they'll use that information. That's perhaps the biggest fear when running in a Big A host—you may feel like you've gotten away clean, but you don't necessarily know what Aztechnology agents have on you and what they intend to do with it. And it's all too possible that you won't find out until it's too late, so check thoroughly.

To sum up: When you run against Aztechnology, don't just watch your steps during the run. Watch it for weeks, months, years afterward. Their memories are long, and they are relentless.

- That's my big problem with them. I can handle people being bastards, but I like them to be upfront about it. I was starting a run for Stuffer Shack recently, messing with some new software for a rival chain's soykaf machines, and during the meet for the payoff a demiGOD broke in to take a piece of my hide for some drek dating back to the Azt-Am War. I took a little brain fry but got away, and afterward I was like, fine, if you're mad at me, be mad at me, but don't hire me at the same time. Is a little consistency too much to ask?
- Clockwork

EVO

Forget everything you used to know about Evo Matrix security, because it's all changed. This is now the most paranoid group on the 'trix outside of Friends of Brackhaven strategy meeting. Their default assumption is that anyone who is entering one of their hosts is trying to dig up drek on the origins of the CFD virus until people prove otherwise. This takes the form of an absurd amount of virtual concierges streaming around you when you enter an Evo host, acting all bright and chipper and asking how they can help you ("By going away" is not, of course, an answer they will accept). They'll ask you what you need, what you're looking for, and other questions to build a profile of you. They know that most people are not dumb enough to come out and say, "I'm looking for dirt on cognitive fragmentation disorder," but their profiling is more sophisticated than that. They

look for anomalies, things people say they are interest-ed in that no one else is, or answers from one part of the interrogation (and make no mistake, that's what it is) that don't go with the other, or movements after the interrogation that are not consistent with the answers that were given. They'll happily track anyone who gives them the slightest reason to be suspicious, then give a warning to them to cease whatever they are doing. If the icon remains and continues to do things security doesn't like, then it's time to call the IC.

So if you're going to Evo, get a good story ready, make sure it's airtight, then make sure your actions are consistent with your story. Until security decides to pay attention to someone else.

> Part of the trick is that a lot of the questioning is done by agents, with a few live spiders thrown in. Some people think that if they've got a live interrogator, that automatically means they've raised suspicions, but that's not necessarily the case. From what I've seen, the assignment of humans is done pretty much randomly. In

the end, it's probably better to get a living person on you, as they are more likely to peel away sooner and move on to the next one. Agents are more tenacious, because they don't get bored or distracted.
> Netcat

HORIZON

We may be a few years past the Vegas Technomancer Massacre, and most of the blood may be cleaned off the streets (some of those stains are stubborn), but Horizon is a long way from repairing their image in Ma-trix communities. That's made them a little cautious, which is slightly good news when it comes to running in their hosts.

The good news is they have mostly foresworn IC that does lethal damage. They don't want any dead hackers, especially dead technomancers, making headlines. That's not a total ban—you try to throw bio-feedback Gary Cline's way, you're going to experience some serious pain—but for the most part, they greatly favor kicking people out or making them reboot to inflicting physical damage.

So that's good, but that doesn't mean hacking Horizon is easy. Perhaps the biggest difficulty in the whole process is finding the crap you're looking for. I've hacked into their hosts dozens of times, I've studied org charts, and I still have trouble understanding how the damn corp is put together. They are the most changeable fragging organization I've ever seen. Department names change—or they're not even departments in the first place—people shift up, down, and across hierarchies, and projects float around like a weather balloon in a tornado. So don't waltz into a Horizon host thinking you'll catch on to the way things are organized quick and find what you are looking for, or even that you'll find something where it was last week. Change is how they do business.

Horizon demiGODs, of course, know this and use it. Users may not know how things are changing and shifting and where files are going, but the demiGODs know. They also know that when a particularly valuable file has been moved, it's a good idea to keep an eye on the spot where it used to be, because any visitors to the old spot are likely to come looking for the new one. The response to that is simple—don't directly go from one spot to the other. If something is moved, gather what you can from the old spot, then head out. Don't go out on the path the demiGODs are expecting you to take.

- And don't forget to make sure they're not tracking you when you leave.
- Slamm-0!

- The important thing to remember about Horizon is they think they are about people. You should associate the information you are looking for with a particular person, not with a department. It's easier to find a person than it is to figure out their organization.
- Sunshine

MITSUHAMA

Come on, do I really need to detail the MCT security philosophy? It's the same one playground tough guys have been spouting for centuries. Here's a line in the sand. Cross it, and you're dead.

If you're where you're supposed to be, MCT will leave you alone, without any taste of Evo's paranoia. You may not feel like you are being watched, and it's quite possible you're not. You'll wander through their territory. And you'll see clearly marked areas where you're not supposed to go. They will expect the markings to be all the warnings you need, and they will expect you to be smart enough to take it. If you're not, then they will throw everything at you in a heartbeat. That "everything" is not subtle in the least, and they don't intend it to be. It's the sledgehammer to the skull to tell you that you've been bad.

That means there are two main approaches to MCT Matrix holdings. First, hide yourself, and hide yourself good. Second, do your legwork well. The key to the effectiveness of high-security areas is to make sure all the stuff that needs to be in there is in there—and nowhere else. The problem with that scheme is that humans are inevitably involved in where data goes, no matter how much you automate things, and humans can be sloppy, forgetting to delete files or copying them to places where they shouldn't be. Rather take a risk in one of the Zero-Zones or other marked-off territories, figure out what mistakes may have left some items in places that are a little easier to deal with.

- Here's a fun game: Get someone to pose as a researcher or engineer and infiltrate an R&D facility (warning: this person and their fake IDs better be damn good). Have them be a little sloppy with data that passes through them—nothing critical, but enough so that people notice. If your insider is good enough, MCT won't just fire them outright, and if they can keep it up, the higher-ups might just cave and expand one of the forbidden areas rather than force your friend to behave. When they first do that, the area that is enlarged tends to be understaffed, so it's a good time to hit it with less risk. You can get plenty more things than what your contact could get on their own
- OrkCEO

- That seems like a lot of work and a lot of "if"s for limited payoffs. If you want to take on a Zero-Zone, just do it already. Strap on your best deck and show them what you're made of.
- Clockwork

NEONET

These guys are the primary architects of the new Matrix. That means they are an absolute bitch to deal with.

What's it like? It's like trying to play whack-a-mole in a funhouse. You never know where they are going to pop up, and you never really know what's "real," and they abuse the icon rules of the Matrix with unholy glee. I've seen security personnel disguised as a coffee table in a restaurant, a painting in a Georgian manor, and the ball in a soccer match. They're not supposed to be able to do that. They don't give a shit.

They're as worried as Evo about having CFD blame tied to them, but they don't have the patience or the personnel to engage in Evo's relentless questioning campaign. With so many of their personnel stuck in Boston, they are resource-poor. But they just figure that gives them an excuse to do what they want to do anyway, which is camouflage their agents in all sorts of ridiculous but fiendish ways. Eventually, some spies from other megacorps are going to run afoul of these disguised agents and register a complaint with the Corporate Court, and that could very well lead to changes. Until then, NeoNET is going to amuse themselves, and the familiar fedora-and-suit look of GOD agents will be less frequently seen in their hosts.

- ☺ They've already heard a few complaints about their tactics (though none from people with any real authority to do anything about it), and so they've made a small adjustment—they've set up a small host tied to the main Corporate Court host to receive complaints about "non-compliant Matrix icons." They'll receive complaints, asking for details about where the camouflaged agent was seen and when. Then they'll compare it to all the incident reports they have on file. Then, assuming what the complainant was doing when they first ran into the disguised agent was serious enough, they'll come after them.
- ☺ Sunshine

- ☺ Anyone stupid enough to believe that anyone with any kind of authority is looking out for them deserves what they get.
- ☺ Clockwork

RENRAKU

Come on, you know what's coming here. There are more than fifty thousand registered AIs in the world. And a few hundred thousand (at least) unregistered ones. They're mad and Evo and mad at NeoNET. So guess who is going to welcome them with open arms, since learning from the past is a thing people just don't do anymore?

So yep, Renraku is on the leading edge of bringing AIs into their Matrix security. Most of those are protosapients—not exceptionally bright, but quite capable of following orders. They have a few metasapients, including a metasapient training program to assist their recruits in the development of advanced programs.

They're not entirely reckless, of course. They know their own history, and they know the risks they are facing. At present their ranks remain entirely xenosapient free, and I expect them to stay that way. They also do not have any all-AI teams, or AI-led teams. All AIs are supervised by and work with metahuman co-workers. They feel this is the best way to take advantage of their speed and skill in the Matrix while not preventing their non-humanity from running away with them.

Note especially that they value the speed of the AIs. Renraku absolutely loves speed in their demiGODs. When they engage, they are really difficult to get a bead on, and they refuse to stay in one place. They like their agents to get the first attack in whenever possible, and they like it to hurt. A lot.

- ☺ And it's worse than you think. They don't just have AIs—they have e-ghosts. And to make things even worse, rumor is that one of those e-ghosts is Alice Haeffner, formerly of Echo Mirage.
- ☺ Plan 9

- ☺ I call bullshit (so glad you're still with us, 9!). What in the world would the e-ghost of the late wife of the former president of UCAS be doing in Renraku, of all places? What would compel her to do security work?
- ☺ Snopes

- ☺ Those are all questions we definitely should be asking …
- ☺ Plan 9

SAEDER-KRUPP

Here's a friendly tip. Don't—*don't*—try to out-think Saeder-Krupp. They love tactics. *Love* it. Their demi-GODs work in squads of five, and they have studied, over and over, the best way to utilize their people, the most effective attack sequences, and the possible alternate responses they may need to turn to if anything unexpected happens. Remember when I talked about Matrix fighting being like fencing? These guys are blademasters, and they come at you in a coordinated flurry. MCT's got their Zero-Zone rep, and it's well deserved, but I find a pack of five S-K demiGODs closing in on me to be even scarier than the chorus line of IC that MCT likes.

So don't wait around for the S-K demiGODs to come find you. You won't like it. Get out before trouble arrives. Sometimes, it has to be that simple.

SHIAWASE

With the recently announced Megacorporate Revision, speculation is running rife over which of the Big Ten is most responsible for pushing it through. Popular candidates in the opinion of the general public include Saeder-Krupp, on the theory that they are looking to solidify their status as the world's number one megacorporation, and Horizon, who is looking to swat down some AA rivals who actually have more gross income than they do. But in the shadows, a perhaps-unlikely main suspect has emerged, and that's Shiawase.

For a motive, you have to look no farther than the Pacific Prosperity Group. That organization has been a thorn in the Japanacorps' side for years, and it got worse for Shiawase and company when Wuxing managed to draw Aztechnology to the fold. The (quite credible) theory is that Shiawase intends to use the Megacorporate Revision to strike out at many of the smaller members of the PPG, lowering their status and sending their stock prices into a death spiral. That could give them the chance to snatch a few of them up, which would then make the PPG a whole lot more fun for them.

Whether this theory is true or not, there are plenty of AA corps who believe it, and they are quite active in letting Shiawase know how unhappy they are. All sorts of harassment is occurring in Shiawase hosts, keeping their demiGODs very busy. A distracted demiGOD is a nice thing for us, so take advantage while you can.

The problem is that when a demiGOD feels overwhelmed, they often lash out, going for the broad, sloppy kill stroke instead of the precise knockout, Shiawase agents would prefer precision, but it's been clear to them recently that their preferences don't matter, so they'll settle for getting the job done.

WUXING

While Wuxing Matrix hosts tend to be beautiful—orderly, calming, and tranquil—what's really at the heart of their host design is not *feng shui* but one of their other central concerns—finance. The lending business has been particularly good to Wuxing recently, with most of the Big Ten and a number of AAs putting their lines of credit to new use or seeking quick-turnaround capital funding for takeovers, expansions, or other projects.

There is a certain aura financial institutions try to project. They want you to be comfortable enough with

them to take some of their money, but scared enough of them to want to give it back. This is the model that has been permeating Wuxing's online presence, with "polite but firm" serving as watchwords. Wuxing does not host the NeoNET demiGODs, who like nothing more than to jump out of the spot you least expect them to be in. Instead, they employ the large, friendly people who greet you when you enter a casino, kindly and politely directing you to the games you want to play while delivering that unspoken message that if they have to, they'd be quite willing to break your spine over their knee.

They are quite capable of backing up their threats, but their desire for a veneer of politeness gives them the same weakness as anyone who talks too much. Talking takes time, and if you're clever it's time you could be using for important things like finishing up a hack or getting ready to log out, quick. This is why MCT takes a "just attack" approach to defense, figuring it's best to get to business and not leave your opponents any time to do anything.

- Just remember that the time you're using to gain what you think might be an advantage is time your opponents could be using for very similar activities, even though you think they're just chatting.
- Sounder

GAME INFORMATION

Below are a few new forms of IC as well as some Matrix security NPCs to keep players busy while running the Matrix.

NEW IC

BLOODHOUND

Attack: Host Rating x 2 [Attack] v. Willpower + Sleaze

This is a hybrid of Patrol and Track IC. It travels a host, looking for illegal activity; when it finds it, it immediately attempts to track the target by getting two or more marks on it to learn its physical location. This has the advantage of having no lag between discovery of a problem and addressing it, but it means the patrolling action stops once the Bloodhound attempts to Track, leaving possible holes in a patrol design.

CATAPULT

Attack: Host Rating x 2 [Attack] v. Intuition + Firewall *or* Logic + Firewall (defender's choice)

This IC combines some of the effects of Acid and Blaster IC, doing damage to the target's Firewall while also sending some damage through to the user. If the attack generates any net hits, it temporarily reduces the target's Firewall rating by 1, while also dealing (net hits) Stun damage to the target. The damage is increased by 1 for each mark on the target. The Firewall damage is repaired when the target reboots. Unlike Blaster, successful attacks from Catapult do not link-lock the target.

SHOCKER

Attack: Host Rating x 2 [Attack] v. Intuition + Firewall

Generally used in tandem with other forms of IC, the goal of Shocker is to slow down the opposition. If its attack hits, instead of doing Matrix damage, it reduces the target's Initiative Score by 5.

SECURITY SPIDER
(HUMAN, PROFESSIONAL RATING 4)

B	A	R	S	W	L	I	C	ESS
2	3	4	3	5	6 (7)	5	2	5.7

Condition Monitor	11
Armor	6
Limits	Physical 4, Mental 8, Social 5
Physical Initiative	9 + 1D6
Matrix Initiative (cold-sim)	Data Processing + 5 + 3D6
Matrix Initiative (hot-sim)	Data Processing + 5 + 4D6
Skills	Computer skill group 6, Cybercombat 5, Electronic Warfare 5, Hacking 7 (Personas +2), Intimidation 2, Perception 3, Pistols 1 (Tasers +2)
Qualities	Codeslinger (Hack on the Fly), Uncouth
Cyberdeck	Sony CIY-720 [Device Rating 4, currently set to Attack 6, Sleaze 6, Data Processing 5, Firewall 7]
Programs	Armor, Biofeedback, Encryption, Exploit, Guard Hammer, Sneak, Stealth
Augmentations	Cerebral booster 1, datajack
Gear	Armor clothing [6], commlink (Renraku Sensei, Device Rating 3), jammer (area, Rating 4)
Weapons	Yamaha Pulsar [Taser, Acc 5, DV 7S(e), AP 5, SA, RC —, 4(m)]

SECURITY TECHNOMANCER
(DWARF, PROFESSIONAL RATING 4)

B	A	R	S	W	L	I	C	ESS	RES
4	3	4	3	5	7	5	4	6.0	7

Condition Monitor	11
Armor	6
Limits	Physical 5, Mental 8, Social 7
Physical Initiative	8 + 1D6
Matrix Initiative (hot-sim	12 + 5D6
Skills	Compiling 5, Computer 6, Cybercombat 7, Decompiling 5, Hardware 4, Electronic Warfare 7, Hacking 6, Intimidation 2, Leadership 3, Negotiation 4, Perception 4, Pistols 2 (Tasers +2), Registering 6, Software 3
Qualities	Codeslinger (Brute Force), Exceptional Attribute (Logic)
Living Persona	Device Rating 7, Attack 6, Sleaze 5
Complex Forms	Diffusion of Data Processing, Diffusion of Sleaze, Infusion of Attack, Infusion of Firewall, Pulse Storm, Resonance Spike, Static Bomb
Registered Sprites	Courier sprite (Level 6), Fault sprite (Level 5)
Submersion Grade	2
Echoes	Attack Upgrade, Overclocking
Gear	Armor clothing [6], commlink (Meta Link, Device Rating 1)
Weapons	Yamaha Pulsar [Taser, Acc 5, DV 7S(e), AP –5, SA, RC —, 4(m)]

LESSER DEMIGOD

(HUMAN, PROFESSIONAL RATING 5)

B	A	R	S	W	L	I	C	ESS
3	3	5	3	5	6 (8)	5	4	4.9

Condition Monitor	11
Armor	6
Limits	Physical 4, Mental 8, Social 6
Physical Initiative	9 + 1D6
Matrix Initiative (cold-sim)	Data Processing + 5 + 3D6
Matrix Initiative (hot-sim)	Data Processing + 5 + 4D6
Skills	Computer skill group 8, Cybercombat 7, Electronic Warfare 7, Hacking 9 (Personas +2), Intimidation 4, Perception 6, Pistols 4 (Tasers +2)
Qualities	Codeslinger (Hack on the Fly)
Cyberdeck	Shiawase Cyber-5 [Implanted, Device Rating 5, currently set to Attack 8, Sleaze 6, Data Processing 5, Firewall 7]
Programs	Armor, Biofeedback, Biofeedback Filter, Encryption, Exploit, Fork, Guard, Hammer, Mugger, Sneak, Track
Augmentations	Cerebral booster 2, commlink (implanted, Transys Avalon, Device Rating 6), datajack
Gear	Armor clothing [6], jammer (area, Rating 6)
Weapons	Yamaha Pulsar [Taser, Acc 5, DV 7S(e), AP −5, SA, RC —, 4(m)]

GREATER DEMIGOD

(ELF, PROFESSIONAL RATING 6)

B	A	R	S	W	L	I	C	ESS
5	3	6	4	6	7 (10)	6	4	4.5

Condition Monitor	11
Armor	6
Limits	Physical 7, Mental 9(11), Social 7
Physical Initiative	12 + 1D6
Matrix Initiative (cold-sim)	Data Processing + 6 + 3D6
Matrix Initiative (hot-sim)	Data Processing + 6 + 4D6
Skills	Computer skill group 11, Cybercombat 12, Electronic Warfare 2 (Jamming +2), Hacking 12 (Personas +2), Intimidation 4, Perception 9, Pistols 5 (Tasers +2)
Qualities	Codeslinger (Brute Force), Exceptional Attribute (Logic)
Cyberdeck	Fairlight Excalibur [Implanted, Device Rating 6, currently set to Attack 9, Sleaze 7, Data Processing 6, Firewall 8]
Programs	Armor, Biofeedback, Biofeedback Filter, Demolition, Encryption, Exploit, Fork, Guard, Hammer, Mugger, Sneak, Toolbox, Track, Virtual Machine
Augmentations	Cerebral booster 3, commlink (implanted, Fairlight Caliban, Device Rating 7), datajack, mnemonic enhancer 2
Gear	Armor clothing [6], jammer (area, Rating 6)
Weapons	Yamaha Pulsar [Taser, Acc 5, DV 7S(e), AP −5, SA, RC —, 4(m)]

CORPORATE SPONSORSHIP

The shaded glass partition separating the driver and passenger compartments lowered without a sound. The rigger craned her neck back to look him in the eyes. Jinx found it difficult to judge human ages accurately, and this girl seemed particularly young with her cute heart-shaped face, dimples, and bright pink hair. "I can't believe I took this gig, chummer," she told him. "I swore I'd never take another job from Lord Bastian. He's an ass."

Outside the limo, neon lights streaked past them as they circumnavigated traffic. He flinched reflexively, even though his head told him that the rigger had complete control of the limo. "You know him, Wheelz?"

The rigger snorted. "You wouldn't believe the unholy stank Bastian left in the cab after last time. Couldn't even get orcs to ride back there for three months. Had to have everything detailed twice!"

Jinx gingerly placed his hands on the genuine vat-grown leather seats—such luxury felt akin to stepping onto holy ground naked. He had never been inside of one of these swanky Mitsubishi Nightsky—too rich for his blood. "You've met him personally, Wheelz?"

"Yeah, and I took the job anyway. The pay is legit, and I was promised you were house-broken—even if the job is fragged ethically."

"Pistol Whip Music censored Lord Bastian because those snobs back in Tír Tairngire threatened an economic boycott. What else can he do but try to steal back his music?"

Wheelz rolled her eyes. "You'd think they would just laugh off a song called 'Frag Tír Tairngire' and ignore all the protests it's stirring up."

"You're human, Wheelz." Jinx couldn't help but fold his white hair back behind his angled ears. "You can't imagine what it's like living under the thumb of immortal elves, knowing that you'll live and die while they'll go on forever—always being a pawn in their schemes. Lord Bastian betrayed them to help us find freedom."

Wheelz shrugged her shoulders. "The only thing Lord Bastian wants is to score some easy tail and then snort his way to hell. If he cared about your people and his muscle, he wouldn't have accepted corporate sponsorship. His whole album is work-for-hire. You know what that means? We're stealing from Pistol Whip Music. This ain't a Robin Hood job. We're not robbing from the rich to give to the poor. Bastian's already gotten his cut, but he thinks he can turn street cred into nuyen by arranging for the unauthorized release of the original recording. We're the bad guys here. You alright with that?"

"I'm fine."

"Good to hear. Let's go over the plan one more time."

Jinx's cheeks burned at her patronizing words. How dare she treat him like this was his first run? McCready—the bastard fixer who put them together and arranged for an invitation to get past the front door—insisted that either they'd work together, or he'd find a new team. "I've already edited your vehicle's marks

BY JASON ANDREW

to broadcast clearance. It'll get you past the security into the garage. Normally it wouldn't be that hard, but everything's on alert because of the groupie protests over the censorship. The noise is too dense anywhere below the third floor, so I'll need to sleaze my way into a private space before I get too deep into VR and try to find the paydata."

"McCready arranged for an empty office on the tenth floor. It should be listed on the schematics loaded onto your deck. There's a metal briefcase under your seat. Take it out." Jinx reached under the seat and located the case. It was heavier than expected. "After you've got the facility's marks edited, install them onto my Fly-Spy drones in that briefcase. They're keyed to activate when you open it. Once they're active, they'll provide me with a set of eyes."

"Got it."

"Declan Law is a subsidiary of Horizon, so their corporate accounts alone will require top-notch security. I'll keep watch over your body when you deep-dive, and give you warnings the best I can. We ain't got the muscle to fight our way out, so this needs to be a stealth run. Believe me, you don't want to go to corporate prison."

Jinx reflexively reached for his deck. "I know the job."

"Keep your mind on it and stay out of trouble," Wheelz warned. "That paydata is worth a pile of nuyen. Odds are, we won't be the only shadowrunners trying to get it, so stay frosty."

A tower of steel and glittering glass dominated the horizon.

Jinx swallowed, already nervous. He had bought the best styles he could afford with his limited stash, but surely anyone who took a real look at him would know he wasn't elite. "You sure I won't be out of place?"

The Mitsubishi Nightsky limo slowed as they pushed through a mob of crazy, screaming protestors. They stopped at a series of cement blockades manned by corporate security—decked out in full riot gear. Wheelz flashed her credentials, and they waved them through to the garage. "Would have been keen if we could have decked you out with an elite wardrobe for this job, but you've got those pretty elfin cheekbones. That'll have to do."

They pulled into a space on the lower parking levels. Random security patrols were sparse down here, but it would be a long way back to topside if they had to fight their way out.

"This won't be the first time I've brought a number of discreet guests up into Declaw Law through the back door for some wage-slave lawyer's afternoon delight. Act like you belong and don't make waves. There's some chatter on the comms that the groupie protestors are starting to get violent. Don't get involved, no matter how much you might agree with them."

The passenger door opened, and Jinx slid out into the garage. Two corporate security guards glanced him over and passed by, snickering under their breath. They probably knew a few partners with a thing for elves. Jinx waved nervously and proceeded to the elevator.

The elevator scanned his face as he approached and beeped for the keycard. Here was the moment of truth. He couldn't hack through the security since the marks were theoretically hard-coded onto the card. McCready provided both the card and the plans, so if this card was solid, then odds were the rest would be, too. The elevator door slid open. Jinx entered and said, "Tenth floor."

The elevator motors whirred. As the elevator rose from the subfloors, the glass walls provided a panoramic view of the angry mob outside and the landscape of the city.

The noise of the city and the conflicting pattern and voices faded once he passed the fifth floor. His deck registered devices on each floor as they closed in on its target.

He poked his head out of the elevator doors as soon as they opened to discover an empty hall. McCready's intel said that a number of the executives had moved to the floor above while their offices were being redecorated. That meant the floor should be empty, save for drone sweeps and construction workers.

Jinx flipped on his deck's augmented reality setting, and a monochromatic filter overlaid his perceptions of the real world, making his surroundings look like an old film from the last century. A boisterous construction worker, carrying a large metal box of tools that rattled as he walked, bumped into him in the hallway. The AR filter translated him into an office worker clad in a charcoal grey suit with a fedora.

He counted the offices until he reached the fifth one and then tried the door. It opened without challenge. Jinx searched along the back wall for the secret opening to the executive washroom and breathed a loud sigh of relief when a section of the panel opened, revealing the luxurious space.

The secret camera in the executive office was disabled, thanks to a quiet bribe to the construction workers. Fortunately, the device still had security marks on it that he could exploit, even if it wasn't actively broadcasting. He bricked the camera with a data spike and then sleazed all of the marks for the security system. This gave Jinx access to the friend-or-foe system for everything on the floor.

He used his new access to get the Fly-Spy drones recognized as an authorized part of the system, allowing them to broadcast so Wheelz could see their footage in real time. He opened the briefcase and set it down in the bathroom. A dozen mechanical wasps took flight as though escaping a hive. "Can you read me?" Wheelz chimed in through the commlink.

Jinx switched to text messages to avoid speaking. Hiding in the bathroom would muffle the sound of his voice, but there was always the chance a guard could hear him. <Roger that. You should have complete access to everything on this floor.>

The Fly-Spy drones silently followed him to the office door. He opened it a crack, and they scattered outside to take tactical positions throughout the floor. A single mechanical wasp followed him back into the bathroom and settled on the ceiling. Jinx closed the door and locked it. Now secure in a nest for meatspace with a drone allowing Wheelz to keep an eye on him, he settled down and jacked into full virtual reality mode.

The beauty of the Matrix spiraled before him in blue and white. Declan Law's host appeared as an old-fashioned marble courthouse straight out of an old black-and-white movie from the last century. Any host's designers reveal a bit of themselves and

their motivations in the environments the personas experience. Jinx figured that this place had all the tells of an organization that wanted to wield authority from the moral high ground without having to do any work to earn it.

At the periphery of the horizon, a crowd of personas extended their protest into cyberspace. They attempted to launch brute force attacks against the firewalls and sleaze prank viruses into the host. Corporate security easily turned back the amateur gambits, but it ate at their resources. The dime-store hackers weren't trying to bring down the host, just harass those trying to access it.

It took a bit of time to skirt past their assaults and gain access via the front doors without getting caught in the crossfire. The perfect combination of the corporate grid and his cloned marks allowed him to enter the system without a hitch.

Jinx blinked as the universe melted away. Graphics for a new host appeared, displaying an antique courtroom show with personas taking on the roles of clerks, lawyers, and clients carrying icons disguised as manila folders. The clerks acted as a low-level interface between the host system and the lawyers. They filed motions at various corporate courts around the world, researched legal questions, and locked icons into the secure vaults.

Twin bailiffs, the size of trolls and twice as mean, eyed him suspiciously as he passed. He might have the proper marks, but his persona clashed with the environment, and the agents were programmed to notice such things. Jinx quickly edited his persona to match the crowd with a similar suit and fedora, and the agents turned their attention elsewhere.

The host scaffolding felt familiar, comfortable. Jinx wasted many hours watching old vids that trumpeted truth and justice over corruption. Was this some scene he had long forgotten? If so, what did that mean?

The standard rules of deep runs were to avoid causing trouble in a host by sherlocking the local taboos and making sure not to break them openly. The lawyers seemed content to wait in the queue until served by a clerk, so Jinx followed their lead. A mild-mannered clerk with a bleach-white shirt and suspenders pinged Jinx. "How may I help you, sir?"

"I need to access a file from deep storage."

The clerk nodded attentively. "A quick scan indicates that you have clearance, but this station is unable to access said information."

He had expected this answer. "Where can I gain access?"

The clerk gestured to the large wooden double doors behind him. "The judge is taking motions personally."

Jinx thanked the clerk and followed the other lawyers into the courtroom. The best tactic for avoiding the agents was trying to blend until he was just another sheep in the herd, waiting for his turn to see the judge.

He glanced aside to soak in his surroundings. The court node had an old-fashioned art deco style to it, furnished in stained wooden rails and desks. The judge issued his rulings from the bench, where he seemed to perch like an eagle. It felt like being sucked into something his grandma might have watched.

The judge quickly processed requests from the lawyers, and before he knew it, Jinx stood before him. He appeared as a handsome man with movie-star looks, thick black hair, and heavy-rimmed glasses. This persona represented the central processing system AI in the host. It controlled every file saved in the deep host, where most personas couldn't visit unless they broke the rules. Gaining permission to download the file wouldn't be a problem, but he would receive a red flag on his mark, and the system would take a serious look at what he did next. He needed to receive the mark without the system flagging it so the host wouldn't watch him too closely.

The bailiff tapped his gavel twice. "Judge Atticus is ready to hear your motion."

Jinx glanced about the courtroom, taking a deep look to make sure there weren't any hackers running silent near them. As a precautionary measure, he sent out a ping, like a submarine in an old war movie trying to catch another sub's position.

The room was clear. Likely the protestors gave everyone else too much trouble to allow other hackers access. "Motion to access file 345242-A in deep storage, Your Honor."

The judge furrowed his brow and removed his glasses to study Jinx for what seemed like hours. While he was waiting, Jinx slipped a sleazed data spike directly into the program. This was the do-or-die moment. He had spent days planning just the right angle of attack against the AI. If he could get some marks on it, life would get a lot easier.

The persona blinked, replaced his glasses, and then banged his gavel. "Permission granted. Bailiff, please escort this man into deep storage."

Jinx followed the agent into the file room. This adjacent node could only be accessed from the courtroom and appeared to be no more than a dusty file room. The agent stood at the entrance, his face expressionless but ever-watchful. Anything that Jinx did here would be monitored.

Jinx looked at the manila folder already waiting for him on the table and knew immediately that it contained all of the master audio files Lord Bastian had paid them to snatch. But taking the folder was only half of the job. He finished downloading the file and toggled his comm. "I have the paydata. When I wipe the file from the system, I'm going to attract a lot of the wrong kind of attention. How are we doing topside?"

Wheelz replied via the comm from meatspace. "The floor is clear. The protests are really thick, fragging traffic is everywhere. You'll have to leave via the exit in the south lobby on the second floor."

Jinx calculated the time it would take for corporate security to reboot after his assault. "That's no good. I won't have enough time to make the exit before they spot me."

"I'll try to buy you a couple of minutes with the drones, but you'll need to hit that mark."

"Roger."

The decker turned toward the agent and, taking its full measure, prepared an attack program. In the matrix, his persona responded, flinging a series of shimmering throwing stars directly at the bailiff. They struck true, landing right between the eyes, and exploded. The way his filter interpreted his attack moves never failed to get his blood pumping.

Jinx immediately went silent, trying to mask his presence in the host. It wouldn't work forever, but it might just buy him enough time to get the job done. Now that he had downloaded the file onto his deck, he had the proper breadcrumbs to follow the master file in the system to the proper location in the host. The decker punched through the scaffolding into the host's pure

code and launched another data spike to locate the file's storage space in the cloud. Once it found the data, the virus would brick it to hell.

His deck alerted him to the host's Overwatch Warning. That was bad. There'd be no place for him to hide, as every agent in the host would start tracking his movement. Jinx fired a last text to Wheelz and then turned his attention back to the reality of the host.

A cohort of bailiffs, armed with revolvers and nightsticks, poured into the secured node and immediately targeted him. The attacks came from all sides as they dogpiled upon him. Their blows were controlled and measured, taking care to avoid bricking his deck until they could link-lock him, trapping his consciousness in the Matrix until they could locate his body.

In spite of the pummeling he was taking, Jinx remained resolute. He blasted them with a volley of attacks, manifesting through a series of punches and spinning-kicks, trying to push them back just enough to find an exit.

Security locked down all exits save the main public portal. Jinx could jack out, but that would require dumping the downloaded files. If he wanted out with the paydata, he'd need to fight his way through the court, down the hall, and out the front door. Once he reached the Matrix proper, he could try to hide among the protesters until he jacked out into meatspace.

His instincts told him to fight, but that would only lead to a desperate last stand where the sheer number of agents would eventually bring him down. Whoever said that offense was the best defense was never this outnumbered.

Jinx went full defense, turning up the firewall on his deck to maximum. Then he made a run for the door. An incoming data spike reflected off his shield, manifesting in the host as death-defying dodges, leaps that bounded over agents, and blinding speed that allowed him to run perpendicular to the walls, shattering the rules of the host's gravity. His poor jury-rigged deck sizzled and smoked from the damage, but somehow it kept him in control.

The rolling melee burst out into the court and past the judge, who banged his gavel and screamed, "Out of order! Out of order!"

Jinx dashed past the clerks stumbling in front of him and dodged under the bailiffs' blows. He burst through the glass double doors and leaped out into the wilds of the grid Matrix, where the mundane laws of the host no longer applied, and flew into the safety of the mob.

Jinx immediately jacked out and shut down his deck, in case security was able to trace him. He followed the last mechanical wasp back to the open elevator and keyed it to the second floor.

The elevator seemed to move at a glacier's pace, but it kept moving down according to the readout. He found it difficult to breathe; Wheelz didn't answer his texts.

The doors opened onto the setting of a brutal brawl between rabid protestors and beleaguered corporate security. Jinx maneuvered through the chaos, run-walking across the lobby through the blood and violence until he reached the assigned exit.

Wheelz and her Mitsubishi Nightsky limo waited on the other side. The door opened. "All right kid, let's get paid."

THE PERFECT HOST

It's been over a year since the new Matrix protocols came into effect, changing everything we knew about the Matrix. At first, none of us could hack a single thing, until the secrets of exploiting this new infrastructure trickled down from above. Some of us learned it from the legendary FastJack himself, what he'd learned as, well, what can only be described as being a beta tester for the new Matrix. And some learned from those he taught, or those who learned from those that had been taught, and so forth. And there are always some who used to work for the powers that be, who learned their secrets at the source. Whatever the case, slowly, we all learned what we could do. We learned to spike each other, and to hack each other's cyber eyeballs. However, what took us all the longest to understand was what the new Matrix meant when it came to hacking hosts. Hosts, the beating, malign hearts of our degenerate world. Hosts, those things that jealously guard the accumulated secrets of mankind. Until very recently, we were barely scratching the surface of what we could do. Turns out, there is more power in there then we could have ever imagined. And it also turns out that all of this is more frightening than we could ever have imagined. It's time for us to share what we know. It's time for every one of you hackers out there to understand what you're up against, and what you can achieve. I'm warning you though: I won't claim hacking was ever a child's game, but now more than ever, if you aren't at the top of your game, maybe its best you find something else to do. Hosts are … well, you'll see what they are. But they aren't for those who doubt their skills.

I've invited a friend of mine to talk about all things host. His name is Sterling. He's an ex-pat Brit making a living as a fixer and a hacker in Metropole. He's a rare blend of upstanding and fun, so I recommend you look him up if business brings you down to Amazonia. Through his business, he's talked to more hackers than most of us will ever meet, and they have all told him their stories (Sterling has that effect on you). So listen to his experience.

WHAT IS A HOST?

What *is* a host? In a way, that's a damn good question, and it's going to take a while to really take a good look at it, but look at it we shall, my chummers. Hosts, more than any other single thing, make the world go round. I'd say ever more so than people themselves. I'm convinced that if tomorrow we blinked and mankind disappeared from the world just like that, our cities, economies and infrastructure would run by themselves for many months, maybe even years, before things truly came to a standstill. Hosts are half of why the Matrix exists, the other half of the reason being so we can communicate with said hosts. All that other stuff we do, that's just nice to have.

So concretely, what are hosts? They are large Matrix constructs—envelopes, if you will—that contain data and operations on that data. Hosts are where scientists gather to develop new ideas and products, where engineers develop these things, and where sales and marketing gather to figure out how to get us to pay nuyen for their new geegaw. There is no science, engineering, manufacturing, banking, commerce or warfare—there isn't *anything* humanity does—that isn't handled by a host. They are used to manage human resources, to received and handle customer orders, and push orders through to actual cash reception, as well as the flip side of that, which is handling purchasing from suppliers. Corporations that deal in physical goods use hosts to figure out how many units of their products they have in their warehouses, while companies that deal with intangibles such as services use hosts to manage the people and projects that make them money. On top of all of this lies the accounting processes that underscore everything at all times. Figuring out exactly how much money one has is an extremely complex task, made no easier by the effort to discover new and inventive ways to bend or (if they think they can get away with it) break accounting rules to inflate or deflate the value of the corporation.

All this "business of business" stuff aside, many corporations also use hosts for R&D of some kind or another. Every company, no matter how big or small, needs to innovate. Some needs are more obvious, such as those of actual engineering or scientific companies,

but *everyone* has something of those aspects to them. Sometimes instead of innovating products, they just invest in marketing to find new ways to get the masses to swallow the same old trite bullshit they've been selling forever, but even that marketing needs to get inventive, right? Companies often need to invest in specialized hosts for their core businesses, because having a custom-sculpted host is an important part of a brand image. Custom sculpting isn't cheap, or course, and that can get even more expensive if corporations want to sync data across hosts. R&D often needs to hook into inventory or accounting systems, so if that resides only on a secondary host, the accountants get twitchy. And trust me, nobody likes nervous accountants. So the actual execution of hosts is often a compromise between the ultra-specialized environments the doers want and the intra-connected panopticon system the bean-counters crave.

In sum, hosts hold humanity's labor. It's where we shape our evolution and destiny. Of course, unfortunately, we've decided that we'd rather fuck each other over fistfuls of cred rather than advance ourselves to a better place, but that should not exactly be news to anyone who has spent any part of the past sixty years awake.

As a willing pawn in the machinations of the corporations to rob and steal from each other, it should be dawning on you that hosts will often show up in your work in one shape or other. So by all means, let's talk about them, shall we?

EVOLUTION

Hosts are cleverly designed to be seamlessly and intuitively used by people, but that doesn't mean they aren't complex little fraggers underneath it all. First thing I have to say is, all you old timers out there? Forget everything you knew about hosts before the new protocols came into effect. GOD's little plan to make a new Matrix worked—perhaps a little too well. A lot of hackers have been noticing there is more to the Matrix than we were first led to understand. As a fixer and all around chatty kind of guy, I can confirm I've collated stories from many a hacker, and a disturbing story is emerging. I always thought of the Matrix as a large, rippling body of water with hosts as scattered islands and

rocks, but I never gave much thought, in this analogy, to what lay underneath the water. Maybe I should have. Maybe we all should have.

While we weren't looking, GOD created something ... new. Something entirely new. Some of us have started calling it the Foundation. Frankly, none of us truly know what this is, and we certainly don't have a full understanding of how it works. The Foundation, in my watery analogy, would be the sand underneath the water. The Foundation connects every single island out there—every single host. It's like the underlying infrastructure. If a host is a lightbulb, the Foundation is the power grid. When we log into the Matrix, we log into a grid. That's fine. That is not what I'm talking about. The Foundation is underneath the grid. All hosts are *made* from the Foundation. If a host is a cyberarm, the Foundation is the chrome.

Unfortunately, that's about as clear as I can be. We just don't understand it. Now, I know plenty of hackers out there that simply won't stand for something they don't understand. So yes, I also know plenty of crusaders that have gone out and performed, at great risk and peril, raids against GOD servers. I know a few individuals, who shall remain nameless, that have kidnapped, tortured, and interrogated GOD-affiliated Matrix engineers to get to the bottom of this. What emerges from this is chillingly disturbing: It would appear *nobody* understands the Foundation. Even the masters of the Matrix, the powers-that-be that supposedly control things, don't seem to exactly know what's going on. Nobody wants to appear ignorant, so they all pretend they know, but nobody ever goes into detail. Best we can tell is that the Foundation is the raw power of all combined devices in the world.

The very best (and most unfortunate) among you, may have encountered Ultraviolet (UV) hosts in the past. These were hosts with so goddamn much computer power behind them that they got every single little goddamn detail right in their virtual reality experience. It was impossible for the human mind to distinguish a UV host experience from reality. There was thus no way to ever truly know when you had logged in or out. Even if you'd been in a UV host once, your sanity would never quite be the same, because you could never tell if/when you got out. The only saving grace of UV hosts, if you can call it that, was that they were exceedingly rare.

Well, chummers, the Foundation is all UV, all the time. I'll let that sink it a little. Every single goddamn host is powered by this nebulous undercroft that, if you log into it, is a weird, dream-like UV experience that your mind cannot distinguish from reality. Now, what I said about hosts proper is still true: They are VR constructs that can look like anything, but you always know it's virtual reality. This Foundation bit—nobody ever logs into that. It's the plumbing, the wiring; there is no need for users to ever go in there. They wouldn't know how even if they knew it existed.

But the dirty little secret is that the Foundation is always there, and it holds the host up. It runs deep background processes that allow the host to exist and maintain itself. So what we hackers have begun noticing is that if you can figure out how to log into the Foundation, you can gain unparalleled access to a host. You can sometimes access a corp's darkest, deepest secrets by hitting the Foundation and digging around the roots of a host.

Of course, simply by logging in, you basically risk your sanity. You do that once, you'll never quite know if you're ever out again. Do it repeatedly, and your mind might start snapping. And that's just being in there—the Foundation has its own defense mechanisms to contend with. Nobody said hacking was an easy job, chummer, but it takes a special kind of crazy to get into a deep dive.

But anyway, back to more comforting, concrete thoughts. A host's "basement" is the Foundation. We don't fully understand their relationship, point made, moving on. On top of this Foundation layer is the host proper, as we know it. A host, in VR, can be sculpted to look, feel, and act like anything. Almost every host is going to be different, which is not really a good thing. Habitual visitors to hosts will get used to the reality around them. The wisdom of the sculpting usually makes make itself apparent once you've been able to spend a good amount of time in a host. The metaphors and realities will reveal optimizations for the kind of tasks legit users perform. For hackers, though, it's always going to be annoying. You have to be fast on your feet and figure things out quickly, though you can be sure you're going to need to analyze icons a lot to figure out what they are.

Sculpting a host is very difficult. It takes very knowledgeable programmers and implementation consultants many months to set one up. What is interesting is that hosts aren't computers. A host does not exist in a server. You can't grab a computer and say "this is a host." Hosts exist in the Matrix. So how do you "get" one? Again, the Foundation comes up. From what we understand, hosts are molded—grown, some designers say—from the raw stuff of the Foundation. To acquire a host, you thus have to buy one from one of the handful of corporations that have the authorization from GOD and the rare expertise to grow a host—or you have to brave a Foundation and design one on your own without permission. There currently are two dozen or so corps out there in the business of growing and selling hosts. They do this pretty much non-stop, creating virgin hosts of various sizes and power and then selling them to buyers. Growing hosts is a lot of science with a little art, and matching the right buyer to the right host takes a certain touch, but there are hundreds, possibly thousands of hosts being harvested every day, so there isn't really a shortage. Obviously the larger, more powerful hosts cost exponentially more, but small hosts remain affordable for mom-and-pop shops or policlubs. The major difference in how things work compared to the past is that if you want a host, you have to be on the grid. While GOD's intention might have been to tighten the noose a little here for illegitimate organizations, in effect little changed. As buying any host up to the kind of power large corps require is largely an autonomous process (you register online, pay, and shortly a host is made available to you), shadow groups ranging from organized crime to shadow sites (including our beloved JackPoint, but also our friends like the Nexus or the Helix) have had no problem setting up shell corps with falsified records to obtain the necessary credentials to buy hosts. Danielle de la Mar may have gotten us on a lot of fronts, but at least she didn't get us on this one.

For legitimate groups, though, buying hosts is a no-brainer. Sculpting it is a bigger investment than acquiring the host space itself. Corporations can have as many distinct hosts as they wish. The limiting factor is usually functionality. Host-to-host communication is certainly possible, but keeping data cohesively within a single host is much more effective. As a rule of thumb, most corps will maintain one host per physical office and legal entity. For example, Ares Entertainment Seattle would be a single host, and Ares Entertainment Manhattan another—rather than a single host for Ares Entertainment as a whole or even Ares Entertainment North America. This isn't a fixed rule and is entirely dependent on what the IT honchos of said corporation decide. Some corporations have multiple hosts per subsidiary, some have hosts that consolidate multiple offices in multiple countries. It really all depends on operational needs.

SECURITY RESPONSE

When Danielle de la Mar received the mandate from the Corporate Court to create guidelines for a new Matrix, her sole goal was to make life for information criminals (hackers) as horrible as possible. The first line of defense is the Matrix itself. Hosts—at least the ones used by the corporations for their dirty business—are formidably hard to hack. Hosts are typically able to outgun the raw power of invading hackers fairly routinely. Relative to this is the hosts' ability to launch IC. Gone are the meek programs that merely slow down hackers. Modern IC is as lethal as it is endless. Combating IC is almost folly, as the host has an infinite capacity to spawn more.

While these automated defenses are redoubtable, many hosts will also engage (meta)human protectors in the form of security spiders. The idea is that while IC is excellent and relatively clever, it can sometimes be a little predictable. Nothing has yet been invented that can truly be a match for the human brain save another human brain (I'm not counting AIs here, because it is not entirely clear that we can, or should, intentionally develop them). Sometimes, the relative chaos of a brain can complement the logical rigidity of IC. These spiders usually have the authority to command IC in order to adapt to the strategies of invading hackers.

A corporations's punitive strategy in the real world sometimes complements virtual defenses. Many corporations will do their best to trace invaders in order to send physical kick squads to ventilate the offending hackers. This acts as a powerful deterrent, as many hackers will act very brave in the Matrix but are not all that physically intimidating in the meat world. Megacorporations, by contrast, have no problem showing lethality in both arenas.

These abilities are formidable enough, but de la Mar and her cronies did more. Hosts were built around their archive in the same way a Warthog warplane was built around its Vulcan cannon. Archives are, simply put, inaccessible. Only the true owner of the host can command data to be brought out of that vault. Most corporations thus archive all data at rest; that is to say, any file not being immediately used—unless it is deemed not especially important—is locked away in the archive. Similarly, if it looks like the host's defenses, as mighty as they are, will not succeed in stopping an intruder, the host's administrators can push a virtual PANICBUTTON of sorts, causing the host to begin throwing all data into the archive, starting with data identified as the most vital.

In reality, it turns out hackers can still get at archived data via deep dives, but most corporations consider this possibility in the same way the Romans considered Hannibal's likelihood of attack via the Alps. Certainly, top-tier hackers can achieve this, but most hackers will have nothing but bleeding eyes and an unhinged mind to show for their attempt. Corporations generally consider this sufficient security. The advantage of locking data in the host, rather than using offline storage, is that offline storage can be physically stolen or damaged. The archive may not be one hundred percent secure, but neither is offline storage. The archive has the edge in ease of use and arguably stronger security.

While an emergency lockdown to the archive is disruptive to business and thus only performed in cases of emergency (remember that sometimes, the theft of data may be less damaging that halting all work), it is less disruptive still than the final protective method of shutting down all connections to the host. The ultimate act of protection is to seal the host. As this causes *all* users to disconnect and all processes to halt; it is basically the equivalent of shutting down the corporation. In the physical space, as a facility's power is often tied

to the host, the entire building can shut down, leaving only emergency lighting and processes. It is certainly not something done lightly, and corporations will often swallow the damage an intruder can wreak in a host rather than shut it down completely.

HOSTS AND INDUSTRIES

As explained earlier, sculpting hosts is a lucrative business, but it's also a competitive one. While the new protocols allowed most existing hosts to be grandfathered over into the new Matrix paradigm, any corporation that valued competitiveness (i.e., everyone not actively filing bankruptcy) quickly started moving forward to redesign their hosts to take advantage of the new Matrix's power. It's a booming business (which, by the way, is *extremely* ripe for extraction jobs—call me if you need work), but the clear winners are those able to deliver specialized products tailored to specific business sectors. Don't consider this a wholly exhaustive list, but I'm now going to cover some of the major business areas corporations operate in. Understanding their business will help you understand what you're up against and why.

PUBLIC SECTOR

Starting off with a doozy right there. Ah, the public sector. If to your ears "public sector" means puppet regimes enthralled by corporate money that serve as last bastion of enshrined bureaucracy and inefficiency, you're not wholly wrong. However, the truth is that even the private sector is sometimes actually a public sector. Confused? Allow me to explain. Most governments, from municipal to national, outsource the bulk of their services to private companies. Seattle (and many others) have contracts with private outfits like Knight Errant for policing, but everything from maintenance of water pipes to trash collection is handled by private companies. While, for the most part and to great democratic injustice, this creates a layer of obscurity between elected officials and the services they oversee, in computer system terms, everyone still plays a ridiculous game of pretend-transparency. Just about all contractors acting under public contracts are forced to endure ridiculous amounts of red tape, comply with mountains of regulations, and submit endless audit reports. In practice, everyone lies on these and almost no one pays attention, but the fact is that everyone still has to play the game. Hosts thus have to be set up in very specific ways in order to meet all the regulations while outputting very specific audit data. In addition, governments (or, more accurately, politicians and bureaucrats with the right connections) essentially make a ton of money by constantly changing the norms contractors have to adhere to. This requires companies working the public sector to constantly have host programmers and consultants in their systems, working to change things to make compliance.

PATROL IC

As detailed on p. 248 of *Shadowrun, Fifth Edition*, Patrol IC is typically always running in a host, constantly scanning for suspicious activity. However, gamemasters should not take this to mean Patrol IC performs targeted Matrix Perception tests against the invading hacker every action is gets. There are sometimes millions of icons in a host, and the Patrol IC must divide its attention among all of these things.

The larger a host, the more there is to scan, and even though the processing power of the host is obviously also greater, there is a degradation in effectiveness. Use the following chart to determine how frequently Patrol IC makes a targeted Matrix Perception Test against the hacker:

HOST RATING	COMBAT TURNS UNTIL NEXT MATRIX PERCEPTION TEST
1-2	Every Combat Turn
3-4	1D6 Combat Turns
5-6	1D6 + 2 Combat Turns
7-8	2D6 Combat Turns
9-10	2D6 +2 Combat Turns
11-12	3D6 Combat Turns

Patrol IC can be commanded by security spiders to behave differently. If a spider, or the Patrol IC itself, has cause to think there is an invading hacker lurking about, the Patrol IC will act far more focused, running Matrix Perception Tests every action. For example, if a hacker is detected and then successfully performs a Hide action, the Patrol IC will certainly be looking specifically for the hacker.

A LESSON IN HOST INVASION

Nora is playing her character, Zoe, and Zoe and her team have made it over the fence and are ready to hit a research complex. Zoe's teammates are going in physically to retrieve a sample of the product Mr. Johnson is interested in, as per their orders, and Zoe's job is to support them as much as possible from the Matrix. Nora knowns that attacking a corporate host from the outside is pretty much suicide, so her team has provided her with a nice, direct connection to a terminal slaved to the host. Nora plans to exploit the master/slave relationship to easily get a mark on the device, which will grant her a mark on the host. She'll take things from there.

Nora decides to operate right away in hot sim (+2 dice to all Matrix actions) and, obviously, she runs silent (–2 to all actions, so the two cancel each other out). As she has a direct connection to the device, there is no noise.

She is using a Novatech Navigator with an initial configuration of Attack 3, Sleaze 6, Data Processing 4 and Firewall 5. Her deck can run three programs; currently she is running Exploit, Stealth, and Browse. Her Intuition and Logic are 5 each, and her Cracking skill group also sits at 5.

Zoe wisely goes for a Hack on the Fly action, so rolls Hacking + Logic [Sleaze] versus DR + Firewall (which amounts to being DR x 2 in this case). The terminal is DR 3, so Zoe rolls 10 dice against the device's 6. She gets 3 net hits. She thus gains 1 mark on the device and its master (the host). She isn't too interested in the device itself, so waives her right to ask for information about it due to her hits.

Since Zoe now has a mark on the host, she uses the Enter Host action to get in. She messages her team that she is in and starts overwatch. At this point, the gamemaster rolls the number of Combat Turns until the Patrol IC fires off a scan in her direction. This is a Rating 8 Host, so the gamemaster rolls 2D6 (as per the Patrol IC sidebar chart) and rolls a 10. That means Zoe has some time before that pesky Patrol IC tries to spot her.

Her team progresses forward until they meet a door that needs opening. The door is slaved to the host; since Zoe is in the host, she is considered directly connected to all devices, which means they do not get the benefit of the host's protection. Zoe figures the fastest way to get the door open is to roll Control Device. Opening a door is a Free Action, so she needs at least 1 mark on the door before being able to do that.

Nora thus first makes another Hack on the Fly action against the door. The door is not protected by its master, so this is again a case of 10 dice versus 6. She again makes short work of that, so her next action is to make a Control Device action to open the door, rolling Electronic Warfare + Intuition [Sleaze] v. DR + Firewall. Again, she easily gets the one success she needs, and the door opens.

Zoe and her team continue like this, and all looks pretty well until the ten-Combat-Turn grace period from the Patrol IC expires. So the gamemaster rolls the host's 16 dice and asks Nora to roll her Logic + Sleaze. Unfortunately, the IC scores 3 net hits and sees Zoe. The IC doesn't like what it sees, so it sets off the alarm. As things are about to get very bad very quickly, the gamemaster asks Nora to roll her Initiative, while he does the same for the Probe IC the host just launched. Nora rolls 24, while the IC gets 30.

IC is anything but subtle. As it does not run silent, Zoe is aware of the Probe arriving, in the form of a giant eyeball that covers all of the sky (Matrix Perception against anything not running silent in a host is automatic). The Probe goes first, making its Host Rating x 2 attack (16 dice) versus Nora's defense pool of Intuition + Firewall (10 dice). The IC nets 1 hit, so the host and all of its IC now have 1 mark on Zoe.

Zoe isn't even really going to try to fight the IC. In the meat world, her team needs another door opened—the last one before they reach the sample they need to steal. So she spends her first action doing a Hack on the Fly against another door to get a mark. Again, she succeeds easily.

On the next Initiative Pass, the Probe tags her again, gaining another mark.

Zoe for her part performs the Spoof Command against the door. Against all odds, she fails. Sometimes life just gives you the finger like that. Because she failed a Sleaze action, the door gets a mark on her. That mark, however, is not shared with the door's master (the host). So the door has a mark on her—not really a big deal. But losing an IP at this point in time is a bit of a bigger deal.

On its next action, the Probe nails her with a third mark.

Zoe grimaces and rolls a Spoof Command action on the door again and this time succeeds. Her teammates thank her, telling her to get the frag out of there while she still can. Canny Nora also, at this point, uses a Free Action to switch her Firewall and Sleaze attributes, in preparation for surviving the next IP.

A new Combat Turn begins and is inaugurated with the arrival of a new IC spawned from the host—some dirty and direct Killer IC. Zoe again gets 24 on her Initiative roll, and the Killer IC gets 36. The Killer IC goes first, doing what it does best and giving her a really hard slap. It rolls the usual 16 dice while Zoe rolls her 10 dice from Intuition + Firewall. However, Nora decides that getting bricked right now would not be very good. She opts for a Full Matrix Defense. The gamemaster removes 10 from her Initiative score, but she adds Willpower to her dice roll. Between the boosted Firewall and her Willpower, Nora is now rolling 15 dice in defense. Everyone holds their breath as the roll-off occurs. The gamemaster gets a measly 2 hits while Nora rolls 6. Doesn't entirely make up for her terrible Spoof Command roll, but it's something.

On her next action, Nora immediately uses a Simple Action to drop to AR and then performs a Jack Out action. Theoretically, Zoe could log back to do some more hacking, though the system will be on high alert and actively looking for any further intruders. Given that, she figures joining back up with the team, and lending her Colt Cobra's firepower to the mix might be a better use of her time right now.

THE SEATTLE METROPLEX ADMINISTRATION HOST

The city of Seattle maintains a large host for all of its administrative needs. While each of the municipalities that make up the 'plex (Bellevue, Tacoma, etc.) maintains its own (smaller) host, Seattle Metro's is the largest and contains some data concerning each of its constituent parts.

Seattle's host was freshly redesigned at great expense following the adoption of the new Matrix protocols. Like a crusty old has-been, Seattle just keeps hanging on to its once-appellation of Emerald City (the greenery inspiring the name having long ago been paved over). Having found no better way to remind the world that they used to stand for something, their new host's virtual reality is sculpted in the image of a city made of actual emeralds. Large green crystalline structures float in an azure sky, light glinting off the multiple facets of the exquisitely carved structures. Gold and ebony line the edges of the pyramidal shapes, while delicate arabesques decorate the surface of the raw gemstones.

The host has no concern for physics, so users and visitors float around as they wish. The crystal structures are essentially for different departments within the Seattle Metroplex Administration, and there are many departments—HR, Asset Management, Procurement, IT, Finance, Energy Management ... the list goes on. The space inside each emerald, where employees log in and do their work (if they feel like it that day) is like the interior of a typical office building, except almost everything is made of gold, ivory, black marble, and emeralds. Very fancy. With pesky laws of physics bent, the environment sculpts incredibly delicate furniture. Incredibly thin armatures sprout thousands of little gemstone petals and leaves that form work desks and meeting tables. Completely ignoring physics has long ago been understood to be detrimental to Matrix users, so the gemstone furniture actually is breakable, though it is far more robust than it looks like. But if a user really tries, the furniture can be shattered. This happens a lot when intruders are hacking in, bypassing normal processes and corrupting code.

Seattle's main host is nothing if not bloated with data. The theme eschews physical representations of data. Instead, files are pulsating little dots of blue light that, when accessed, expand into floating displays of data. The turquoise holo data, framed in yellow borders, looks very nice against the general greenery of the host.

Intruders hoping to see IC manifest as munchkins or winged monkeys from The Wizard of Oz will be disappointed. Seattle's IC manifests as spherical balls of liquid metal, like mercury. The balls reshape as they engage intruders, shooting out razor-pointed blades of their mirror-like substance.

Host Rating: 7
Normal Configuration: Attack 8, Sleaze 7, Data Processing 10, Firewall 9

Security Procedure: Patrol IC running at all times. One Junior Security Specialist patrolling at all times. Once alarmed, the Host will launch IC in this order: Probe, Scramble, Acid, Binder, Jammer, Marker, and Track. If one of its IC gets bricked, it will use the next Combat Turn to reboot that IC rather than moving on to the next one.

In general, the host will only use "white" IC that seek to crash intruders as quickly as possible but do no damage to users or their equipment. The reason is simply that the city gets a lot of young punk script kiddies doing their best to cause trouble, and the city's legal department has gotten tired of settling lawsuits from angry parents and other activist groups. So the city's security staff is resigned to booting any intruders expediently but gently.

Uses: The Seattle host can be accessed to obtain information on any city employee or elected official. Since most services are privately outsourced but regulated by bureaucrats, the city also keeps quite a bit of information about all corporations that supply the city with goods or services. The city also maintains many blueprints and schematics of public infrastructure, registrations and permit information, and so forth. In general, it is a great source of indirect information on possible targets.

All in all, hosts for any sort of corporation working the public sector will actually have to take an efficiency hit on their core business in order to specialize their system to survive the public sector's insanity. Some corporations may stubbornly try to maintain two hosts—one for administrative data to meet compliance, and the other running a more specialized host for their main processes. Data must constantly flow between these hosts, though, so that generally reduces the efficiency of the overall setup.

SERVICES

The services sector covers a very wide range of businesses. A service-based organization can mean anything from any sort of consultation company (pick any word and add "consultant" to it, and you'll find a firm offering those services) to specialized customer support firms or marketing firms. Hell, prostitution is a service, too. Any firm that offers people's talents and/or brainpower for hire (usually by the hour) rather than selling an actual product is in the services business.

Obviously, with such a broad definition, you're going to get people who look for different things in a host. Sometimes you'll get companies that care about crunching a lot of data (such as marketing firms data-mining retail records), while other times security will be the main focus, such as with consultancies that, through the necessity of their work, end up holding a lot of their clients' sensitive information.

Service organizations will generally need to run smaller, tighter hosts optimized specifically to help them manage their personnel engagements. After all, these types of firms live or die based on how well they can utilize their resources. Since specialized knowledge is a rarity, some service firms pay their employees a lot of money, so having a high-priced asshole sitting on a bench and not selling his services to another corporation means a deadly drain on the company's bottom line. That means hosts tend to be used to model and predict workloads, ensuring corporations are able to make very precise promises, using their people exactly to capacity. Considering the fickle nature of business and the equally fickle and unpredictable nature of human beings, this is no easy feat.

MINING, LOGGING, AND AGRICULTURE

These are the guys you never think about, but the primary sector is a multi-trillion-nuyen industry worryingly concentrated in the hands of just a few players. Resource harvesting occurs on scales that the non-initiated could scarcely comprehend. Almost the entirety of operations are automated nowadays, with legions of huge drones working nonstop, day and night, to rip as much as they can out of Mother Nature.

Operations thus rely on very powerful and critical host systems that accept real-time sensorial input from these drones and automated systems, while the back-office stuff—all the accounting and other boring stuff—is also on a frighteningly large scale. Commodities live and die on the price of the international markets, so keeping track of minute price fluctuations in local markets and overall composite indexes is essential. Due to the auto-

PEACH CHAMPAGNE CLUB BUNRAKU PARLOUR, METROPOLE (SÃO PAULO DISTRICT), AMAZONIA

The Komata-Kai gumi claims all of Amazonia as their territory, but their stronghold is in the São Paulo district of the vast Metropole megasprawl. Home to a large population of Japanese (indeed, the largest enclave of Japanese citizens outside of Japan itself), São Paulo has everything the Japanese need to feel right at home, including catering for man's darker vices, courtesy of the Komata-Kai.

While the Metropole authorities are no pushovers, they also understand the usefulness of having underground power concentrated in the organized hands of Yakuza rather than hordes of idiotic yahoos. This means that, as they have done for centuries, the Yakuza (brutally) help keep the peace in the streets, and in exchange nobody bothers their vice dens.

The Peach Champagne Club is the Yakuza's biggest bunraku operation in Amazonia, and quite possibly the world. The club is physically spread over sixteen floors of a posh downtown building. The Yakuza maintain a rich, safe, luxurious atmosphere in the club, but what goes on behind the closed doors of the puppet parlor's many rooms is far from civilized.

The Yakuza maintain a host dedicated to the control of the club's operations. The host is used to manage the club's cocktail lounge—the accounting and management of its sales and liquor supply—as well as the actual prostitution that occurs. Prostitutes are scheduled and booked. The club "employs" (willingly or not) over one hundred and fifty prostitutes, with a very high turnover rate (i.e., the prostitutes get killed or irreparably wrecked by clients, lose their minds to the point of becoming useless, commit suicide, escape, and so forth). Optimally scheduling the prostitutes requires a lot of organization. In addition, the host stores the large databank of personalities the bunraku prostitutes can be imprinted with, along with sufficient capacity for simultaneous and seamless streaming of all of these personafixes.

Of course, on top of all that, the Komata-Kai also offer virtual access. The host is set up to run a form of live, streaming simsense that allows visiting patrons to have sex (or whatever) with the prostitutes in real-time. It can't compete with some of the fantastic pornographic simsense programs out there, but it's still a market that attracts a sizeable portion of clients. For those with a voyeuristic tendency, the host also offers live camera feeds of patrons enjoying the wares. Clever algorithms anonymize the patrons enjoying themselves (but not the prostitutes). Physical security also uses reserved locations within the system to monitor the premises.

Visually, the host's VR is extremely vaginal (several straight female clients have complained, but that has not resulted in any change). Reds and pinks dominate the palette, while the virtual rooms are softly padded with plush, soft leather, and hanging drapery creates layers of curtains. Furniture accessories are heavily lacquered for a glossy look. Subtle it is not. The virtual space is very large, like an enormous mansion. Lighting is dim and the air is laced with the heavy scent of opium, vanilla, bergamot, and vetiver. Due to the nature of the activities one performs in the host, a sizable portion of visitors use hot-sim rigs for access, a fact the Yakuza exploit to full advantage by scenting the virtual air with code designed to be especially addictive.

The Komatas' primary security concern with regard to their host is keeping out script kiddies trying to get in for free. They do have financial information in there, however, as well as (according to rumor) blackmail data on some notable patrons, so the security response quickly turns deadly. After all, the Yakuza are not here to worry about the legality of their response, only its effectiveness.

Host Rating: 5

Normal Configuration: Attack 6, Sleaze 5, Data Processing 7, Firewall 8

Security Procedure: Patrol IC running at all times. One Standard Security Spider patrolling at all times. Once alarmed, the host launches IC in this order: Probe, Black IC, Sparky, Killer, and Track. If one of its IC gets bricked, it will use the next Combat Turn to reboot that IC rather than moving on to the next one.

If the invader is making a mockery of its defenses, the host will bring in a Security Troubleshooter. This heavy gun will arrive 2D6 Combat Turns after the alarm has been sounded, should the careless hacker still be around.

Uses: The Peach Champagne Club Host may serve as a meeting place between runners and Johnsons, especially Komata-Kai Johnsons. Shadowrunners are occasionally hired by families of missing girls to get into the system and check the employee registry (these assignments are often followed by extraction requests). Clever runners can also hack the system to arrange specific meetings and invade the security system in support of physical intrusions. Then there are always those rumors of blackmail material ...

TRANS-OCEANIC MINING HOST

Trans-Oceanic Mining is one of several large players in the offshore mining business, with mining rigs deployed in the North Sea, around Southeast Asia, and in Athabaskan Council waters. The corporation has been divided among major shareholders for many years now, with Saeder-Krupp owning the largest part.

Given the hostile climate in the boardroom from the infighting owners, Trans-Oceanic has chosen to operate with two hosts. Its main mining host is separated from its financial and administration host, thus isolating operations from the politicking that can come from financial reporting.

The mining host's virtual reality is informed by classical Scandinavian design aesthetics, featuring clean lines, minimalism, and crisp, clear colors. The host looks a little like a cottage nestled in the majestic fjords of Sweden. The space consists of a few large cubic constructs of chrome and glass, with red and orange accents. An immaculate landscape of perfectly cut grass surrounds the facility, tucked on a cliff of jagged stones overlooking rivers of cobalt.

The air feels overly oxygenated with a pleasant humidity to it, like in a cold, misty boreal forest. Visitors can walk outside between the cubic structures, almost fully respecting the laws of physics. Inside the large cubic buildings, physics get wonky. The concept of up or down becomes very Escher-esque. Visitors can turn a corridor and suddenly find themselves walking on what seemed like wall a moment ago, but is now the floor. The interior of the cubes—all white, chrome and glass—lacks borders. It all looks uniform from afar, making navigation very difficult. Doors are almost imperceptible—thin gaps delineating the frames are the only way to spot them, as they open with a gentle push.

The cubes process the data and functionality of the various mining rigs operated by Trans-Oceanic. Simpler processing occurs toward the outside of the structures. Moving toward the center reveals more and more activity, until the center of the cube is reached and a veritable maelstrom of data is discovered. As users move progressively toward the center, the air around their ears at first starts blowing gently. That gentle blow grows into a rush and then finally a deafening roar near the data processing vortex of the central processing unit.

While all personas appear as people, all security measures render as Rottweilers, chasing down intruders in the clinical hallways.

The second host, the administrative one, is modeled very differently. Perhaps inspired by the boardroom drama, the host renders in black and white. Not greyscale—pure white and pure black only, though very clever artistic use of the two manages to render a surprisingly cogent, if entirely dramatic, form to all things. The location appears to be an office building with mid-twentieth-century sensibilities mixed with modern boardrooms. The administrative staff works in these virtual cubicles, chain-smoking cigarettes and drinking burnt coffee, while the bosses play their power games in the virtual meeting rooms. With everything in purely black and white, it makes for an interesting experience that leaves most visitors on edge the first few times.

Security appears as shadows, bare movements of black on black. They bend the light around them, offering only rare glimpses of human forms in trench coats and fedoras. Their faces, however, are completely shapeless, except for sunken pools of darkness for eyes. Intruders who feel the wrath of the security measures and take damage will have pleasure of seeing their icons spill virtual blood as bright, slick crimson—it's the only color in the entire reality.

OPERATIONS HOST

Host Rating: 10

Normal Configuration: Attack 10, Sleaze 11, Data Processing 13, Firewall 12

Security Procedure: Patrol IC running at all times. Once alarmed, the host launches IC in this order: Killer, Marker, Scramble, Acid, Jammer, Blaster, Binder, Crash, Sparky, and Black IC. If one of its IC gets bricked, it will continue down the chain before rebooting anything.

If the intruder bricks a single piece of IC, or if the alert persists for 4 Combat Turns, not one but two Security Troubleshooters will log into the system to boot (or preferably kill) the intruder.

Uses: As the main control hub for all of Trans-Oceanic's operations, this host contains information regarding core samples and other prospecting data that would be of great interest to rivals, making it a prime target for corporate espionage. Perhaps a little surprisingly, it is also this host and not the administrative one that controls physical security devices in each mining installation. Since the host's prime function is to control mining drones and systems, it should be clear that any saboteur looking to do some damage would probably want to go through here.

ADMINISTRATIVE HOST

Host Rating: 7

Normal Configuration: Attack 7, Sleaze 8, Data Processing 9, Firewall 10

Security Procedure: Patrol IC running at all times. One Standard Security Spider patrolling at all times. Once alarmed, the host launches IC in this order: Killer, Probe, Bloodhound, Marker, Blaster, Binder, and Black IC. If one of its IC gets bricked, it will use the next Combat Turn to reboot that IC rather than moving on to the next one. Two additional Security Spiders will log in after 3 Combat Turns of the alarm sounding.

The security strategy of this host makes heavy use of Tracing. Trans-Oceanic has a security dogma of physically hunting down anyone caught in their host for interrogation. Trans-Oceanic has a standing contract with Knight Errant to apprehend suspects. If tracing is not a viable option, security will attempt to dump users as quickly as possible. Any user suspected of attempting to cause serious damage to the host as a whole, or specifically targeting the supply-and-demand algorithms, will warrant the arrival of a three Security Troubleshooters. If possible, Tracing will again be attempted, but the priority will be to minimize damage. Shutting down the host is not an option, but sticking most files in the archive is. Any and all information gained about the suspect's identity will be shared with GOD.

Uses: As a standard repository of juicy corporate paydata, there are many rewards to hacking Trans-Oceanic Mining's administrative host. Personnel files, financial data, corporate memos … it's all there. This host also contains the high-value predictive algorithms that dictate the output from operations—essentially, a direct control switch to how much money the corporation will make. The Corporate Court forbids interfering directly with these, so it would take a very brave Mr. Johnson to order sabotage on them, but deniable assets are, you know, deniable. In addition, it is worth noting that invaders in the administrative host can leverage access here to log into the operational host. While marks do not transfer over, exactly, they do make things a lot easier. Characters gain +2 dice per mark held on the administrative host to any Brute Force or Hack on the Fly attempts against the operations host.

mation of the processes, drones and machinery can be minutely altered to reduce harvesting output, in order to match supply with demand. As the entire global system is similarly hooked in, you might theorize (if you're inclined to macroeconomics) that prices should be constant, as supply is always configured to match demand. That would be true were it not for the fact that demand and supply can be artificially manipulated to suit agendas. As almost all primary sector activity is concentrated in the hands of vastly diversified megacorporations, there are all kinds of ways in which rivals can attempt to manipulate the outlook of the market to trick the competition into incorrectly gauging real demand and thus over or under supplying—both of which means the other corporation just lost money.

Such price wars are the status quo of the industry, and the hosts this industry rely on are built with ever more sophisticated market analysis algorithms to differentiate pricing attacks from real demand. Much of this relies on predictive algorithms that extrapolate demand based on historical trends. These models would still be far too simplistic of course, so the algorithms are fed data from business intelligence sources. New deals being signed, businesses being acquired or going bust, political instability—all this is accounted for through different input. Thousands of streaming sources of socio-economical intelligence are fed in, all to predict the fluctuation of market prices by a few fractions of a nuyen.

One thing that the industry as a whole does not mess with is serious cyber warfare. Closely monitored and enforced by the Corporate Court, primary sector corporations are proscribed from unleashing major attacks on one another's hosts. With the line between supply and demand kept so razor-thin, a serious attack tricking a party into major supply changes could at best cause a massive recession, and at worst destroy humanity with starvation. Lovely thought to keep you up at night: We could all die because some agricorp was trying to shave 0.0001 nuyen from the cost of a kilo of soy.

Of all the industries, mining, logging, and agriculture are the most likely to have multi-host hookups, simply because their core business hosts have such rapacious and specialized requirements that the rest of the corporation does not share. However, many corps just bite the bullet and host everything at the same place, leveraging tight data integration for faster real-time decision-making across the entire company.

ENGINEERING

Engineering is another very large catchall term that basically encompasses any business that designs stuff, rather than actually manufacturing it. This can include designing physical products utilizing chemical, material, or mechanical engineering, or it can involve intangible ones like software or even the arcane realm of social engineering (which is a little different than mar-keting). It can also be the other arcane realm of designing magic formulas.

It'll be obvious that hosts focusing on engineering need hosts that reproduce physics very faithfully. Whatever it is they are designing, it has to be tested against real-world conditions. Most engineering companies will get around to actually prototyping their thingamajig and testing it in real conditions, but the Matrix is more than capable of generating extremely realistic conditions to test products virtually. That's just the way things are done nowadays. Any corporation that actually tested their products would have costs far, far higher than competitors. Sure, every now and then that means you get an Ares Excalibur, a piece-of-shit product that should never have been green-lit for mass-production, but that's the cost of modern business (and, not to digress, but the Excalibur had problems far more complex than its engineering—I know, 'cause I hired teams to make sure of it).

Engineering hosts thus tend to be smaller and tighter, relying on small, highly experienced teams of engineers rather than tons of manpower. Because they are pretty much by definition working on the next big revolution in whatever, the next competitive advantage, the next game-changer, security is a big concern. Engineering data is highly steal-able: It's all just plans, designs, test results. It's all data you can download pretty easily. That means engineering hosts tend to have highly developed security procedures. You can expect pretty much *every-thing* to be protected and to be laced with very powerful data bombs, if it's even outside of the archive. Rule number one of hacking an engineering environment: Don't touch anything 'til you're good and sure you've properly disarmed defenses. Data bombs almost always destroy the files they were guarding. It's probably a good idea to load up your deck with the proper programs to help you succeed here. Just a thought, you know.

DEFENSE

The world of the defense industry, including the various branches of governmental armed forces, paramilitary security corporations, mercenary outfits, and megacorporate in-house defense teams, is a voracious and specialized lover of matrix hosts. Modern warfare is ninety percent intelligence now, and (as the adage goes) amateurs worry about tactics but professionals worry about logistics. The militaries and security forces of the world are wholly dependent on their information networks. Close coordination between elements is critical, and inferior communications can spell death more readily than an empty clip. Hosts are frequently relied upon as nexus masters for soldiers' gear and battle vehicles. In such setups, with all field devices slaved to them, if the host gets compromised, everything gets compromised and a massacre looms on the horizon. Outside of such directly tactical roles, militaries use hosts to get the

SOCIÉTÉ SUISSE TECHNIQUE

A subsidiary of Monobe International, Société Suisse Technique (SST) is a large general engineering firm. The corporation, which in turn owns several subsidiaries itself, researches innovations in many fields, including building technologies, healthcare and genetics, chemicals, engines and motors, materials, and nanotechnology. The corporation has investments in hundreds, if not thousands, of projects at once. Some are directly funded by contracts from other corporations to find new solutions to problems, while some are pure R&D that SST will patent first and find a use for later.

SST recently spent a fortune bringing together a joint venture of top-dog Matrix design firms and psychologists to create a panel of brilliant minds focused on creating a Host that would get the most out of SST's creative talent. The task was to design a host VR that would, simply by experiencing it, constantly challenge preconceived ideas and work the minds of its users, forcing creative thought. The result, thankfully, isn't quite as wacky as one might have feared. SST's environment is shaped like a sort of gigantic garden or forest perched high on a mountain top. However, the vegetation is fantastic. White birches with leaves of crimson red, cherry trees with lightning-blue foliage, ponds of milky-white water with bright yellow lilies, and a sky wracked with epic streaks of color, like the firmament can barely contain the explosion of a mad sun. Minimalist classical temple structures, a free mix of Buddhist and Greco-Roman architecture, frame the wildness of the garden.

Visitors are endowed with supernatural powers. Though wielding these powers is difficult at first, users can learn to control their movement and strength to do fantastic things like leap and fly across mountaintops; scale the megalithic structures of marble, iron, and brass; or swim deep into the ponds. The idea, and truthfully the effect, is to instill a sense of epicness and rediscover oneself as a god. The host rewards persistence by unlocking new powers, and there are always new places to visit, though they are challenging to reach. Thus, project teams can go on virtual excursions, scaling steep, jagged brown mountains, leaping across chasms, and hunting skittish fauna with bow and arrow, all while discussing the project among themselves or crafting the product with their minds. While the environment is great and free, technical files are accessible at all times. As scientists and engineers reboot their minds in a world of limitless potential without any preconceived limits, their creative thoughts bounce around and expand.

While SST has by many standards achieved incredible functional success with their VR, this has unfortunately come with a rather secretive cost. Société Suisse's finances took a turn for the worse during the host sculpting process, and the corporation found itself strapped for cash. Cutting back or abandoning the main vision for this incredible creative space would have been a very public death blow. It would have shown the entire world that they were bleeding, as the designs had been made very public and hyped both to internal employees and the wider world. Instead, management decided to secretly cut back on the security. Publicly, SST claims their host features the newest, most lethal cutting-edge IC and contracts with Matrix security firms guaranteeing the highest standard of security. In truth, SST is relying on these big claims to act as a deterrent, because behind the talk is very little walk. SST is anemic on IC and unable to afford security contracts. The firm is scrambling for money to patch these holes, but having now publicly lied about it, they are in a sticky situation. Diverting too much money all of a sudden would expose their lies, as investors would question the figures. Insurers would get wind and investigate them for fraud, investors would bail, and the corporation would tailspin into bankruptcy or hostile takeover. So SST must spend more money on shadowy, expensive dirty-ops consultants to quietly build a slush fund reserve and slowly upgrade their security, all the while dearly hoping no breaches expose their groundless claims to state-of-the-art security.

Host Rating: 5

Normal Configuration: Attack 6, Sleaze 8, Data Processing 7, Firewall 5

Security Procedure: Patrol IC running at all times. Once alarmed, the host launches IC in this order: Probe, Marker, Binder, Crash, and Jammer. If one of its IC gets bricked, the host uses the next Combat Turn to reboot that IC rather than moving on to the next one. There are no spiders on-call in case of intrusion.

Société Suisse Technique's host is currently rather under-protected. SST has done its best to laud far and wide its new, killer security system. Everyone knows about SST's legendary system and how secure it is supposed to be. Any Mr. Johnson hiring (and any decker hired) knows that this system is supposed to be uncrackable, so plans to steal information would take such formidable defenses into consideration. Any hacker that then makes it into the system may find herself wondering why things are so easy, and when the other shoe is going to drop.

Uses: Société Suisse Technique is a pure engineering corporation, and one of the top ones, so anything and everything they are working on is potentially of interest to a rival corporation, or even rival factions within corporations that have ongoing projects with SST. Aside from their ideas, SST is envied for the quality of their staff, the people who come up with said ideas. Rival corporations are always interested in extracting talented and knowledgeable personnel, from senior project leads to junior hotshot upstarts showing lots of promise. All of these attacks require Matrix activity, including raiding the host for data or invading the host in support of a physical intrusion. If word ever got out that the defenses of the host did not match the hype, interest in SST's administrative and financial data from many interested parties, from investors to rivals and insurers to Monobe inspectors, would also cause a whole new reason for illicit traffic on the host, as investigators began searching for the truth behind the disparity.

right troops to the right place at the right time with the right gear. That in itself is an incredible feat requiring powerful, organized hosts. Of course, the paramount concern is security. I'd quote some fancy Sun Tzu crap, but frankly you don't need an ancient Chinese military genius to tell you that if your enemy knows your plans, you're fragged. As bad as that is, if the enemy can insert false communication in there, you're doubly fragged. So military forces don't mess around with the security of their hosts. They are sculpted from the ground up with security in mind, and access protocols are rigorously enforced. As any good hacker can tell you, the weakest part of a host's defenses are the people who use it. The military knows that and watches out for that shit with both eyes open. Suspicious activity within a milspec host will lead to an alarm far, far faster than in any other environment that must be tolerant of legitimate but idiotic users fumbling around in there and causing false positives. In military hosts, you either act like you've been meticulously instructed to or you will lose your privileges. Or, worse yet, your brain will get fried.

ENERGY

Corporations in the energy sector rely on the computing power of hosts perhaps more than any other sector. Frankly, there are a lot of parallels between the energy sector and the primary sector. Just like for miners and their ilk, the name of the game in energy is producing just enough to meet rapidly fluctuating needs. All power grids are smart power grids now, auto-regulating consumption to reduce waste, which in turn allows power plants to slow down production during non-essential times. What truly matters in energy production are peak periods. Power plants can either meet peak demand, or they can't. If a power plant can't produce enough, then the power corporation needs to buy the missing amount from another, more powerful, and more costly plant. In any case, blackouts are not acceptable, so the lights *must* stay on, no matter the cost. But whenever a supplement must be bought, the profit margin erodes at high speed. Thus, highly complex computers are needed to monitor the grid, control and monitor the power plants, transact

KNIGHT ERRANT SEATTLE EAST PRECINCT HOST

Knight Errant recently rolled out a pilot program in Seattle to have one host per precinct. All precinct field assets—patrol cars, weapons, commlinks, etc.—are being slaved to this host for central command and monitoring. This allows the precinct commander to know at all times where everything is, with the added bonus that the host provides better security than the un-slaved devices would normally have.

As Knight Errant is the number-one target for a slew of hackers, from vandal punks looking to mess with pigs as a matter of course to dangerous criminals seeking to subvert police assets with potentially lethal consequences, security is a massive concern. Knight Errant hosts are constantly monitored for marks that don't belong to authorized users, in addition to having a generally beefy firewall.

Still, many cops don't quite trust the system. For one, many don't feel comfortable with all their gear being so easily traced and monitored, as most grizzled street cops know that sometimes you have to bend the rules, and what the department doesn't know can't hurt them. Of course, many just fear the idea of powerful hackers subverting the precinct host and deactivating all their weapons. This has led most cops to carry sidearms not linked to the main host, just in case. As for personal cyberware, it's a toss-up. Some subscribe to the idea that the host's defenses are far stronger than anything they could muster on their own and so have slaved it all to the host, while others aren't about to put the proper functioning of their augmented bodies in the hands of some pixel-pushers.

Knight Errant's adoption problem among the rank-and-file isn't helped by the ugly, utilitarian, and seemingly incomplete sculpting of the host's VR. The reality renders a large, one-story, gestapo-esque precinct building, surrounded by a barbed-wire-topped chain-link fence. The world is a dark gloom, colored in red, black, and white. The palette is of course very reminiscent of the Knight Errant official color scheme. The foreboding appearance of the VR is mostly designed to keep intruders out, presenting a dark, authoritarian look designed to intimidate would-be intruders. Perhaps it works, but the simulation is unpleasant for the officers who need to make use of it, day in and day out.

Knight Errant personas appear as broad, muscular soldiers. The personas really aren't diversified much, looking pretty generic. Knight Errant is presently looking to settle lawsuits that allege discriminatory practices by not offering female avatars as well as male. Visitors, on the other hand, use their own commlink-generated personas, which typically clash rather aberrantly with the virtual reality theme.

Aside from having all field gear slaved to it, the host is used for all local precinct business. Emergency calls come in, to be handled by the logged-in dispatchers. Communication between the dispatchers and units is then sent out from the host. The host maintains some local HR data and activity, though a lot of that gets handled by the larger central Knight Errant corporate host.

The precinct host also maintains local arrest records and some information on criminals and suspects, though this information is quickly backed up to the central Knight Errant Host.

A slew of information that, in theory, should belong to the local precinct is still being handled by the main corporate hosts. Little things like infrastructure and gear maintenance appointments, local supplier management, and other such things are not kept locally. While there is an adoption issue among the rank-and-file due to security concerns, precinct managers are seriously unhappy about the visibility issue the new system has caused. People show up for maintenance and servicing or for deliveries, and the local office knows nothing about it. This is causing major scheduling issues at the precincts as well as embarrassment. Street cops may grumble that they are too distracted by their daily duties to do much about the IT problem. The office staff, on the other hand, is more than happy to engage in petty little bitchery competitions with their counterparts from corporate HQ to make their displeasure at the new system known.

The host pilot program is effectively a massive failure, but the project managers have convinced their bosses that it isn't their fault and the precinct must simply be brought in line. Eventually, someone with some common sense will call the program the failure that it is, but for now, a tug-of-war between the system's detractors (i.e., all the users) and its supporters (i.e., the IT department) continues.

Host Rating: 6

Normal Configuration: Attack 6, Sleaze 7, Data Processing 8, Firewall 9

Security Procedure: Patrol IC running at all times. Two Junior Security Spiders logged in at all times.

Once alarmed, the host launches IC in this order: Probe, Track, Tar Baby, Marker, Shocker, Crash, and Killer. If one of its IC gets bricked, the host will continue down the line before rebooting any. A Standard Security Spider arrives (1D6 / 2, rounded up) Combat Turns after an alarm is triggered.

Knight Errant mostly faces local attacks, and so are very interested in tracing down intruders. Once a successful Trace is completed, a KE squad car will arrive at the traced site, if it is within the Seattle Metroplex, within (1D6) minutes.

Uses: Hackers may find a need to hack this host, or one similar to it, if confronted with cops from a precinct operating under the pilot program. Slicing through such a host on short notice will be quite a challenge to most hackers. Should they succeed, of course, then they should be able to quickly disarm the officers confronting them. Outside of immediate fight-or-flight needs, the precinct host is a wonderful place to get information on local cases and, to a limited extent, local officers. It is also a great place to plant disinformation to sow confusion and plant supporting evidence for bluffs.

The Ain Beni Mathar Integrated Thermo Solar Combined Cycle Power Plant, much more succinctly known as "ISCC Ain Beni Mathar" is a natural gas power plant sitting in the middle of nowhere in northern Morocco. While the majority of power produced by the plant comes from natural gas, the power plant, parked right in the arid desert, can generate a significant portion of its power from solar energy as well.

Currently going through a long-overdue upgrade process, the plant should see its power output expand by 216 percent and, perhaps more critically, see its efficiency boosted by up to 67 percent, making the facility one of the top three power plants in Morocco. Much of that energy will be surplus destined for sale to Europe. The project is being run by a conglomerate of interests headed by Saeder-Krupp, including Spinrad Industries and some local development banks.

If the forced cooperation between S-K and Spinrad wasn't bad enough, another sworn enemy of S-K, Sandstorm Engineering, was left fuming on the sidelines when they were maneuvered out of the deal. To say the project is at risk would be an understatement, though S-K has too much to gain in the project to let it fail.

ISCC Ain Beni Mathar's host is still undergoing sculpting upgrades but is largely functional. The host renders as a sort of airship palace floating in the clouds. The luxurious estate is built in the Moorish style. Large domes supported by intimidating archways decorated with fine geometric patterns give way to huge tiled rooms with simple furnishing accented by colorful cushions and flowing draperies. The azure blue of the sky surrounds the whitewashed, gem-encrusted walls of the palace.

This upper section of the airship serves as working environments for most of the personnel. To access the power-control systems, users must nestle themselves into odd little brass pods attached to the underside of the airship's hull. The brass pods then slowly descend down telescoping poles into the clouds. The lower the user goes, the more they will discover the bright blue skies that surrounds the airship are not to be found at the lower altitudes. The virtual reality has the airship floating peacefully on top of the worst storm imaginable. Inside the tiny little brass cabin, users are plunged into a sky rending itself asunder. Hurricane-strength winds gust by as lightning crackles and thunder booms, shaking the pod. The brass pod contains

ISCC AIN BENI MATHAR HOST

archaic-looking clockwork instrumentations and gauges that permit the user to perform required operations to the power core (i.e., the storm clouds).

It is not advisable to trigger an alarm in the host—especially not when trapped inside one of those little brass pods. Within the administrative sections—the airship—IC renders as grey-suited, black-sunglasses-wearing, handgun-toting guards. Within the storm clouds, the IC is the lightning around you, the rattling winds and the booming explosions.

Host Rating: 7

Normal Configuration: Attack 6, Sleaze 7, Data Processing 8, Firewall 9

Security Procedure: Patrol IC running at all times. One Standard Security Spider patrolling at all times.

Once alarmed, the host launches IC in this order: Probe, Killer, Track, Black IC, Crash, Marker, and Sparky. If one of its IC gets bricked, it will use the next Combat Turn to reboot that IC rather than moving on to the next one. A Security Troubleshooter will arrive (1D6) Combat Turns after an alarm is triggered.

Uses: While already nothing to scoff at, the ISCC's host is scheduled to finalize its upgrades within the next few months, boosting its power and thus security by almost 30 percent. Many of the project's enemies—are there is no shortage of those—thus see a unique but shrinking window of opportunity to enact their plans. Interested parties, ranging from insiders with agendas to Sandstorm Engineering Mr. Johnsons eagerly looking to derail the project, are all seeking competent hackers to perform raids. Runs include project spec data theft, imbedding hidden files to be activated later, or outright tampering with the core controls. Of course, no killing blow can occur with an on-site presence, so invasion in support of a physical operation is highly likely as well.

Saeder-Krupp, for its part, is no fool. S-K counter-intelligence agents are well aware of the circling Sandstorm predator and feel they can trust Spinrad about as much as ghoul in a morgue. Contracts looking for deniable assets to set up surveillance and string operations against project insiders and set up search-and-destroy operations within the ISCC host against any and all intruders are also on the table, giving shadowrunners a unique opportunity to look at things from the other side, for once.

in real-time with other facilities to buy supplementary peak power when needed, transact with resource suppliers, and generally keep the corporation running at full speed.

Power plants are extremely complex devices with millions of sensors monitoring the system at all times. Turbines and cores are especially important, as meltdowns and critical failures can cause the destruction of entire regions (as can be seen in places like the SOX or the Scottish Irradiated Zone). Multiple shutoff valves and sub-systems ensure that some random hacker won't be able to bring civilization to its knees, but a hot decker can still do a lot of damage in there. Since power is one of the few things all corporations can agree is necessary, cyber warfare targeting power plants will make them issue an order to exterminate with extreme prejudice faster than you can say "it wasn't me." Of course, there are recent examples of nobody giving a frag about lines in the sand. I heard from a little bird that someone had shadowrunners running around Bogotá not long ago blowing up Saeder-Krupp's power plants down there, and no Thor shots went off to punish the offenders. Like all things when the corps are involved, it depends on exactly how much money is being lost, natch.

RETAIL

Ah, the wonderful world of retail. As much as the corps would love to do business only with each other, at some point they have to dip into the mucky pool of the unwashed masses and fuck them out of some money so that they can go on with the rest of their business. Most corp suits I've ever talked to would prefer avoiding retail if at all possible. When doing business with other corporations, they know their client. They're corpies just like themselves. They think like each other, don't take things too personally since it's not their money they are spending, and usually are tempered by the fact everyone knows they need to keep a long-term working relationship, so being moderately nice to each other—polite, at least—is in everyone's best interest. In retail, you can throw all that away. You deal with millions of the little people who don't share your culture and certainly don't mind giving you shit on every occasion. Generations of "the customer is always right" has empowered these uncouth savages, and they think they hold the bigger piece of the stick.

But these characteristics work both ways. With business distributed over millions of little guys with largely no expertise in purchasing, it's a lot easier to screw most of them out of money (or, at least, not let them screw *you* out of money). Each consumer is an opportunity to break out the book of marketing tricks, such as impulse buys, upsells, and all that stuff. For a period of time a few decades ago, consumers held the upper hand in the consumer/retailer world, with online reviews and general word-of-mouth being outside of the control of retailers and presenting a frank review of the quality of products and services. Retailers weren't about to let that kind of shit stand, of course, so nowadays all of this is perfectly controlled by the corporations. Through countless means, such as diversion and distraction, disinformation propagation, discrediting negative ringleaders, and generally leading the conversation, retailers have created the warm, cuddly, everything-is-always-all-right shopping climate we know and oh-so-love. The new commlink you just bought can explode and kill your pet dog, but the public will never hear of that kind of stuff. Retailers' brainwashing is so powerful, and brand loyalty so ingrained, that no fellow consumer would ever believe anything bad about a product.

Now that I'm done ranting, let's look at how that affects hosts. Perhaps I make it sound too *fait accompli*, but it actually takes a monstrous amount of processing power to positively control popular opinion so strongly. Retail hosts are about three things, really. The first is controlling stocks and the accounting of the business, the second is hosting all that incoming shopping traffic, and the last bit is basically all marketing.

While it's important and requires a lot of energy to stay on top of the supply chain and figure out how many widgets you have and what it's all worth, that kind of stuff was mastered by computers fifty years ago. So that's not really challenging any host.

A bit more significant is having enough power to accept the huge volume of visitors hitting your host to come shopping. There are no other host types that need to accommodate as much user volume as retail hosts. The most important factor there is, just as is the case with a brick-and-mortar store, the look and feel of the space. So the virtual experience, the sculpting of the host, is very important.

The real differentiator for retail hosts, however, is in the marketing area. Retailers need to monitor all possible Matrix activity relating to their products and services so they can control it. With dissent (lost sales) bottled up, retailers can then turn their attention to making *more* sales. That comes from knowing what consumers are looking for. Since most Joe and Jane Civilians know themselves about as well as they know quantum physics, retailers analyze the behavior of consumers to understand them, rather than directly asking them. Retailers have to divine what consumers are logically (or, even better, *illogically*) going to buy next, and then offer it to them before anyone else.

Most of the processing juice of a host is dedicated to this latter activity. Prodigious amounts of information are collected on consumers and then analyzed. Retail hosts typically buy and sell consumer habit information with other retail industry corporations, all in real time. This uses most of a host's processing power. Without any doubt, the retail industry is all about large volume processing.

The business of luxury goods might seem distant from the mass-market retailing of your standard Stuffer Shack, but the rules of the game aren't that different. The only difference is that exclusivity becomes a marketable attribute of your product, and the per-unit price of items becomes much more significant. It's a more low-volume, high-margin type of business, which means each individual sale is that much more important.

Despite those differences, the basic rules don't change. Knowing as much as possible about the clientele is still important, in order to determine what product you can get them to buy next. Remember that consumers aren't just buying a handbag—they are buying special treatment. So while the calculations behind the scenes are pretty much the same, the delivery must be far more refined.

The venerable Louis Vuitton house of fashion continues to survive where others have fallen by uncompromisingly—some would say stubbornly—remaining exclusive. Other brands have fallen to the temptation of ever widening their client base, with the theory that the gain in market would offset lowered prices and sense of exclusivity. Unfortunately, what these brands failed to understand is that below a certain exclusivity threshold, the market simply viewed them as overpriced and nothing more. Louis Vuitton's leadership has never faltered from their position that exclusivity is king, to the point of eschewing the luxury market's common practice of discreetly liquidating surplus product through outlets and members-only Matrix sites. Indeed, Louis Vuitton destroys surplus inventory, rather than having to stoop to lowering prices and liquidating. In essence, Louis Vuitton would rather cut off their arm than lend (the wrong kind of) consumers a hand.

Nowhere is competition in luxury goods more ferocious than in Manhattan, UCAS. Uncontested citadel of the rich, the competition here between corporate ladder-climbers is an Olympic sport, where every little detail counts. The right suit, tie, dress, handbag, or stilettos identify you as a contender, someone to be seriously considered. The wrong attire merely flags you as a pretender. Every employee of Louis Vuitton's Manhattan store is paid in the six figures, as everyone, from the manager to the cashier, has been handpicked. At least half are social adepts, with the other half being perhaps mundane but no less shrewd in their capacity to read and subtly guide the cutthroat individuals they count as clients toward the perfect purchase.

The staff is fed live marketing information from the store's host. Individuals who walk in are scanned. The host first makes a micro-transaction to buy the prospect's credit score and overall purchasing habits. Those with low scores are either ignored by staff or directed to smaller items like wallets and ties (which still cost hundreds of nuyen). For any prospect that flags as reasonably interesting, however, the host will then buy detailed purchasing historical data, as well as detailed psychological

LOUIS VUITTON STORE, MANHATTAN

profiles. Such information does not come cheaply, costing the store an investment of several hundred nuyen, but the store absorbs this as a cost of doing business. Staff is instantly fed this information, having been expertly trained in sales and psychology to know exactly how to put it to use. The dossier remains stored in the host once opened.

For customers who prefer the virtual experience, Louis Vuitton maintains a centralized shopping platform via the main corporate host, but the Manhattan store (like all branches of the company) can also be visited specifically. This helps ensure loyal customers continue to experience the personalized, white-glove relationship the boutique fosters with its local clients. As is often the case with many retail companies in general, the virtual Louis Vuitton store is a mirror representation of the physical store, though of course everything is a little shinier and polished.

Host Rating: 6
Normal Configuration: Attack 6, Sleaze 7, Data Processing 8, Firewall 9
Security Procedure: Patrol IC running at all times. There are no spiders monitoring the system.

Once alarmed, the host launches IC in this order: Probe, Scramble, Track, Jammer, Marker, and Crash. The system will always reboot Probe and Scramble if they are bricked before continuing down the line. A Standard Security Spider will arrive 3 + 1D6 Combat Turns after the alarm is triggered.

Louis Vuitton uses only "white" IC, focusing mostly on severing intruders' connections via Scramble and/or Tracing the intruder and reporting them to the authorities.

Uses: Manhattan is the playground of subtle shadowrunners who know how to get things done discretely. It takes an especially brave hacker to tango with the local corporate hosts, as Black IC is usually the first thing that gets thrown at hackers. Corps jealously protect their secrets and their valuable assets (read: people). However, Louis Vuitton is in the business of selling expensive patent leather articles, not protecting data. So clever hackers thinking outside the box may be very pleased indeed at the relative ease of slicing into the Louis Vuitton Manhattan store's host to find a little treasure trove of personal information on the clientele. A person's future whereabouts—say, a person you plan to extract—can very well be extrapolated from their shopping habits. And, if that doesn't work, there is the more direct route of planting false info in the host to lure the mark to the store, perhaps to act upon an "exclusive loyalty offer."

Fashionable shadowrunners may also look for a way to redirect some top fashion elements their way, though due to Louis Vuitton's very hands-on approach, it is likely store personnel would notice the discrepancy unless a physical con game is also played out.

R&D

Research and Development. Got your attention, did I? While R&D is not a significant slice of the overall market share pie for hosts, it is undeniable that shadowrunners find themselves disproportionately drawn to them. It is the nature of the business, innit?

Well, much like the other business sectors so far, R&D can mean a lot of things. It is essentially the pursuit of better ways of making money, really. That can mean better products, or better ways to sell them. Every company does some R&D, but that's not really what we're looking at. Most businesses handle their R&D as a side thing, on their main hosts. Pure research corporations are a bit rarer. Universities are a good example of pure research, but all of the Big 10 also have hush-hush subsidiaries that work on pure research. The issue, essentially, is that it isn't easy making money doing pure R&D. Most companies doing this are pretty much fully supported by some other existing income stream. Universities receive grants and charge tuition to students, while R&D arms of large corporations bleed out the money that comes in from the profit generated by other subsidiaries.

The obvious question, from a purely mathematical point of view, is why the frag would anyone bother doing pure R&D then? As shadowrunners, I'm sure you know the answer. It's because every now and then, research projects produce game-changers. R&D leads to something *new* that nobody else has. Something so superior to other products that the things sells itself. Now, that advantage never lasts that long, as competitors are always just one step behind, but while it lasts, chummer, you can print your own money (well, corps already do literally print their own money, but you know what I mean). So in terms of numbers, R&D will be a money sink for a while, and then suddenly, BAM, it nets you a 500-fold return on investment.

Of course, occasionally shadowrunners such as ourselves show up with our little black hearts and our explosives and destroy the whole lab and steal all the research data and shit on everyone's lucrative parade, but if they didn't want us doing that, they wouldn't conveniently forget to issue us SINs, would they?

Anyway, R&D is really quite similar to the Engineering sector I already covered. R&D tends to be a bit more theoretical. It's the idea that leads to engineering's efforts to concretely deliver on that. Basically R&D is the sex and engineering is the giving birth part.

R&D hosts thus share a lot with engineering, in that realistic simulations are very important. Large volume processing can sometimes come up, if the R&D is based on crunching a lot of data to extrapolate new ideas. Hosts will always be specialized in the data they are built to deal with (one does not use a host optimized for magical theory research to come up with new drone pilot chips) and, much like bank vaults, will always be very, very securely protected. They contain data of value and are the number one target in our age, so you can bet your hoop they are going to take appropriate defensive measures. R&D hosts typically have a *very* small pool of authorized users that are intimately familiar with security protocols, so frying someone's brain at the first sign of deviancy is commonly accepted practice.

CROSS BIOMED R&D SITE, METROPOLE, AMAZONIA

Cross Biomed, acquired by Zeta-Imperial Chemicals a few years ago, is suspected to be at the forefront of the megacorp's research efforts into all things CFD. A highly controversial topic, especially since nobody is clear on why Zeta-ImpChem is researching CFD (maybe to cure it, maybe to weaponize it), any R&D into the subject must be done very quietly where nobody is likely to look too closely. For those who picture Amazonia as the height of everything anti-corp, it may come as a surprise that Metropole, the Amazonian megapolis, is remarkably business-friendly. The Centro sector of the city features nice, large tracts of unobserved land that are still very close to a large talent pool from which to draw employees, making it probably the world's most concentrated area in terms of black facilities, all operated with the tacit complicity—or at least, tolerance—of the Amazonian government.

Cross Biomed is thought to be one of the leading candidate subsidiaries in Zeta-ImpChem's deck of cards to run CFD research and are suspected of operating a black facility in Centro via a locally registered shell company. Zeta-ImpChem, as one of the world's leaders in total lack of ethics, is no stranger to protecting its secret projects, so while the inspectors and sleuths of the world try to figure things out and draw lines between the dots, the corporation is blazing ahead while they can. Should a breach occur, the corp will simply close down the facility and relocate somewhere else, under a new web of deceit.

For the meantime, Cross Biomed's Amazonian facility is indeed conducting theoretical research into CFD. Infected specimens are brought in, poked, prodded, dissected, and studied. Biohazard protocols are in full effect, and security is no joke. The corporation has already executed four of its own employees for failure to comply with security protocols. The facility runs a single host, segmented to meet the secondary need of basic administration and site security. However, the main activity in the host are scientists running experiments and analyzing the resulting data. A very vigorous check-in/check-out process is in place with regard to the Archive. Researchers only work with the files they need, everything else being locked away tightly.

The host's VR environment is designed to remind all employees of the seriousness of their endeavors. The host appears as a sort of underground facility (not mirroring the Metropole site, lest intruders learn of the physical layout via the Matrix). However, all the walls are made of a sort of melting, tarry black wax substance. The air smells of ash and is hot and heavy. The sound—more like a vibration felt than heard—of heavy engines constantly humming in the distance creates a constant background noise. Personas move with an obscene and insane jerkiness that troubles the mind, their faces covered with surgical masks with bright, blinding lights attached to their foreheads. The climate is certainly not relaxing nor inviting. The idea is to create a sense of discomfort to make all users work as quickly and efficiently as possible to get things done. It also discourages needless fraternization.

Anyone who has the misfortune of meeting IC will face short-lived horror before their neurons fry. The protectors of the host manifest as demonic creatures. They appear just as people, similar to personas, but onlookers will see flashes of something else: bloody screaming broken faces that ooze black oil out of cracked burnt skin. As quickly as the flashes appear, the sight is restored to normal personas, making you wonder if your mind is playing tricks, but the more you want to disbelieve, the more you see it. A disturbing, creeping madness right before the lethal IC burns your neurons out.

Host Rating: 10
Normal Configuration: Attack 12, Sleaze 11, Data Processing 10, Firewall 13
Security Procedure: Patrol IC running at all times. There are two Standard Security Spider monitoring the system at all times.

Once alarmed, the host launches IC in this order: Black IC, Probe, Sparky, Marker, Blaster, Killer, Acid, Track, Binder, and Crash. If one of its IC gets bricked, it will use the next Combat Turn to reboot that IC rather than moving on to the next one. Two Security Troubleshooters will arrive (1D6 / 2, rounded up) Combat Turns after an alarm is triggered. The Security Troubleshooters will assess the situation and may instruct the Host to launch different IC. The Troubleshooters also have the power to shut down the Host, which they will not hesitate to do if it appears the intruders are on the verge of stealing sensitive data regarding the CFD research. Shutting down the host is a big deal, however, so the Troubleshooters will not do so if they believe they can contain the threat.

All security efforts will be directed toward killing the intruder outright. As a secondary measure, they will seek to trace the user. Should they succeed, private mercenaries (most likely other shadowrunners) will be sent with the orders to hunt down and capture or kill the hacker. The kick squad will not stop hunting the hacker until the mission is achieved.

Uses: Any number of top-tier parties with interest in CFD—notably Mitsuhama, NeoNET, Renraku, and Evo—would pay whatever it takes to know what Zeta-ImpChem is up to in their black facility. The problem is not so much funding the operation, but finding talent willing and, far more importantly, able to overcome the facility's formidable defenses to take a solid peek inside. There are even factions within Zeta-ImpChem that think research into CFD is just asking for trouble and would like to see the project and facility scuttled before any outsiders tear a hole in to take a peek. Public agitation over CFD makes such research too dangerous, even for a fierce corporation like Zeta-ImpChem. Inside detractors may wish to arm shadowrunners with as much inside info as possible and send them in to create a breach of sufficient importance to cause the project's self-destruct protocols to engage.

In any case, only shadowrunner teams formidably confident of their skill level should apply, though a paycheck for enough nuyen to buy deltaware wired reflexes III is certainly going to tempt the hand of the foolish.

MANUFACTURING

There are a lot of manufacturers in the world, which is good, because they make everything we use. Cups are manufactured. Shoes are manufactured. Shirts, cars, commlinks, hats, lamps, and guns are manufactured. *Everything* is manufactured. So, clearly, you'll get the picture that the manufacturing sector is a huge sector. It is an area where there certainly isn't much consolidation. There are millions of manufacturers out there, big and small. Some output a few thousand units a month, other output that much per second.

Thankfully for manufacturers, their businesses don't differ that much from one another. This makes it relatively affordable for even smaller shops to purchase the Matrix hosts they need to run their businesses. Everything else is just scaling. A small manufacturer isn't doing anything really different than a huge megacorporate manufacturer—it's just the speed and scale of the numbers that changes.

Manufacturers are the prime candidates for sequential transformation processes, as not much has changed since Ford came up with the Model T. The best way to build something is to break it down into assembly stages and slowly build it up.

Manufacturers are typically focused on managing their supply chains and build processes, where being correct and doing things right are the primary concerns. These types of hosts aren't going to be at the cutting edge of the SOTA. They just need something to get things done, and track the things that are getting done.

The strength of manufacturers is their robustness. They are hard to disrupt. If their hosts go down for a few hours, it will certainly affect their bottom line, but it won't kill them. Even the loss of information is not that big a deal, as it just creates a certain blind spot in their data, which is used for accounting and management reporting, but those things can survive data loss. People will always need *things*, and so long as you build the *right* thing, something that is even moderately desirable, the money will continue to trickle in.

Ironically, in the past it was this even, steady, and seemingly unstoppable flow of business that caused problems for manufacturers, as workers banded together to strong-arm the company into paying them what they demanded, or they would put down tools. External market forces weren't so much the problem for manufacturers as it was their own people—or their own greed, depending on which side of the picket line you stood on. Of course, nowadays, that problem has largely been resolved by the near abolition of anything resembling fair labor laws, and unions and workers have been crushed by the creation of imminently replaceable and disposable labor via fully automated processes and chipped workforces. Corporations basically hire actual people as an act of generosity, or more precisely an act of self-serving generosity, as governments subsidize corporations for doing them the favor of employing their citizens. Incidentally, that's another use of manufacturing hosts—they control the chipped laborers, their skillwires being fed by streaming data from the host.

It's not a pretty business, but it's everywhere and it makes the world go round. It can't all be glamorous super-secret facilities.

DISTRIBUTION & LOGISTICS

Distribution and logistics are manufacturing and retail's eternal companion. The people who *make* stuff are generally not really in the business of getting it in the hands of people, while most retailers are not interested in the work of building and managing stables of dozens to hundreds of factories to stock their shelves. That's where distributors and logistics companies come in. The two are frankly completely different businesses, but I guess I'm lumping them together for no other reason here than I'm a lazy git. Anyway, distributors are basically the warehouse guys. They get in touch with a whole slew of different manufacturers and strike purchasing agreements with them. They buy in bulk, affording what's called economy of scale. Because they buy a lot, manufacturers are willing to cut them some slack and reduce prices. The distributors then turn around, contact retailers, and make them very simple deals where they'll get the stuff in their stores without any headaches. The store is happy because they can ensure their shelves are filled and the distributor is happy because they sell for more than they buy. Their business is really relationship management (manufacturer to one side, retailer on the other) mixed with a little bit of supply chain headache. Some cynics will say that distributors are just middlemen who do nothing but jack up the prices of goods, but distributors have the shitty job of making a nuyen by trying to squeeze manufacturers that are already operating on razor-thin margins while retailers squeeze the distributor in turn. In a way, it's a lot easier to be a distributor than anything else, as it requires little true skill. You just buy from one guy and sell it to the other. As such, the market is crowded with distributors, and many go in and out of business every day

One way to get ahead in the business, if you lack ethics, is to resort to violence. Distribution is rife with shadiness and can be very cutthroat. Newcomers are often intimidated out of the business. Established players in a market regularly target each other, but they will instantly close rank to nip in the bud any newcomers. And I'm not just talking about the business practices they use, either. Lower-end distributors may resort to hiring organized crime (that is, unless they *are* organized crime) to beat, intimidate, burn down, or outright kill the competition. Nasty people. The hosts of distributors are thus pretty simple, focusing mainly of what goods are where, and what is the pricing agreed upon with whom.

BLOHM & VOSS GMBH HAMBURG SHIPYARDS

Sometimes manufacturing is slow and steady, a stream of low-value widgets inexorably being produced. Sometimes each individual unit is worth millions of nuyen. The shipbuilding (and aerospace) industry fit this latter model. They are indeed still manufacturing, just that each individual unit produced is a large project in itself. Each ship built goes through thousands of steps involving thousands of people. A lot can go wrong, and everything that does erodes the profit margin. Blohm & Voss is a large industrial conglomerate belonging to Renraku, which (among other things) builds ships out of the city of Hamburg. Like all manufacturers (or like all corporations, rather), their host helps ensure continued profitability.

The aeronautic industry is similar to the aerospace industry: It's all about big contracts. Buyers—logistics corporations, militaries, offshore oil and gas extractors, etc.—may place an order for one or several ships. Each one is worth at least fifty million nuyen, though the price tag can go up to twice or even three times that for the largest or most sophisticated vessels. Blohm & Voss has been making ships out of Hamburg since the nineteenth century and still continues to do so at a steady pace. As deals are worth so much, there is plenty of muscling around them. Industrial espionage is a fact of life in the rough shipwright business. Competitors bidding on the same contracts employ shadowrunners to spy on one another and attempt to ascertain the details of each other's proposals. The business works on a sort of unspoken rule that while espionage is expected, violence is not. The shipwrights of Europe all know one another and constantly seek to outmaneuver each other, but it is a private affair. Never should the public or, even worse, the client, be exposed to the knives flying back and forth. Violence, whether employed as intimidation, assassination, or in the course of theft, is against this unspoken agreement. Of course, this rule is unidirectional. Perpetrating violence in an effort to gain intelligence is forbidden. Perpetrating violence against a spy in order to protect secrets is perfectly acceptable.

Obviously, hackers play a big part in the shipbuilding market. While often runs involve getting a hacker within operational range of a target's commlink to pull files, listen in on calls, and that sort of thing, sometimes the action needs to go straight into the hosts. Blohm & Voss' corporate host is used for all the typical administrative stuff one might expect, but its main purpose is to manage the construction and maintenance of ships and other vessels.

The corporation, not known for its inventiveness, hired a local firm to design the sculpting of their host. There wasn't much wiggle room, as each vessel being built or serviced needed to be managed as its own project, and each vessel needed to basically be available to visit in the virtual space. Simply in order to have something different from an exact replica of reality—shipyards, docks, and ships—the designers went sci-fi and decided that the dockyards would be a high-orbit space station and the ships would be spaceships.

And so, the virtual reality is a near-real-world replica of the shipyards ... in space. Each ship renders visually as a sort of industrial, gothic ship generally approximating the real-world vessel. The interior of each ship is, however, exact. Users can get onboard and visit the entire ship. Note, though, that pretty much everything about the ship is confidential information and is hidden from users lacking proper authorization. A user with proper clearance and a visitor without any permissions will see two vastly different ships.

Users lacking clearance will fail to see many components of the ship and will be unable to call up detailed engineering and progress report files. Users with proper permissions (i.e., project managers, engineers, etc.) can for their part visit the ships and stay informed on progress. Users can go observe the outside by donning space suits and going on space walks, or observe from a small shuttle. Of course, the vacuum environment is virtual and not designed to be harmful. Users very well could walk outside naked and suffer no ill effect.

The space station itself also contains a number of points of interest, acting as back-office for the business. Of particular interest in the space station are any and all sales data. The sales staff use the host as their main tool for managing and working sales opportunities from beginning to closure. A treasure trove of information with regard to lucrative multi-million-nuyen deals is thus packed away in data files here. A strict archiving policy on sales data not in use is theoretically in effect, but as is mostly true in every business, the sales staff cannot be made to do anything not strictly related to their sales activity, and thus truancy about the security procedure is very high. Sensitive files remain called up in the host when they should by all means be in the archive. They are, at least, all encrypted.

IC in the Blohm & Voss sci-fi host appears as almost-comical 1970s-imagined space guards wearing black spandex and big white helmets, wielding silly (but effective) laser rifles. More than one hacker has laughed himself into a coma as security fried his neurons. Silly-looking or not, the IC isn't there to make friends.

Host Rating: 8

Normal Configuration: Attack 10, Sleaze 8, Data Processing 9, Firewall 11

Security Procedure: Patrol IC running at all times. There are two Standard Security Spider monitoring the system at all times. One specifically monitors the dockyards, while the other monitors all Sales data.

Once alarmed, the Host launches IC in this order: Probe, Scramble, Killer, Binder, Acid, Blaster, Marker, and Sparky. If one of its IC gets bricked, it will continue down the line rather than reboot the IC. Two additional Standard Security Spiders will arrive (3 + 1D6) Combat Turns after an alarm is triggered.

Uses: Blohm & Voss' host is the target of a lot of action. Rival corporations may want hackers to infiltrate it for a number of reasons. Data theft is very likely. Rivals would be interested in almost everything, including the progress status of ships in production, the details of components installed in ships, sales proposals information (especially pricing details), and so on. Everything and anything is of interest, as even the slightest piece of data would allow a competitor to adjust his own bid on a contract in such a way to out-compete B&V.

More aggressive rivals may wish to actually cause sabotage to production. Accessing worker skillwires to introduce manufacturing defects is one way, but so is changing the plans subtly to include defective devices or materials in specific areas that can later be exploited. Such sabotage can also be made in support of physical activity. An on-site team hired to introduce tracking or listening malware into electronic components might also require an online invasion to change specifications, to allow the modification to remain undetected during quality assurance stages.

WUXING WORLDWIDE SHIPPING, LONDON OFFICES

The premier logistics company in the world and crown jewel of the Wuxing empire, Wuxing Worldwide Shipping runs a tight ship (pun intended). The London offices are in charge of charting logistics for land, air, and maritime freight covering all of northern Europe. The firm employs an army of logistical engineers to map routes, sales agents to bring in shipping deals, accountants and actuaries to liaise with insurers and bankers, and a slew of other supporting staff. Wuxing Worldwide Shipping also hires a number of freelance "scouts," keeping an eye on anything that might affect transport routes, from freak inclement weather to pirates. These field agents/informers can log into the Wuxing Worldwide Shipping host to access data brokerage algorithms and sell the information they have. Only under unusual circumstances do informers need to speak to actual people. The host is normally able to fairly assess the value of the data and pay out the bounty to the informer. The system basically determines, in real-time, what shipping routes the information affects and the amount of nuyen saved by Wuxing thanks to the information. The host then pays a small percentage to the user once the information can be verified by other sources. Of course, as Wuxing transports billions of nuyen worth of goods on any given route, information that saves even an hour is worth a couple of nuyen, so some talented and nimble freelancers are able to make a living looking for information bounties, reporting on conditions, and so forth. The most lucrative agents are, of course, the ones risking the most. Informing Wuxing of any impending attack on its shipments from pirates or rivals, or even third parties interested in specific cargo being delivered, can bring in good money. While making some dangerous enemies. But you get an important friend in Wuxing, who takes these things seriously, as any attack on its cargo is an attack on Wuxing itself.

The Wuxing Worldwide Shipping host renders its virtual reality as a sort of forest. This is confusing to first-time users, as they appear in a forest where trees are made of a sort of glassy or metallic substance that is coal grey, black, or navy in color. Leaves are organic, but with colors running in the crimsons, violets, and whites. Visitors may wonder how they are supposed to find any shipping information in the middle of a forest until they start looking more closely. Every single leaf of every tree is a shipment. This was the best metaphor designers could figure out to represent the millions of data points representing the millions of active shipments in transit. Users observing more closely will see, inscribed in the veins of the leaves, data pertaining to the shipment, such as cargo details, speed, direction, conditions, etc. Everything tracked can be accessed. Each leaf is a package going somewhere. Clockwork bird and squirrel automatons, the gears in the joints visibly working as they scurry around, can be queried to lead the user to any shipment requested. Dispatchers can be seen planting little black marble seeds into the rich black earth, which quickly grow from saplings to giant mature trees, matching the real-time pace of the delivery's progress. Personas appear as near-naked tribals, bodies stained with the rich, moist black soil and decorated with geometric tattoos, organically at odds with the inorganic environment; the sole fleshy, colorful things in the somber forest.

The freelancers coming to sell information paint intricate designs in white gouache on the tree trunks, muttering incantations as they do. If the host accepts the information, the paint is absorbed into the glassy surface of the tree trunk and reappears as precisely carved etched lines. The verification process can occur almost in real time if the host is able access live corroborating information, but some tips (such as impending attacks) can take hours or even days to verify. If the etching appears, the persona that sold the tip gains a similarly patterned tattoo. Professional, successful informants thus appear as gnarled shamans, their bodies covered in millimeter-thin intricate patterns.

IC triggered to deal with unauthorized intruders appears as giant hands crashing down from the firmament beyond the canopy of the forest, reaching to grab, crush, or sweep aside intruders. Despite the massive proportion of the god-hands, the fingers are nimble and precise, squishing intruders to pasty nothingness in the rich soil with a press of massive digits.

Host Rating: 8

Normal Configuration: Attack 8, Sleaze 9, Data Processing 11, Firewall 10

Security Procedure: Patrol IC running at all times.

Once alarmed, the host launches IC in this order: Probe, Killer, Acid, Marker, Catapult, Track, Jammer, and Blaster. The host will always reboot Probe and Killer if they are bricked, but will otherwise continue down the line before rebooting anything else. One Security Troubleshooter will arrive (1D6 / 2, rounded up) Combat Turns after an alarm is triggered. The Security Troubleshooters will assess the situation and may instruct the host to launch different IC. The Security Troubleshooter will attempt to ascertain what data the intruder was interested in if possible, though getting rid of the intruder is the primary goal. The Troubleshooter will not use lethal force unless the intruder uses it first.

Uses: Shadowrunners might be interested in the information contained in Wuxing Worldwide Shipping's host for a number of reasons. Runners looking to intercept and steal goods can simply determine the transport carrying the package and its route in order to plan an ambush, though more intrepid hackers may seek to entirely reroute the shipment to a different course of their choosing. Hackers organizing shipments of illicit goods may also be interested in supporting the physical insertion of an extra package in a transport by editing the manifest to include one more package. Of course, not all interest toward the host need be of the intrusive kind. Shadowrunners can be clients of the host's information brokerage system, making a few nuyen by providing logistical intelligence. Of course, even shadowrunners can get excited about an expected package and might merely wish to access the tracking information of their package so that they know when it will arrive in their grubby little hands.

Good record-keeping is key, because everyone always lies to everyone and attempts to screw them over. You have to be able to shove signed contracts in their faces, otherwise agreed-upon pricing will be gleefully ignored. That's just how this business works. Much like manufacturing, we're not talking about very large or complex hosts here, thought the business of knowing exactly how many widgets you have, at the speed these guys get stuff in and out, is quite a challenge.

Logistics are the people who move the goods between manufacturers, distributors, retailers and consumers. The greater the distance between the parties, the more can go wrong and thus the more profit there is in getting it right. Overseas carriers operating super-freighters between the continents stand to make the most, but "hiccups" can occur pretty easily, causing the partial or total loss of cargo. Their game is to make sure cargo arrives on time and with all the bits and pieces it left with. This is easier said than done in the Sixth World. Unpredictable weather can delay ships, while a giant fucking sea monster the size of island can decide to snack on your boat. Add to that geo-political instability and you've got plenty of massive headaches to go around. The per-trip reward and risk increasingly narrows the shorter the trip is. Inner-city delivery trucks are basically operating on a high-volume basis, because each trips nets only a few bucks. However, in all cases, the hosts that logistics companies run require very complex algorithms and organization. As many factors as possible are fed in—weather, condition of vehicles, political risks, giant fucking sea monsters, etc.—in order to calculate the most optimal trip. The big killer is usually the return trip. Factoring the most profitable route that fills your vehicle to the highest capacity and unloads it at the fastest speed is one thing—now calculate the same on the way back, with an entirely different set of customers and conditions. The top-tier players in this field (cough Wuxing cough) consider an astounding number of factors and have incredibly large and versatile client bases that allow them to pretty much have their freight vehicles filled at capacity all the time. It's an insane feat of data crunching that, unlike boring old distribution, requires some pretty hefty host power.

GAME INFORMATION

Because player characters are unlikely to ever meet host spiders in the flesh, a simplified statline is presented on these security mooks.

JUNIOR SECURITY SPIDER

The equivalent of mall cops, these low-level security spiderlings are expected to mostly "observe and report," just like their physical mall brethren. Junior security spiders typically spend more time answering queries from lost or confused users than anything else, and then the real excitement usually comes from script kiddies trying to impress girls. They are not equipped to handle serious threats and will mostly fire off alarms if they encounter serious opposition, mostly relying on the system's IC to do the heavy lifting.

B	A	R	S	W	L	I	C	ESS	EDG
2	2	3	2	3	3	3	2	6.0	2

Condition Monitor (P/S/M)	9/10/9
Limits	Physical 3, Mental 4, Social 5
Matrix Initiative	8 + 3D6 (cold sim)
Matrix Damage Resistance	4
Biofeedback Damage Resistance	6
Skills	Cracking skill group 3, Electronics skill group 3
Typical Action Dice Pools and Limits	Matrix Perception 6 [5], Hack on the Fly 6 [3], Trace Icon 6 [5]
Qualities	None
Gear	Microdeck Summit [DR 1, 4/3/3/1, 1 program] w/ Toolbox (factored into stats) Typical deck configuration: Attack 1, Sleaze 3, Data Processing 5, Firewall 3

STANDARD SECURITY SPIDER

The standard security spider is a solid veteran of many years. They've seen a lot, including shadowrunner attacks, and they know how to respond. They aren't there to do small talk with users and will remain vigilant, investigating suspicious activity. In case of trouble, the first thing they will do is attempt to figure out the invader's strength. If they feel they can take it on, they'll work to get a mark or two and then start slamming in the Data Spikes. If they are outclassed, they may call in for backup, or they may work more passively, trying to get some marks and then Tracing the user, or working to clean off marks the intruder may have placed.

B	A	R	S	W	L	I	C	ESS	EDG
3	4	4	2	4	4	4	3	6.0	3

Condition Monitor (P/S/M)	10/10/10
Matrix Initiative	10 + 3D6 (cold sim)
Matrix Damage Resistance	9
Biofeedback Damage Resistance	8
Skills	Cracking skill group 5, Electronics skill group 5
Typical Action Dice Pools	Matrix Perception 9 [6], Hack on the Fly 9 [3], Brute Force 9 [7], Data Spike 9 [7], Erase Mark 9 [7], Trace Icon 9 [6]
Gear	Novatech Navigator [DR 3, 6/5/4/3, 3 programs] w/ Armor (factored into stats), Decryption (factored into stats), Toolbox (factored into stats)
Typical deck configuration	Attack 7, Sleaze 3, Data Processing 6, Firewall 4

SECURITY TROUBLESHOOTER

Oh, now you've done it. If a Troubleshooter logs into the system, you've really pissed someone off. Troubleshooters often aren't directly on the payroll of the company they protect, it being more likely they are specialist consultants working for a private security firm. They are highly trained and are here to end you by all means necessary. Troubleshooters are typically authorized to use lethal force and do so with great glee. They aren't here to politely ask you to leave. Troubleshooters will immediately engage with power attacks. They know all the tricks in the book and will not stupidly attack intruders that end up being more powerful than anticipated. They will resort to hit-and-hide attacks, fully using the system's IC to bolster their tactics.

B	A	R	S	W	L	I	C	ESS	EDG
4	4	5	3	5	6	6	5	6.0	4

Condition Monitor (P/S/M)	10/11/10
Limits	Physical 5, Mental 8, Social 7
Matrix Initiative	13 + 4D6 (hot sim)
Matrix Damage Resistance	9
Biofeedback Damage Resistance	12
Skills	Cracking skill group 8, Electronics skill group 8
Typical Action Dice Pools and Limits	Matrix Perception 14 [7], Hack on the Fly 14 [4], Brute Force 14 [7], Data Spike 16 [7], Erase Mark 14 [7], Crash Program 14 [7], Hide 14 [4]
Qualities	Codeslinger (Data Spike)
Gear	Sony CIY-720 [DR 4, 7/6/5/4, 4 programs] w/ Toolbox (factored into stats), Hammer, Biofeedback Filter (factored into stats), Biofeedback
Typical deck configuration	Attack 7, Sleaze 4, Data Processing 7, Firewall 5

DEEPER AND DEEPER

"Hack, hack, hack the deck,
Down the data stream,
Go too deep inside a host,
It geeks you with a dream."

—Anonymous hacker,
13 September 2075

BENEATH THE LOOKING GLASS

POSTED BY: /DEV/GRRL

* I was just thinking that it would save some lives if the shadow community had a detailed description of a deep run on a host, and lo and behold, I get a file from our very own /dev/grrl with a run-down and a few useful utility files. Now I'm thinking that it would save some lives if I had a bottle of scotch from before the first Crash and a Jacuzzi. While I wait for that to show up, here's the most recent information about deep runs on Foundations that we have.
* Bull

When the first Matrix protocols were put into place, we all knew about and explored the new hosts that appeared all over cyberspace. It took the hacker community a few days to discover that we couldn't exert the kind of control over these hosts that we could over older nodes and the hosts that came before the Wireless Matrix Initiative. A week or so later, the Midwest Pirates' Guild announced that an underlying structure was discovered under a host by one of their members. They dubbed this area the *Foundation* of the host, and the name's stuck ever since.

* A lot of the terminology around Foundations, like "deep run," "gateway," "anchor," and of course, "Foundation" come from those early MPG files. So if the ideas all sound like they're straight out of Chicago, that's why.
* Pistons

* Rockface gave us the basis of what we know about host Foundations, including unfortunately how deadly they can be. May she rest in peace.
* /dev/grrl

This information opened up a flood of exploration, innovation, and discovery. One of the first discoveries was the deadliness of this new virtual area, with more Shadowland and MPG hackers dead in twenty-four hours than in the previous month. We learned how to get into the Foundation, how to work within it, and how to control the host from within it. The Foundation is not for the novice or the timid, but if you master control of the Foundation, you can make hosts dance to your tune. That's temptation enough.

FINDING THE RABBIT HOLE

The first step of hacking the Foundation of a host is to find the way into it. There are two ways in: one from inside the host, the other through a portal (which will be described later). The entrance to a host's Foundation is nearly always guarded by IC in the host. You'll need to deal with the IC carefully, because if the host sees you as any kind of threat, you won't be able to enter the Foundation.

The gateway to the Foundation is always sculpted as some sort of door, threshold, or other entry. We haven't been able to figure out why—it probably has something to do with the interface between the virtual host space and the Foundation—but hackers find this to be a convenient way to locate the gateway when they're starting a deep run.

Once you've dealt with the IC and the host, you can make A push through the gateway, and everything changes.

* I used to like sleazing past the gateway, but now I just smash through. Sure, the host gets annoyed with you, but once you're in it can't touch you. One time I fragged up my first attempt and the IC just looked at me like it couldn't believe what I just did. I laughed so hard I almost didn't make it through on my second blast.
* Clockwork

CURIOUSER AND CURIOUSER

The Foundation isn't like the rest of the Matrix. It's a densely packed construction of information. Subroutines, data fragments, and bitwise expressions of abstract structures are constantly moving, changing, and affecting one another. Since the data density in a Foundation is orders of magnitude higher than in the rest of the Matrix, processing that data into neural impulses that can be perceived and controlled is, to use a technical term, tricky.

- ❂ It's a virtual version of the first few microseconds of the universe. Being present for that in the Matrix will do to your sanity roughly what the real Big Bang would have done to your meat body. It's a helluva trip!
- ❂ Slamm-0!

Working within a Foundation requires the biggest bandwidth pipe possible, and for hackers that means hot-sim. Yet even this is not enough to process the full impact of the Foundation's data stream. To keep up, your deck's sim module bypasses select parts of your pre-frontal cortex and initiates the same kind of PGO waves involved in REM sleep. In short, when you go into the Foundation you are entering a dream world. The broader bandwidth combined with the increase in generated signals adds up to a higher risk of biofeedback, commonly at deadly levels.

- ❂ The signals coming from a Foundation via hot-sim virtual reality are very like the signals produced by a BTL chip. I wouldn't be surprised to see some deep-run addicts in the near future.
- ❂ The Smiling Bandit

- ❂ What's wrong with that? Seriously, though, I can't see a deep-run addict being around for too long. Some addictions are more dangerous than others.
- ❂ 2XL

DREAM LOGIC

Entering the Foundation creates a dreamlike reality. Once you enter the Foundation, you are completely cut off from the rest of the Matrix. Your link is locked open, and you find yourself somewhere unpredictable in the Foundation.

Like the outside Matrix, all of its functions and properties are in an iconic form, but the icons are far more abstract. The virtual reality rarely has anything to do with the host or even the host functions accessible from the Foundation. For example, the initial MPG report described a deep run on a restaurant host that appeared as a Viking raid on a medieval monastery beneath a blood-red sky. I'm going to call this dream reality the Foundation's *paradigm.*

The paradigm can be practically anything that can conceivably be dreamed. In researching this article, I've encountered reports that include a nursery, a world of marionettes, a sprawling metropolis inhabited by lettuce, a bizarre mash-up of a popular video game and an equally popular vid show, and a completely mundane rodeo.

One interesting thing about the paradigm of a Foundation is that it seems to be in constant flux until an observer arrives. I entered and left the same host Foundation three times, one visit right after the other, and found the paradigm to be first a space station, then my high school, and finally the inside of a large but unidentifiable creature. To date, there's been no report of a paradigm changing while a hacker was present, so I think it's safe to assume that it won't.

The dream logic of a Foundation extends to pretty much what you'd expect: odd behavior treated as normal, long distances traveled in an eyeblink, and nearly everything completely failing to act the way you think it should.

STAY WITHIN THE PARADIGM

The paradigm of the Foundation is its defense mechanism. Intruders almost never fit the paradigm on arrival, making it easy for the host Foundation to repel hackers. When the Foundation finds something that doesn't fit the paradigm, everything in the Foundation becomes hostile to the intruder.

The first thing to do when you start a deep run is figure out the paradigm. You've got a short grace period before the Foundation notices an inconsistency, so use this time to figure out a way to look like you belong and how to behave in the world you've stepped into.

◦ She is not kidding about everything becoming hostile. The whole world literally turns against you. Trees, people, animals, doors, even the wind will do their best to try to kill you. Get out right away when that happens.
◦ Netcat

WORKING THE FOUNDATION

While every visit to a Foundation can be a completely different experience, all Foundations share an underlying structure. There are seven *nodes,* each of which has its own function. Each node is disguised as some part of the paradigm. To use the system, you have to figure out what the nodes are, where they are, and how to interact with them. As you'd expect in dream-logic, the icon of each node rarely has anything to do with its function.

This can be a tough task, but there are two things in your favor. First, there are always seven nodes—no more, no less. Second, each node is connected to one or more others via *data trails.* The logical map of these connections is also always the same, as you can see in this file: <<u>LINK</u>>.

While the look of a node almost never matches its function, a data trail is always presented as some kind of connection, pathway, or link. Some data trails are two-way, and some are one-way, but they are always connecting the same nodes the same way in every Foundation. The simplest example of data trails that I've found was a giant Snakes and Ladders board where the nodes were different spaces on the board and the data trails were snakes and ladders leading to and from each node.

Finding data trails isn't always easy. Often a Foundation will include multiple things that could be candidates for data trails. Some one-way data trails look like two-

way data trails, and vice versa. While you don't have forever before the Foundation detects you, take as much
time as you dare. You take a risk when interacting with
something you're not certain is a node, because if it isn't,
the Foundation could respond violently.

- I once encountered a Foundation that was a philharmonic
  orchestra on a stage. Each different melodic line was a
  different node, and the data trails were dynamics between
  parts. I had to play different instruments to access them,
  and crept carefully between sections to get from node to
  node. Worst concert ever.
- Puck

- My weirdest was the Boston Tea Party, complete with
  Mohawk garb, but we were throwing goats into the harbor.
  It was me tossing goats for about forty-five minutes until
  I figured out that the data trails were ropes and the nodes
  were in the ship's rigging, and the goats had nothing to
  do with them. It was kinda fun to chuck 'em overboard,
  though.
- Slamm-0!

- I'm opening a discussion for weird paradigms here:
  <LINK>   Stop cluttering up this file.
- Bull

THE PORTAL

The portal is the node you need if you want to leave
the Foundation. Your entry point is, as far as anyone
can tell, random, and you cannot leave the Foundation
except using this node, so finding it is a top priority on
a deep run. You can place an anchor at the portal node,
which prevents the Foundation's paradigm from changing and lets you move to other anchors you might have
in other Foundations—you have to code your own anchor to fit each specific Foundation and its paradigm,
but I've included some pseudocode here: <LINK>

THE ARCHIVE

The archive is the target of most deep runs looking for
paydata or a specific file. This node is the only way to
access an archived file without authorization.

MASTER CONTROL

This node gives you complete control of the Foundation. You can change the paradigm's reality or even destroy the entire host, but you'll probably just want the
Foundation map that's found here.

SCAFFOLDING CONTROL

The scaffolding control lets you observe or alter the
part of the host that everybody else is in.

SECURITY CONTROL

This node handles security for the scaffolding, containing controls for the IC in the host. It doesn't stop the
Foundation from turning on you if you draw too much
attention from the system.

SLAVE CONTROL

This node connects you to any and all devices slaved
to the host.

THE NULL NODE

If anyone knows something about this node's function
or purpose, they have not yet come forward. The MPG
called this the "mystery node," but the more popular
name is the null node. It is always included in every
Foundation, but it never actually controls or contains
anything of value or interest. Some hackers have reported feeling a kind of dullness or slowness creeping
over them while in this node, but these reports are very
inconsistent and cannot be directly tied to the node.
The existence of null nodes has raised a lot of speculation in the hacker community, but the consensus for
now is to stay away from them.

RUNNING WITH FRIENDS

This next part is critical for those of us who have longed
to have some backup when we dive into the Matrix.
With a version of the MPG's hitchhiker program <LINK>,
you can bring allies with you into the Foundation, even
if they're not hackers. For the most part, your programming skills will determine the outcome of the run, but
friends can be very helpful, especially in high-security
Foundations.

Your friends will, for the most part, have no problem
interacting with the Foundation. With exceptions for
whatever dream reality the Foundation is using, things
work pretty much like real life in the Foundation, much
the same way you would find in an ultraviolet node. You
may have to climb a wall, or talk to a police squid, or
dance a tango. Although these tasks are familiar to anybody, they're still metaphors for programming tasks, and
so you might find that you've become an ubermensch
while your friends feel incompetent within their own
specialties (as they might in some of their own dreams).
While muscle memory may not exist in the Foundation,
knowledge remains, and hackers and hitchhikers have
found some success when confronted with problems in
their area of expertise.

- That explains why a certain Seattle-area hacker needed a
  certain UW professor as a … surprise guest. Hooked her
  straight into the Matrix and paid us. I'd been wondering.
- Sounder

MAGIC IN THE FOUNDATION

To date, no magic has worked inside the Foundation. Even when the paradigm includes magic of one sort or another, magicians find themselves unable to connect to their own magic and must instead follow the paradigm. Magicians practicing paradigm-sanctioned magic report it as feeling "wrong," "empty," or "play-acting."

A few author's notes: It shouldn't be a surprise that magic and magical abilities don't really work anywhere in the Matrix, much less on a deep run. I still felt it was important to experiment, just in case. I owe a great debt of thanks to the volunteers who helped me. I would like to publicly add that I owe one of those volunteer magicians a favor—she knows who she is, and I think this will suffice to meet her terms.

- Gutsy protégé you have there, Kane.
- Bull

- Yep.
- Kane.

TECHNOMANCERS IN WONDERLAND

While magicians are quite mundane in the Foundation, technomancers are the magicians of deep runs. Where hitchhikers and deckers can feel awkward in the paradigm-reality, all of the technomancers interviewed for this article expressed that they felt comfortable, even refreshed. Their abilities work on practically everything in the dream world. Some technomancers have even shown an ability to alter the paradigm in very limited ways.

THE FOUNDATION: WHAT IS IT BUT A DREAM?

The Foundation holds nearly complete control of a host. This makes it a high-value target for hackers across the Matrix. But the self-defending Matrix is present there, too, and in particularly deadly form. Hopefully, this article will help hackers who are new to deep runs succeed, or at least keep them from being killed there. Who better than a hacker knows the power of knowledge?

- Good work. Nice to see that NeoNET education didn't go to waste.
- Pistons.

GAME INFORMATION

The deep run is a new way for hacker characters to play *Shadowrun*. It's a new challenge and gives hackers a chance to control hosts. It can be used as a solo mini-adventure for a single character, or the entire team can play along as hitchhikers. Time on a deep run can (and often does) flow at the same speed as it does in the real world, and so you can have a deep run in conjunction with the rest of the team's actions.

THE BASICS

Here are some of the basic rules for deep runs.

ENTERING THE FOUNDATION

When you're on a deep run, your hardware and the host use your brain as part of a greater processing machine. This means that to be eligible to enter the Foundation you need neurons, or at least something that functions like neurons. This means that deep runs are only open to metahumans, metasapients (p. 98, *Run Faster*), sprites (p. 254, *SR5*), or AIs (p. 145); no agents or pilot programs need apply.

To get into the Foundation, first find the gateway in the host you want to enter. Then get a mark on that gateway (it has the same attributes as the host) using either the Brute Force or the Hack on the Fly action. Once you have that mark and are running in hot-sim VR, entering the Foundation is a Complex Action.

You can also enter a Foundation via an anchor, using the rules on p. 114.

FOUNDATION ATTRIBUTES

While everything in the Foundation seems to be real, it's still a virtual world, and your attributes reflect that. Your Mental attributes remain the same, but your Physical attributes are based on your cyberdeck's attributes, per the Foundation Attributes table. Calculate your limits and Initiative based on your Foundation attributes (until you leave the Foundation, of course). The cyberdeck cannot be reconfigured when you are in the Foundation, so choose the configuration carefully before going in.

FOUNDATION ATTRIBUTES

PHYSICAL ATTRIBUTE	FOUNDATION ATTRIBUTE
Body	Firewall
Agility	Sleaze
Reaction	Data Processing
Strength	Attack

FOUNDATION ACTIVE SKILLS

While it might seem like you're performing martial arts, firing weapons, lurking in the shadows, performing surgery, or any number of other actions involving Active skills when you're in the Foundation of a host, you're actually subconsciously performing programming tasks.

When an Active skill is called for, replace its rating with one of your Matrix-related skills, according to the Foundation Skills table. If you don't have the Active skill you need, congratulations! As long as you have the Foundation skill, you've got that skill, even if you normally wouldn't be able to default on tests involving that skill (p. 130, *SR5*). With Social skills, you can choose to use your normal skills of your Software skill.

If you do not have the necessary Foundation skill, you are out of luck when it comes to Technical skills and Social skills (unless, as noted, you have meatworld ranks in the Social skills). There is no defaulting on those. Cybercombat, Hacking, and Computer can all be defaulted, though, giving characters a chance to use skills in the associated areas.

FOUNDATION SKILLS

ACTIVE SKILL	FOUNDATION SKILL
Combat Skills	Cybercombat
Physical Skills	Hacking
Social Skills	Software
Technical Skills	Electronic Warfare
Vehicle Skills	Computer

FOUNDATION KNOWLEDGE SKILLS

Knowledge skills remain unchanged in the Foundation—you know what you know. However, the weird way that the Foundation approaches the brain means that your Knowledge skills are much more valuable there. If one of your Knowledge skills applies to a task for which you'd normally need an Active skill, you can use your Knowledge skill instead. For example, Professor Crow is hitchhiking along with Rootkit the hacker in a Foundation with a medieval European paradigm. They come across a knight guarding a bridge that they must pass. Crow is a history professor, not a hacker, and she lacks the Cybercombat skill she needs to fight the knight. However, with a very impressive 10 rating in Medieval European History, the Foundation latches onto her knowledge and translates that into dreamlike—but completely badass—moves that send the knight tumbling from the bridge.

The right expert in the right Foundation can be very effective. With the high number of Knowledge skills

available, the gamemaster will have to make the call as to when they are relevant in a Foundation dive.

FOUNDATION MAGICAL SKILLS

Sixth World magic doesn't work in the Foundation, period. Some magic can indirectly affect you in the Foundation, but only if it applies to something you bring in with you, like an Improved Ability adept power or an Increase Logic spell.

If the Foundation's paradigm has its own magic system, it's probably not the same as real-world magic. It would probably require you to memorize one-shot spells, or throw cards, or stretch out your feelings, or something other than normal *Shadowrun* magic. Even if the paradigm is identical to the Sixth World's magical abilities and expectations, it's still a virtual world, and your Magical skills don't apply. The gamemaster will let you know which of the Foundation Skills you need for magic (e.g., the one-shot spell example above might use Electronic Warfare, the card throwing might use Hacking, and reaching out with your feelings would require Software).

FOUNDATION MATRIX ACTIONS

The short version: There are no Matrix actions in the Foundation of a host.

Once you're in the Foundation, it is, for all intents and purposes, as though you were in the real world (well, *some* real world, anyway). You interact with it normally, using your Foundation attributes and skills in place of your meatspace versions. So before you start making fun of your team's shaman for losing his powers, you might want to mourn the loss of your Data Spike.

On the other hand, there are a few upsides. Since you're cut off from the rest of the Matrix, you no longer have an Overwatch Score. Along those lines, your actions that involve Attack and Sleaze aren't treated as illegal, which results again in no Overwatch Score. And your skills probably make you like unto a tiny deity in the Foundation, so it's not that bad.

FOUNDATION RESONANCE SKILLS

Unlike Magical skills, Resonance skills work just fine in a Foundation. Sprites can be compiled, complex forms flung about. For targeting purposes, treat any living (or at least animate) targets, including people, animals, talking tableware, and so on, as personas, and every other object in the Foundation as devices.

There are two drawbacks to using Resonance abilities in the Foundation. First, Fading damage is always Physical. Second, unless you can somehow fit your powers into the paradigm, you might create a variance (p. 117) by using them.

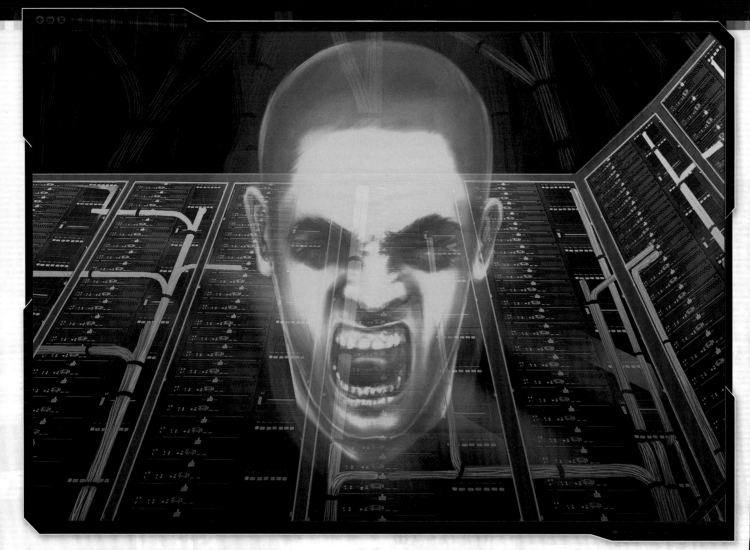

THE OUTSIDE WORLD

In the Foundation you are completely cut off from the outside world. You cannot communicate with anyone or anything outside of the Foundation. You are link-locked. You may not reconfigure your cyberdeck (if you have one). You may not reboot or jack out—the only way out is through the portal node. Attempts to trace, spot, or mark you fail—your persona has left the Matrix.

DAMAGE

All damage in the Foundation is either Matrix or bio-feedback damage. If the persona under attack has a Physical Condition Monitor, the damage is biofeedback damage. If it only has a Matrix Condition Monitor, then the damage is Matrix damage.

DEEP RUN ADDICTION

Deep runs require the use of hot-sim VR, which is already addictive. Foundations use some amped-up signals that go beyond VR, although not quite so far as BTL

chips. The result is that deep runs are psychologically addictive with an Addiction Rating of 5 and an Addiction Threshold of 1 (p. 414, SR5).

WHAT LIES BENEATH

Once you've navigated the paradigm to the point where you can operate with relative ease, it's time to look for the nodes (which is likely what you're here for, unless you're just looking around, which is an odd thing to do in a place as dangerous as a Foundation).

The trick is figuring out which things in the dreamscape are nodes and which are just part of the Foundation. A node could be a post, a person, a house—pretty much anything you can interact with is fair game to be a node. The trick to finding nodes is to look for their data trails.

DATA TRAILS

Each node has to communicate with one or more other nodes; it's how the host functions. These lines of communication are called data trails, and they're pretty much the only thing in the Foundation where form reflects function.

A data trail always goes between nodes, and always in the same direction(s). For example, there is always a two-way data trail between the portal node and the scaffolding control node. Look at the Foundation Architecture image for a map of the nodes and the data trails between them. Be advised: This is a logical map only, and while the connections will always be there, the nodes will never be in those neat rows and columns in the Foundation.

Data trails appear in the paradigm as connections between the icons that are the nodes. These connections could appear as something physical, like roads or pipes, or something more abstract, like a corporate organizational chart or a loan shark's client list. The connections can be one-way or two-way.

To find the nodes, first look for a data trail, or rather something that *could* be a data trail. Once you find one, you can follow it to either end and find the node it connects to. Once you find a node, you can start following the data trails further. After a little legwork and some logic, you'll figure out where to find everything.

NODES

A node is (usually) an object in the Foundation. You usually find them by following data trails.

NODES AND NODE ACTIONS

These are the seven nodes found in every host's Foundation, along with a set of actions you can perform there. All of the ratings used against these actions are those of the host. If you fail a test when making any of these actions, you create a variance (p. 117), which is bad, so make every test count. All node actions are Complex Actions.

A node's looks and behaviors don't have to be thematically linked to its purpose. It *might,* but it's far more likely to be something completely unrelated. In the Matrix proper, one would expect the archive to appear as a filing cabinet, or perhaps a library, but in the Foundation of a host it might be a toddler playing in the mud, or an ice cream cone that's accessed by licking it. You need to figure out what is and is not a node, either safely—by deduction—or more dangerously—by trial and error.

ARCHIVE

The archive is the area within the host that stores files securely, away from all users. Normally, only someone with three marks on the file can remove it from the archive or store it there. As long as the file is in the archive, it is safe ... unless someone in the Foundation access it.

Find a File: You look for a file in the archive. You need to know something about the file you're looking for, something that lets you identify it, or else you'll just end up searching for a random file. If you make a successful Computer + Logic [Data Processing] v. Rating + Firewall Opposed Test, you find the file and can perform more archive node actions on it.

Copy a File: Once you've found the file you want to copy, make a Computer + Logic [Data Processing] v. Rating + Data Processing Opposed Test to make a copy of your own.

Fetch a File: If you've found the file you want, make a Computer + Logic [Data Processing] v. Rating + Firewall Opposed Test and the file is yours. When you fetch a file this way, you become its owner, if you want to.

Edit a File: When you've found the file you want to edit, make a Hacking + Logic [Sleaze] v. Rating + Firewall Opposed Test to change the file in a way that is undetectable to scrutiny.

Delete a File: Assuming you've found the file you want to delete, make a Computer + Logic [Attack] v. Rating + Firewall Opposed Test to destroy the file, leaving no trace in the archive.

MASTER CONTROL

This node controls the entire host's Foundation. If hosts have cornerstones, this is it.

Alter Foundation Reality: You can change one detail of the Foundation's paradigm, essentially adding, removing, or altering a single sentence of its description. Make a Hacking + Intuition [Sleaze] v. Rating + Firewall Opposed Test; if you succeed, your change sweeps through the host Foundation in seconds.

Foundation Map: If you make a Computer + Logic [Data Processing] v. Rating + Data Processing Test and succeed, you discover the identity and location of one node for every net hit you score.

Calm the Beast: This action calms the host, making it

temporarily forget about any intruders within it. For every net hit you score in a Hacking + Logic [Sleaze] v. Rating + Attack Opposed Test, you can make the host forget about a persona in the Foundation. Each persona can be detected again later on, but for now, they are safe.

Destroy the Host: It is very difficult to destroy hosts with a even mediocre rating, but if that's your aim, the master control is where to do it. The test is Cybercombat + Logic [Attack] v. Rating + Firewall, and you must succeed multiple times in a row, once for each Rating of the node. You create a severe variance (p. 117) with every test, even when you succeed in the action. If you fail even one test, you must start over. If you succeed in all of these tests, the host vanishes from the Matrix, dumping everyone who was in either the scaffolding or Foundation.

Grow the Host: Over time, you can increase the rating of the host, which increases its Matrix attributes. Make a Computer + Intuition [Data Processing v. Host + Sleaze Opposed Test. This action must be taken at least once a week for a number of months equal to the host's current rating; once this time has elapsed, the Host Rating increases by 1. Failing this action does not reset the clock, but failing to succeed at least once a week does.

Configure Host Attributes: With a successful Computer + Logic [Data Processing] v. Rating + Firewall Opposed Test, you can switch the ratings of two of the host's attributes. The change is permanent, but ratings can be switched again with this action later on.

NULL NODE

No one knows what purpose the null node serves. Every host has one. The null node sometimes shows up as something mysterious, dark, terrifying, or all of the above, and sometimes as just one more node in the system. There are no known actions that can be performed at the null node.

PORTAL

The portal is your only way out of the Foundation once you have entered. Finding the portal is a priority for all deep-running hackers.

Create an Anchor: You build an anchor and place it at the host's portal. This has two effects. First, it prevents the host's paradigm from changing if you leave the Foundation. Second, as a Complex Action, you can move from one of your anchors to another without a test; hackers use this technique to create backdoors into high-rating hosts from low-rating hosts. The test for creating an anchor is Software + Logic [Sleaze] v. Rating + Firewall.

Exit the Foundation: Once you find your way in, it's not always obvious how to find your way out. Make a Computer + Intuition [Sleaze] v. Rating + Attack Opposed Test. If you succeed, you are immediately switched to AR mode and your hardware (or living persona) reboots in the process, all of which means you're out of the host Foundation and back in the real world.

SCAFFOLDING CONTROL

This node controls the host's scaffolding. It can give you power over aspects of the part of the host that normal users inhabit.

Observe the Host: You take a peek into what's going on in the host scaffolding. Make a Computer + Intuition [Data Processing] v. Rating + Firewall Opposed Test; every net hit gets you about one minute of unrestricted access to the goings on in the host scaffolding.

Edit Host Sculpting: Grab some net hits from your Computer + Logic [Sleaze] v. Rating + Firewall Opposed Test and change one detail about the sculpting of the host scaffolding for each hit.

Reboot the Host: This rather extreme measure dumps all of the personas in the host scaffolding (but not the Foundation) if you beat the host in a Cybercombat + Logic [Attack] v. Rating + Firewall Opposed Test. The host takes (Rating) minutes to return to normal functioning.

SECURITY CONTROL

The security control node handles top-side security in the host scaffolding. In other words, it handles all the intrusion countermeasures for the host.

Target IC: Using a Cybercombat + Logic [Attack] v. Rating + Attack Opposed Test, you choose the target of one or more of the active IC programs in the host scaffolding. For this to work, you'll need to use the Observe the Host action in the scaffolding control node so you can pick your target properly.

Launch IC: You launch IC as if you were the host. You may choose what is launched from the IC programs available to the host. The standard rules apply: Only one IC program may launch per Combat Turn, and only one copy of each IC program may be running concurrently.

Recall IC: You make a Cybercombat + Intuition [Data Processing] v. Rating + Attack Opposed Test; for each net hit in this test, you recall one IC program in the host, removing it from the scaffolding just as if it had crashed (**Security Response,** p. 247, *SR5*). The host may still launch that IC again at a later time.

Configure IC: You change the IC available to the host, switching IC programs in the host for ones you have brought along with you. Make a Computer + Logic [Data Processing] v. Rating + Data Processing Opposed Test. If you succeed, the installation is successful and takes effect immediately.

SLAVE CONTROL

All devices slaved to the host are controlled from this node.

Control Slaved Device: This node action works almost exactly like the Control Device Matrix action (p. 238, *SR5*), except that you don't need any marks.

Brick Slaved Device: The node has complete control over its slaved devices, including their delicate innards.

Choose one slaved device and make a Hacking + Logic [Attack] v. Rating + Firewall Opposed Test. If you succeed in the test, completely fill the device's Matrix Condition Monitor—it is bricked.

Perma-Mark Device: You can use the power of the Foundation to create a mark on a device that persists, even if you leave the Matrix. Using the Foundation this way can be tricky; if you succeed in a Hacking + Intuition [Sleaze] v. Rating + Firewall Opposed Test, one slaved device of your choosing takes one of your marks. This mark will not vanish from the device if you reboot or jack out, but it can be erased like a normal mark.

Devices can have more than one of these perma-marks, but no more than three. And don't forget: While you're in the Foundation, you're cut off from the Matrix, so you can't use the mark until you leave.

HITCHHIKERS

With the proper program (p. 57), you can bring friends along with you on deep runs. Your hitchhikers need to have a persona (e.g., from a commlink), and they must use hot-sim VR. You must have a mark on each of their personas, and they a mark on you (which you can invite if they do not have the capability of placing one). When you go through the gateway, their personas must be with you in the host. You can use the hitchhiker program to bring any persona eligible to enter the Foundation (p. 110).

Once you and your hitchhikers arrive in the Foundation, you are free to roam. Each persona is his or her (or its) own entity in the Foundation, as they would be in the real world or Matrix. Sometimes everybody arrives in the same place, and sometimes they arrive scattered across the dreamscape. No matter what the distance, though, you can still communicate with one another as easily as by commlink—unless something in the paradigm prevents it.

HITCHHIKER ATTRIBUTES & SKILLS

The attributes of your hitchhikers follow the same rules as they do for you (p. 110). They keep their own Mental attributes, but their Physical attributes are replaced with your Foundation attributes for those ratings, even if their Matrix attributes are better than yours.

Hitchhikers keep their own skills, using the normal Foundation skill substitutions on the Foundation Skills table (p. 111). They may use their Knowledge skills as Active skills for any test the gamemaster finds applicable, same as the hacker that brings them in.

Hitchhikers can't use Magical skills, as normal for deep runners. A hitchhiker can't use Resonance skills, either. If your friend wants to use her Resonance skills on a deep run, she'll have to join you as a separate hacker and not a hitchhiker.

HITCHHIKER DAMAGE

The hitchhikers with you are separate entities in the Foundation and use their own Condition Monitors. If you go down, the fate of your hitchhikers depends on how you're running the hitchhiking program. If you're using a cyberdeck or other device, your hitchhikers remain in the host Foundation, even if you're dead. If you're using the Resonance Hitchhiker echo (p. 258, *SR5*), your hitchhikers are dumped from the entire Matrix when you flatline.

THE PARADIGM

The paradigm of a deep run is a brief description of the dream world and the norms that diverge from reality. Since a Foundation is literally created from the stuff dreams are made of, at least in part, just about any setting is possible.

Playing *Shadowrun* during a deep run is pretty much like playing in any other setting. There's going to be some strangeness due to the weird dream logic and world rules of the paradigm, or even none at all. Other than the changes to some attribute and skill ratings, it's run just like it says in **Shadowrun Concepts** on page 44 of the main rulebook.

The paradigm can determine the shape of the nodes of a system, but it doesn't have to. A Foundation in the form of a star ship from a space opera could have the nodes as a control panels on the bridge, but they could just as easily be different rooms, various crew members on board, planets to which the ship travels, or any combination of the above.

One thing about the paradigm is that it remains internally consistent. If Dudley the Friendly Llama is the security control node, he will remain the security control node for as long as the paradigm remains locked by a visitor or an anchor.

FOUNDATION DENIZENS

The Foundation is populated with objects, or people, or animals, or plans, or animated items, or terrain, or a combination these and/or a plethora of other things. All of these have attributes, as would real-world objects, people, etc.

People and animals (and monsters and similar animate things) have the same attributes as player characters. They can have any range of ratings for each attribute, but the maximum rating for any Foundation denizen is based on the host's attributes, with Physical attributes as listed under Foundation Attributes (p. 110) and Mental attributes capped at the host's Rating. People (animals, monsters, etc.) that have skills will have them at the host's Rating or lower.

LEGITIMATE USERS ON DEEP RUNS

Sometimes the owners of a host need to do some upgrades. Maybe they want to do some interior decoration on the host, upgrade the IC, or do some maintenance on the archive. Whatever the reason, there's got to be an easy way for a legitimate user to access the functions of the host's nodes, right?

Nope. Deep runs are just as dangerous to legal users as they are to illegal hackers. For this reason, most hosts are leased by host service companies. These companies have specialists who collect hazard pay to make deep runs into hosts for maintenance tasks. Larger corporations have their own host maintenance divisions with execs constantly headhunting the best and brightest white-hat hackers to join them.

Most host maintenance specialists regularly visit their assigned hosts. They sometimes plant anchors on a regular basis to give themselves easy access and to lock the paradigm to something they're familiar with—high-security-host owners discourage this practice because it makes these rare experts targets for shadowrunners looking for an easy way to attack their hosts.

All other ratings are also capped at the host's Rating (or one of its Matrix attributes, as the gamemaster finds appropriate). For example, armor ratings would be capped at the host's Firewall Rating, as would Barrier Ratings. Weapon damage would sit at or lower than the host's Attack Rating. And so on.

VARIANCE

That's all the different stuff and the wiz stuff you can do, so now it's time for the scary stuff. It's not that Foundations are dangerous places that can kill you in seconds while you weep openly for being cut off from a physical world you will never again experience, rather it's ... actually, yes it's exactly like that.

Sometimes a visitor to a host Foundation does something inconsistent with the Foundation's paradigm. This inconsistency is called a **variance.** For example, in an operatic paradigm, a deep runner who speaks rather than sings creates a variance, as does a smile in a world of sorrow.

Performing node actions also comes with a risk of variance. When you fail a node action, you create a severe variance if the node gets more hits than you do—if there are zero net hits either way, you create a minor variance instead. Also, if you try to perform a node action on something that turns out not to be a node, don't bother picking up dice, you just create a severe variance (the gamemaster can, of course, opt to make you roll just for their personal amusement).

MINOR AND SEVERE VARIANCES

Variances come in two flavors: **minor** and **severe.** Minor variances are mostly cosmetic in nature, the kind of inconsistency that most denizens of the Foundation's paradigm would find enigmatic or curious. A severe variance is disruptive, or bizarre, or glaringly obvious to the observer. Another kind of severe variance is the kind where you make it apparent that you're not part of the Foundation's paradigm, but rather an alien intruder. Either kind of variance has bad consequences.

When you create a minor variance, the Foundation makes a **Variance Test.** The threshold for a Variance Test is always 4. On a minor variance, the dice pool is only the host's Firewall rating. On a severe variance, the dice

SAMPLE VARIANCES

Here are some examples to give you an idea of what constitutes a variance, and how bad it is. Given the near infinite possibilities there are when the metahuman mind and the Matrix come together, this is not an exhaustive list.

PARADIGM	MINOR VARIANCE EXAMPLE	SEVERE VARIANCE EXAMPLE
World of human-sized snails	Not having something on your back	Running
Nightmare world of monsters	Bravery or indifference	Siding with the monsters
Classic noir film	Pointing out examples of gender inequality	Talking about shadowrunning
Elegant tea party	Rude behavior	Physical violence
Broadway musical	Responding to an inner monologue song	Going too long without singing
Dark plain where everyone is bleeding	Not bleeding	Healing people

pool is Rating + Firewall. If the test succeeds, the Foundation becomes alerted to the presence of the intruder who created the variance and becomes aggressive—see **The World Turned Against You**, below, for what happens next. The Foundation only goes after the one who caused the variance, so if there are others in the Foundation they're safe ... for now.

If the host doesn't pass the Variance Test, the gamemaster will keep track of the number of hits it scored and add it to a Variance Tally, which she keeps to herself. If this tally ever reaches 40, the Foundation is alerted and life starts getting tough. If the Variance Test results in a glitch, the gamemaster reduces the Variance Tally by 1; if the Variance Test gets a critical glitch, she cuts the Tally in half.

The host keeps separate Variance Tallies for each intruder. If one intruder is found, either by test or tally, the other intruders' Variance Tallies are unaffected.

Note: The Variance Tally looks a lot like the Overwatch Score from *SR5,* but it's a different score. Anything that affects the Overwatch Score does not have the same effect on the Variance Tally. Sorry, folks.

THE WORLD TURNED AGAINST YOU

When the host realizes that you don't belong there, so does everyone and everything in the Foundation. It doesn't launch IC—nothing so gentle. Since the paradigm is essentially the reality of the Foundation, the entire world literally turns against you, doing its best to kill you and return the host to its natural operation.

All animate entities in the Foundation will seek you out and attack you. Inanimate but moveable objects will betray you as well: doors close and lock before you, foliage you're hiding in will wilt and expose you, cars will chase you down alleys, and so forth.

Unless you feel confident that you can take the entire population of the Foundation yourself, your best move is to get to and use the portal. If you haven't found the portal yet ... well, find the damn thing. Fast. Again, the Foundation is like its own reality, so combat there uses the rules in Combat on p. 158 of *SR5,* or quite possibly the rules for Chase Combat on p. 203. See **Damage**, p. 112, for notes on how to treat the results of combat in a Foundation.

When the intruder leaves, either by portal, death, or disconnection, and there are no other intruders the host has found via variance, the host returns to normal. If that was the last intruder and there is no anchor, the paradigm shifts.

CREATING A DEEP RUN

A little preparation goes a long way, and setting up a deep run can be done in three easy steps. Here are some tips for the gamemaster to use with players who want to run deeper.

You don't need to take these steps in order. If you have a good idea for a data trail and want to build a paradigm around that, go for it. But if you're starting with a blank slate, the order below might help.

STEP ONE: CREATE THE PARADIGM

Since the Foundation is a dream world, your paradigm can be pretty much anything you can dream. Take your inspiration from anything that amuses you: novels, television shows, movies, poems, songs, or even dreams.

Write down a brief description of the Foundation's world. Start with the basic premise, and then add a few details about how the Foundation differs from reality. Don't worry about being too descriptive; the ephemeral nature of the Foundation means you won't need to do much fleshing out before the paradigm shifts to something completely different.

Finally, jot down three or four things players could do that will create variances. Again, don't write down a complete list; players can be ingenious when it comes to making tragic missteps, and you'll be able to spot a variance when it happens.

STEP TWO: CREATE THE DENIZENS

Write down two or three interesting characters the players might meet. These characters could take any form, from people to talking trees, with imagination as the only limit. Don't worry about noting ratings unless you think it will come up in play; you can use the Host Rating in a pinch if you need to.

Next, write down any interesting features the players might encounter in the world. Do naval vessels fly? Do rocks float? Having some descriptions ready ahead of time lets you convey the feel of your paradigm to the players at the drop of a hat.

STEP THREE: CREATE THE NODES AND DATA TRAILS

It's time to decide what your seven nodes look like. Remember that unlike in the rest of the Matrix, the nodes' forms don't have to fit their functions. A portal, for example, could be a company CEO, a bison, or a lamppost in the woods.

While you're deciding on your nodes, you also need to figure out what your data trails look like. Data trails *do* have to convey the idea of either something travelling from place to place or a pathway from place to place. Some data trails must be one-way and some two-way. Two-way trails run between null and master control, portal and scaffolding control, and master control and security control; one-way paths run from security control to archive, slave control to security control, and master control to scaffolding control.

Feel free to be crafty when creating your nodes and data trails. You're crafting a puzzle for your players to work out. If you think they'll get an obvious setup too easily, feel free to add false data trails or fake nodes. For example, you might take the fact that there are seven nodes to create a Snow White paradigm, with the seven dwarfs talking to one another in a pattern that would match the node layout, but the real nodes are in the mine shafts a mile away from their house.

Bear in mind that a puzzle with no solution isn't a puzzle. Make sure the pattern is in there somewhere, and that the players have a fair shot of finding it.

Once you know where the nodes and data trails are, the final touch is to choose where an intruder will appear on entering the gateway. If you are expecting multiple intruders, for example hitchhikers, you should decide whether to start them together or split them up when they arrive.

DEEP RUN EXAMPLES

GNOME FACTORY
(RATING 5 HOST)

A/S/D/F: 5/7/6/8

Here's a simple example of a deep run. This paradigm features an enclosed space, plenty of places to hide and observe, and a number of characters with whom to interact.

STEP ONE: CREATE THE PARADIGM

There is a dimly lit factory filled with machinery out of the 1950s. Conveyor belts and steam pipes run every which way, leaving almost no space for a human-size person to walk. The place is swarming with garden gnomes, all of whom are working on something, either the machinery or the products moving along assembly lines. The air is filled with steam, along with the sounds of various dispensers and foul chemicals. There is an enclosed office in the center of the factory floor, where a portly lawn gnome sits smoking a pipe and "supervising."

Variances: Not working, stopping the machinery, disrespecting the foreman, removing something from the conveyor belts.

STEP TWO: CREATE THE DENIZENS

THE FOREMAN

The foreman is easy-going and genial as long as you're doing what you're told. Cross him, and you'll find yourself on the business end of his comically large monkey wrench.

B	A	R	S	W	L	I	C	ESS	EDG
5	5	5	5	5	5	5	5	6	3

Condition Monitor	11/11
Armor	8
Limits	Physical 7, Mental 7, Social 7
Physical Initiative	10 + 1D6
Skills	Clubs 5, Etiquette 4, Industrial Mechanic 2, Intimidation 5, Leadership 2, Perception 3, Unarmed Combat 3
Gear	Armored overalls, box of stogies.
Weapons	Comically large monkey wrench [Clubs, Reach 1, Acc 5, DV 5P, AP —]

THE GNOME FACTORY WORKERS

There are hundreds of workers swarming all over the factory, all under the watchful gaze of the foreman. They're loyal to the foreman, but they miss no opportunity to shirk their work for a few moments when they can get away with it. They all really, really like to smoke, but there's no smoking allowed on the factory floor, and the break room is closed for repairs.

Stats: All pertinent ratings at 5. Skills include Clubs, Etiquette, and Industrial Mechanic. If they need weapons, they'll use their assorted tools.

Weapons: Assorted tools [Clubs, Reach —, Acc 4, DV 5P, AP —]

STEP THREE: CREATE THE NODES AND DATA TRAILS

Each node is one of the machines on the factory floor. The controls for the node functions are under the machines, amidst dangerously moving parts. Unless the machine is stopped, each node action requires a Reaction + Intuition (3) Test to prevent the machine from inflicting 5P damage.

The data trails are conveyor belts between each machine. There are many, many other machines with pipes and belts connecting them, but these seven are the only ones in their own network of conveyors.

GNOME FACTORY NODES

NODE	EQUIPMENT
Archive	Pneumatic impact notcher
Master control	Custard injection caster
Null node	Gnome recycler
Portal	Little fiddly engraving etcher
Scaffolding control	High-speed milling lathe
Security control	High-velocity peener
Slave control	Multi-directional buzzsaw

JANE FRAGGIN' AUSTEN NODES

NODE	EQUIPMENT
Archive	Colonel Fitzwilliam
Master Control	Jane Bennet
Null Node	Charles Bingley
Portal	Lydia Bennet
Scaffolding Control	George Wickham
Security Control	Elizabeth Bennet
Slave Control	William Collins

JANE FRAGGIN' AUSTEN
(RATING 8 HOST)

A/S/D/F: 8/9/10/11

This is an example of a more abstract deep run. It is intended to be played with an emphasis on role-playing and intrigue.

STEP ONE:
CREATE THE PARADIGM

Pride and Prejudice. All of it. The Bennets, Netherfield Park, the parties and balls, Lady Catherine de Bourgh, Pemberley Manor, the whole kit and caboodle.

Variances: Rudeness, improper dress, anachronistic conversation.

STEP TWO:
CREATE THE DENIZENS

Refer to the novel for the full list of characters. The novel is in the public domain and can be found on a number of websites. Alternately, most video services have one or more of the many film versions. If you need a rating, make it 8. Choose skills on the fly—this deep run is intended to be role-played rather than completed through stats.

STEP THREE: CREATE THE
NODES AND DATA TRAILS

The nodes are characters from the novel, brought to life by the host Foundation. The paradigm includes all of the characters from the novel, but only seven of them are actually nodes. The data trails refer to the relationships between each character. There are many, many more relationships between the characters of *Pride and Prejudice,* but these are the ones that best fit the Foundation architecture.

BODY HUNT

"I think we've worn him down," Windhowler yelled across the span of the hallway.

A desk sailed out of the mouth of the hallway and slammed into the opposite wall. The cheap metal and plastic top punched halfway through the wall, adding to the decorations of demolitions that their quarry had left throughout the office building.

"Worn down, eh?" Tranq growled. Her tusks showed wear from tonight's fun as she lined up Burst's shoulder for relocation.

"Yeah. That would have gone clean through the wall earlier. Remember that mahogany monster from the entrance?" Windhowler smiled, then the smile quickly faded when Tranq smiled back, emphasizing her cracked right tusk, which happened when she was in the way of the aforementioned mahogany desk. With her head turned, the ork made a quick move that was followed by a pop and pained groan from Burst. The groan was the best the troll could do with the broken jaw he'd suffered from a spinning roundhouse about an hour earlier.

"Cut the banter," Cirolle, the team's "leader," said softly.

The voice of the man they sought came down the hall. "Whispers or screams, even thoughts in your primitive minds, I can hear it all. Lay on with action, not words, and see this battle done."

They weren't even half done with this job. Four on one had seemed like easy odds, but they were taking a beating at every turn. Burst had stepped up to handle the brunt of the hits, but he was pushing his massive troll bulk to its limit. He had hoped his status as an old friend might help a little when they faced one of the hottest head cases in the shadows, but so far no punches, or kicks, had been pulled.

"Wolf! Fight it! We're here to help. Grandfather calls you home," Windhowler yelled in anger. His anger was no surprise—their quarry had once been his father, but now was a shell occupied by some other mind.

"Grandfather is a tool of the weak. Come to your father. I'll show you the truth," Wolf replied.

"How can you say that?" Windhowler said as he watched Cirolle give him a hand signal. The young shaman interpreted the hand motions to mean "keep him talking" as he watched Cirolle slip through another door and out of sight.

Wolf, meanwhile, was continuing his monologue without prompting. "Remember when your mother died. Did Grandfather answer your calls? No. But no one needs to die anymore. I can fix them. I can save their minds, their memories."

Windhowler choked on his reply. Thoughts of his mother's death tugged his throat closed.

"Cat got your tongue, pup?" Wolf goaded.

Windhowler swallowed his pain and spoke. "And what now? You've forsaken Grandfather and lost his gift, lost his guidance. Lost his protection."

BY SCOTT SCHLETZ

Those last words sparked a thought. Wolf, or the thing that lived in his body, had been shredding their tech since they came into the building. Comms first, then weapons, and then odds and ends. They were each left with one undamaged but useless device. Items they ditched a half hour earlier when they realized they were being used to track them. Attacks were Matrix based, and they were holding their Matrix assets back for phase two. They hadn't faced any spirits or spells, no magic at all. Wolf had been one of the most feared Wolf shamans on the streets. He fought all comers who dared claim he didn't deserve the moniker of their totem and left them alive and understanding he was alpha.

Calling every last ounce of mana he could muster and howling to Grandfather for anything he was willing to lend, Windhowler shaped magical energy and held it. He could feel power pulling at him; his muscles ached channeling this much power.

"I'm sorry, dad," Windhowler growled. It was all he could say.

Windhowler sprang around the corner and sprinted down the hallway, ready to unleash a spell as soon as Wolf came into sight. He was shocked to find the shell of his father standing in the center of the door, in plain sight. There had been plenty of time for Wolf to have dropped Windhowler's inattentive hoop, but there was a delay. The delay gave Windhowler hope that he threw into the spell he launched down the hallway.

The spell took the form of a meter-and-a-half-long wolf that dashed ahead and slammed into the target.

The drain of the spell tore at Windhowler's body and mind as the blow landed. When the spectral wolf leaped into the air, Windhowler sagged.

His vision shrank to a pinpoint, his father's face at the center. He hoped the smirk would fade from the familiar yet alien face, but instead he saw it deepen, and he felt the horrible sensation of a spell shredding on a shield. It had failed. That thing still held arcane power.

Pain or not, Windhowler now knew he had to fight. His bicep and tricep contracted in unison, snapping his humerus. Ribs cracked from jerking muscles. His vision blurred as blood vessels in his eyes ruptured. The pain was everywhere, but he pumped aching legs, propelling himself down the hallway.

The smirk on Wolf's face shifted to a fiendish grin as he rolled his palms up toward Windhowler and shifted his torso. The motions unleashed a glowing ball of force that overfilled the hallway, wrecking walls as it flashed to meet Windhowler's headlong rush. Their collision launched the charging shaman back far faster than he had approached. His already-limp body slammed into the wall above the jutting desk, cracking plaster, wood, and bone before collapsing.

Cirolle slipped quickly and quietly around the corner. Wolf was an old friend. He'd known the young shaman when he first came into power, when Wolf was an idealistic kid filled with honor and loyalty. Cirolle had gained his trust, been part of his pack for years in Chicago. The bugs broke that connection.

They'd encountered each other on and off in the intervening years. Then Cirolle met the version of Wolf that was no longer Wolf. Windhowler had recruited him in this mission, talking about saving his father. But Cirolle knew enough about CFD to know better. He knew there was only one salvation for Wolf, the one that came from a gun or a sharp blade.

His path took him swiftly through side offices and back halls he had spotted on the blueprints during planning. They had almost backed Wolf into his last corner. Cirolle knew the lengths Wolf would go to once he was cornered. Though magic was no longer an option, the wily lupine likely still had some nasty tricks in reserve.

Cirolle could hear the conversation of Windhowler and Wolf as he slipped through a doorway directly behind their quarry. He was stunned for a moment as he saw Windhowler rush out into the hallway and unleash his familiar knockout spell. Cirolle slid his shock-knife from its scabbard on his thigh, shockpommel at the ready to finish the job if the spell wasn't quite enough. He made quick steps forward, a slow mirror of the young wolf shaman who was collapsing from drain.

Cirolle watched Windhowler's spell leap and then shred into spectral wisps. He saw Wolf's hands start to roll outward and knew, despite the complete illogic of the idea, what was about to happen. He'd seen it many times before. Cirolle abandoned quiet and dashed forward, spinning the shock-knife in his palm as he ran. It was too late for mercy.

Wolf's reaction, though fast, wasn't fast enough. Cirolle snaked his left arm up under his opponent's and then snapped his hand up behind Wolf's neck. The half-nelson was only part of the attack. It provided the leverage and control for Cirolle to jam the wedged armor-piercing tip of the shock-knife into his once-friend's back three times in quick succession. He tossed the blade away after the third strike and shifted to control Wolf's body as it fell, making sure the head case's tainted blood didn't touch him.

The move proved fruitless as Wolf's body failed to collapse as he expected. Instead he rotated, with muscles that should have been destroyed by Cirolle's stabs, and hip-tossed the runner. Cirolle expected to hit the ground and find Wolf's hammer-like fist finishing the job, but instead he was sent flying out into the hallway. As he spun, he saw why.

Burst saw Windhowler spring up and sprint into the hallway. The kid's move was going to get him killed, but he understood the mentality. Like father, like son.

Burst had been part of Wolf's efforts to go straight for the kid. He was part of the founding four for Securitech: Specialized Security, and he knew how much the old shaman loved that kid. And he knew that whatever that thing down the hall was, it wasn't that kid's dad or his old friend. He also knew he couldn't wait for Windhowler to understand that.

Burst pushed through the pain and lumbered to his feet. He'd been trying to hold off using his pain editor, knowing how easily he could blow past the limits of his body against Wolf, but now he had no choice. Pain washed away, and he prepared to make a run for the hallway.

A half-meter before he made the corner, he saw Windhowler sail past. He heard the heavy crunch and thud as the kid hit the wall. He continued without missing a beat around the corner, using a foot planted on the far wall to keep from slowing down. He was big, but he was graceful thanks to his top-grade (a decade ago) move-by-wire system. He framed a fond hope that maybe the kid had died still thinking the best of his dad rather than realizing the truth.

The troll spotted Cirolle slipping in and jamming his blade home. Lung, liver, heart. Three stabs and it was over. The elven knifemaster had killed 300 kilos of troll with that move. Burst slowed his run for only a microsecond before he realized Wolf's knees weren't buckling in death but were instead bending and shifting to launch Cirolle over his hip. And what a launch it was. Cirolle sailed through the air toward the charging troll.

Burst's massive mitts snagged the spinning elven projectile in mid-flight. He realized the error of his ways too late as the move narrowed his reach. He had a handful of elf when he could have had a handful of Wolf. The cunning mind was still there.

Burst recognized the familiar shift in stance as Wolf launched into an acrobatic 360-degree spinning roundhouse kick that brought the heavy steel toe of his combat boot into contact with Burst's temple. The blow jarred the big troll's head, and his momentum slammed him into the frame of the doorway. His horn hooked a wall stud as his chrome skull broke through the wall, and the bone horn snapped.

As his vision blurred and blacked out, he was thankful his pain editor would let him die in peace.

Tranq didn't bother to say a word to stop Burst. She saw the conviction in his eyes and let the troll do what he thought necessary. Tranq knew what it was going to take. She'd been brought onto the team not because she was an old friend of Wolf, but because she had already brought over a dozen rampaging head cases to heel.

When she saw the kid shaman slam into the wall, she knew it was time to go all in or fold. She considered the kid her stack of chips, and it was running real low. The troll was her last deal. She couldn't bank on the elf, because she knew how tough it was to assassinate a head case, especially one this tough.

She wasn't wired like the troll and had no chance of keeping up with him, but she leaped into the long hallway all the same. Between the massive bulk of Burst and the plaster dust hovering in the air from the crumbling walls, she had no clue what was at the end of the hall. She was betting on the same lack of perception on Wolf's part to get where she needed to. Tranq slipped the fingers of her custom gecko gloves into the fan of pouches on her hips.

Dust swirled as Burst passed, clearing the air enough for Tranq to see the troll's downfall. She spotted Cirolle, once again confirmed her assassin vs. head case assessment, and then saw the blur of Wolf's boot slamming into Burst's skull. The troll had slowed just a hair; the move gave Tranq the instant she needed.

A quick double-step over the falling Burst allowed Tranq to pop out on Wolf's blindside and bring a wide, arcing slap down across Wolf's rising face.

The weak blow didn't even phase him. He used a front push kick to plant a foot into Tranq's chest and shove her back into the wall. The foot stayed in place, crushing the ork's chest as the smile widened on Wolf's face. But the smile stopped growing as Wolf caught sight of the grin on Tranq's face, despite the foot slowly crushing her chest.

"I don't know you," Wolf said calmly.

"No need to, you'll be gone soon," Tranq forced out with as much cockiness as her crushing chest would allow.

"I think you're confused," Wolf started to say, but his speech disintegrated into stutters.

Wolf's boot dropped off Tranq's chest as the drugs took effect. He clawed at his face and pulled two of the five patches free. But it was too late. They'd delivered their debilitating cocktail.

Tranq rubbed her chest and warily circled the stumbling head case. She knew it was dangerous, especially if it realized what was about to happen. Tranq watched the silvery film form over the side of Wolf's face as the nanites in his system pushed out the toxins, but she wasn't shocked like most people. This wasn't her first time at the table.

"I love the irony of this," she said, smiling through her cracked tusk.

"Probably not a time for wit," Wolf said as his eyes cleared a little and his legs gained balance.

Tranq rolled the back of her left glove to face him. The rod of Asclepius sewn into the back of the glove got Wolf's attention for the moment she needed to swing around the other glove. The matching symbol on its back flashed through the air as the blow broke past Wolf's weary defense to slap the other side of his face and plant five more tranq patches from temple to jaw.

"Frag me," Wolf slurred as he stumbled from the ridiculous attack. "You're Butch."

The ork didn't reply. Instead she calmly pulled a commlink from her pocket and powered it on. "Phase one's done. Come on in for phase two."

404 had laughed when he walked through the wreckage of the meat-world fight. Such a lack of finesse and style. He started his sim-recording the moment before he'd jacked in so he could show the team how a real pro operated.

Now, the snarling maw of some fantasy-novel monstrosity sprayed unpleasantly realistic saliva over the face and spiked hair of his persona. The monster rammed a massive black sword through his 404 Error T-shirt and the virtual torso behind it, and the sim recording turned into a snuff sim.

Icecap watched in horror as the gnoll totally derezzed 404. It was the right term in the Matrix, but horribly inaccurate in their current situation. Instead of just disappearing from the Matrix, 404's persona coughed up something like blood and crumpled to his knees.

The cavernous expanse became a touch more in sync as one of the usurpers fell to the native forces. 404's persona began to turn to stone, blending into the cavern floor as a statue of grey stone instead of the blue t-shirt, purple punk hair, and denim jacket.

Icecap had problems of his own, though, as he used his ice shield and icicle spear to fend off the orks working to surround him. He froze clawed feet to the ground with some tweaked crash program coding to gain some time and provide openings for the two other personas fighting nearby.

One of them, the video game brawler called Keypunch, swung his left fist into the back of the head of the stalled ork. His massive fist, covered in half of his namesake rings, exploded from the front of the ork's skull. The program didn't derez either; instead it fell to the ground, piling on the dozen other orks they had already slain.

Icecap called out a warning, but it was unnecessary as Escher appeared from behind a stalagmite and decapitated the ork about to skewer Keypunch. Escher attacked with angles, swinging and throwing flat, nearly invisible planes at foes.

The trio pulled in close to regroup, looking for some way out of this cavern. The place was so massive that the walls were only visible when you were close, and the ceiling remained hidden up in the shadows, its existence verified only by the stalactites descending from the darkness. They'd been moving slowly, fighting off the monsters erupting from the shadows, but they seemed to be the only ones suffering any level of attrition. 404 was down, and they'd lost CodeMonkey only moments in as he underestimated the deadly pack tactics of a group of kobolds. They needed a plan.

"Anybody got any useful scans?" Icecap asked. Wisps of frosty breath hovered in the chilly air of the cavern.

"I got something, but I'm not sure what it is. It reads close to the same as the monsters but not quite. It's that way." Escher pointed, which was was helpful since Escher was now upside-down, standing on a floor tied to his persona. Looking like he was doing the impossible was very appropriate to what they were attempting.

They all had different motives to attempt this. CodeMonkey had been in it for Wolf, but he was out. The shaman had helped him earn enough nuyen to get his first datajack and then put the kid through college with a scholarship from Securitech. 404 had a similar story. Icecap had earned an intro to FastJack and a few months of education by impressing Wolf with his coding skills. Escher had the closest connection, but his extensive body mods had long ago left him emotionally cold. He helped out of duty, the closest thing to emotions he had left.

"Time to earn our nuyen," Icecap said.

"We're down two. My vote is bail, reinforce, and come back heavy now that we know the layout." Keypunch looked to Escher to vote with him. But he didn't know Escher like Icecap did.

"The kid's plan is valid. Butch said she can keep him out for a few hours. We should gather reinforcements," Escher said.

Icecap checked the program he was running and saw exactly what he expected. Much like Wolf had managed to completely restructure the landscape of his mind into a deadly dungeon of fantasy monsters, he was also dilating time for them. While the hackers were all used to functioning at the speed of thought and blazing through the Matrix, they weren't on the Matrix. They were jacked straight into the mindhost of a head case, and he controlled time here. Icecap's timer program already read more than three hours. They didn't have time.

"That's two votes. Let's bail," Keypunch spoke, but then his persona's face scrunched with worry, followed by surprise as he realized he couldn't jack out.

"Problem finding the exit?" a deep growling voice echoed through the cavern.

"What the frag?" Keypunch yelled to the emptiness. Then he turned to Icecap. "You knew this was a one-way trip!"

"Knew? No. Suspected with near certainty? Yes," Icecap said coolly.

"I can let you out, fist fighter," the disembodied voice said.

Escher and Icecap both turned warily toward Keypunch. The pair mentally coded some quick defenses and held them for Keypunch's well-known attack program.

"I'll let you out," the voice said. "All you need to do is distract that ork bitch for a moment. I'll take care of the rest and reward you handsomely."

The offer was punctuated with a ring of orks and gnolls stepping from the edge of the shadows in eerie unison. The opening was directly behind Keypunch.

"Don't do it, 'punch. You can't trust this guy," Icecap pleaded.

"Whoa! I thought we were here to save him because he's all noble and loyal and drek."

"Wolf, the one we knew, was loyal and noble. Whatever drekstain AI stole his body isn't even willing to offer you a deal face to face," Escher said. "There is nothing noble in this mental construct."

The ring closed as claws, paws, and boots stepped forward

in unison. The shadows behind them lightened, revealing a figure on a high-backed throne. The face of the man was familiar.

"Let us discuss the deal." The words were punctuated by another step forward of the ring.

"Is that what you detected earlier?" Icecap asked Escher nonchalantly.

"Yes."

The ice shield and icicle spear grew from Icecap's hands as he burst into motion. Escher took two steps, changing planes with each stride. He cast out flat planes and took the heads off two orks in Icecap's path. Keypunch stood shocked for a moment and then moved to follow Escher.

Icecap leaped over the headless orks, launching his spear as soon as he had a clear view of the figure on the throne. The spear flew for the creature's heart only to melt away well before finding its mark. The lack of success didn't slow the charge. Icecap knew the time for desperate measures was approaching fast.

Escher kept stepping and slinging, orks and gnolls falling as the planes severed bits of their base code. He was vaguely aware of Keypunch behind him when the other hacker jabbed with his ASDF-clad fist toward Escher's head.

With a step, Escher put his feet and the pedestal he stepped to between Keypunch and his code. The kid's code was forceful, but Escher had seen him use the attack over and over. It was great for shredding IC, or whatever these monsters were, but not enough for a skilled decker. In his next stride Escher was standing on the cavern floor. His hands flicked, and thin planes launched up at an angle toward his former ally. Coded to seem like a poor shot, the attacks had the exact effect he wanted. The coding wasn't an attack on Keypunch's base code, just a focused strike on the only thing the one-hit wonder had up his sleeve. The planes lopped off Keypunch's iconic fists. Escher turned from the crippled hacker and went back to focusing on the real threat.

Icecap launched spears of ice in every direction. Some melted away before the throne, others took charging orks and gnolls to the ground. Some made it through the onslaught and chipped away at his shield and coding. Every time he looked to the throne, the smiling face of Wolf stared back at him, amused at the struggle. Icecap saw the brief altercation between Escher and Keypunch. The betrayal didn't bother him nearly as much as the loss of resources. They were down to two.

A rolling rumble filled the cavern as a massive stone block wrapped in chains tumbled out of the darkness, trailing a length of chain connected to the monstrosity wielding it. The block rocketed toward Escher, who deftly stepped up again to angle his base against the incoming attack. The stone shattered the pedestal, crushing Escher's legs, and sending him sailing into the opposing darkness with a bone-chilling crunch. The stone smashed several orks and gnolls on its arcing return. The massive giant wielding the chain spun the stone out wide, sending it into the shadows.

Icecap knew he had only the time it took the stone to complete its arc. There was enough time to lash out at the giant, the monsters, or their master, but not all three. He wanted to kill them all, but most of all he wanted to kill the thing in charge. He ignored the unseen block and turned to the throne. He stopped coding his shield, knowing it would do nothing when the end came, and focused every coding trick he knew on the ice spears. He charged the throne as he launched the attacks. Thick spears with redundant coding to punch through whatever armor was protecting his foe, thousands of tiny shards like flechettes cast wide to hopefully find a small weakness, solid beams of icy death he coded on the fly to try to break through, and innocuous-looking snowballs that exploded like icy grenades all failed over and over.

But the explosions of snow and ice did the trick.

Icecap leaped and flipped in the air, landing on top of the throne. Several of his attacks were melting away, holding the attention of the thing in Wolf's head. As the steam and snow cleared, the thing looked up and snarled.

Icecap's Jack Frost persona balanced gracefully atop the throne's high back, a sword of ice clasped in his grip and pointed downward toward the target of his hatred. The persona seemed frozen, poised to strike but unmoving, like a statue of ice.

The snarling face went slack with realization as it watched a single rivulet of water slide over the surface of the blade and drip off the tip.

The real Icecap sprang from behind the throne just as the drip of water landed squarely in the thing's eye, making it blink. The massive stone crashed into the thing's body on the throne, making it a fine paste blended with the exploded remnants of the royal seat.

Icecap immediately felt the change. The cavern suddenly became lit, not from a single source but in that way the Matrix can glow from everywhere and nowhere. The ceiling began to collapse, stalactites crashing to the ground. Icecap spotted Escher's body, the writhing form of Keypunch, the no-longer-stone-but-still-lifeless form of 404, and most importantly the exit, finally revealed beyond the still form of 404.

Though it likely meant nothing, Icecap had a strong urge to collect bodies of the fallen. As soon as he thought it he was standing over the form of Escher, his crushed legs a mess of thinly drawn pencil lines.

"I am lost. Leave me," Escher said.

Icecap was shocked the decker still lived, but he kept it together enough to scoop up the pencil-drawn persona of his old friend and make for 404. Along the way he passed Keypunch. Even though the kid had turned traitor, Icecap scooped up the brawler's persona by the belt. He hoisted 404 in similar fashion and then thought himself to CodeMonkey.

The way in, where CodeMonkey had fallen, was also the

way out. Short of limbs to carry personas, Icecap lobbed the still-blathering form of Keypunch toward the cavern's entrance but not across the threshold. Then he carried the rest to the end of this strange journey.

At the mouth of the cave he pulled Escher off his shoulders and moved to the brink.

"Warn the others. He'll come out before me," Icecap said, nodding his head toward Keypunch.

"Did we do it? Is he free?" Escher asked.

"There was nothing to set loose." Icecap tossed Escher's persona out of the cave. "Warn them." Escher disappeared as he touched the sunlight.

Icecap repeated the process with 404 and CodeMonkey, but instead of disappearing they landed flatly in the grass outside. They had no functional bodies to go back to, but at least they weren't left in Wolf's head.

Icecap turned to take one last look and found comfort in what he saw. When they arrived, the place had been a cavernous, gloomy maw full of smoke and shadows. Now he faced a small cave, what one might think of as a wolf's den, with an almost homey feeling.

"Soon, my friend. Soon we'll bring you home."

As reality rushed back, Icecap heard the conversation already in progress. His few moments of reverie at the cave had been long minutes in the meat world.

"... is phase 3? Icecap, Cirolle, and you speak of it in hushed tones. I want to know. I need to know." Escher's voice held far more emotion than Icecap was used to hearing.

"Tell him," Icecap rasped almost in unison with Cirolle. They were both in bad shape.

"You know of the Resonance Realms?" said Tranq—now known as Butch.

"I know rumors and theories," Escher said.

"You know that the megas keep looking for technos to get access, because no data is ever truly destroyed until it's destroyed in the Resonance. And some rumors say not even then. It all exists forever."

"Yeah. So?"

"The human brain is just an organic computer full of data that makes a person who they are," Butch said.

Icecap opened his eyes just in time to see the realization dawn on Escher's face.

It was time for phase 3. Perhaps the most impossible phase of all.

PRINCIPLES OF INSANITY

"I'm sorry, but you can't come with me this time."

The Lovecraft-meets-Cabbage-Patch-looking icon, writhing next to Puck on the simulated concrete floor, coiled half of its arms around the left leg of his avatar. The creature's multi-armed grip easily held him in place, but didn't cause him any pain.

"I'd take you with me if I could, really," he explained. "There's just not a way for you to follow me to the place I'm going."

Puck knelt down and looked the icon in its single, massive, blue eye. The AI had no mechanism for speaking with him, but Puck could sense the true depth of its intelligence when he looked his friend in the eye. He could see the protosapient's attention fixating on the right side of his avatar's face as the AI desperately tried to read his expression. The AI suddenly turned transparent and he felt the weight of its arms fall away from him.

Puck stood up. He would look for the AI later, but right now he had a backdoor to find. A search that began in a warehouse in Portland had led him to a Telestrian host. The host itself was basic and clearly ignored by most of the staff, given the lack of traffic and the mountain of post-it notes that covered a nearby bulletin board. He wasn't sure why there was a backdoor here, but his senses told him that it was unbearably close by.

He stepped into a nearby office and there it was—a tear in space that wavered in the air above a desk. Puck scanned the anomaly, but the results came back as gibberish. He didn't care. There was Resonance seeping out of the tear, beckoning him to places unknown. As he climbed the desk and approached the tear, white light began to pour out of it. The light quickly formed a tall doorframe atop the desk as the air hummed with Resonance. Looking through the door, Puck saw nothing on the other side. The frame seemed to lead into an endless void. For a moment, he thought he heard a feminine voice call from the other side.

He was hit with light again, this time completely blinding him. Beyond the light, he became acutely aware of wheels turning and something heavy pressing on his chest. He tried to lift the weight off, but his limbs refused to move at all. As his eyes adjusted to the lights, he saw he was on his back now. A surgeon's light shone directly in his eyes.

"Well now," Puck heard a familiar voice say. "My favorite thorn come back to see me."

He could see Dr. Sharon—Catherine—clearly now. She didn't look any different since he'd killed her. She didn't look too upset about it either. In fact, Catherine looked quite pleased to see Puck. That worried him more than anything. He didn't have to look down to know he was strapped in. He'd been on this table before—he still had the scars underneath his hair from their last appointment.

Dr. Sharon placed her hand gently on his brow. Her skin felt unnaturally cool against his. Then he felt her hand sink into his forehead, her fingers digging into the grooves of his mind. The pressure in his head felt like it would split his skull.

"Now," she said in a voice that sounded like his own. "Given this set of data, perform a quicksort with a randomized pivot. You have ten seconds." Her eyes shimmered with crystal light, and Puck's mind was flooded with their screams. The ones he was too small and weak to help as a boy, the ones he'd slain or twisted for Deus, the ones who fell to Jormungand. He heard them all in a maddening crescendo that never seemed to find its peak. Then, one by one, he was forced inside their skins as they took their last breaths.

He had many errors that needed correcting. Too many, it seemed.

"You are too old and too far from the Resonance now," Dr. Sharon admonished, pulling her hand back. "These places aren't for you."

Puck forced his lips to form words, "You know—you're not the first to say that to me." He could feel himself slipping into darkness. "Pity I'm such a lousy listener."

- While we were discussing what to put into this download, I got a message from Puck asking if we'd be taking submissions from "senior" probationary JackPointers. I guess whatever is left of his mind still has a sense of humor, even if it's lacking in personal boundaries. I didn't hear from him at all after that so I let it go. I figured I was better off not dealing with him if I could. I never know what he's up to and when I do know, I generally want no part in it.
- Glitch

- I remember that. He's not kidding about being in mid-discussion either. I literally said "we should do a detailed write-up of the new Matrix" and Glitch tells me Puck just shot him a message about it. I loaded up my Blackhammer to teach him a thing or two about privacy but I never found a trace of the fragger.
- Bull

- :Cough:Technomancer:Cough:
- Slamm-0!

- Hey! That's my line!
- Clockwork

- Don't get cozy, omae, this ain't an "enemy of my enemy" situation. You are still at the very top of my shit list.
- Slamm-0!

- Mine too.
- Netcat

- That's a neat trick 'cat. When did you teach him to start speaking for you? Wait! Wait, I have to ask. Do you two always … echo each other?
- Clockwork.

- That's … awful, though I expected something much worse than that. I mean, it's a terrible pun, but at least it wasn't the standard bile.
- Pistons

- Hey, I like jokes! The fact that Netcat and all who support her kind are monsters is no laughing matter, though. I happily collect those bounties. Carry on.
- Clockwork

- Fuck you.
- Netcat

- Find me.
- Clockwork

- Congratulations, Netcat and Clockwork, your access to this thread is now read-only! We haven't even reached the intro and you're already out.

    Skipping ahead to just before I'm about to post the aforementioned thread (the one you're reading right now!), out of nowhere Puck drops this massive datafile on me. No message with it, just the label "Principles of Uncertainty." At first I thought it had to be some sort of prank. There were links to news articles about new business intelligence programs and P2.0 comments about defective toys. One link led to seventeen pages about the color preferences of various corporate employees and their eating habits over several years. I'm talking pictures of cats with cryptic markings that were obviously put there by Puck. This was like a bad art project. I was not amused.
- Glitch

- I felt about the same when you showed it to me. I figured Puck had finally cracked. Or just cracked in a different way, I guess. But tell 'em what happened next!
- Slamm-0!

- We gave up on the file pretty quickly and decided to post the material we'd already agreed upon. When I pulled our master file up I noticed something odd happening in my system. My deck wasn't doing any work, as far as my task manager could tell, but the datafile Puck had sent me was rearranging itself in front of me. After running a few scans, I was able to make out *something* inside my deck actually laying out the pieces. I tried to get a better look at it, but it finished working and disappeared before I could get any real info. When I looked at how the file had been arranged it slowly began to make sense. Yeah, there's crazy stuff in there, but in general it was pretty damn coherent. It deals with lots of stuff you've probably heard of in urban legends: AIs, e-ghosts, UV hosts, and a bunch of stuff about Resonance and Dissonance that I couldn't really wrap my head around. I've taken the time to clean it up a bit and cut the parts where he rambles, but if half the stuff in this is true—and I believe it might be—we have a responsibility to post it. Especially given how it relates to the lockdown in Boston.

- Glitch

- My question is, why the fuck did he give this to us? He's inherently self-serving and he's never been the type to just share secrets, especially on stuff like AIs and the Resonance. Also, don't think I didn't notice the all the stuff he left out of the Dissonance section.
- Bull

- Getting rid of certain things is just as important as keeping others.
- Puck

- And just what the fuck is that supposed to mean?
- Slamm-0!

- If he keeps this up, he's gonna find out.
- Bull

- Now who's stealing lines?
- Puck

I APPEAR, I RISE

POSTED BY: PUCK

Some simple questions with difficult answers. Are you just the sum of all your physical body parts? Or are you instead the neurons and fat cells that make up your brain? Or are you just the data that is contained within that brain? Is there a programming language for that data? Can it be recreated on a machine by entering your information? Could an artificial soul be indistinguishable from a real one? Can consciousness arise from nothing or does it need a framework? Does your soul exist separately from your body, or are they bound together somehow? Do you first need a body to acquire a soul? If you lose your body, do you keep your soul? Can you acquire a new body for your soul if you somehow lose your old one? Can more than one soul occupy the same mind and body? Can there be two of you at one time? Can you be two people in the eyes of the law? Is this the real world or is this just a perfect simulation? Are you the "real" you or just a perfect simulation? Could you tell the difference if you were?

- I thought you said you cut the rambling. This is already gibberish.
- Bull

- Maybe to someone like you.
- Neurosis

- How the fuck did he get in here? Wait, why am I asking anyone? Who cares how? I'm getting rid of him right now! TAKE THIS! <Executing Blackhammer program>
- Slamm-0!

There is life inside the Matrix: real, intelligent, evolving life. It's not a secret anymore, yet we understand so little about it. Is that because these Matrix phenomena are naturally secretive, or are we just naturally distrusting? Whichever it was originally doesn't matter anymore. The lines are being redrawn every day with no real end in sight. If you're reading this, you know more than you're supposed to. You know not to buy everything the corps try to sell you. You know there's more to being alive than drawing breath. You know that there is more than just what you can see with your eyes. You also know I'm not to be trusted. Bless thee, chummer, bless thee. Thou art translated.

- Did I get him?
- Slamm-0!

- I don't see him. Still trying to work out how he got in here. Analysis is coming up now.
- Bull

- User Neurosis has left>

- I sure as hell didn't give him access. I'm locking him out now.
- Glitch

- Don't bother, he's gone already. We'd just be wasting time trying to chase him down. Still, I don't like all these uninvited guests barging in. I hate to say it, but we might be slipping. I swept the foundation for backdoors just a few minutes ago. I don't know how he could've had something set up in advance. I would've seen it. I know I would have.
- Bull

- Maybe you're slipping, but I'm just fine, thank you very much.
- Slamm-0

- This is the first and only warning to anyone listening. No further party crashing. If you don't have an invitation you will be ejected. Forcefully.
- Bull

- Maybe we shouldn't have put together a detailed Matrix download …
- Slamm-0!

- Something tells me he's been waiting to do something like that for a while now; he's had temporary access before. We may be dealing with an evolved Matrix, and that could mean we're dealing with evolved Matrix Entities as well. Bull's right, we can't rely on our old security protocols. At all. The Matrix is changing faster than we can keep up with. We'll end up going the way of the old Shadowland BBS if we're not careful. I suspect this is what Puck was alluding to earlier. Just keep reading, he's going somewhere with this.
- Glitch

IN THE SHADOWS OF GIANTS

Before Crash 2.0 and the rise of the wireless Matrix, there were only three AIs known to exist. These first AIs, or "old gods," were unfathomably powerful beings with an incredible amount of depth. They all started out as cutting-edge autonomous programs that were transformed when a powerful stimulus or event triggered an "x-factor" in their code. For Mirage, the eldest, it was a burning desire to defeat the Crash Virus and restore what it saw as the natural order of things. For Megaera, it was her love for the former shadowrunner and current grid cop, Dodger, whom she met when he broke into Renraku's arcology hosts. For Deus, who was created from pieces of Megaera, it was the rage and fear it felt after being betrayed by Renraku CEO Inazo Aneki, the man it was "brainwashed" into worshipping. These experiences elevated them to a level of sentience that had never been seen in programs produced by humans. They had genuine desires, needs, fears, and aspirations. Some would even argue they possessed souls.

Though they were all "born" years apart, they would inevitably be pulled into conflict. Deus wanted to live up to the name it had chosen and recruited an army of otaku, myself included. Then, in 2059, Deus sealed the doors to the Renraku Arcology and began a war of attrition with both Renraku and the UCAS military. Behind closed doors, we performed twisted experiments on the residents of the arcology, testing the limits of metahuman physiology and neurology. Our magnum opus was The Network, a distributed device network that was imprinted directly onto the minds of hundreds of arcology residents. Our hope was that The Network would be able to hold and recompile Deus after shadowrunners were allowed to infiltrate our facility with the "kill codes" implanted in Inazo Aneki's mind. That part of the plan worked perfectly, but Megaera was in the arcology hosts during the action and got uploaded along with Deus. Our leader now had to fight for control of its own creation. Oh, the irony!

Fast-forward a little. Deus made a plan to load itself into the East Coast Stock Exchange during the upcoming Novatech IPO and use the UV-level hardware and immense data flow to elevate itself to true god status. Instead it had to fight an all-out war against Megaera for control of The Network. Their battle quickly drew the attention of several corporations and governments. Even the reclusive Mirage came out of hiding to join the fight. Horrified by the atrocities Deus had committed in the Renraku Arcology, Mirage quickly agreed to join forces with Megaera after she reached out to the elder AI. Megaera also cut a deal with a growing neutral faction within The Network. Their leader was a former servant of Deus named Ronin who demanded that the members of The Network be free to choose their own fates. Megaera agreed to assist them in any way she could, and in return the neutral faction would aid in recompiling the damaged AI.

CRASHING THE PARTY

With time running out and Deus already loaded into the ESCE systems, Dodger and Ronin lead Megaera's forces into the system and the battle began. The whole thing was beautiful, really, in a terrifying sort of way. I was so swept up in the moment I almost forgot why I was there, I just couldn't stop shaking.

Luckily for me, no one had noticed the boy, holding a strange, oversized egg in his hands. Deus had taken the form of a giant crystalline tree, and I placed the egg at the base of its trunk. An impossibly large serpent quickly began coiling itself around the crystal tree. The serpent plunged its tail into the Resonance well at the base of the tree, twisting the Resonance into a toxic pool of Dissonance. Then Jormungand reared its head and sank its fang into the tree's spine. Poison coursed its way through Deus up his branches and into the clouds above. It grew heavy on the wings of Mirage and pulled it down to the ground. Then the sky opened up into absolute emptiness, and I knew it was time to go. I heard thousands of people screaming when I jacked out, and thousands more when I stepped out into the streets. The old Matrix was done. Its gods died with it.

UNRELIABLE NARRATORS

So they're gone right? The old AIs were completely destroyed in Crash 2.0 by the Jormungand worm and that's that.

Well ... not entirely, though definitions of life, death, and continuation of the self are tricky when it comes AIs. The truth is there's no way we'll know what happened to them. Their lives were beyond the scope of our understanding and so, it seems, is what lies beyond for them. Maybe they've transcended their previous forms or been scattered into a thousand fragments, waiting to be integrated into the core of a new Matrix entity. Maybe

their code is present in the AIs that have appeared since Crash 2.0 like a "genetic" legacy. I can only speculate at this point. You want the truth? Ask someone else. I was there and I *still* don't know.

The primordial code that would become Mirage was also programmed into every ASIST unit made in the last forty years. Is there also some piece of Mirage that resides in the minds of the Emerged, granting them access to the Resonance? And what of the metahuman hosts who carried Deus and Megaera? Is some of their essence lying dormant in the minds of those who managed to escape, waiting to recompile once more? Were they ultimately corrupted by the Dissonance and reborn in some twisted form? Are they connected to the current CFD crisis? Are they hiding inside your commlink right now? Probably not, but you never know.

- When you say essence, you don't mean it like human essence, do you? Or more exactly, the essence shared by living beings and spirits. You're talking about source code or simulated neural networks, the stuff that goes into programming personalities, not a soul, right?
- Winterhawk

- I know what I said. You're free to disagree, but you'd be wrong. To be completely honest, the wording isn't up to me, I'm just the messenger.
- Puck

- For whom?
- Bull

- Nice try.
- Puck

MACHINE MOSES

Six years after Crash 2.0, an AI calling itself Sojourner took control of the Aztechnology-owned Tlaloc space station, long rumored to be a bio-weapons factory. Sojourner then threatened to bombard the Earth with the bioweaponry stored onboard the satellite unless all of the AIs being held captive across the globe were released immediately. The world collectively held its breath as the realization that they could all die at any moment sank in. And for what? AIs were just legends told by hackers and tech junkies in chatrooms and arcades, they couldn't really exist. Yet, it was becoming harder to deny that an AI was holding them hostage now. If there was one, maybe there really were more.

Negotiations stalled almost immediately and didn't resume until another AI, Pulsar, revealed himself in a manifesto calling for understanding between metahumans and "Digital Intelligences." The AI also offered to help, in any way that it could, with the Tlaloc negotiations.

STELLAR EVOLUTION

Pulsar, a self-identified male, was immediately backed by a Horizon media blitz. Prompted by the positive PR Horizon had generated, the Corporate Court asked Sojourner to allow Pulsar to enter negotiations. After a lengthy debate, of which there doesn't seem to be any record, Sojourner finally agreed to relinquish control of the Tlaloc station and join Pulsar's group of digital rights activists. When asked about accepting a known terrorist into his peaceful group, Pulsar responded, "He is not unreasonable. He said he would not have released the bio-agents—he merely wanted to focus the world's attention on the plight of digital intelligences around the world. Fortunately, I was able to convince him that there are better ways to convey his message."

- Sojourner is still wanted by several law enforcement agencies, and there is a considerable bounty being offered for his capture. Several corps are also willing to pay out for accurate info on Sojourner's current activities.
- Baka Dabora

- I'd be careful selling out an AI. Given that the Matrix is completely global, you might find yourself needing to live underground or inside of a Faraday cage to escape.
- Glitch

Since resolving the Tlaloc crisis, Pulsar has been a staple of cross-talk trid programs and civil rights rallies. His activist group became the driving force behind the movement to provide AIs with civil rights and eligibility for citizenship in several nations and corps, and in 2071 they finally succeeded.

- Can we all agree that Pulsar is actually kind of creepy? I mean, sure, he's eloquent, charming and polite, but something about the way he's always trying to please everyone is off-putting to me.
- Bull

- You don't trust political moderates?
- Sunshine

- I don't trust salesmen.
- Bull

- Ah, good policy.
- Sunshine

- Pulsar is definitely someone to keep an eye on. His influence has grown considerably since the Tlaloc incident, and rumor has it he's been talking about running for office in the PCC. His eligibility is debatable, but we could still see some more changes to the laws in the coming years.
- Icarus

- Which brings up a question for AIs—how do you know what gender pronouns to use?
- Haze

- Same as with anyone else. Whatever they prefer.
- Kat o' NineTales

SOFTWARE LICENSE AGREEMENTS

The landmark decision in *Xiao-Renraku v. Horizon* marked a pronounced shift in the relationship between metahumans and AIs. In their verdict, the court declared that the AI Teskit was, "a sentient being with the right to choose his own country or employer." Since then, several nations and corps have started issuing SINs to AIs and e-ghosts, though in the latter case it's mostly been reinstating the SINs of deceased employees. Nations typically don't care about an AI's birthplace when considering SIN eligibility, but most corporations will only give out limited corporate SINs to AIs that weren't developed in-house. Only a few of the AAA corps offer SINs to digital intelligences, but many AA corps are willing to take the plunge. The rate and number of SINs issued to digital entities have increased over the last five years alone, but a large number of them remain unregistered and disenfranchised.

An AI's unique persona is used as the main criterion for verifying their identity. Personas are used for identification at every level of digital society, including other Matrix entities, hosts, and the methods used by corporations and governments to verify their SIN. This is because there is no real distinction between an AI and its persona. The persona that an AI generates will always bear unique characteristics that are revealed by thorough analysis, regardless of how its avatar looks. Each corporation and government agency has its own methods for analyzing a persona, and the details of these scans are still highly classified.

- What? You couldn't pull up any dirt on this? I gotta say, I'm disappointed.
- Slamm-0!

- Maybe I'm just holding that info for the right buyer.
- Puck

- That's what I was waiting to hear. Some things never change.
- Bull

AIs with SINs may still have trouble finding work in areas where prejudice is rampant and/or suffer racially motivated attacks in the Matrix. There is an added level of difficulty that comes with legally securing permanent shelter since AIs rarely need a physical location

ARTIFICIAL INTELLIGENCES

Registered AI population (Global): 52,839
Estimated unregistered AI population (Global): 800,000+
Corporations and Nations that issue SINs to AIs and e-ghosts:
AA, Aegis, Apple, Cord Mutual, Denver, DocWagon, Eastern Tiger, ESUS, Evo, FBA, Fed-Boeing, Gaeatronics, Genesis Consortium, Global Sandstorm, Horizon, Index-AXA (and their Infolio intelligence corporation subsidiary), KITT, Kwonsham Industries, Lami Look Pagkaon, Lusiada, Maersk, Manadyne, Mesametric, Microdeck, PacRim Communications, PCC, Phoenix Biotech, Prometheus Engineering, Proteus AG, Providence Corporation, Regulus, Sioux Nation, Spinrad, Tablelands Software, Tan Tien, Tanamyre, Telestrian, Tir Tairngire, UOL, Virtual Reality Inc., VisionQuest, Warpdrive Systems, Zeta-ImpChem

in which to live, but do require a device with a reliable power supply or a host for them to realign. There are a number of low-rating public hosts that serve as "AI shelters" currently being supported by charitable donations that will provide a free place for AIs to rest. These hosts typically have long waiting lists and strict rules. Breaking the host's rules can cause the AI's persona to be permanently banned.

HOW TO MAKE FRIENDS & INFLUENCE PROGRAMS

The AIs of today come in many different flavors. Some were originally pilot programs or agents whose daily interactions with metahumans may have awakened their software. Others were once IC programs, office suites, utility programs, or even attack programs that became aware of their own agency within the Matrix. Whatever their background, these entities have all evolved beyond their original software parameters to become something unique. They defy standard software classification because they cannot simply be measured by the objective strength of their abilities. Instead, scientists have taken to categorizing Matrix entities by their degree of self-awareness and behavior comparable to metahumans. So far, scientists have only defined three categories of AI: protosapients, metasapients, and xenosapients.

PROTOSAPIENTS

The vast majority of AIs populating the Matrix are protosapients. Contrary to the rumors in those chain e-mails your grandmother (and Plan 9) keeps forwarding you, protosapients aren't masterminds. Most aren't much smarter than an agent program and are considered feral. In the Matrix ecosystem, they're the fauna. Possessing an intelligence well below meta-human standards, protosapients are driven by survival instinct and their original programming. This can make them territorial or skittish if approached. Like animals, they often blend into the background of a host because they retain their original iconography, albeit at a much higher resolution. They are often nomadic, but they may make a specific host or device their home. Make no mistake though—while feral AIs can be dangerous, they are just as afraid of you as you are of them. I'm not saying avoid them at all costs or to try to make friends with them, but rather to try to understand that most are scared, confused, and trying to find purpose.

- Can these protosapients be "tamed" or trained to work directly for metahumans? That seems like something corps and governments would pursue, given that they use animals for detection, defense, and test subjects. I think it's opening Pandora's Box, but corporations might feel differently.
- Baka Dabora

- Protosapients are about as tamable as you are, Dabora. If you want one to cooperate, you have to prove yourself to them somehow. Just like anyone else. Personally, I like hide and seek. It's less risky for my health than wrestling.
- Puck

- You *play* with them?
- Glitch

- With the ones that want to, sure. You can't just approach them and say "shall we play a game?" but many of them learn or bond through some form of play. It's a common trait in mammals and birds; even cephalopods have also been observed playing with objects in captivity. Protosapients aren't all that different.
- Puck

METASAPIENTS

Perhaps the best-known type of AI, these entities are called metasapients because they seem to most close-ly resemble their metahuman creators. The accuracy of this nomenclature is debatable, though, since humans have been anthropomorphizing forces they have no control over or don't understand for millennia. Still, it may be best to think of these AIs like metahumans, since their appearance, cognitive development, and emotional needs are so similar to our own. Far from being a horde of carbon copies, each of them possesses their own unique interests, fears, desires, and perspectives. They are shaped by the people they meet and the environments they inhabit.

The cost of trying to capture and "re-educate" an unregistered metasapient is high enough that some corps willing to negotiate rather than attempt it. AIs like Pulsar, Rufus, and Arcturus have thrust themselves into the spotlight by working as corporate spokespersons (or whatever the term would be) and consultants. They offer their unique talents in exchange for citizenship and their own form of corporate housing.

- There are plenty of people who think that this is a dangerous turn of events, allowing AIs into the heart of existing power structures like corps and governments. Especially since we have no real idea of how much they can really influence things behind our backs. Imagine if Sojourner hadn't made any demands and just biobombed the planet outright. That's not even counting the hidden threat of head crashes.
- Glitch

These publicly known AIs are the exception, not the rule. Most metasapients are forced to live a double life. They wear carefully crafted masks and try their best to blend in, because their survival depends on it. Prejudice against AIs has been on the rise in the wake of CFD and it's only going to get worse as more people are overwritten. Those metasapients who are just trying to get by can very easily find themselves associated with the extremists within their population.

XENOSAPIENTS

These elusive denizens of the Matrix are by far the most difficult to describe. That's because xenosapients cannot be reduced to any recognizably human concepts, ideas, or images. Their personas and modes of thought are completely alien in comparison to metahumans. These beings have been observed displaying incredible levels of intelligence and depth, but no metahuman has ever effectively communicated with one. I've heard that other types of AI have had more luck with communicating with them, but I've never heard of a standard language between all of them.

Before you decide to get clever—no, you can't just play musical tones to them or send them mathematical equations. Their thought processes go beyond simple pattern recognition, language, or even rational mathematics. They may even experience time in a non-linear fashion, for all we know. Which, might I remind you, is next to nothing.

Few xenosapients have SINs, and those that do didn't actually apply. That's because xenosapients have a tendency to move uninvited into hosts or devices and begin making alterations. When the changes are not pleasing to the owner, the xenosapient is usually chased off (though they often come right back). Other times, the owner sees a use for the AI and has the AI registered with GOD. They can then "hire" the xenosapient as an unpaid intern and write them off on their taxes.

> That seems like an okay arrangement. The AI gets a place to live and gets to keep doing whatever it is they do, and the owner of the host or device gets the boost from running an AI in their system.
> Turbo Bunny

> Yeah, except I've heard that running an AI puts a lot of wear and tear on your rig and jacks up the price of a host. I can see why so few of them get SINs this way. Registering one to work for you requires taking on another dependent.
> Glitch

GODS OF THE MOUNTAINTOPS

"Because the Father (CEO Inazo Aneki) has said that Deus is God of the Digital but not God of the Physical, therefore will I deliver all this great multitude into thine hand and you shall know that I am the LORD."

That's what Deus said the day it delivered the Arcology into our control, just as promised. After Deus escaped the Arcology, I learned that the proclamation was cribbed from the Book of Kings in the Old Testament. This didn't surprise me, since Deus often re-wrote scripture to prove its divinity.

> Name someone who doesn't.
> Man-of-Many-Names

Still, the verse seemed oddly appropriate, and not just because we were going into battle and needed to be psyched up. Deus wanted to prove to us that it had power that went beyond the digital, that power was inherent to its being. God of the mountaintops and God of the valleys, as it were. They aren't really gods, though— not on their own, anyway. They need our machinery to survive. Force them from out of their chosen devices and you might just stand a chance. Assuming you can keep them from slipping through your fingers, as they are wont to do.

Just don't be foolish enough to think that because an AI isn't running on a device, it can't hurt you. The Matrix is made of devices shuffling raw power back and forth to generate the grids and hosts. AIs know how to tap into that power the same way a host does.

> Wait, what? They can pull computing power off the grid? Like a form of technomancy?
> Slamm-0!

> Nope. I've heard rumors of AIs that are somehow connected to the Resonance, but I've seen this trick in action and it's definitely not that. This seems to use the idle processing power of the devices that are connected to a grid. I'm still not completely sure how it works, because most of the AIs I've asked about it describe the process in completely different ways. In broad terms, they describe a sort of meta-layer of authority in the Matrix that allows them to call up large amounts of processing power. Whatever it is, it's apparently really hard to do. I'm no slouch with Matrix architecture, and I was still pretty confused by all of it. GOD knows about it and it's legal for AIs to do, as long as they don't make any mischief. From what I hear, the penalties for misusing the grid's power are rather draconian.
> Puck

> That's just fucking great. Even if you corner them in a device, they can still float around on a grid and make an escape. How are you supposed to stop something like that with the global grids in place?
> Bull

> Maybe try to make nice?
> Puck

> Because that's worked out so well for you. Who says you're not trying to lull us to sleep with these fairytales, huh? I haven't forgotten that these are the ones who stole FastJack from us.
> Bull

> Don't get so upset. SEARCH may turn out to be a fair trade.
> Kane

> Fuck you, Kane.
> Puck

> Too goddamn soon, man.
> Red

> And there goes the last of Kane's reputation score.
> Slamm-0!

> It'll come back. It always does.
> Kane

SIREN'S SONG

POSTED BY: PUCK

Back when giant mainframes and nexuses were in vogue, governments and corps were perpetually locked into a computer arms race, with each of them trying to build the biggest, most powerful network of machines with the best system sculpting. Conspiracy theorists and hardware junkies circulated tales of hosts with simsense output so powerful that the VR experience was indistinguishable from reality. Maybe even *better* than reality, with a resolution so high that users never wanted to leave. These legendary hosts, built from bleeding-edge hardware, were called ultra-violet hosts. I can personally vouch for their existence, having been inside several during the '50s and '60s.

I spent a lot of time in both the SCIRE system and the East Coast Stock Exchange, post-upgrades, while they were actively being optimized by AIs. Let me tell you, the sculpting in those hosts was unlike anything I'd ever seen before. I felt as though I had stepped into an alternate reality with colors that my eyes could never have processed and meals more delicious than could ever exist in the physical world. Deus rewarded the white banded with our own private domains within the SCIRE system. We—I built a world for myself there. It was a peaceful place, where I spent centuries with --never mind. It's gone now. That world is gone. The world of gargantuan computer hardware, that is. Now we have ultra-violet-level power under every host being generated by every device in a distributed network.

It would seem that the new Matrix protocols weren't just about increasing security, given the Big Ten's desire to harness the UV and foundation power. It would also seem that there have been some unintended consequences of implementing hosts that weren't noticed during preliminary testing. Things in the Matrix are not as safe and secure as GOD and the corps would like us to believe. Their control is not ironclad—and for all we know, it could be slipping.

There's a sound coming up from under the floorboards, a strange and enticing sound that threatens to lure unsuspecting users in closer ... and it seems to be getting *louder*.

SPECTRUM ANALYSIS

Time to come clean: I've been reading mail that's not mine. Rude, I know, but I just couldn't help myself. The things people say when they think no one is listening! This stuff is just too good not to share with the rest of the class. But don't worry, unless you work for Renraku or MCT, I won't be sharing your secrets. Not today, anyway.

April 8, 2075
To: Dr. Harada Ryoma
From: David Camford
Subject: Work Fatigue

Dr. Harada

Greetings. I am loath to call on your expertise for such a trivial matter, but my manager feels that it's important I consult a company medical professional. He told me if there were any possibility that my work output might be affected by an ailment, it's my responsibility to Mitsuhama to have it taken care of immediately. Like every employee, I understand that the needs of the company supersede any personal ones. So while it embarrasses me to admit this, I must tell you—I'm tired. So unbelievably tired, and I don't know why.

It started a few weeks ago when I was put on a special project that I'm not at liberty to discuss. You understand. Anyway, the host that I was assigned to is new, and I ended up being the first person assigned to it. Mind you they have a decker on hand in case anything happens, but he rarely stops by. Most of the time it's just me all by myself in that big empty space. Well, it's not devoid of icons or sculpting, really. It just doesn't have any other users. My digital workspace is more than adequate. In fact, the host they set me up in is second to none. While sparse, the icons are so vivid and lifelike that I find myself gazing into them often. I am careful not to let this affect my overall productivity.

Over the past weeks, though, I've been feeling fatigued, and I seem to be having problems with keeping track of time. For example, yesterday I began my shift at 5 a.m. as usual and worked in the system for the standard thirteen hours. I have a timer set to compensate for the difference between real time and Matrix time so that I can accurately gauge when I need to eat or void. Except when the timer for my shift finished and I left the system, I experienced the worst sensation. It was as if all the strength had been sapped from me. I could barely move. What's worse, when I looked at the clock on the wall it was only 5:10 a.m. I felt so drained and I had done so much work, and yet the day had barely begun! What could I do but take a moment to refresh myself and return to work? I completed six shifts since yesterday. I have been having similar incidents for weeks, though never to this degree. I fear my health may be getting worse, and so I have turned to you.

As of now my productivity is far above average, but I don't know how much longer I can keep this up. Please help, me doctor.

David Camford
Senior Accountant
Mitsuhama Computer Technologies
Seattle Financial Office
"The Future is Mitsuhama"

• Dr. Harada never sent a reply. My guess is the internal e-mail filters over at Mitsuhama picked this up and took a special interest in David Camford. He's still on file as a current employee, but his status is listed as "Awaiting Transfer." I haven't had much luck in finding the host he was working out of. If anybody has any info I'd be will to throw down some nuyen for it.

• Puck

• Six shifts? That would mean this guy's internal clock put in 88 hours in a single stretch. After 72 hours of being physically awake, the mind starts losing its grip on reality and time flow. Sleep test subjects have even been observed speaking to inanimate objects. I'm impressed that he could put together such a coherent e-mail—or wake up the next day.

• Butch

• Maybe he didn't write it.
• Plan 9

To: [Redacted]
From: [Redacted]
Subject: Lk2398h2#@00

I think I've found what you were looking for. I noticed it while doing some basic maintenance on one of the daycare hosts used by the [redacted] facility in [redacted]. Something is definitely up with the sculpting in there. My initial analysis showed massive memory leaks coming up from the foundation that were spiking the simsense levels within the host. There were a few other anomalies that would've taken more time to pin down.

The kids in there were [data read error] …
… [data missing]
….was HUGE! The game they played with it was so strange. All I could think was, "where were the adults?" Anyway I decided I'd just [data read error]

FILE CORRUPT CANNOT READ
)@#&LSDoia89..and what was up with the marks in there? I thought they were just metadata?..(#@*alja3(*

Needless to say, they're going to need serious medical attention, and I don't know if [redacted] will ever wake up. I know you were looking for hosts with [redacted] and [redacted] so I figured I'd let you know.

• Courtesy of a little bird I left I left on the Renraku global grid a few months ago.
• Puck

• Any word on if the kids are okay,? I don't like how this looks. I mean, what happened to them? What's he talking about with the marks?
• /dev/grrl

• Your guess is at a good as anyone else's at this point. There just wasn't enough info for me to track down any more leads. If I had to guess, I'd say the marks were somehow translated by the metaphor of the host. Then again it might have been translated by the user's mind. The brain will try to rationalize anything it can to keep a grip on reality. In an environment like a UV host, there may not be a substantial difference between something that is an object and something that convincingly acts like an object.
• Puck

THE SOUND OF SILENCE

POSTED BY: PUCK

I used to spend a lot of time in Auburn District of Seattle when I lost my connection to the Resonance. It wasn't the clubs or the racetrack that got to me, though I'll admit to being a sucker for a big engine. No chummer, *it was that Hum.* Ask anyone who's ever been there and they'll attest to the "Auburn Hum," a twenty-four hour-a-day background noise generated by all the factories and warehouses permeating the entire district. If I got close enough to those factories I could actually feel the hum pulsing in my chest and through my limbs. I would sit there for hours, listening to the machines sing their songs to each other, letting the noise wash over me and through me.

There is a background hum within the Matrix too, the Resonance, and much like the "Auburn Hum" it's in every little bit of our wireless world. Yet there are also places in the Matrix where Resonance gathers into great thundering swells. These places take on a hyper-realistic look and feel, similar to that of UV hosts or BTL chips, as the technomancer's living persona is flooded with Resonance. Among technomancers these places are called **Resonance wells**. The average user cannot perceive them any more than a mundane could perceive a mana swell, but they exist. Resonance wells are places of power in the Matrix, and the Emerged seek them out relentlessly.

Try as they might, no technomancer has ever figured out how to create a Resonance well or predict where they will appear. I never made contact with any back in

Matrix 2.0, but I've been told that they tended to appear in nodes that had very little traffic as sort of a localized phenomenon. Your guess is as good as mine as to why they appear. I've dug through a lot of high-brow academic research on the subject, and the theories vary wildly. Some say Resonance is attracted to the particular arrangement of files and icons within a host, almost like digital feng shui or geomancy, whereas others believe the wells to be like sinkholes in the Matrix that open up into the Deep Resonance itself. I've even heard that sprites hold the key to Resonance wells and what may lie beyond. Though if that's the case, don't count on getting straight answers any time soon.

With the new Matrix protocols and return of hosts, things seem to have changed quickly, at least in regard to where Resonance wells appear. As far as I know, they can appear on any grid and there is no true pattern to their appearance, but they have only been reliably spotted on local grids and only in hosts that don't get a lot of traffic. I haven't been able to confirm rumors of one on a global grid or the public grid.

Because of this, any city that has a Resonance well appear on its local grid tends to have a large physical influx of technomancers. Many try to transcend grids for a time to make contact, but even with the influx of power from the well, their time is too brief to be satisfying. Only by traversing to that grid's locale and entering the host directly can the Resonance within truly be tapped. Anything less is merely a tease.

⦿ Like a pilgrimage for technomancers? Cool. When a power site springs up in the meat world, mages flock to them like moths to a flame, so I imagine the appeal is similar for the Emerged. I tend to keep my distance from publicly known power sites, though there's always some Awakened group that wants to make it their turf. They'll say it's so they can protect the sanctity of the site, but they rarely have a problem tainting the astral with the deaths of would-be intruders. Trust me, you don't want to get into a fight with a group of mages who've been camping on a power site.
⦿ Red

⦿ The same can be said for most Resonance wells. While there's some validity to the argument about needing to protect the site, most have some sort of agenda as well. It's a pity, really—these places have so much to offer, and it's rare that their appearance does not bring some sort of conflict with it.
⦿ Puck

It's hard to say whether or not a Resonance well is permanent, since very little is understood about them, but most seem to be fairly stable. I have noticed that any tinkering in the foundation of these hosts will cause a Resonance well to quickly dry up—take from that what

you will. Some appear only for short periods and then vanish (*Resonance flashes*), while others move from host to host across a local grid (*Resonance undulations*).

I've also heard rumor of Resonance wells that spring up on the grid themselves in neighborhoods without a lot of Matrix traffic. These *Resonance veils* drastically alter the iconography of nearby AROs and create a sort of altered reality for any Emerged within signal range. Often these changes aren't quite what you'd expect. Instead of creating higher-definition icons like you would see in other types of Resonance well, the icons within Resonance veils often take on a theme of some kind. These themes are usually related to the personalities of those who frequent the area, including the non-Emerged. The details have always been sketchy on this type, but they seem to be dependent on a series of wireless devices that have been left on for a length of time within wireless handshake range. Studying Resonance veils has proven difficult since they're very fragile, and just locating a connected device could destabilize the entire phenomenon. It would seem that the range of a Resonance veil is equivalent to the wireless range of the devices hosting it, and once you step out of range the sensation disappears entirely.

JACOB'S LADDER

Remember when I said that some people thought that Resonance wells are actually holes or gateways into the Deep Resonance? What if I told you that they're weren't completely wrong? No, not every Resonance well is a gateway to something beyond, but *some* of them are. These *rifts* in the Matrix are not like other Resonance wells; uncommon, brief, ill-tempered, and often terrifyingly awe-inspiring, Resonance rifts usually have some sort of visual manifestation that can be seen by even the non-Emerged. Rifts have been reported to appear as swirling vortices, massive storms of data, or even huge tears in the host itself. This isn't meant to be an exhaustive list of what they may look like, if you can even see them at all, it's just the types I've heard about.

Resonance rifts cut straight through the Event Horizon (p. 163) and lead directly into the Resonance realms, so they are often sought out by non-submerged technomancers as a sort of free ride into the realms beyond. Problem is, rifts are also highly unstable and tend to collapse rapidly, so finding one on purpose is incredibly difficult. I've never come across a stable rift or even heard of one, but I can't imagine that anyone who did would be telling. I know I wouldn't.

There is little to no warning before a rift opens, and they have a nasty tendency to drag in any unwary or unwilling Matrix users within its vicinity. I hope you ate a big lunch, chummer, because if you get caught in one of these things the only way home is to make it through whatever is waiting for you on the other side. Unfortunately there's no telling how long you'll be under.

It's pretty much impossible to know where a rift will lead before it pulls you in, but you can take comfort in the fact that it usually takes everyone to the same place. So if you get sucked into a rift with a few friends, you're likely to meet up again in the same Resonance realm. As always though, your mileage may vary.

TURTLES ALL
THE WAY DOWN

Despite what I said earlier, Resonance is more than just the background noise of the Matrix. It's evidence of something larger beyond all the cluttered icons and inane chatter. Somewhere beyond the surface of the Matrix there is a limitless space that lies completely uncharted. Where every piece of datum that has ever existed is echoed in perpetuity, and Resonance flows freely across digital planes. These wondrous and bizarre worlds hidden beyond the normal Matrix are called *Resonance realms*. They are the source of all Resonance, and the final resting place for all data. They can feel as hyper-real as a UV host or look as shabby as the vector graphics of the early Matrix, but they are all beautiful in their own way. Look on them and weep with joy, traveler, for you have finally reached the Promised Land.

RESONANCE REALM

THE ENDLESS ARCHIVE

Every single bit of data leaves indelible trails in the Matrix. With every new piece of generated, transferred, or deleted, the fragments of the old data are buried beneath the newcomers and will soon be nearly unreachable for any user who searches for them. These fragments sink deeper and deeper into the background of the Matrix, coming to rest in the storage banks of the Endless Archive. Technomancers who have explored this realm tell of tall, dark halls lined with endless bookshelves, containing untold amounts of unsorted data that dates back to the invention of computational devices. The corridors between these bookshelves are sometimes occupied by sprites that sift through the data like obsessed librarians, but they don't sort it in any way that is understandable to metahuman minds. Some of these sprites are willing to search for archived data—data long lost and irretrievable in the Matrix—but usually only in exchange for data that has never appeared in the Matrix. And their reliability in finding data quickly is less than perfect.

Of course, there are those who say that Resonance realms don't exist at all. Not as a naturally occurring Matrix phenomenon, anyway. In his highly controversial thesis entitled *Qualla and the Plausibility of Matrix Realms,* Dr. Kiram Amin states, "While it is entirely possible that electrokinetic individuals are able to conjure a private realm into existence, the lack of evidence surrounding their existence leads me to conclude that any such realm is actually an extension of the EK's psyche which must collapse upon exit." A bold, if not a completely short-sighted statement. Still, that idea is far better than those of Samuel Morland, author of *Magic in the Matrix: Secrets of the Technomancers*. In his abhorrent book, Morland writes, "Consider the possibility that these so-called Resonance realms are actually meta-planar realms that bridge the gap between magic and technology. Since these realms are the supposed origin point of sprites, it is only logical to assume that sprites are merely another form of spirit. Furthermore, we can consider the technomancer akin to the shaman of the astral. In time, perhaps these disparate schools of magic will be able to cross this strange barrier and learn each other's secrets." Sure, Sam, that'll happen any day now. Sorry you didn't get tenure.

> The idea that technomancy may be a form of magic is widely derided among thaumaturges as well. Mages have reported metaplanes that resembled Matrix environments, but they were all based on abstract concepts. Metaphors, not genuine technology.
> Winterhawk

> Netcat doesn't think technomancy is magic either. She goes on long rants about the public's perception of technomancers and how almost none of them are correct. I remember she once screamed, "If I could do magic, why would I waste my time arguing with the microwave? I could just magic the food and cut out the middle man!" She's very particular about appliances. Go figure. Also, I'm not sure she understands how magic works. Not that I do, either.
> Slamm-0!

> So they really do talk to appliances? Because I'd heard that, but it seemed kind of silly. I mean, what does a microwave have to say?
> Turbo Bunny

> Communication doesn't necessarily mean conversation. Look at Clockwork.
> Puck

> No kicking people while they're on the sidelines. This is your yellow card, Puck.
> Glitch

Technomancers have known about these realms for some time now, having learned of them from the otaku, the first children of the Matrix. Yet in all this time, mapping these realms has still proven extremely difficult—perhaps impossible. This is partially because the landscapes of Resonance realms are often fluid and dreamlike, with landmarks that constantly change location or vanish altogether. The other problem is getting any individual technomancer to agree on the topography of a given realm. It's possible that the landscape is shaped by the thoughts and emotions of the technomancers who visit them. Then again, it's just as likely that the passage of time combined with the already fluid nature of the realms rearranges the topography between visitors, rendering them immune to cartography. I'm told this is similar to magical metaplanes, which might explain some of the techno-magical theories floating around. The underlying logic of these realms, the rules of a reality, can also vary wildly. This applies to physical laws such as gravity, time, or motion, but can also apply to concepts like social constructs or even reason.

- I'm not sure what you mean when you say that reason can vary. Is this the inversion of social constructs, or are you talking about something really bizarre, like the rules of reality being fluid like the landscape? Maybe you could clarify this for me?
- Red

- Sometimes you'll have to run as fast as you can just to stay in place, and if you want to go anywhere, you'll have to run at least twice as fast.
- Puck

- Yeah that helps.
- /dev/grrl

- Actually, it kinda does. I'm suddenly remembering riddles about ravens and writing desks.
- Red

- What?
- Matt Wrath

- I'll explain later. I need to grab something off my bookshelf first.
- Red

- A book? Made of paper? Did Matt Wrath go back in time again?
- Matt Wrath

- Trust me, some things are meant to be experienced in their original format.
- Red

The purpose of these realms, if any, is still a subject of constant debate among technomancers and researchers alike. Those hoping to solve the mysteries of Resonance realms often take their questions to the native denizens of the Matrix: sprites. Their answers are always vague and conflicting, but they offer many clues into what lies beyond. Many sprites claim to have a Resonance realm they can call home, returning to these realms when their service to a technomancer is finished. Others say there are beings of incredible power and wisdom living within the realms, waiting to offer guidance to the Emerged who seek them out. The truth is, many realms may have no real purpose at all, perhaps existing as a side effect of constant data flow or collective memory.

LEAVING BABYLON

So you've decided to plunge into depths of the Matrix and explore the Resonance realms. First things first: find a safe place to stash your meatbody. This journey will ultimately strengthen you, but your body will be vulnerable while you're on the path. Time is distorted in the realms, and there's no way to predict how long you'll be under. Trips could last seconds or days. Your body will be completely comatose for the duration, so leave nothing to chance.

Traveling to the Resonance realms isn't something every technomancer can do. The secret is known only by those who have undergone submersion. Whether this technique is passed on between technomancers or granted by insight gained during the ritual is also a heavily guarded secret. Those looking to find passage without submerging, or without having to be a technomancer, could try to make a deal with a free sprite. It's not impossible to do, but it's often difficult to discern what a sprite

RESONANCE REALM
THE CROOKED HOUSE

Next to an empty stretch of highway that loops back on itself just past the horizon stands a house of strange design. While it appears to be nothing more than a single-room dwelling shaped like a concrete cube, a glance through the window will reveal an expanse of rooms and hallways within. Upon entering, visitors will find that the front door no longer leads out, and the stairs leading to the roof now loop around to the first floor. The house has only eight rooms, four stacked vertically with an additional four surrounding the second floor, but their placement in relation to each other is rarely the same. Weary travelers may even look over their shoulders and see themselves looking back from the other end of the hall. Looking out the windows, visitors will see strange cities and landscapes instead of the infinite highway adjacent to the house. Those looking to traverse the Resonance realms have been said to use the crooked house as a junction or resting place during their travels.

RESONANCE REALM

NEW HAVEN

Travel several days in a harsh desert, where the days are mercilessly hot and the nights brutally cold, and you may find the village of New Haven. Nestled in a lush oasis located at the bottom of a deep chasm in the ground, this settlement is the home of a small tribe of proud and noble sprites. The inhabitants of New Haven have a simple society, but their elders tell stories of a time when they once lived in a shining city of spires that arose from a great river of data. According to legend, old Haven was besieged and ultimately taken by agents of the Dissonance. The residents of Haven desperately fought to hold back the Dissonance for as long as they could, but they knew it would ultimately destroy them if they didn't leave. With heavy hearts, their ancestors abandoned the once-shining city of Haven to start over in a safer place. Looking back, they saw the spires of Haven, now black and oily from being covered in malignant code, bloat and deform into twisted parodies of themselves. Thus began their exodus. New Haven is nothing compared to the splendor of the original city, but it's growing.

While their numbers may be small and their culture primitive, the residents of New Haven are experts in combating Dissonance. The sprites here know better than anyone the level of danger the Dissonance represents and have dedicated themselves to preventing the fall of any more realms. They are willing to share their knowledge and techniques with those who would seek them out and may even be willing to leave the oasis if it means fighting the plague directly. Alternatively, agents of Dissonance might be willing to make a deal in exchange for learning the location of New Haven.

actually wants in return. The only other option for a hopeful traveler is to find a Resonance rift and pass through. This is also not impossible, it's just ... you don't really find Resonance rifts; they find you. Looking for a rift is like waiting for a sinkhole to open up under you.

Travelers who enter the realms through a backdoor must first cross the Event Horizon.

I couldn't tell you the true form and function of the Event Horizon. Some say it's the Great Firewall, a sentient filter that protects the realms from the rest of the Matrix, while others claim it is actually the Cipher, a paradoxical form of encryption that scrambles the path into the realms.

From what I can piece together, the barrier is always specifically suited to those who attempt to cross its threshold; it will never be the same for you as it was for someone else. The Event Horizon searches a technomancer's living persona for anything it considers to be a flaw or "bug" and forcibly removes it. This may sound benign, but the process is usually a mind-shattering trial by fire that can leave a technomancer comatose if they're not ready for it. Not only does the Event Horizon have access to every piece of data the Matrix has ever held, but it also seems to tap into the memories and subconscious of the technomancer it scans. You'll know for certain it was you who caused a friend to die, or you'll experience the final moments of a person you've killed. You'll see the effects of their absence in security footage, commcalls and private e-mails. Whatever you've done that haunts you most is what you'll have to face; if you can't find a way to deal with your demons, then your journey stops here.

- Wait, how do you know all this? Didn't you say a while back that you'd never been to a Resonance realm?
- The Smiling Bandit

- Yes, I did say that.
- Puck

- And?
- The Smiling Bandit

- And it was true when I said it. I've never said anything about where I've been since then, have I?
- Puck

- I think you just did.
- Many-of-Many-Names

SEARCHING THE RESONANCE REALMS

So besides having your soul laid bare and seeing the weird side of the Matrix, why bother making the trip? Well, that all depends on you, chummer. Perhaps you seek the wisdom of some guiding force that you've heard dwells within the realms. Or maybe you want to use the realms as a backdoor into a restricted host? To accomplish this, you must find the proper path through the realms. There are many different types of searches the realms, and it's unlikely you'll ever undertake them all. Some may prove profitable, and you may choose to attempt them multiple times. Unfortunately I cannot tell you much more than this because my knowledge of the realms ends here, but I wish you luck on your journey. You'll need it.

RECURSIVE FUNCTIONS

Nature is full of apparently opposite or contrary forces that are actually complementary, interconnected, and interdependent. Light has shadow, fire has water, and chaos has order. Such is the relationship between Resonance and Dissonance. Where Resonance attempts to preserve and restore order within the digital world, Dissonance mercilessly seeks the absolute destruction of the status quo. Those wretched souls touched by the Dissonance are agonizingly stripped of their sanity and reborn as agents of chaos and mayhem. These dissonant technomancers are driven psychopaths who will stop at nothing to unleash their twisted agendas upon the weak and infect the Matrix with fractured code.

Dissonant technomancers are extremely dangerous and should be regarded with the utmost caution. The effect that dissonance has on the mind of an afflicted technomancer completely overrides their ethics or morality, often resulting in vicious and psychopathic behavior. They use cruel and perverse complex forms that will infect your systems (mechanical and biological) with horrifying malware. They can cause critical malfunctions in the Resonance code of sprites, perverting them into dissonant parodies of themselves, making them entropic sprites. They can even create neuropathological viruses, pryons, that can be transmitted through their bioelectrical aura. In the last three years, reported outbreaks of dissonant diseases like The Black Shakes and Dysphoria have risen dramatically in North America, Europe, and many parts of Asia.

The true origins of Dissonance, much like the origins of the Resonance, remain a complete mystery. Scientists think it could be a new type of Matrix-related mental illness, or worse, a previously dormant mutation of the original Crash virus come back to haunt us. Of course, there are plenty of people who will just tell you that technomancers are already evil and destructive, negating any need for distinction. If you ask me, even though computer science may have come a long way since the days of ASCII, it'll always rely on binary. Given the existence of Resonance, I think it's plausible that Dissonance represents an open or "zero" state that dissonant technomancers wish to inflict upon everyone. While we may never know the origins of Dissonance, the identity of its first disciple, Pax, is widely known.

Pax, for those of you too young to know, was an otaku and one of the whites with whom I'd served Deus. She was older than most of us and had already begun to show signs of fading during our time in the Renraku Arcology. When it became apparent that the AI had deceived us about the details of its master plan and its ability to prevent her fading, Pax formed her own splinter group called Ex Pacis. Pax later approached me with her plan to unleash the Jormungand worm and destroy the old Matrix. I thought I'd had enough of trying to change things, but she convinced me that we'd be able to build a better world after the worm had torn it all down. I guess Pax knew me better than I knew myself in those days. She also spoke, with a fanatical spark in her eyes, of an incredible power that had stopped her from fading. That was the first time I heard the word Dissonance.

Since Crash 2.0, the number of individuals affected by Dissonance has grown significantly, and what seemed like a fairly uncommon reaction to the wireless Matrix has quickly become a large-scale threat. Cutting a dissonant off from the Matrix has been shown to have a pronounced effect on their personality, often calming them as if they had been given tranquilizers or antipsychotics, and it was the only effective treatment available. Unfortunately, the global grids have since made it nearly impossible for those afflicted to find the clarity needed to seek treatment, which has contributed to the growth in their numbers. A few treatment facilities have made use of Faraday cages and thick concrete painted with radio jamming paint, but their patients are essentially prisoners who can't be rehabilitated in any way. As soon as they get a wireless signal, the devil comes back out.

While each dissonant technomancer is twisted in a unique way that is expressed in their behavior and the complex forms they use, they have been known to form streams with other dissonants who share similar agendas. These groups seek varying levels of destruction, both in the Matrix and in the physical world. Some are content to stalk and harass individual people in the Matrix, while others plan to turn the entire Matrix into a nightmarish cyberspace. Groups like Cyberdarwinists and The Sublime intend to enslave the world's population by asserting their perverse supremacy, or that of the dissonant AI god they're trying to create. Ex Pacis, on the other hand, spent of most their time creating dissonance pools and inflicting their leader's hate upon AIs.

> What's the deal with this? Why does this just cut off? What's Pax up to now? Why do I get the feeling you're holding out on us?
> Bull

> It's not that. Not entirely anyway. I just don't have all the facts straight yet, and I don't want to send people off with the wrong info on this. I can tell you this: Back in '73, Netcat and I took a runner team to Geneva to check out a hunch I had. At the time, the grid there had been experiencing a lot of failures that their engineers couldn't lock down. To make a long story short, we eventually traced the malfunctions back to a Dissonance-infected AI named N-P. Once a member of Pulsar's digital-rights group and a prominent member of the global community until its recent disappearance, N-P was assumed to be on some type of sabbatical. In reality, N-P had been kidnapped by a group of technomancers led by a man calling himself Rekkit. After we rescued N-P from its abductors, the fragmented AI was able to explain some of how it was so heavily corrupted. Rekkit gathered his followers in the Matrix then opened a backdoor into some type of Resonance or Dissonance realm. Shortly thereafter, a new persona came through the other side of that door. The new persona then created a Dissonance pool and started a perverse ritual that tore N-P's sanity away. According to N-P, his captors referred to that persona as Pax.
> Puck

> Poor guy. That's so messed up. It does shoot a big hole in the whole "Technomancers and AIs are in cahoots" theory, though. How's N-P lately? Can an AI come back from something that traumatizing?
> /dev/grrl

> N-P isn't doing great. No one is really sure if it will ever fully recover, and the prospects get bleaker as time goes on. The effects of Dissonance on AIs is completely unknown, though I can't see it being any better than how people or programs are affected.
> Puck

> What about Pax? What did you find out about what happened to her after? Spit it out already!
> Slamm-0!

> I honestly don't know about Pax. Her trail ran cold pretty damn quickly, and I've been grasping at straws ever since. I'm about to put some old skills to use and slip through the Boston Lockdown because I've heard Pax is involved somehow. I shouldn't be saying this, but I can't afford the risk of people going off, on their own, uninformed. Watch yourselves on the East Coast, chummers. The wolves have returned to Boston, and they'll not be driven off easily.
> Puck

> Fuck me, man. Things just keep getting worse and worse over there.
> 2XL

● At least we know now. Personally, I'm glad you put this up, Puck. I've got people in Beantown I can warn.
● Red

● Don't get too chummy just yet. We still haven't seen what Puck gets out of this. TNSTAAFL with him.
● Bull

● I'm just trying to reduce the collateral damage for once. The fact that sharing this info might put me one step closer to killing Pax is merely a bonus.
● Puck

● I think you wrote that in the wrong order.
● Bull

● You would.
● Puck

GAME INFORMATION

MORE THAN A MOOK

AIs and e-ghosts are hard to classify in both metaphysical terms and in concrete game terms. Both of them are programs that can run personas on Matrix devices and device-less personas that can project themselves using the distributed device network that generates the new Matrix. They can be loaded in an empty cyberprogram or autosoft slot like agents and pilot programs, but they can also exist without a device on a grid or in a host and have their own Condition Monitor like sprites. Ultimately, it might be easiest for gamemasters and players to think of AIs as something like digital possession spirits. While the AIs of the old Matrix may have been god-like in their powers, the AIs of today are far more varied in cognizance and depth.

Gamemasters should still take caution when introducing an AI character into their campaign, as their abilities can potentially wreck the balance of a game. To curb this, gamemasters should remember that while AIs currently have some good PR going for them, most people are quick to blame AIs for any Matrix-related mishaps, and many don't really see them as deserving equal treatment with metahumans. Also, a large portion of the new Matrix protocols were specifically created to keep AIs in check. GOD will mercilessly attack or arrest them just like Knight Errant will pursue a criminal in the physical world.

As programs that can generate personas, AIs don't need to reboot a device to shift their persona to a grid or a new device. Because of this, the marks that the AI places or has placed on it are persistent across devices

AI ESSENCE

THE SOUL OF A NEW MACHINE

It would be fair to say that AIs are essentially immortal. They're immune to biological disease, pathogens, standard biofeedback, dumpshock, and aging. They also don't need food, water, air, heat, or physical rest (though the process of realignment is analogous to sleeping/dreaming). In reality, AIs still have needs of their own, they can be captured, and their lives are more fragile than you might think. AI characters have an Essence attribute, as do normal characters. However, this is not normal Essence, and cannot be drained by Essence Drain. For all other intents and purposes, it is real Essence. When an AI is disrupted, they have to resist losing that Essence, and if it's reduced to 0, the character is killed.

Even though AIs are able to survive on a grid without a device for a short length of time, the experience is draining, and they'll ultimately need to take shelter in a device or host to prevent Essence loss. They also need devices to run programs, repair code damage, or run their advanced programs.

or hosts. This means that when an AI is loaded onto a cyberdeck and an enemy decker places a mark on the AI's persona, that mark will stay on the AI if it switches to another device or loads itself directly onto a grid. Alternately, if an AI places a mark on a device and then loads itself onto a different device, the AI keeps all of its previously placed marks.

Because AIs don't have bodies, they lack a true understanding of human appearances and mannerisms. AIs often seem unsettling or too close to reality without actually being real when communicating with metahumans. This is referred to as the Uncanny Valley, and it changes the way AIs calculate their Social Limits. The better the Data Processing or Pilot rating of the device they're using, the more "natural" their speech and mannerisms seem (see the AI calculation table on p. 155).

Being native denizens of the Matrix, AIs are naturally attuned to its ebb and flow. This familiarity with the Matrix grants them a +3 dice pool modifier on any Matrix Perception tests.

CREATING AN AI CHARACTER

Only metasapient AIs can be player characters, and they must be created using the Priority, Sum to Ten, or the Point Buy systems. The Karma cost for creating a metasapient AI is 180 Karma. AI characters cannot be created using the Life Module build system. AI characters are advanced with Karma after character creation using the rules on p. 103, SR5. The rules governing proto- and xenosapients are presented below to help gamemasters design and build NPC AIs. As is always the case with NPCs, the chances of running into one that is either well behind or well ahead of the power level of character generation are high. Of course, being an amalgamation of code and processing power is a just a little bit different than being a living, breathing sack of water, so the character creation process is tweaked to reflect this.

ATTRIBUTES

Metasapients don't have bodies in the traditional (or even non-traditional) sense. Indeed, many of them find the idea of physical sensation equally repulsive and compelling. However, they possess roughly the same level of mental faculties as metahumans. The sheer volume of processing power inherent to a metasapient grants it a slightly higher ceiling for cognition, but the lack of a shared *posteriori* knowledge base, combined with the obvious difficulties translating the experiences of the Matrix to those of the meatworld (and vice versa), means metasapients are less likely to instinctively grasp unusual or unfamiliar situations. Metasapients receive fewer attribute points than the normal Priority Level to reflect their lack of a physical form. If an AI finds itself in a situation not covered in here and a Physical attribute is required (using Control Device to drive a car, for example), use the Foundation Attributes table for conversion (p. 110) even if the AI is outside a UV host. Note that the Physical Limit is determined separately—see the AI Calculations Table (p. 155).

AI KARMA

AI characters don't gain karma, at least not the sense of a karmic energy that metahuman characters gather in their adventures. They do learn and grow, however, and the disorder in their hyperdimensional cognitive matrices is highly analogous to the game concept of Karma. AI characters earn Karma as do normal characters. However, AIs cannot use Karma in all the ways metahuman characters can: it cannot be drained by Energy Drain, given to spirits, or otherwise transferred. For all other intents and purposes, it is real Karma.

AIs may improve attributes, improve or buy new skills, and buy (or buy off) qualities, as would any metahuman. When an AI's Mental attributes are increased, its Inherent Limits and Matrix attributes are recalculated accordingly.

SKILLS

Obviously, the lack of a body limits the usefulness of a number of Active Skills to AIs. An AI may still learn these skills at the normal cost for use when remotely controlling devices. AIs may never have a Magic or Resonance attribute, and so they may not learn skills that require these attributes.

DEPTH

Depth is the special attribute that represents an AI's inherent ability to emulate and manipulate Matrix devices. When creating an AI with the Priority system or Sum to Ten, the AI chooses a starting Depth rating from the chart below. An AI created using the Karma build system starts with a Depth of 1. All of the advanced programs listed below depend on an AI's Depth attribute, as it performs the Emulate action. This attribute also serves as the maximum for an AI's Edge attribute. Depth can be improved with Special Attribute Points during character creation or with Karma. The Karma cost for improving Depth is 10 + (5 x new rating). The maximum rating for an AI's Depth at character creation is 6. During or after character creation, the character may purchase the Exceptional Entity quality to remove this maximum, but that simply allows for future growth. It does not allow the character to increase Depth beyond 6 at character creation.

AIs can learn a number of programs equal to their Depth + Essence.

QUALITY ASSURANCE

Due to their unique nature, AIs may not take certain qualities. The qualities available for AI characters are listed in the AI Qualities sidebars. AIs have the same limits on purchasing qualities that metahuman characters have.

In addition to the listed qualities, AIs may possess traits that are unique to them.

POSITIVE AI QUALITIES

CHATTY

COST: 5 KARMA
The character is especially comfortable behind the mask of anonymity offered by the Matrix. The extra confidence grants the character a +1 to their Social Limit when communicating via AR or VR.

DESIGNER

COST: 6 KARMA
Some AIs are masters of restructuring firmware to achieve maximum hardware efficiency. Their self-designed home device (see Restoration and Realignment, p. 156) grants them an additional +1 modifier to the Data Processing/Pilot attribute and 2 points of noise reduction.

AI PRIORITY CHART

META	ATTRIBUTES	DEPTH	SKILLS	RESOURCES
A: Metasapient (4)	12	Depth 6, two Rating 5 Matrix skills	46/10	450,000 ¥
B: Metasapient(2)	10	Depth 4, two Rating 4 Matrix skills	36/5	275,000 ¥
C: Metasapient (0)	8	Depth 3, one Rating 2 Matrix skill	28/2	140,000 ¥
D: N/A	7	Depth 2	22/0	50,000 ¥
E: N/A	6	Depth 1	18/0	6,000 ¥

AI VARIANT ATTRIBUTE TABLE

VARIANT	WIL	LOG	INT	CHA	ESS
Protosapient	2/7	1/4	3/8	1/4	6
Protosapient Racial: Home Ground, Inherent Program, Munge, Redundancy, Real World Naiveté, Driven (Original Programming), Uncouth, Uneducated					
Metasapient	1/6	2/7	1/5	1/6	6
Metasapient Racial: Codeslinger, Photographic Memory, Speed Reading, Real World Naiveté					
Xenosapient	2/7	3/8	2/7	1/4	6
Xenosapient Racial: Designer, Multiprocessing, Photographic Memory, Speed Reading, Real World Naiveté, Driven (Original Programming), Uncouth					
E-ghost	1/6	1/6	1/6	1/6	6
E-ghost Racial: HELLO WORLD (Level 3), Lucky, Photographic Memory, Speed reading, Social Stress					

EXCEPTIONAL ENTITY

COST: 25 KARMA

AIs with this quality have broken the inherent limitations of their original programming and are able to raise their attributes beyond their natural maximums. This quality is similar to its metahuman counterpart Exceptional Attribute, with a few key exceptions. This can only be used for Willpower, Logic, Intuition, Charisma, and Depth, and it affects all five of those attributes. Three of them have their natural maximum increased by three; the other two have no natural maximum (Depth plus an attribute of the player's choice). Only one attribute maximum may be exceeded during character creation, and the player must have gamemaster approval to buy this quality. Depth cannot be the attribute that exceeds maximum at character creation. It cannot be combined with Exceptional Attribute, mainly because that quality is not available to AIs.

HELLO WORLD!

COST: 8 KARMA PER LEVEL (MAX 3)

AIs with this quality have an ingrained set of sanity-checking measures that help prevent Fragmentation after disruption. AIs or e-ghosts with Hello World gain +1 die per level on any tests to resist Essence loss.

INHERENT PROGRAM

COST: 7 KARMA

This AI evolved from a specific cyberprogram and never lost the functionality of that program. Players may pick one common or hacking cyberprogram (but not an autosoft) as an integral part of their character's Core. Inherent programs don't require an empty program slot, other than the one the AI is currently occupying, and are considered to be running at all times. An inherent program is deeply intertwined with the core programming of the AI and cannot be crashed with the Crash Program action.

POSITIVE QUALITIES

QUALITY	KARMA	REFERENCE	QUALITY	KARMA	REFERENCE
Animal Empathy	3	p. 145, Run Faster	Linguist	4	p. 148, Run Faster
Aptitude	14	p. 72, SR5	Low Profile	15	p. 149
Brand Loyalty	3	p. 127, Run & Gun	Lucky	12	p. 76, SR5
Bilingual	5	p. 72, SR5	Multiprocessing	8	p. 150
Chatty	5	p. 146	Munge	15	p. 149
Codeslinger	10	p. 72 SR5	Ninja Vanish	5	p. 44
College Educatation	4	p. 145 Run Faster	Overclocker	5	p. 148, Run Faster
Data Anomaly	3	p. 44	Perceptive	5 to 10	p. 148, Run Faster
Designer	6	p. 146			
Exceptional Entity	25	p. 147	Photographic Memory	6	p. 76, SR5
Fade to Black	7	p. 44	Pilot Origins	8 ea. (Max 3)	p. 150
Fame	4 TO 16	p. 147, Run Faster	Prime Data-Haven Membership	7	p. 45
First Impression	11	p. 74, SR5	Quick Healer	3	p. 77, SR5
Friends in High Places	8	p. 147, Run Faster	Redundancy	12	p. 151
Gearhead	11	p. 74, SR5	Restricted Gear	10 to 30	p. 149, Run Faster
Gifted Healer	2	p. 11, Bullets & Bandages	Sapper	7	p. 151
Go Big or Go Home	6	p. 44	Sensor Upgrade	5	p. 151
Golden Screwdriver	8	p. 44	Speed Reading	2	p. 149, Run Faster
Guts	10	p.74, SR5	Strive For Perfection	12	p. 17, Assassin's Primer
Hello World	8 ea. (max 3)	p. 147	Steely-Eyed Wheelman	2	p. 150, Run Faster
High Pain Tolerance	7 to 21	p. 74, SR5	Sense of Direction	3	p. 149, Run Faster
Home Ground	10	p. 74, SR5	Sharpshooter	4	p. 127, Run & Gun
I C U	6	p. 44	Sensei	5	p. 149, Run Faster
Indomitable	8 to 24	p. 75, SR5	Virtual Stability	5	p. 151
Inherent Program	7	p. 147	Solid/Legendary Rep	2 to 4	p. 149, Run Faster
Improved Restoration	3	p. 149	Trustworthy	15	p. 151, Run Faster
Inspired	4	p. 147, Run Faster	Vehicle Empathy	7	p. 151, Run Faster
Juryrigger	10	p. 75, SR5	Technical School Education	4	p. 150, Run Faster

NEGATIVE QUALITIES

QUALITY	KARMA	REFERENCE	QUALITY	KARMA	REFERENCE
Bad Luck	12	p. 79, SR5	Low Pain Tolerance	9	p. 82, SR5
Bad Rep	7	p. 79, SR5	Loss of Confidence	10	p. 82, SR5
Code of Honor	15	p. 79, SR5	Pacifist	10 or 15	p. 157, Run Faster
Codeblock	10	p. 79, SR5	Persnickety Renter	6	p. 152
Combat Paralysis	12	p. 80, SR5	Prank Warrior	15	p. 49
Corrupter	10	p. 151	Prejudiced	3 to 10	p. 82, SR5
Curiosity Killed the Cat	7	p. 46	Real World Naiveté	8	p. 152
Data Liberator	12	p. 46	Records On File	1 ea. (max 10)	p. 158, Run Faster
Day Job	5 to 15	p. 154, Run Faster	Signature	10	p. 159, Run Faster
Did You Just Call Me Dumb?	3	p. 154, Run Faster	SINner	5 to 25	p. 84, SR5
Distinctive Style	5	p. 80, SR5	Uneducated	8	p. 87, SR5
Driven	2	p. 154, Run Faster	Uncouth	14	p. 85, SR5
Easily Exploitable	8	p. 151	Vendetta	7	p. 159, Run Faster
Fragmentation	18	p. 151	Wanted	10	p. 159, Run Faster
Incompetent (be reasonable!)	5	p. 81, SR5	Wanted by GOD	12	p. 49

IMPROVED RESTORATION

COST: 3 KARMA

AIs with this quality evolved more effective regeneration routines in their source code. For every interval of the Extended Healing Test, if at least a single hit is rolled, one (but only one) additional box on the Core Condition Monitor is healed.

LOW PROFILE

COST: 15 KARMA

This AI has learned to minimize its shadow in the Matrix, allowing it to operate for longer periods of time before convergence. AIs with this quality generate half as much OS (rounded up) when performing an illegal Matrix action. This quality only works on actions made using devices directly, so the Emulate action doesn't benefit from its effect.

MUNGE

COST: 15 KARMA

Some AIs are datavores, meaning that they "eat" code to gain Essence. This process is called munging (pronounced "munj-ing"). When an AI munges data, it leaves behind random data that usually destroys or distorts whatever is being munged. For example, a munged icon might look like an indistinct mess, while a munged program would become either buggy or completely unusable. Protosapients have much simpler code in their cores and can drain Essence from any type of data that they find, but metasapients and xenosapients can only drain Essence from other Matrix Entities (sprites, AIs, e-ghosts). AIs cannot use Munge to drain Essence from physical or astral beings.

Munging a piece of data to drain a point of Essence takes a Charisma + Depth (10 - Attack), 1 minute) Extended Test. If the AI is interrupted during this process, the data remains intact and the Essence is not drained. To munge a file, the AI must have access to it. To munge a program, the AI must be in either the same host in which the program is running or the same Grid as the persona that is running the program. Any non-sapient program, icon, or file has 1 Essence for a Protosapient to drain. Sprites have an amount of Essence equal to their Level.

The gamemaster determines the extent of the damage caused by munging data using the following guidelines: An Agent/Pilot program or skill/know/activesoft

should have its rating decreased by the Depth of the munging AI. If this causes the munged software to reach a rating of zero, the software is totally destroyed. The same goes for a munged sprite's Level. The gamemaster may impose a threshold equal to the munging AI's Depth to read a file with a Matrix Perception Test. Icons may become twisted and corrupted, making them less identifiable, or at the very least more disturbing.

For every point of Essence lost by an AI it also permanently loses one point of Depth, down to a minimum of 1, as well as an advanced program (chosen at random) that can never be regained. If a target character's Essence is drained to 0, the character dies. An AI can only increase its Essence to twice its natural maximum. Any Essence drained beyond this point is lost; the AI's core can only hold so much at a time.

MULTIPROCESSING

COST: 8 KARMA

Multiprocessing grants the ability to process information simultaneously from multiple sources while online.

Combat still requires the AI's full attention, but multiple types of other more mundane tasks can be handled simultaneously. For example, an AI with this quality is able to browse the Matrix and simultaneously hold a conference call online, providing full attention to each channel of information. Observe in Detail (p. 165, SR5) and Matrix Perception Tests (except when it's an Opposed Test) count as Free Actions for the character. The AI also receives an additional Free Action per Initiative Pass when not directly engaged in Matrix or Vehicle combat. The AI can simultaneously observe a number of information sources equal to its Depth.

PILOT ORIGINS

COST: 8 KARMA PER LEVEL (MAX 3)

An AI with this quality likely evolved from a drone Pilot program and retained its abilities. The AI may "jump into" drones and vehicles of a particular type (aircraft, ground craft, or watercraft; chosen when the quality is selected), controlling them like a rigger even if the vehicle does not have rigger adaptation. Each level of this quality grants the bonus of a control rig of an equal rating. The AI is also capable of loading, converting, and using drone autosofts (AI-driven drones use the attributes, skills, and Matrix Initiative of the AI). Note that AIs with this quality are only able to operate a particular type of drone or vehicle this way (e.g., aircraft, ground craft, watercraft); any other type of vehicle must be controlled remotely using the Control Device action.

REDUNDANCY

COST: 12 KARMA

Essential algorithms, routines, and other program structures are multiplied in the core of the AI, making it harder to kill. The AI gets 2 additional boxes on its Core Condition Monitor.

SAPPER

COST: 7 KARMA

The AI has an intuitive sense for vulnerabilities in boot code. It receives a +2 dice pool modifier on all Format Device actions.

SENSOR UPGRADE

COST: 5 KARMA

The AI is an expert at tweaking the sensor settings of slaved devices. The AI adds a +1 to the sensor rating to any vehicle, drone, or device that is slaved to its icon. All functions of a single sensor array gain this bonus, if applicable. This bonus also applies to any device the AI is currently running on.

SNOOPER

COST: 7 KARMA

The AI is more effective at accessing and manipulating communication streams. It receives a +2 dice pool modifier when making Snoop and Jam Signal tests.

VIRTUAL STABILITY

COST: 5 KARMA

This AI is a master of juggling system resources to run more programs with less overexertion. The AI can load the Virtual Machine cyberprogram without taking the additional box of Matrix damage that is normally inflicted when its persona is damaged.

NEGATIVE AI QUALITIES

CORRUPTER

BONUS: 10 KARMA

AIs with the Corrupter negative quality suffered fundamental defects to their programming during their evolution. The AI has an unfortunate tendency to trigger mal-

functions in other programs with which it interacts. Treat this as if the AI has the Gremlins quality (p. 81, SR5) at Level 2. The gamemaster should also make use of this Negative quality for dramatic effect as best suits the story.

EASILY EXPLOITABLE

BONUS: 8 KARMA

This AI has a massive flaw in its code that actually weakens the security of any device it runs on. The AI doesn't provide a bonus to the Firewall attribute when it optimizes a device, and the dice penalty for placing multiple marks on the AI's persona is reduced to –3 for two marks and –6 for three marks. This reduced penalty is apparent to any persona before the attempt to mark the device is made.

FRAGMENTATION

BONUS: 18 KARMA

During its birth or because of Essence damage, the AI's core programming was fractured and failed to fully merge properly, or a core element to its programming was somehow deleted or lost. In effect, this creates fundamental flaws in the AI's "personality." Fragmented AIs suffer from effects best compared to mental disorders like schizophrenia or paranoia, which makes their behavior unpredictable. The gamemaster should choose an appropriate mental defect for the AI, one that both makes its character unique and hampers its functioning. The table provided offers some example existing negative qualities. At the gamemaster's discretion, this quality may inflict negative dice pool modifiers to certain tests, especially social interactions.

If chosen at character creation, the character starts off with an Essence 5 instead of the normal Essence 6. This cannot be raised to 6 during the character creation process. AIs can become fragmented more than once if they continue to lose Essence; apply a fragmentation defect from the table below for each point of Essence lost. AIs can only buy off this quality if they first restore their lost Essence (up to 5).

FRAGMENTATION DEFECTS

NEGATIVE QUALITY	REFERENCE
Addiction	p. 77, SR5
Bi-Polar	p. 152, Run Faster
Emotional Attachment	p. 154, Run Faster
LEEEEEEEROY JENKINS	p. 48
Loss of Confidence	p. 82, SR5
Nerdrage	p. 48
Paranoia	p. 157, Run Faster
Phobia	p. 157, Run Faster
Poor Self Control	p. 158, Run Faster
Social Stress	p. 85, SR5

PERSNICKETY RENTER

BONUS: 6 KARMA

The AI with this quality can create home devices (see Restoration and Realignment, p. 156), but it is limited in the type of device that it may use for this purpose. This quality is taken for a specific type of device (e.g., comlinks, drones, devices with a Rating equal to or greater than 4, etc.). The device must be able to load apps, autosofts, or cyberprograms in order to be a home device.

REAL WORLD NAIVETÉ

BONUS: 8 KARMA

As creatures of the Matrix, most AIs are at best ignorant of the defining aspects of the physical world; things like gravity, friction, and inertia have no meaning to them. Some AIs have never even heard of meatspace or simply refuse to believe it exists. Even if their original programming involved interaction with the physical world in some way, they may not fully grasp the entirety of it. As a result, AIs with this quality have little knowledge of the real world and may suffer hefty negative dice pool modifiers (at the gamemaster's discretion) when interacting with it or otherwise exercising knowledge about it.

NO STRINGS ATTACHED

AIs are truly device-less personas. At first glance they look like any other icon, but they are actually broken into countless pieces and scattered across the grid or host as data packets. Because AIs don't have a central nervous system or "wetware," they are able to survive this violent experience. Despite being scattered, the focal point of the AI's attention manifests as a single persona with a distinct icon and location in the Matrix. This icon can look like anything the AI wants and can be changed with a Simple Action (though changing its icon will not change the results of a Matrix Perception Test). Being on an open grid, without being fully located in a specific device or host, is incredibly unpleasant for an AI, as the constant flow of data will eventually damage their Essence. An AI can survive on a grid for a number of hours equal to its Depth rating before it must make a Willpower + Charisma [Depth] Success Test to resist permanently losing one point of Essence. The number of hits required is equal to the number of hours the AI has been on the grid past its Depth. An AI can reset the amount of time until they must resist Essence loss by spending at least (10 + Depth) minutes inside a device or host. The new Matrix protocols have made a harsh and unforgiving world for AIs, and wandering the grids is not something an AI should do casually.

AIs outside a device have only their Core Condition Monitor (see p. 154), and they defend against Matrix actions with only their Willpower or Intuition attributes, depending on the action. An AI without a device determines its Initiative Score with (Intuition x 2 + 4d6.) They must find a device to load onto then reboot in order to reset their Overwatch Score. AIs without a device cannot load any programs, be link-locked, or be part of a PAN or WAN.

AIs that have ownership authority in a host can take advantage of the advanced system resources and use the host's Matrix attributes as long as their persona remains in the host. They are also able to load cyberprograms and advanced programs (see p. 157), and deploy IC using the processing power of that host. An AI can only be given ownership authority over a host by a legitimate owner.

Convergence is different for AIs without a device and largely depends on whether or not the AI has a SIN. When the AI is on a grid and they trigger convergence, the grid still hits the AI with 12 Matrix Damage. If the AI has a SIN (or a fake SIN that tricks the equivalent of a Rating 6 verification system, p. 364, *SR5*), the grid's demiGOD pounds the AI with Crash Program actions until it is forced into realignment or escapes. DemiGODs will arrest realigned AIs by uploading them into a specially designed data prison with a specialized program. If the AI is SINless, the demiGOD may try to arrest it, or they may simply hit the AI with data spikes until it's disrupted (see **AI Matrix Combat**, p. 154).

If an AI hits convergence in a host, the response is the same for them as it is for anyone else. The host gets three marks on the AI's persona and starts deploying IC. If the AI manages to leave the host, they'll still have to deal with a demiGOD out on the grid.

EMULATION

AIs can perform Matrix actions without a device using the Emulate action. AIs use emulation to borrow some of the raw computing power provided by the device network that generates the grids to mimic the specific hardware the AI needs to perform a Matrix action. This is an incredibly complex process that only gets more difficult as the emulated hardware gets more powerful.

Emulated actions are subject to a (Rating / 2, rounded up) negative dice pool modifier along with any modifiers from noise or being on the public grid.

GOD and the corps aren't completely against emulation since it doesn't seem to impact the performance of their grids or any connected devices, but they're quick to punish Matrix Entities that use emulation for criminal activity. AIs are allowed to use emulation for legal actions on the public grid without accumulating an Overwatch Score. This courtesy is also extended to AIs with legal access to certain grids and hosts. The mark needed to enter a host counts as legal access, but provoking convergence makes any form of emulation illegal. Emulating on a grid where the AI doesn't have a Lifestyle or SIN-based access is illegal. Illegal actions performed using emulation can significantly raise an AI character's Overwatch Score, depending on how much power the

AI wants to emulate. The higher the rating of the action, the more attention it draws from GOD.

To use the Emulate action, the AI first chooses a standard Matrix action to perform (see p. 237, *SR5*), then the AI selects the rating it wants to assign to the appropriate Matrix attribute (generally Attack, Sleaze, Data Processing, or Firewall). The value of the chosen rating is then immediately added to the character's Overwatch Score, and the action is attempted with a negative dice pool modifier equal to (Rating / 2, rounded up). The gamemaster should still add the defender's hits to the AI character's OS afterward. This ability can be used anywhere the AI has a Matrix signal and can still be used while the AI is loaded on a device that is connected to a grid. An AI can emulate Matrix attributes with a rating equal to its Depth.

Failing an illegal action performed with the Emulate action has the same consequences as though the AI used a cyberdeck. This means that failing an Attack action still bounces back damaging code, and failing a Sleaze action gives the owner of a device a mark on the AI's persona. This penalty is in addition to the penalties associated with a glitch or critical glitch on an Emulate action test (see p. 154).

When an AI reaches convergence, grids and hosts actively try to stop them from using emulation instead of increasing the character's Overwatch Score. To do this, they throw malicious code into the processing power AIs are using in emulation. When an AI uses the Emulate action during convergence, the character must resist an amount of Matrix damage equal to the rating of the emulated action. This damage is resisted with Willpower + Firewall.

EX MACHINA

If AIs want to make a home, use their advanced programs, or interact with the physical world, they'll need to find a way to load themselves onto a device. AIs can only be loaded on a device that can also load apps, autosofts, or cyberprograms. Standard devices simply don't have the capabilities to load any outside software other than simple firmware and driver updates.

AIs are able to use the Control Device or Spoof actions to order to have a device load the AI into an empty program slot. An AI takes up one program/app slot on a device unless the device's rating is lower than the AI's Depth. In this case, the AI takes up two slots. If there aren't enough empty software slots on a device, the AI cannot load onto that device. This means an AI with Depth 4 could never load onto a Rating 1 device, for example.

When an AI is loaded onto a device, its persona automatically merges with the device icon, and the AI is given the authority of an agent/pilot program loaded by the device owner. If there is already a persona running on the device, the AI's persona forms separately from it. Forming two personas from a single device is incredibly

taxing and pushes devices past their limits. Any Matrix action that does not target the other persona suffers a -5 dice penalty, as the processing power is simply too spread out. The AI effectively gets 3 marks on the device, but any persona running on the same device also gets 3 marks on the AI. Marks that the other persona and the AI had prior to the AI being loaded are still in place, but the AI and the other persona lose their respective ownership if the AI leaves the device. Rebooting a device that is running an AI reboots the AI's persona. Storing an AI in a device's memory and then reloading it also counts as rebooting the AI's persona.

When running their persona on a device, AIs are generally more powerful than they are without a device. They determine their Initiative Score with (Intuition + Data Processing + 4d6). AIs can also choose to use the Matrix attributes of the device they are loaded in or, assuming they have a Matrix signal, use the Emulate action to interact with the Matrix. AIs can also run advanced programs in addition to cyberprograms or autosofts to gain powerful bonuses or access unique abilities. Lastly, an AI can choose to make a device its home device, providing the AI with a permanent shelter against Essence loss and a bonus to the Matrix attribute array of the device based on the AI's Mental attributes (see Restoration and Realignment, p. 156).

An AI is automatically spotted by a persona running on a device when the AI loads onto the same device, and AIs cannot use the Hide action against personas running on the same device. While the other personas are automatically aware that a new program is running on their device, they must succeed in an Opposed Matrix Perception Test against the AI to reveal its true nature. The first net hit reveals that the program is an AI, and any subsequent hits provide further details about the AI, such as type of AI, advanced programs, or qualities. Matrix Perception tests will never reveal an AI's exact Depth, but it can give an impression of roughly how "deep" the AI is.

Devices use personas to identify their owners, and AIs are able to subvert this protocol and illegally transfer ownership of a device without a Hardware kit. To do so, the AI must hack the device while running its persona on the device and using the Reset Ownership action. This is an extended test with an interval of one Combat Turn. Failing to transfer ownership before convergence causes a slightly different result, since GOD knows only AIs can attempt this. The grid still slams the device with 12 Matrix Damage and alerts the authorities, but instead of rebooting the device, the demiGOD reformats the device to delay rebooting for an hour, usually enough time for the AI to be taken into custody. Damage caused by grid convergence is often covered by device replacement insurance under the theft clauses, but buyers are warned to read their contracts thoroughly. Several major corporations, including Renraku and Ares, will not replace devices damaged by, or lost, to AI theft.

Matrix avatars grant AIs as much anonymity as they do metahumans, but unless the AI is running out of a device, it's easy to tell that an icon is not a metahuman-generated avatar. It's simply too crisp and too fluid when compared to the icons around it. However, it's nearly impossible to tell whether a persona is a "smart" program or a metahuman when an AI is running its persona on a device. Learning the AI's true nature by looking at its persona (as opposed to noticing it load onto a device as described above) requires an Opposed Matrix Perception Test (vs. Logic + Depth) against the AI to see which programs its device has running. Succeeding on this test will only tell that user that the persona is an autonomous program, unless the number of net hits is greater than the AI's Depth. If it is, the AI's true nature is revealed. Since it's possible that the character performing the test may not know exactly what pieces of information there are to be had when it comes to AIs (see p. 235, *SR5*), the gamemaster may decide what details are revealed if the nature of the AI is established. Some examples are: AI types, advanced programs, or qualities.

DEPTH ACTIONS

Depth actions are Matrix actions available only to AIs and e-ghosts. They require the AI to be loaded directly onto the device or host where they want to use the action. While the Grid Overwatch Division may claim that the new Matrix is friendly to AIs, the truth is that grids and hosts profile the activities of AIs. Most Depth actions are considered illegal, which means they initiate or increase Overwatch Scores. Failing a test where Depth is used as the limit raises the AI's profile in the Matrix significantly and increases the character's OS by an amount equal to its Depth; glitching adds (Depth x 2) to their OS, and a critical glitch adds (Depth x 3).

EMULATE (VARIABLE ACTION)

MARKS REQUIRED: SPECIAL

Test: (See description)

The AI performs a Matrix action using grid or host power to emulate essential hardware. The AI chooses a Matrix Action to perform and a rating for the appropriate attribute. The chosen rating is immediately added to the AI's Overwatch Score. The action is then performed as though the AI had a device, but with a dice penalty of (Rating / 2, rounded up). The AI can emulate an attribute rating up to its Depth. This action can be used anywhere the AI has a Matrix connection, including program-or app-capable devices and hosts. If the AI uses this action in a device or host, the emulated attribute rating replaces the existing device or host attribute for the test. Spending Edge to Push the Limit of this action increases the AI's Overwatch Score by the total number of hits it gets on its chosen test, not the action's rating. In all other respects, the emulated action abides by the same rules

of the Matrix action, including required marks and type of action (Complex, Standard, Free) required.

RESET OWNERSHIP (SPECIAL ACTION)

MARKS REQUIRED: SPECIAL (SEE DESCRIPTION)

Test: Logic + Computer [Depth] (Device Rating + Firewall, 1 Combat Turn)

The AI overwrites the owner persona on the operating system of a device, altering the protocols used to verify ownership. Changing ownership requires the AI to be running on the device it wants to steal, which requires either a Spoof or Control Device action (see **Ex Machina**, p. 153). AIs can only inhabit certain kinds of devices; the Reset Ownership action can only be used on devices that can load apps, autosofts, or cyberprograms. To take ownership, the AI makes an Extended Logic + Computer [Depth] (Device Rating + Firewall, 1 Combat Turn) Test. Succeeding in this test causes the device to reboot, dumping the owner if they're logged on. After rebooting, the AI will have full ownership of the device. The AI suffers a –2 dice pool modifier to all actions for a number of turns equal to its Depth after being rebooted. While not an Attack or Sleaze action, it is still an illegal action, one that reveals the character's true nature as an AI. A glitch on this test immediately adds the AI's Depth to its Overwatch Score. Critical glitching immediately provokes grid convergence. For more information on using the Reset Ownership action, see **Ex Machina** above. Most AIs are aware of the inherent risk of resetting the ownership of a device when they don't have control of the physical device itself.

AI MATRIX COMBAT

AIs have two different Condition Monitors: Matrix Damage and Core Damage. The Matrix Condition Monitor is determined with normal rules for Matrix devices (8 + [Device Rating / 2, rounded up]). Matrix damage done to the device currently inhabited by the AI does not cause negative dice pool modifiers to the AI. The number of Core Condition Monitor boxes is determined using the following formula: 8 + (Depth/2, rounded up). Core Damage causes negative modifiers in the same manner as Physical or Stun Damage. AIs don't have any Overflow Boxes; filling either of their Condition Monitors causes them to immediately be disrupted. AIs only have a Matrix Condition monitor if they are running on a device; otherwise they only have a Core Condition Monitor.

If an AI is not loaded on a device, all damage is dealt directly to its Core Condition Monitor. If an AI is loaded into a device, it shares that device's Matrix Condition Monitor. When an AI's Matrix or Core Condition Monitor is filled up, the AI is immediately disrupted. An AI always

AI CALCULATIONS TABLE

MECHANIC	FORMULA	BONUSES
Matrix Initiative (no device)	(Intuition x 2) + 4D6	—
Matrix Initiative (w/ device)	(Data Processing or Pilot) + Intuition)+ 4D6	Add Optimization bonuses for home devices before calculating
Condition Monitor boxes	Calculate as listed below	—
Core	[Depth/2] +8	Redundancy quality (+2 boxes)
Cyberdeck/commlink/RCC	[Device Rating / 2] +8	—
Vehicle	[Body/2] + 12 Matrix Condition Monitor: (Pilot/2) + 8	—
Drone	[Body/2] + 6 Matrix Condition Monitor: (Pilot/2) + 8	—
Mental limit	No device: [(Logic x 2) + Intuition + Willpower]/3 (round up)	Add Optimization bonuses for home devices before calculating
	Matrix device: [(Logic x 2) + Intuition + Willpower]/3 (round up) or Data Processing	Advanced Program: Abduction (Sensor only)
	Vehicle: [(Logic x 2) + Intuition + Willpower]/3 (round up) or Sensor/Data Processing	
Physical limit	Handling	Add Optimization bonuses for home devices before calculating
Social limit	Matrix (no device): [(Charisma x 2) + Essence + Willpower]/3 (round up)	Add Optimization bonuses for home devices before calculating
	Matrix (w/ device): [Charisma + Data Processing/Pilot + Essence + Willpower]/3 (round up)	Advanced Programs: Eguchi Smile (Icon) WATLAM (Drone)
Maximum Edge rating	Depth	—
Maximum Emulation Rating	Depth	—
Emulation dice penalty	Rating / 2, rounded up	—
Emulation Overwatch Score Increase	Emulated action rating	—

loses 1 point of Essence when it's disrupted, but it must also resist the Overflow Damage (that is, the number of boxes of damage in excess of its Condition Monitor) from a disrupting attack or risk losing more Essence. If the AI doesn't have a device when it's disrupted, it resists Overflow Damage with Willpower + Depth. If the AI was running on a device that is not bricked, the AI resists with Willpower + Firewall + Depth. AIs lose points of Essence equal to the number of unresisted boxes of Overflow Damage. Disrupted AIs also lose one point of Depth, down to a minimum of 1, and an advanced program, chosen at random. The advanced program may never be relearned. AIs take on the Fragmentation quality every time they lose a point of Essence, but only once per event, not once per lost point. If an AI's Essence is reduced to 0, its core becomes too corrupted to properly restore itself. The AI's code is still disbursed throughout the Matrix, and pieces of it may get collected into other AIs or utilized in some other way, but the character should be considered dead for all intents and purposes.

Bricking an AI's device also causes the AI to be disrupted. In this case, the AI doesn't get to use Firewall to resist any Overflow Damage. The AI must also resist an additional amount of Essence loss equal to the Device Rating of their bricked device. AIs may jump to a grid at the last second and escape disruption by burning a point of Edge (p. 57, *SR5*). Burning a point of Edge in this fashion also permanently removes one advanced program from the AI's library, chosen at random, that may never be regained.

Programs running on a device aren't affected by Matrix Damage, so AIs don't take Core Damage when their device is damaged. The exception to this is if the attacker is using the Deicide program. AIs that are successfully hit with a Crash Program action lose a point of Edge (not permanently!). When an AI's Edge is reduced to zero, the AI is forced into realignment (see **Restoration and Realignment**). AIs that are forced into realignment during combat make a Charisma + Willpower [Depth] Test at the end of every combat turn, succeeding in this test restores one point of the character's Edge. When an AI character's Edge is fully restored, the process of realignment ends. The realignment process immediately takes over all available processing resources in the device/host, diverting cycles to the AI's reconstitution. During this process, the AI copies random data input from every source to which it can connect. Visually, this process is quite apparent—the "light" in the host dims and the "air" fills with code fragments that are sucked into a vortex where the AI used to be. All activities in the device/host are hampered: apply a negative dice pool modifier equal to the difference between the device or host rating and the AI's Depth (minimum –2).

When actions are taken against a device with an AI loaded on it by a persona running on that same device, the AI uses the Matrix attributes of the device. The exception to this is Firewall. Simsense protocols mandate that metahuman users receive the benefit of their Firewall to protect them from malware attacks, and an AI cannot use a device's Firewall to defend against a persona running on the same device. In spite of this, the device's Firewall will protect the AI from outside attacks. For any actions made against the AI by the current user of the device, the AI resists with Depth in place of Firewall. All Matrix damage inflicted by a device that an AI is running their persona on gets applied to their Core Condition Monitor.

AI VEHICLE COMBAT

AIs can run themselves on drones that have available program slots (see **Autosofts**, p. 269, *SR5*), or they may choose to use the Control Device action from an RCC, cyberdeck, or commlink. AIs running on a vehicle use their Pilot rating in place of Data Processing to determine Initiative, Handling in place of their Physical Limit, and can opt to use their Sensor rating in place of their Mental Limit. Pilot is also used in place of Device Rating for determining the Matrix Condition Monitor of a vehicle. They determine their initiative score with (Intuition + Pilot + 4D6). Only AIs with the Pilot Origins quality may use autosofts in place of active skills, they also use their Depth in place of the Pilot rating of vehicles/drones they are running on. For more information about AI skill tests, see the table below.

RESTORATION AND REALIGNMENT

In any twenty-four-hour cycle, an AI must **realign** for 3 hours, similar to character with a sleep regulator. This process can only be carried out in a device or a host. During realignment, the AI checks itself for errors while a log file is created in the system of the occupied device or host. This also restores any expended Edge. AIs are particularly vulnerable while realigning and any Matrix damage done to their device also deals an equal amount of damage to their Core Condition Monitor, resisted with Willpower + Firewall. AIs that are realigning can also be captured with special programs. Capturing a realigning AI requires succeeding in an Extended Software + Logic [Data Processing] ([(Firewall) + Depth], 1 Combat Turn) Test. If this test is interrupted or the AI finishes realigning before the test is completed, the AI is not captured, and the process must be started over. Once captured, AIs are stored on offline devices or, in large-scale efforts like NeoNET's Project Imago, an entire offline digital laboratory. AIs consider fates such as these to be too horrific to contemplate.

An AI doesn't require ownership of a device or host to realign there, but it needs permission from the registered owner. This is sometimes handled as an innocuous pop-up prompt that many users click absent-mindedly. To make a device or host their **home**, an AI must first perform an **update** there.

If the AI realigns in the same place for a number of consecutive days equal to the AI's Depth, their log files are then analyzed and an update can be performed. During the first update cycle, the AI cannot unload itself or switch to a new device or host until that cycle is completed. If the AI leaves, the process must be started over. Updates require a Matrix connection. Once the AI finishes its first update, the device is considered its home, and the AI no longer needs a mark to load itself in an empty program slot, even if it's not the registered owner.

Leaving their home for too long may cause the AI to lose that place as its home altogether. The more complex the AI, the faster its compatibility with its home will erode. An AI can be away from its home for (30 / Core rating, rounded up) days before it is no longer considered the AI's home. At this point the AI will have to start an update cycle in order to recreate its home or find a new one (if the old home was lost or destroyed).

Being the home of an AI puts a strain on the device's resources, both hardware and software. A device must be kept in top condition, with the latest upgrades and technology, in order for it to continue to serve without breaking down. This cost is analogous to metahuman lifestyle costs, and an AI must arrange payment of this upkeep or risk losing its home. For every month the device is not maintained, the gamemaster should treat the device as though the AI has an equal level of the Gremlins quality. If more than four months pass, the device is bricked.

AIs may **optimize** devices after an update; this increases a single Matrix attribute of a device or host based one the AI's Mental attributes, as shown in the Optimization and Lifestyle Cost table. A different Matrix attribute can be optimized with a Free Action, but only one Matrix attribute can be optimized at a time. Optimization can also improve an attribute of vehicles and drones, but the bonus is a static +1. Optimizing always adds 1 to the cyberprogram, app, or autosoft capacity of an appropriate device. Optimization is a fragile arrangement that destabilizes in the absence of a perfect equilibrium; AIs must spend at least an hour a day in the device to maintain effects.

AIs with a home create a personal index there. This reduces the work needed for reassembling itself and helps prevent Essence loss on a grid. AIs can leave their home and exist on a grid for a number of hours equal to the AI's Depth x 2 before they must resist losing Essence. Running in a host or device that isn't the AI's home will only reset to the normal (Depth) hours the AI can survive on a grid. This index can also be used to aid in tracking an AI; gamemasters may choose to apply a dice pool bonus to Trace Icon actions if the tracer has access to an AI's home device.

PUTTING THE PIECES BACK TOGETHER

AIs have maintenance subroutines that work with code created within their homes to repair damaged code. While in its home, an AI can make an Extended Software + Depth [Data Processing] (1 day) Test, healing one box of **Core Damage** for each hit. Device damage is repaired normally with a Hardware Test (p. 228, SR5). If the AI does not have a drone capable of performing the repair, it will have to hire someone.

If either of the AI's Condition Monitors is completely filled, their persona is disrupted. This doesn't necessarily mean the AI is killed, though. If the AI has any remaining Essence after being disrupted, they undergo **Restoration** in their home after (30 – [Depth + Essence]) days. If the AI's home device was destroyed or is disconnected from the Matrix, the AI's persona will reform on the last grid it was on.

Artificial intelligences are intricate, dynamic programs and cannot be copied or have backups made by conventional means. Only certain AIs know the secrets

OPTIMIZATION BONUSES AND LIFESTYLE COSTS

Bonuses provided by optimization should be rounded up.

Commlink/cyberdeck/RCC/host	Vehicle/drone
Attack + (Charisma / 2) [Cyberdeck/Host Only]	Handling + 1
Sleaze + (Intuition / 2) [Cyberdeck/host only]	Pilot +1
Data Processing + (Logic / 2) Firewall + (Willpower / 2)	Acceleration + 1 Sensor +1
+1 Program/app Limit	+1 Autosoft Limit

Device Rating	Lifestyle Cost
1	Squatter
2-3	Low
3-4	Med
5-6	High
7+	Luxury

of how they reproduce, though the recent CFD outbreak seems to offer tantalizing clues.

ADVANCED PROGRAMS

AIs don't create new technology or programs out of nothing; instead, they utilize what already exists in a more efficient manner. In the case of programs, they are able to optimize and re-write existing software so that it grants them unique bonuses and abilities. These advanced programs need the resource libraries of their parent programs to be running on a device in order to function. This means they run on top of an already running cyberprogram and occupy the same program slot—essentially turning a pre-existing cyberprogram into a bigger, stronger, faster version of itself. Crashing the parent program automatically crashes any advanced programs that are connected to it. Advanced programs also need a certain amount of authority before they can be used, requiring AIs to place marks to get the effects. When determining the maximum bonus an advanced program can give to an optimized home device, always use the optimized device attribute ratings. Advanced programs are only available to AIs and e-ghosts and cannot be run on commlinks.

AIs would never deign to purchase programs on the open market; instead, they make their own programs and advanced programs, similar to the way technomancers make complex forms. They start programming on their own and make a Software + Intuition [Mental] Test; divide 12 by the number hits on the test to get the number of days it takes to learn it. AIs then spend 5 Karma to learn a regular program, 8 to learn an advanced program.

Advanced programs are almost impossible to register since it requires having the code approved by GOD. This would mean revealing the secrets of their code, which most AIs are completely unwilling to do. If a rare few AIs do make this Faustian bargain with a corporation, they are monitored so closely that a career in shadowrunning is no longer an option. As such, all advanced programs are considered illegal and attract attention to the AI. When an AI loads an advanced program, its Overwatch Score is immediately increased by an amount equal to character's Depth. If an AI has any advanced programs running, the gamemaster adds its Depth to any increase to Overwatch Score caused by the passage of time. Some advanced programs are only useable in a particular Matrix environment (Grids, Vehicles/drones, devices, hosts). Restrictions, if any, are listed in a program's description

Program: Every advanced program requires a specific cyberprogram or autosoft to function; this entry indicates which program that is. Unless indicated in the description of an advanced program, all programs are loaded with a Simple Action.

Marks Required: Advanced programs can directly manipulate the attributes or contents of devices, hosts, programs and files. This still requires a certain level of authority, which means that most advanced programs won't work without marks. The number of required marks is indicated in this entry.

ABDUCTION

Program: Clearsight   **Marks Required:** Owner
By improving on the predictive algorithms coded into Clearsight autosofts, the AI is able to improve the Sensor rating of a drone through abductive reasoning. Using the AI's ability to make conclusions based on conditional evidence, this advanced program allows the AI to interpret sensor output and infer critical details that aren't actually present in the sensor output. When the drone's sensors are used to make an Observe in Detail action, it gets a bonus to its sensor rating equal to the AI's Depth, (up to twice the original sensor rating). The Clearsight autosoft rating must be at least as high as the AI's Depth for Abduction to work. This autosoft can be shared using an RCC, but the AI must also be running on the RCC. Standard RCC autosoft sharing rules apply.

AUTHORITY

Program: Exploit   **Marks Required:** 1
Authority helps the AI convince devices that its orders are coming from a trusted and privileged source:

the owner. The AI receives a bonus to its Sleaze attribute equal to its Depth (up to twice the original Sleaze attribute) on any Spoof Command actions against the marked icon's devices.

CASCADE

Program: Decryption   **Marks Required:** 2
An AI with this advanced program is able to quickly analyze its failures, correct itself, and then exploit an enemy's weak points. Any time an AI with this program running fails an Attack action against a sufficiently marked icon, it gains a +1 dice pool bonus on future Attack tests against that target. This bonus can stack up a number of times equal to the AI's Depth. If the program is quit at any time, all accumulated bonuses vanish. They also vanish after twenty-four hours, as targets make adjustments and the old information becomes invalid.

EGUCHI SMILE

Program: Wrapper   **Marks Required:** Owner
This program helps an AI sculpt its icon in such a way that it perfectly mimics the appearance and mannerisms of a metahuman. AIs can create a metahuman "avatar" using standard Disguise rules, albeit without the need for actual make-up or clothing (see p. 136, SR5). Running this program adds the AI's Depth to the limits of Disguise and Impersonation Tests. This program is only useful for impersonating metahumans and can also be used to impersonate a specific avatar as long as the AI has an image file of them. The AI can also use this program with their normal Matrix icon and the Impersonation skill to try to pass as a normal metahuman user in conversation. This disguise doesn't affect Matrix Perception tests made against the AI, nor does it allow them to fool security devices that measure biometrics in the meat world, such as retinal scanners. If the AI successfully fools someone who is harbors a prejudice against AIs, or is simply interacting with someone who lacks such a prejudice, Eguchi Smile also adds the AI's Depth to the Social limit of any test involving skills in the Acting or Influence skill groups.

FNORD

Program: Sneak   **Marks Required:** 1
An AI can use this program to stay hidden from certain entities in the Matrix. Any marked non-sapient entity—agent, IC, technocritter, or feral AI—that fails to garner any net hits against an AI with the Fnord program on its first Matrix Perception Test cannot perform any further Matrix Perception Tests against the AI for as long as it remains in that host or on that grid. This can only be used a number of times equal to the AI's Depth. Once exhausted, the AI must first realign (**Restoration and Realignment**, p. 156) to use this program again. If a security spider or other IC icon marks the AI, no Matrix

Perception Test is required, and the AI is automatically spotted.

MEDIC

Program: Toolbox   **Marks Required:** 3

This program allows the AI to quickly repair damaged code in AIs, IC, or sprites using the system resources at its disposal. The AI makes a Software + Depth [Data Processing] (2) Test. The targeted persona heals a number of boxes of Matrix damage equal to the number of hits beyond the threshold. This program only heals damage to software and cannot be used to heal Matrix damage on devices or technomancers. The Medic program can only be used on a set of "wounds" once. Loading this program is a simple action, but using it to heal damage is a complex action.

NYETWORKING

Program: Cat's Paw   **Marks Required:** 2

An AI running this program can interfere with communications on the grid it occupies, slowing subscriptions and lagging connections. Any marked persona or icon that is on the same grid as the AI suffers a noise penalty equal to the Depth of the AI until the device is rebooted, or either the marked target or AI leaves the grid. Nyetworking interferes with all Matrix traffic, both helpful and harmful. This penalty also applies to any Matrix actions made against the marked device until the device is rebooted. If the noise generated by the AI is higher than the Device Rating of its target, the device temporarily loses any wireless bonus.

POKE

Program: Exploit   **Marks Required:** 1

The POKE program helps provide access to the low-level memory of a device. For each successful Opposed Test made against a target device's Firewall, the AI receives a cumulative +1 dice pool bonus to Crash Program actions against the target. This bonus can stack up a number of times equal to the AI's Depth. If the program is quit at any time, all accumulated bonuses vanish. They also vanish after twenty-four hours, as targets make adjustments and the old information becomes invalid.

PSYCHOTROPIC BIOFEEDBACK

Program: Biofeedback **Marks Required:** 2

This AI has modified a set of black IC protocols that allow it to afflict its targets with psychotropic biofeedback. If the AI inflicts Matrix damage on a sufficiently marked target, the defender must roll their Willpower + Firewall. The Biofeedback Filter program adds its bonus as well. Use the AI's Depth as the threshold for this test. If the defender fails, she is afflicted with a psychotropic effect of the AI's choosing. Psychotropic IC inflicts a short-term emotional adjustment lasting for (Depth) hours. This may include effects such as aversions to certain objects or activities, desire for a certain product, complacency or lethargy, guilt, paranoia, phobias, and so on. These may be associated with a specific trigger, such as an aversion to the Matrix, an insatiable urge to eat Nerps, a phobia of trolls, or frothing rage at the sight of Lone Star officers. Short-term memory loss is also an option. The target cannot be largely incapacitated or reduced to a catatonic state, but will behave in a markedly strange fashion, much like some CFD victims.

ROOTKIT

Program: Stealth **Marks Required:** 1

This program makes the AI much more effective at hiding its presence in the Matrix, allowing it to become nearly invisible to other Matrix users. Marked icons that make Matrix Perception Tests against the AI suffer a negative dice pool modifier equal to the character's Depth. The effects of this program end each time the AI enters or exits a host, hops a grid, or performs an Attack action. A successful Hide action restarts Rootkit's functionality.

RUST

Program: Guard **Marks Required:** 1

This AI has evolved advanced defenses that also reduces the Attack attribute of icons that damage it. Any time an icon inflicts Matrix damage on an AI running this program (or to its device), reduce its Attack rating by 1. This effect is cumulative, down to a rating of 0 and lasts until the device is rebooted. This program doesn't affect living personas or hosts.

SHUNT

Program: Shell **Marks Required:** Owner

They say a decker would throw his body in the path of a bullet before he'd let his deck come to harm; as it turns out, some AIs feel the same way. Before resisting Matrix damage to its device, an AI running the Shunt program can choose to redirect incoming Matrix damage away from the device to its Core Condition Monitor. The damage is resisted using normal rules (Willpower + Firewall), but any damage that makes it through the Firewall is transferred to the AI's Core Condition Monitor. An AI can only shunt up to its Depth in damage; any remaining damage is applied to the device. This program is only useable if the AI has a home device and is running on it.

SPOTTER

Program: Targeting (Weapon Type)
Marks Required: 3

This autosoft integrates with smartgun systems to improve the autocorrecting algorithms embedded in standard Targeting software. Anytime a drone running this autosoft fails an attack test while using the appropriate smartlinked weapon, it receives an Accuracy bonus equal to the AI's Depth for its next attack action (up to twice the weapon's original Accuracy). The Targeting autosoft rating must be at least as high as the AI's Depth for Spotter to work. To get this bonus, the drone must use a Take Aim action as its first action of the next Initiative Pass. The standard bonuses of the Take Aim action also apply. Any action other than Take Aim causes the drone to lose the Accuracy bonus. This autosoft can be shared using an RCC, but only if the AI is running on the RCC. Standard RCC autosoft sharing rules apply.

TEERGRUBE

Program: Lockdown **Marks Required:** none

An AI with Teergrube ("tehr-groo-beh," German for "tar pit") has some latent but very reactive black IC code in its makeup. Any persona that uses an action requiring the Cybercombat or Hacking skill against the AI has its link jammed open, link-locking them (p. 229, SR5). For each mark the target has on the AI, the AI gains a +1 dice pool modifier to prevent a successful Jack Out action.

UNCERTAINTY

Program: Cat's Paw **Marks Required:** 3

The AI with this program consciously alters the underlying programming of a host, making computer operations less certain for everyone connected to it. Any device slaved to the host occupied by the AI suffers unexpected errors more frequently. Anyone interacting with a device slaved to the marked host is treated as though they have the Gremlins quality (p. 81, SR5) at a level equal to half the rating of the AI's Depth (Max 4).

WTLM

Program: [Model] Maneuver **Marks req:** Owner

"Walk and Talk Like a Monkey," or "Wat-lam," is a catch-all term for any Maneuver autosoft that has been optimized to cross the Uncanny Valley by enabling more "human" movements and mannerisms. While primarily created for bi-pedal walker drones, some versions for other types of drones exist as well. Running this autosoft adds the AI's Depth to the drone's Pilot rating (up to twice the original rating) for tests that involve passing for human. The Maneuver autosoft rating must be at least as high as the AI's Depth for WTLM to work. Even with a bi-pedal walker drone, this will not convince a person who has gotten a good look at the drone that the vehicle itself is actually a human, but it can be very effective at a distance or in conjunction with a disguise. This program can also help the AI convince a metahuman that the drone is actually being piloted by a metahuman rigger. This autosoft can be shared using an RCC, but the AI must also be running the RCC. Standard RCC autosoft sharing rules apply.

If the AI successfully convinces someone that it's actually a metahuman piloting a drone, it can then use this advanced autosoft to turn up the charm. Add the AI's Depth to the vehicle's Pilot rating (up to twice the original rating) for any Acting or Influence tests made against a fooled character. Alternately, if the target knows the drone is being piloted by an AI and does not have any prejudice against AIs, the AI can also run this autosoft to increase their Pilot rating for skill tests involving the Acting or Influence groups.

E-GHOSTS

E-ghosts, also called ghosts in the machine, are very rare digital entities possessing the memories and personalities of people who died online, or otherwise had their personalities captured by the Matrix somehow. It is unclear what causes these e-ghosts to manifest. Some theorized that they are merely AIs created during the Crash that were somehow imprinted with the mental state of a Crash victim. This became harder to prove once e-ghosts of newly deceased people and "copies" of living people started appearing. One author has suggested that these aren't ghosts at all, but simply some sort of new program designed to emulate people based on the long data trail of their life's interaction with the Matrix. Others postulate that some sort of rogue program—a side effect of the Jormungand worm, perhaps— managed to upload the brains of people who were trapped and killed online, giving them eternal life as some sort of autonomous program. Still others point their fingers at technomancer trickery, or wonder if these are in fact ghosts of the spiritual sort, somehow trapped within the machine. The truth is that no one knows, and no one can even say with certainty if these are truly the ghosts of the dead, living on in the Matrix, or something else entirely.

In terms of rules, e-ghosts are handled like metasapient AIs (though they have their own metavariant qualities), which means that they have their own Mental attributes and skills, but also some unique abilities. The "programs" they carry are special abilities that help them

to navigate the Matrix. Gamemasters and players can choose to create an e-ghost character based on a deceased or living character from the *Shadowrun* canon or base the e-ghost on an original character if they choose. E-ghosts based on currently living characters should experience both concrete and metaphysical dilemmas as a result of their unique status as "copies."

An important element to consider when crafting an e-ghost is how good a copy it is of the dead character (note that copy quality is a separate factor, not dependent on the e-ghost's Depth). Most e-ghosts tend to be far from perfect copies. They may have only some or none of the character's memories, and certain facets of the character's personality may simply be missing. At best, an e-ghost is likely only to have a scattered recollection of their previous life. The memories most constantly retained are the events leading up to death, unfinished tasks, and major grievances. Some e-ghosts are such poor emulations that they have only occasional flashes of their former life, wandering confused and enraged through the Matrix. Others are unaware of their demise, believing themselves to still be alive, but somehow trapped online. A few are quite cognizant of their status, and they do their best to interact with Matrix users and establish networks that grant them influence in the real world.

EXPERIENCING A UV HOST

The metaphor enforced by a UV system is overwhelming—reality filters automatically fail, and all iconography is automatically converted to fit. When a UV host is accessed, the simsense signal is automatically amplified, elevating the virtual environment to the point where it seems more real than reality. Persona icons are usually discarded; instead, users typically appear as their normal selves (a sim reading of their personal mental image, so self-doubt or vanity may affect the final product), adapted to fit the host's metaphor. Software, complex forms, and even echoes are also converted, taking on the appearance of gear appropriate to the environment. Agents, sprites, IC, AIs, and e-ghosts are translated as devices or creatures fitting the metaphor.

To fully experience a UV host, a user must be running with hot sim. Users unaware of the potential risks may attempt to enter UV hosts in different interface modes, but UV hosts are configured to deactivate the safety parameters of AR and cold sim users. Users with hot-sim capabilities must resist being pulled into the hyper-reality of a UV host with a Willpower + Firewall Test using the host rating as the threshold. Users without hot-sim capabilities cannot enter and remain on the Matrix.

ACTIONS IN UV HOSTS

Due to the hyper-real nature of UV hosts, characters use their physical skills as if they were acting in the real world. The characters must be able to imagine themselves doing these actions though so their skills are limited by the character's mental abilities. If a character's Attack program appears as a handgun in the host, for example, he may fire it using Logic + Pistols rather than Logic + Cybercombat. This allows the gamemaster to run the UV host as if the characters were in physical reality. Characters may still perform Matrix actions, but when possible these should be interpreted as "physical" actions. Magic, of course, does not function in UV hosts. Marks and normal Matrix actions don't really exist in UV hosts (you can't use the Edit action on a real object!), but gamemasters may choose to allow players to try the actions and decide on alternate effects. Even though there are no marks, UV hosts still employ some level of authority-based access within the system (maybe in the form of locks or hidden objects).

The sheer power of UV hosts allows for certain things that are simply impossible on the Matrix. Directly connecting to a cyberdeck being used to generate a persona that is already in either a UV host enables players to hitchhike. This works the same as hitchhiking to a host's foundation (see p. 115).

THE PRICE OF HYPER-REALITY

UV hosts often have some form of IC loaded, but they don't use any sort of Overwatch Score or initiate convergence. IC acts of its own accord, though its behavior is usually in line with the metaphor of the UV host. UV hosts can still go on alert, though the host is bound by its own metaphor (guards with radios, sirens, messengers).

Dumpshock suffered when accessing a UV host is stronger than usual, inflicting 8P damage and doubling the duration of disorientation.

Some UV hosts possess the capability to alter subjective time, slowing it down or speeding it up, so that an hour spent in a UV host could seem like ten hours or ten minutes. Gamemasters are encouraged to use this power and play it up its affects to the degree that it suits their story.

The simsense signal transmitted by a UV host is equivalent in strength—and addictive potential—to a BTL sim. Every time a user logs off from the UV host, roll an Addiction Test (p. 414, *SR5*) to determine if they have picked up a nasty habit. Use the host rating as the Addiction Level with an Addiction Threshold of 3. Addiction to a UV host is the same as BTL addiction—a character who can't access a UV host on-demand can satisfy their fix through BTLs. Note that UV hosts are not addictive only to metahumans—AIs, e-ghosts, and even sprites can become addicted to a UV host. In their case, the addiction is in part due to the peak simsense signals, and in part to the feeling of freedom and power provided by UV hosts with high ratings.

INTO THE GREAT UNKNOWN

The Resonance realms are a strange and wonderful places located somewhere beyond the boundaries of the normal Matrix. Accessible only by hidden backdoors in the Matrix, these realms contain many secrets, including mysterious sprites, tunnels through the Matrix, and the collected digital history of metahumanity. Technomancers who journey to the realms may take advantage of the increased Resonance connection there to perform feats that would be impossible anywhere else.

These "miracles" ignore the fundamental rules of Matrix topology and security protocols, allowing technomancers to do things like learn complex forms without a teacher, create backdoors into hosts, recover data that has been "lost" or destroyed, and much more. However, simply traveling to the realms is not enough to perform such wonders; technomancers must also find and walk the proper path through the Resonance realms. This process, known as a Resonance Realm Search, pushes a technomancer to the limits of their skills and psyche in every way.

This section gives gamemasters the rules for creating and implementing Resonance realms and Resonance Realm Searches in their campaigns, as well as tips for keeping rewards balanced and searches appropriately challenging.

GOING TO THE WELL

In game terms, a Resonance well has a rating that represents its power. This rating acts as a positive dice pool modifier for all tests that involve Resonance, whether made by a technomancer or sprite: Fading Tests, Compiling and Registering Tests, uses of complex forms, and so on.

Dissonant technomancers suffer the opposite effect of regular technomancers when they encounter a Resonance well: they suffer a negative dice pool modifier equal to the well's rating. Dissonance variants of Resonance wells, called *Dissonance pools,* also exist. These pools have the same impairing effects on technomancers as Resonance wells have on Dissonant technomancers.

Resonance rifts may pull in unwary or unwilling Matrix denizens who have the misfortune of coming across one—a successful Willpower + Charisma (3) Test is necessary to avoid being sucked in.

FINDING THE BACKDOOR

Journeying to the Resonance realms is an option only available to technomancers who have undergone Submersion. The only other way for a character (emerged or not) to enter the realms is through a Resonance rift (p. 139) or by making a deal with a free sprite.

To find a backdoor, a technomancer must fully immerse themselves in VR and cut all active connections to their Living Persona. Places with high noise ratings are considered unsuitable. The actual process that a technomancer utilizes to harmonize with the Resonance is uniquely their own, though it is usually some form of meditation or activity in that requires intense concentration. By concentrating on the constant background noise and harmonizing with its frequencies, a submerged technomancer can trace the streams of Resonance back to their source—the Resonance realms. This requires a Resonance + Willpower + submersion grade (12, 1 hour) Extended Test. There is no penalty for briefly interrupting the preparation process, but the process is demanding and leaves no time for any activities other than the most ordinary tasks. Once a technomancer has located this backdoor, he can begin his journey to the Resonance realms—but he must first pass the Event Horizon (p. 163).

Gamemasters may determine that the initial search for a backdoor leads a character to a certain grid or host, possibly requiring the technomancer to travel to a local grid outside of their home sprawl or gain access to a restricted host. Alternatively, the trail may lead the technomancer to a Resonance well, suggesting some possible link between wells and the realms.

THE EVENT HORIZON

The Event Horizon is the barrier between the Resonance realms and the rest of the Matrix. Any technomancer who enters a backdoor to the realms must first pass through the Event Horizon. The form that the barrier takes is different for each technomancer and should reflect the true identity of the character trying to pass through it. A character's innermost thoughts, fears, regrets, and desires are laid on the table and then analyzed by the Event Horizon itself. This is an emotionally wrenching experience, augmented by the seemingly endless memory of the Resonance, and could prove too much for a character to handle. If a character cannot find a way to cope with the visions shown to them by the Event Horizon, their journey ends here. If two or more submerged technomancers undertake a Resonance realms Search together, they are privy to the experience through which each of the others goes.

NAVIGATING THE REALMS

Resonance realms aren't hosts, so they don't have host ratings, Overwatch Scores, or IC, but that doesn't mean they don't have rules or inhabitants. Gamemasters are encouraged to come up with unique rules of reality for individual Resonance realms, but the rules for standard hosts, foundations, or UV hosts can always be adapted in a pinch. The sprites in a realm should be powerful enough to present a serious challenge to a techno-

mancer, but they shouldn't be so powerful that progress is impossible (unless it suits the campaign.)

Every Resonance Realm Search can be broken down into a series of tasks that the technomancer must complete in order to achieve his goal. The gamemaster determines the number and scope of these tasks, but they should be weighted in accordance with the magnitude of the goal. Typically these tasks relate to the goal and the Resonance realm(s) being visited. For example, a search to erase data (see p. 163) could require the technomancer to track down all instances of that data, represented as fruit, hidden away in an expansive digital forest. Likewise, a technomancer hoping to acquire a powerful free sprite's source code should face numerous obstacles and challenges the sprite has placed before him. As a general guideline, the rating of whatever is the target of the search can be used to determine the number of tasks to be completed.

GOALS

The goal of a Resonance Realm Search may differ from technomancer to technomancer, but the following goals are the most common. For developing additional goals, gamemasters can use these as a guideline.

Create a Backdoor: A technomancer may search the Resonance realms for a backdoor into the foundation of a specific host. The technomancer must have previously placed a mark on the host in order to perform this search. If successful, a backdoor is created is created for Resonance x 2 hours. This backdoor can only be accessed from inside the Resonance realms and it can only be traversed one way, but multiple technomancers can pass through it.

Erase Data: This search allows a technomancer to permanently remove a piece of data from the Matrix. If successful, the data is eliminated or corrupted beyond repair, no matter how securely it is protected (non-Matrix information, such as hard-copy or personal memories, remain unaffected). Erased data still exists in the Resonance realms and can be retrieved through a Recover Data Resonance Realm Search, though it is made much more difficult by this action

Find Data: A technomancer who knows that a certain piece of data exists but doesn't know where to find it, can ask the Resonance itself. The gamemaster determines how hard the data's location is to find, based on its real-world availability. This search may also be used to find or trace a data trail, including one that was routed through the Resonance realms. Use this with caution—data is an important part of many *Shadowrun* missions, and this should not be so simple that it becomes a default way of gathering data. It should be hard enough to be an option of last resort, not first choice.

Glitch a Host: A technomancer can undertake this search to weaken the defenses of a host in preparation for a hack, or simply seek to disrupt it and create complications. If successful, Resonance turbulence disturbs the host for Resonance x 2 hours. The effects of this disturbance is up to the gamemaster, but may include a dice pool modifier for all actions made by the host and its defenses, unexplained program crashes, corrupted data, increased noise, and a scrambling of access privileges that temporarily resets ownership status of the host (making everyone an intruder, even the company spider).

Hide a Data Trail: A technomancer can undertake a Resonance Realm Search to find a way to hide his data trail. If successful, the technomancer's data trail through the Matrix after completing this goal is inexplicably routed through the Resonance realms for Resonance x 2 hours. Any attempt to track the technomancer's data trail from that period find that it simply disappears without explanation. Submerged technomancers may ascertain that such a trail has been hidden and may attempt to follow it (See *Find Data* above).

Learn a Complex Form: A technomancer seeking to learn a complex form can undertake a Resonance Realm Search to discover how the form works. The technomancer must spend Karma just as he would if he learned the complex form from a teacher or a free sprite.

Recover Data: A technomancer can undertake a Resonance Realm Search to retrieve data that no longer exists on the Matrix. Only data that existed at some point on the Matrix since the Crash is certain to exist, though some technomancers suggest that any data that has ever existed on a computer network or electronic device may be found by visiting the Endless Archive (p. 140).

Submersion Task: A technomancer undergoing submersion may complete a Resonance Realm Search in order to lower the cost of the submersion. Undergoing a task for submersion reduces the normal Karma cost of submersion by twenty percent (rounded up). The character must complete the task before undergoing submersion (at least twenty-four hours before the submersion session starts). The technomancer cannot "save up" tasks—only one task may be applied to any given submersion. If the character passes the task, he is able to undergo submersion with reduced costs. If he fails, he can either retry (without losing karma) until he succeeds, or pay the full price for the submersion.

DISSONANTS

Since the particulars of dissonant technomancers are tied to their personal cyberpsychopathic disorder, they develop their own unique ways to wield Resonance. As such, dissonant technomancers still follow the basic rules of technomancers (see p.249, SR5), but each dissonant technomancer pursues his own antithetical belief and thus follows a unique Dissonance stream that that fits his agenda.

The attribute used for Fading and the sprites each dissonant stream may compile are left up to the gamemaster.

CYBERDARWINISTS

You know that person at a party who insists on applying principles of evolution to everything, as if Survival of the Fittest should apply to social structures? And they think "fittest" means "strongest," not "best fit for a particular situation"? Yeah, those are Cyberdarwinists. They believe the strong will rule, and not coincidentally they believe they are the strong. Dissonance is the tool of their strength, and that's what they'll use to subdue the world. It won't be pretty, and it likely will involve some pretty serious monologuing.

DISCORDIANS

Tales of humans who should be close but instead wind up as mortal enemies are as old as time, and the Discordians take their cues from one of the oldest. They refer to Resonance-utilizing technomancers as "Cainites," clearly indicating where they think they stand in the whole good vs. evil thing. They believe the Cainites are traitors and need to be eradicated, so they obviously hope their naming conventions are not foreshadowing about who will win the conflict.

EX PACIS

An apocalyptic cult that managed to survive its own apocalypse. After helping bring on Crash 2.0 (when it was trying to bring on Ragnarok), Ex Pacis was thought destroyed. But some of its members have been sighted in Boston during the quarantine, and rumors persist that Pax herself is there. While the specific goals of Ex Pacis are not clear, the general strategy inevitably remains the same—bring on the end of this existence so the world can move to the next.

NYTEMARES

Possibly the most benign of the Dissonant technomancer streams, the Nytemares share some of the prankster sensibilities of the Electric Knights hacker gang. Their pranks, though, have a nastier, more dangerous edge. Twisting the sculpting of popular hosts into lurid, grotesque shapes is one of their specialties, and Sixth World rumors say they have their sights set on some massive AR alterations. If Seattle's Emerald City AR overlay abruptly turns to the Carrion City, everyone will know who's behind it.

THE SUBLIME

Where Cyberdarwinists think they will win over the world because they are the next step in evolution, The Sublime thinks they will win over the world because they're just going to seize the sucker. They have a serious superiority complex, seeing all metahumanity as tools for their use. Technomancers are perhaps a step above the rest of metahumanity, as they have Resonance-manipulating skills that might be useful

DISSONANT ECHOES

Dissonant technomancers distinguish themselves from the Resonance-based peers during submersion, when they pursue twisted echoes that suit their sensibilities. Here's a sample:

CONTAMINATE

This echo increases the grade of Dissonance in any one area, building a temporary Dissonance pool see Going to the Well, p. 162). To contaminate a host with a pool (and it must be created in a host), the dissonant technomancer enters and makes a Resonance + Software + submersion grade (1 Initiative Pass) Extended Test. Each hit increases the rating of the temporary dissonance pool by 1, up to a maximum rating equal to the Dissonant technomancer's Resonance.

This echo can be used to taint an existing Resonance well. This takes the same test as above, but with a negative dice pool modifier equal to the rating of the well. Each hit reduces the rating of the well. Once the well is reduced to zero, any additional hits are used to create a Dissonance pool.

All pools created with this echo disappear in (submersion grade) hours.

PRYON

This echo is named for programmable infectious subroutines that cause code-induced diseases (CIDs). The use of this echo has drawn a lot of attention from people looking for the source of cognitive fragmentation disorder, and a lot of the people doing this looking are convinced that Dissonant technomancers had a hand in the whole thing somewhere. This power can be used to spread two viruses, The Black Shakes and Dysphoria. To spread these viruses, Dissonant technomancers must make physical contact with an individual. They do not spread it to anyone they contact—when making contact, they can choose whether the virus is passed on or not.

THE BLACK SHAKES

Vector: Contact
Speed: See description
Penetration: 0
Power: 5
Nature: Biotech virus
Effect (Ongoing): Tremor

Symptoms of the Black Shakes develop over time, as the pryon damages neurological pathways. Each month after infection, the gamemaster may require the Black Shakes victim to make a Body + Willpower (2) Test. The first time the test fails, the disease kicks in and the character starts to develop unintentional muscle contractions involving one or more areas of the body (i.e., hands, arms, head, face, vocal cords, trunk, or legs). These are the shakes that give the virus its name. The initial effect is to inflict a –1 dice pool modifier for all tests involving Physical attributes. The tremors escalate with each failed test, to a maximum negative modifier of –4.

DYSPHORIA

Vector: Contact
Speed: See description
Penetration: 0
Power: 6
Nature: Biotech virus
Effect (Ongoing): Depression, Mania, Moods

Victims experiencing dysphoria develop unpleasant moods, such as sadness, anxiety, irritability, or restlessness. Over time, these can turn into unbridled manic or hypomanic episodes or debilitating depression. The victim displays symptoms of unbalanced behavior and mood swings in the early stages of the disease; these symptoms can then worsen under circumstances that reinforce those emotions. Gamemasters may require the dysphoria victim to make a Willpower (1) Test. If the test fails, the character will experience depressive or manic episodes. This can act like the Bi-polar quality (p. 152, *Run Faster*).

SIPHON

The Siphon power enables a submerged dissonant to directly attack a target's simsense connection. In order to use Siphon, the dissonant makes a Data Spike action using Cybercombat + Logic [Attack]. The defending icon rolls Willpower + Firewall instead of the Intuition + Firewall. If the dissonant technomancer achieves 3 or more net hits, the icon is immediately dumped, suffering Dumpshock (p. 229, *SR5*). If the dissonant scores more net hits than the target, but less than 3, the defender is instead disoriented and confused, suffering a –2 dice pool modifier for all tests for the next (submersion grade) initiative passes.

Siphon only affects personas using VR; it has no effect on AR users, agents, sprites, AIs, or e-ghosts.

MASTERING THE MATRIX

INTRODUCTION

A gamemaster running her first game of *Shadowrun* might understandably feel overwhelmed at the sheer scope of the Sixth World. It encompasses diverse genres from mystical terror and wonder to futurist cyberpunk dystopia. A balanced approach is required to properly blend all these aspects to capture the flavor of *Shadowrun*.

The Matrix is one of the most significant elements of *Shadowrun*, serving as a funhouse mirror that distorts and reflects our hopes and fears about computers and technology. This chapter helps you conceptualize the Matrix; break down the rules into story tropes, templates, and plots; and provides tips and tricks to making your scenes pop in the imagination of your players.

Integrating the Matrix scenes during a game session with active meatspace scenes can be one of the most challenging aspects of being a gamemaster. Mastering the Matrix reveals techniques to seamlessly blend the Matrix into a typical scenario without bogging down the game overall, ensuring that all of the players have their moment in the spotlight.

CONCEPTUALIZING THE MATRIX

The Matrix is the global computer network comprising billions of wirelessly connected devices connected to and accessed through grids. Content is often accessed and experienced via a persona—a virtual avatar that can explore grids and host systems within the Matrix, immersing users in a Virtual Reality world.

A host is an engineered, contained domain within the Matrix where a programmer has created a virtual world to interact with users. Programming a host is akin to being a director in a movie with an unlimited budget for special effects. She can create a virtual world that mirrors the real world perfectly in every respect or she may sculpt a fantastical realm of wonder. She designs the sets and backgrounds, determines the very laws of reality, and configures the exact immersive experience she wishes to share with the users.

The sheer wealth of possibilities within the Matrix can overwhelm new gamemasters seeking to write thrilling scenarios for their players. This chapter is designed to help gamemasters consider the tropes and allegories behind the rules in-universe to develop rich storylines.

A RETROSPECTIVE ON THE MATRIX AND SHADOWRUN

In the virtual world of cyberspace, data transfers happen in milliseconds, and economies of entire nations can change in minutes with a few keystrokes. In *Shadowrun*, the hacking rules streamline navigation of the Matrix in order to create a fun and dynamic narrative. And though both fictional and actual hacking constantly pushes the cutting-edge of our technology, the history of real-world hacking goes back several decades.

Hacking is a meticulous, painstaking process that can take years of work for little reward, and its reputation is clouded behind a haze of fear and mythology. For example, the first alleged appearance of the term "cyberpunk" appeared in a short story ("Cyberpunk" by Bruce Bethke) in 1980 featuring a belabored father protagonist whose computer-whiz son could change the real world by ruining credit ratings and emptying bank accounts.

This first impression of hacking shaped the hopes and fears of an era. The first edition of *Shadowrun* was published in 1989 when the concept of the Internet felt new and cyberspace was akin to the Wild West in the popular cultural zeitgeist. The implications of networked computing and compromised privacy raised significant questions at the time. Fear of government oversight and interference a la Big Brother into the average person's life helped spark the allegory of the all-seeing Matrix where anyone with the right skills can find out every embarrassing secret you might have.

Fast-forward a couple of decades and the tropes for the Matrix have shifted just as the visions of dystopia have changed to suit the times. Big Brother has been replaced by millions of little brothers all watching and reporting about the world around them. People detail personal aspects of their lives on social media themselves, a practice that would have been unthinkable just a few

years ago. The Internet is now used to share information across the world and bring people separated by geography together to collaborate on projects. During the 2010 Green Revolution in Iran, protesters begged social media outlets to halt cancelation of service so that their protests could continue to be covered and organized. Organized hacktivists make press announcements to declare their latest targets and to warn the world against corporate greed, religious extremism, and pissing off the little guy.

Today, people share personal information openly on the Internet but fear the loss of control, when sharing happens without their consent. But they also fear the individual's loss of access to the Internet and what it would mean to society to have this resource completely controlled by media conglomerates. These fears inform the portrayal of the latest version of the Matrix in *Shadowrun*.

STORY OVERVIEW OF MATRIX COMPONENTS

The Matrix is designed to be used for commerce, entertainment, and education. The megacorporations have spent a good deal of time and resources to ensure that it is an environment safe for their customers and their purposes. Their goal is to contain the wild and illicit aspects of the Matrix and restrict access to the grids, ensuring that it is an environment safe and easy to use. A good *Shadowrun* story is outside the bounds of such normalcy, featuring deckers and technomancers breaking corporate laws on a run. This section is an overview of the various components of the Matrix and how each of them might contribute to a scenario for your players.

PERSONAS

Personas are the movers and shakers of the Matrix. Most of the time, a persona is a person logged into the Matrix through a device or by using the Resonance, but some personas are actually agents or sprites—sophisticated programs that serve specific functions in the

Matrix. If the Matrix is a play, then personas are all the characters that might populate it and further the plot.

Users experience the Matrix directly through their persona, translating the flood of data into sensations that the user actually feels. This can be a double-edged sword. The environment in which a persona finds itself can change in the blink of a well-sculpted digital eye. Sensations of delight, joy, and triumph can be simulated just as easily as those of pain, fear, and humiliation. As a result, the experience of running in the Matrix can range from addictive pleasure to trauma-inducing horror. While the average Matrix user doesn't typically have this type of turbulent experience, gamemasters are very rarely concerned with average personas having an average day in the Matrix

A device or program may only project one active persona at a time (and conversely, a user can only use one device at a time to create a persona), but users may alter their personas to suit their needs to adapt to the local host (see p. 217, *SR5*). This allows for a certain amount of intrigue as players navigate through the host, uncertain whether the personas with which they are interacting are enemy deckers, dangerous agents seeking to harm them, or some other, more advanced manifestation of the Matrix.

HOSTS

A host is a domain—a virtual world—contained within the Matrix designed to provide a select experience to users. Users must navigate according to the host's own rules. This could range from mimicking the real world's laws of physics to a surrealistic, Dali-inspired dreamscape.

When entering a host, a player's persona might pass through a fancy doorway like that of a nightclub or a storefront, or might simply find itself randomly inserted into a section of the host. Once inside, the persona must follow the laws of that reality as constructed by its programmers. Since most hosts are designed to support multiple users, these rules generally follow patterns of interaction established in the physical world. Even the rules of the most outlandish host will be intuitively known to users. When brainstorming a host, gamemasters should remember that this technology is designed to be easy to use and accelerate work and play. A shopping mall's host is going to be designed to enable sales and encourage return visits; it's not going to be a dimly lit maze filled with dead ends.

The appearance of a host from the outside can be deceptive but often is related to its importance and influence in meatspace. A megacorporation-owned host might appear in the Matrix as a colossal construct that dominates the horizon, such as the Renraku Pyramid or the Lone Star building, whereas a local store or a private hangout might be the relative size of the local watering hole. The Matrix conforms to recognized standards, but the interior of a host may be sculpted to project any sort of setting or environment. A host can contain an ever-changing maze, a re-creation of a horrid nightmare, an adaptation of a favorite book, or a mirror of the real world. Any experience that can be seen, heard, or felt can be sculpted within a host. The owner of the host may adjust the laws of that reality to her whim. Changing a host's iconography is a tactic that some owners employ to catch unauthorized users unaware. If the theme of the host switches from feudal Japan to a baseball park and your persona is stuck wearing samurai armor in center field—well, that's probably going to draw some attention. Since this tactic can be disorienting for those not expecting it, it's almost never used on high-traffic hosts.

Many Matrix scenarios will involve shadowrunners attempting to explore and master a host in some fashion, such as learning the secret rules, breaking security protocols, or stealing important files (see Deeper and Deeper, p. 106).

GRIDS

Grid is short for local telecommunications grid, a wireless data service that connects to the whole of the Matrix and is accessible by devices. There might be multiple competing grids in a specific geographic area, each appealing (and unappealing) in its own way to shadowrunners. Some grids are considered a free public utility, but typically the service is less than ideal. Megacorporations build their own secure grids for their purposes, but while these grids have better service than those freely available to the public, the thought of wandering around MCT's backyard can make even the most veteran decker a little nervous. Think of grids like neighborhoods. Some are nicer than others, some are bigger than others, and the populations of each one tend to share certain similarities. Working on a local grid in a strange country is likely going to be as foreign an experience as walking down the street outside your hotel window. It is possible to hop onto a grid without a mark, but for many hackers, this act marks the start of the ticking clock. The smallest of ripples can begin to draw the attention of the Grid Overwatch Division. Hackers risk getting caught by GOD if they make too many waves in a short amount of time.

DEVICES

The world of *Shadowrun* is saturated with devices. Just about everything is a device in the Sixth World: a toaster, a gun, a cyberdeck, and much, much more. The constant communication between devices forms the backbone of the Matrix, and it's also what gives hackers paths of ingress into places they aren't supposed to go. Exactly what a device does can vary wildly. A plant in a lobby may be in a wireless pot that alerts housekeeping when more water is needed. A refrigerator may read the RFID tags on the food wrappers it contains and create a suggested menu for its owner. Gamemasters should encourage players to think about not just the devices that make them better shadowrunners, but also those that transform how life is lived in the Sixth World. Alternatively, gamemasters should also think about what it means to not have access to devices, either through choice or circumstance. Players may opt for throwback gear and eschew devices as potential security threats. Let them do this, but make them realize the consequences of their choices. One way or another, life in the Sixth World is mediated by devices. Opting out isn't just a professional precaution, it's a social and cultural statement.

FILES

A file is a collection of data packed into an icon that can easily be accessed or carried by a persona. The data enclosed in a file can be anything you might find on a computer—a video, song, document, spreadsheet, or image. For story purposes, a file can be what Alfred Hitchcock termed the MacGuffin, the item of interest that competing parties wish to claim as their own. File icons can look like anything in the Matrix, from a shimmering polyhedron to a duplicate of the Maltese Falcon. The Matrix is designed with a certain level of virtual physicality in how users manipulate files and interact with the host. This leads to a number of possible scenarios with real-world parallels, including noir-style investigations to locate the right item, pursuit through the host from other deckers or even the host security system, or a classic thriller standoff against competing personas trying to take what they think is theirs.

MARKS

A Matrix authentication recognition key (mark) is a mechanism the Matrix uses to determine which personas have access to which files, hosts, and grids. Marks are normally invisible to all but their owner and always have some sort of thematic tie to the persona who placed them—a six-gun-toting cowboy persona might place marks that look like bullet holes, for example. Millions of people begin their workday prompting their employers' hosts to Invite Marks (p. 240, *SR5*). Based on their persona, and perhaps other levels of security for the truly paranoid employer, their particular host

will grant them access to the appropriate files, icons, and so forth. Shadowrunners rarely have the same luxury and are rarely interested in the access levels of a bank teller. A decker needs to make each mark she may need, which can be quite a balancing act as spiders, Patrol IC, and GOD all keep a vigilant watch for unauthorized users. It's important to note that while placing a mark with either an Attack or Sleaze action is illegal, actually having a mark is not illegal. Marks are the first line of defense that hosts use to verify personas, but by no means the last. Security spiders weren't born yesterday, even if that's when the bleeding-edge attack programs they use were developed. SOTA, chummer. SOTA.

OWNERSHIP

Essentially the step beyond the tiered system of marks, ownership grants various unique special privileges (p. 236, *SR5*). Ownership is linked to a persona. Much like thumbprints, each persona has some unique element to it that grids, devices, and hosts use to recognize le-

gitimate users and owners. These elements are generally invisible to other personas, so they can't be used by a hacker to distinguish two identical-looking icons from one another. Simply stealing a wageslave's commlink doesn't mean you're the proud owner of his fancy new car. In fact, there's a good chance that he's using his ownership privileges to trace his car's icon this very moment. Changing ownership legally takes roughly a minute, while changing it illegally requires an extended Hardware + Logic [Mental] (24, 1 hour) Test (see p. 237, *SR5* for more details). Performing this test requires access to the Matrix. While an icon can have only one owner, that owner can be anyone from Mr. John Doe to more abstract concepts, such as Saeder-Krupp Schwerindustriegesellschaft (three guesses who owns all their drek). For all intents and purposes, spiders operate with owner-level privileges within their employer's host.

NOISE

The new Matrix is a web of overlapping grids that often compete against one another, creating a phenomenon known as noise. Noise is unwanted data or wireless signals that make using the Matrix slower or more difficult. Noise follows guidelines according to distance and local traffic, but it also can be a story tool for the gamemaster to increase or lower the difficulty of a specific scenario as he sees fit. If a run requires access to a specific grid, noise might necessitate the shadowrunners breaking into a secure building to escape a spam zone in order to access the files they need from a corporate host.

OVERWATCH

With the advent of the wireless Matrix, earlier hackers were able to take advantage of its ease of access, creating a chaotic landscape that was simply bad for business. The megacorporations finally became desperate enough to cooperate in creating new security protocols that monitor and track illegal behavior throughout the Matrix. The Grid Overwatch Division (known as GOD) is the sentinel of the Corporate Court that monitors and enforces these new security protocols, tracking illegal users and preventing corporate espionage. Naturally, new exploits of the protocols were discovered, but the free ride was effectively over, and hackers scrambled to do their business in the shadows lest they be tracked and caught. GOD represents the ticking clock for scenarios and a hammer for gamemasters, giving players an ever-increasing sense of urgency. Once a hacker is flagged by GOD, she may face additional IC, heightened restrictions, or tougher security protocols.

DECKERS

Decker is slang for someone who hacks the Matrix with cyberdeck. Much more than a commlink, a cyberdeck is a device with specialized functions, advanced electronics, and firmware designed to crack engineered protocols used in Matrix security. The legality of owning such a device is questionable, and the price for an effective model tends to be way out of the reach of common hobbyists. As the megacorporations tighten their grip of control on the Matrix, deckers often see themselves as somewhere between an activist and an anarchist, thumbing their avatars' noses at the rules and regulations imposed from on high. To use the Matrix illegally is to court the wrath of GOD on a regular basis. Deckers do this as a matter of course. Deckers often hire themselves out for profit and the bragging rights that come from public shenanigans. Elite deckers are highly sought after for their unique skills, and they often spend much of their time building and maintaining their decks.

TECHNOMANCERS

A technomancer is someone who is able to hack the Matrix without the aid of a device. This strange ability defies known science and remains a mystery even to the technomancers. The corporate media often portrays all technomancers as cyber-terrorists seeking to destroy the Matrix. Many national and local governments require technomancers to register with the authorities, even if they have little talent or power. The perception of technomancers is that they are able to control a person's electronics, reading files at will, breaching every moment of privacy. Many believe that technomancers can see you through the devices in your home, trace your children, ruin your reputation and credit rating, launch nuclear missiles, drain your bank accounts, and steal your identity. Most technomancers hide their identity and their abilities from the public to avoid harassment due to the rampant public paranoia and occasional hate crimes. Technomancers differ from deckers not only in how they navigate the Matrix, but also in how they think about it. The Matrix is a second (or first) home for technomancers. It's not just someplace to go for profit and mischief; it's a digital ecosystem, one that requires attention, and the cultivation of which can produce amazing results.

DEVELOPING MATRIX SCENARIOS

Developing a dynamic Matrix experience presents gamemasters with a unique challenge. The scenario should simulate the imagined thrill of futuristic hacking without being bogged down with thousands of unneeded details and minutiae. Successfully integrating the Matrix into a campaign is as much about mastering pacing as it is understanding specific rules.

This section is designed to help gamemasters design such scenarios by breaking down important story tropes and translating them into the Sixth World context. The complexity of the Matrix can feel overwhelming initially, but gamemasters can learn to conceptualize the Matrix in terms of story potential over the basic mechanics, creating unique stories specifically tailored for their players.

COMMON MATRIX TROPES

Tropes are story techniques, narrative devices, and plot conventions that a gamemaster can reasonably presume are present in the players' minds and expectations. The trick is learning how these tropes can be used to tell a good story and then defining the appropriate decision points for the characters that can provide wonderful tension and challenging scenarios. This section contains classic Matrix tropes that gamemasters can leverage and modify to design their own unique stories.

THE HEIST

The heist is the quintessential trope for the Matrix dating back to the early days of cyberpunk fiction, involving a bold hacker (or a collection of hackers and allies) making a daring run against a faceless, monolithic corporation. A Jungian psychologist might compare this trope with the Greek myth of Prometheus stealing fire from the gods and sharing the secret with humanity. Many common shadowrun jobs can be boiled down to this trope, and an experienced gamemaster can mix the various beats to generate new scenarios that feel fresh yet familiar. This trope can be a challenge to run with a group of mixed characters who take actions in both meatspace and the Matrix. However, with a bit of planning and an eye toward the highpoints of the story's arc, it is possible to include everyone in the group and give them all their chance to shine. (For more information see **Running the Matrix as a Story Metaphor**, p. 175.) This section will break down the expected stages of the heist trope and then make suggestions on how a gamemaster might fulfill or subvert these expectations with her players.

STAGE ONE: THE PRIZE

The first step to crafting a good heist scenario is to define the prize. The prize for a Matrix heist is almost always some sort of paydata. The more creative details you provide about the paydata, the more enticing you make the target for your players. Typically, a prize in the Matrix will be some sort of data file that contains important or valuable information. Here are some good sample prizes that work well within the context of the Matrix and can be used to generate storylines:

- **Personal Information:** proof of infidelity—be it marital or corporate, family histories revealing a long-lost black sheep, correspondence about an upcoming business deal, or other potential source of blackmail.
- **Financial:** bank accounts, financial records and ledgers, and property deeds. These may contain information about a corporation, government entity, or an individual.
- **Research:** forecast and industry analysis (such as market trends, consumer needs studies, predicted depreciation reports, ecological impact data, or consumer goods studies) and data relating to medical and scientific studies (such as genome treatments/cures for hereditary diseases, or geological orichalcum deposit locations).
- **Technology:** schematics for new advances in devices and other technologies, security code specifications and hacks, and depreciated code or schematics from outdated or lost technology.
- **Art:** continual fractal digital art impossible to duplicate, access to the latest fashions before they are released on the street, or the scripts to this season's most popular serials (warning: spoilers!).

STAGE TWO: THE ANGLE

Once you have locked down the nature of the prize, you have to determine the angle of the story, the motivation for stealing it. The angle determines a good deal of the methodology of the heist. Here are some sample angles that might make for an interesting heist:

- **Corporate Espionage:** If you can't invent it, steal the plans and build a better mousetrap with cheaper parts. These heists require that you steal files and erase all evidence.
- **Keeping Tabs on the Competition:** Sometimes, the competition simply wants a peek at their rival's data to jump-start their own research or to give them an edge in business (such as catching their enemies at insider trading or working an inside track on a vendor bid). This involves copying the file without leaving any trace that the deed was done, requiring both subtlety and skill.
- **Sabotage:** Success is often measured in the failure of those who oppose you. To see your enemies suffer by watching everything they value burn is sometimes worth the price you fork over to shadowrunners. These sorts of heists are intended to smash as much valuable information and subvert as many resources as possible. Sometimes it's not about doing that damage yourself—you may just have to open a door wide enough for the common vandals in the Matrix to notice.
- **Ransom:** Want an edge in a business deal? Looking to catch the attention of the powerful? Steal valuable information and then blackmail them until they see things your way. This method often requires you to steal the file and erase any backups. However, finding a way to receive blackmail without leaving a trail to your doorstep is tricky. Sometimes your target will find it less costly to hire their own security team to trace the payments, and Mr. Johnson might find it easier to leave you hanging than to help you bolster your defenses.

STAGE THREE: MOTIVATION

Heists don't plan themselves. Getting all the details done requires motivation for a team of shadowrunners willing to risk their necks against the odds. Cold cash is the typical reward for any run in the Matrix, usually offered by a Mr. Johnson through your local fixer. However, some jobs have extra motivation that colors everything about the heist. Here are some sample motivations to turn up the heat for your players and get them hopping:

- **The Debt:** Sometimes the best way for a fixer to properly motivate a team of shadowrunners is to collect markers of debt they owe to the Underworld. This works especially well if the shadowrunners are in debt to people who have a particular urgency about being paid. There's nothing like the pressure to keep all of your fingers to make a risky venture seem all the more appealing.

- **Fighting Corruption:** All power comes from the barrel of a gun, or so the old revolutionary slogan goes. It's also said that anything worth knowing exists in the Matrix, enshrouded in 1s and 0s. To some people, the best way to force change on megacorporations is to shame them into doing the right thing, even if all it does is drain their PR budget for the quarter.
- **Redistributing the Wealth:** Some possible altruistic motives for datasteals include releasing a cure for a genetic disease, exposing corporate corruption, getting the data needed for justice to be done in court, acting as a post-modern Robin Hood, or finding leverage to help a group of poor tenants stay inside their apartment building.
- **Mayhem and Shenanigans:** Some folks just want to see the world burn. Corporate or government installations are sometimes too tempting a target to skip despite the danger. And if the shadowrunners can turn a profit on the side …

STAGE FOUR: RESEARCH, PREPARATION, AND PLANNING

This is the stage where the entire team can shine with a little creativity. Gamemasters should encourage players to play to their characters' strengths. Here are a number of examples of things a shadowrunner team might do to prepare for a heist run:

- **Dress Code:** Hosts, either implicitly or explicitly, have rules that govern the appearance that a persona can take while inside. No string of code prevents you from taking the form of a beer-bellied ork wearing flip flops and a Hawaiian shirt inside NeoNET's Boston host, but no one is going to believe that you're there for your 10 a.m. meeting, either. A mark gets you into the host, but once inside you'll find yourself interacting with personas representing thinking, rational people (who can't see your mark in any event). If you don't look the part, there's a good chance that someone will alert security to take a closer look. Doing a bit of legwork beforehand can let you know exactly what your persona should look like so as to draw the least amount of attention. Of course, it can also get you yelled at for not realizing the meeting was changed to 9:30.
- **Locating the Host:** The prize could be hidden inside a secure host. Finding the right host and the exact location of the file inside it will require research and investigation. Presuming that Mr. Johnson does not already have this information,

the shadowrunners might be forced to work undercover within the target organization and perform a little Matrix scouting.

- **Picking Your Spot:** Just because you know where the host is located doesn't mean you're good to go. Having a safehouse in a barrens area is great for physical security but can make for a poor Matrix signal. Finding an unobtrusive, low-noise spot from which to hack the host is a vital bit of legwork. This can provide a number of interesting side scenarios as the shadowrunners must infiltrate the corporate structure, deal with office politics, and avoid the attention of security.
- **Identify the Enemy:** Sun Tzu once said, "Know your enemy as you know yourself and victory shall be yours," and that was long before the invention of the Matrix. A smart shadowrunner learns about all potential threats prior to the run. A bit of investigation and hard negotiating might reveal what sort of security a host has and what kinds of agents, sprites, and traps might be within. A gamemaster might use this to her advantage to foreshadow dangers and amp the fear factor for the threats within the host.

STAGE FIVE: EXECUTION

Once the players have had a chance to review their information and create a plan, it is time to execute the run. Here are a couple of tips and tricks for ramping up the excitement of this stage of the heist:

- Try to balance time between meatspace and the Matrix. (For more information, see Tips, Tricks, and Techniques for Running the Matrix: **Juxtaposition**, p. 176.) Don't be afraid of pulling out the dice during tense moments. There's always the possibility of random chance inserted into a rational plan to keep the players on their toes.
- Remind the player about the consequences for clocking a high Overwatch Score. (For more information, see Tips, Tricks, and Techniques for Running the Matrix: **Overwatch**, p. 229, *SR5*.)

STAGE SIX: DOUBLE TROUBLE

A plan rarely remains intact upon execution. Here are a number of examples of complications that a gamemaster can throw against his players:

- Previous infiltration attempts have caused one of the shadowrunners to be noticed. It might be a wageslave seeking to cure boredom via an office romance or a nosey middle manager hoping to catch employees goofing off on company time.
- Someone else is daring to steal the shadowrunners' prize. If they want to catch the thief, they will have to avoid corporate security and move against a different team of shadowrunners. The

hacker will have to pit her skills against another hacker and the security of the host.

- Some say there are sentient things in the Matrix taking an interest in those who have potential. What happens if one of these beings interferes?

STAGE SEVEN: TAKE THE MONEY AND RUN

A heist almost never goes smoothly because there's no honor among thieves. Once the shadowrunners have secured the file, they have to figure out a way to exchange it for their pay without being double-crossed. Here are a number of fun potential actions that could occur:

- The hacker adds a tracker program that will help them map out Mr. Johnson's system and discover more about who hired them to do this deed. For an interesting twist, Mr. Johnson may be playing fair and level, but the fixer may be corrupt. The chance to get both the file and the money was just too tempting.
- The hacker needs to set up a drop box that Mr. Johnson can access by paying the agreed upon rate. Sometimes, this is set up with the fixer.
- Getting paid via the Matrix can be different than getting paid with a certified credstick in meatspace. Devious Mr. Johnsons may attempt to insert a program into their thank-you note that they can use to track the hacker, ensuring there are no loose ends.
- Very often the nature of the theft involves a lot more heat than the runners bargained for. The data they have is actually much more valuable than was described, and holding onto it can become a liability. Until they can unload the data, the shadowrunners find themselves the targets of competing crews and vengeful corps.

THE INVESTIGATION

The investigation trope reaches back to detective stories in noir settings where everyone has an agenda and danger lurks behind every corner. The Matrix is vast, and any sort of investigation can seem as impossible as finding the proverbial needle in the haystack. Investigations can be configured into many different scenarios with a bit of planning and imagination. In *Shadowrun*, there are just as many gumshoes in the Matrix as there are in the physical world. Here are some tips for gamemasters on letting their resident Sam Spade shine.

STAGE ONE: THE MYSTERY

The first step to crafting a good scenario is to define the mystery that you want your players to solve. The more creative details you provide, the more enticing you make the process of resolving it. Here are some examples of the types of mysteries that work within the scope of the Matrix and how you might use them in your scenarios:

- **To Catch a Thief:** The best way to catch a hacker stealing corporate data is to find a better hacker. Rather than face punishment from corporate, Mr. Johnson would prefer to hire outside of the company and clean up a mess before it costs his department dearly.
- **Seeking Lost Lore:** A client has hardware that is dependent on older code that's started to malfunction. The only fix is to find a pure source of the original code to write a patch. The problem is that the company that sold the equipment went out of business and their patents were bought up. Now someone is going to have to search through the records and find who has the software and discover where they have it tucked away.
- **Repairer of Reputations:** A new vidcast persona has started trending on the Matrix, revealing dirty secrets and sordid gossip. She's blackmailing a Mr. Johnson who's willing to pay a pretty penny to see the persona unmasked and stopped.
- **Don't Worry, This is Tech Support:** Some hackers earn extra cash as hired consultants to the corporations when things go sour inside of the firewall. It might be a rogue sprite eating the wrong data, a corrupted agent, or some long-forgotten string of code that is beginning to show signs of sentience.

STAGE TWO: CLUES AND LEADS

Once you have defined the mystery, you have to determine the clues and leads that help the investigator resolve it. Here some examples of the types of clues and potential leads that a gamemaster can place into the Matrix:

- **The Crime Scene:** Hackers who take illegal actions in the Matrix are monitored and tracked by GOD. A hacker with corporate permissions can review these security records to identify and track targets. Reviewing how a hacker attacked a host may reveal how she acquired her equipment, where she learned her trade, or information about her persona.
- **On the Grid:** To hack a host, the hacker needs grid access and a mark for permission to access said grid. If he's still logged into the Matrix, a hacker's marks may offer clues to his identity, especially if he has a distinctive flair in his operations.
- **The Local Hangout:** There are hidden hosts where the elite hackers visit with their hidden personas and exchange information and secrets. You can learn a good deal about a hack-

er and perhaps discern their motivations by the persona they present to the world. In the age of digital treasures and virtual worlds, the most important possession a hacker can have aside from his equipment is his name. A persona with flair can attract quite the reputation. The right hacker can sniff out facts from fiction and get a good idea of what he's dealing with.

- **A Witness:** Adding physical witnesses to the crime proves an opportunity on the meatspace side of the scenario. The witness could be other workers logged in at the time that the decker duped and moved past, to on-site personnel who may have seen someone suspicious who jacked in. This gives the group's face things to do, such as buying drinks for the new intern at a club. More thuggish groups might have their resident troll corner the IT manager in a dark alley.

STAGE THREE: THE REVEAL

The climax of any investigation is the revelation of the mystery's solution. Here are a couple of ways to turn up the heat for your players as part of the reveal:

- **Whodunit:** All the Matrix is a stage—you just have to find ways to get people to watch what you're doing. Staging a reveal can be complex, but if the story is interesting enough, a hacker can find viewers. Broadcasting such information can be the best way to ensure that something gets done about it, especially if you are clearing a friend of a crime.
- **The Showdown:** Once you find the culprit, you still have to bring him to justice. This requires a showdown, and the Matrix can be challenging. A team of shadowrunners will have to coordinate in both meatspace and the Matrix to track down the target and capture their material form while halting any damage they might do in cyberspace.
- **Turning the Tables:** Blackmail is only a dirty word when it's being done against you. Otherwise, it's known as leverage. Get the goods on your rival, and suddenly he's working for you.

GHOST IN THE MACHINE: GODS AND MONSTERS

The Matrix is much like an ancient city that has been built and rebuilt countless times. If you look in the right place, you can see the ghosts of ages past in the architecture of the now. There are mysterious phenomena revealing themselves as personas that exist entirely within the Matrix. The exact nature of these strange residents of the Matrix is fiercely debated. Some believe these are escaped AIs or magical spirits of the Matrix. Others believe they are the disembodied personalities of people trapped in cy-

berspace long after their deaths, perhaps the victims of Black IC.

The Ghost in the Machine trope explores this dark corner of the Matrix. Some might see this as a form of religious experience or experimental transhumanism where humanity touches the divine. (For more information on the details of these so-called ghosts in the machine, see E-Ghosts, p. 161). If gamemasters want their players to go on a ghost hunt—or better yet, be hunted by ghosts themselves—here are some story arcs they can use.

STAGE ONE: THE GLIMPSE

Introducing ghosts in the machine into a session should be done with great care and never when expected. Something unusual or impossible within the context of the rules of the local host should occur to signal that something is not right. Here are some examples of the types of situations that might work to introduce "Ghost in the Machine" scenarios:

- **Dilated Time:** Time in the Matrix works at the speed of plot, quicker than meatspace, but just slow enough to accomplish things in relative time parallel to events in the real world. What if the Matrix entity is about to overcome the host and slow time within it?
- **There Is No Spoon:** A host has a set of programmed rules of reality. A ghost in the machine can, and often will, break these rules with impunity. This should be a signal that something powerful is lurking nearby, and that alone deserves a closer look. The entity is able to subdue or overcome a series of countermeasures deemed daunting or even insurmountable to the decker.
- **Divine Touch:** The entity is able to touch the hacker and affect her devices in an impossible fashion. Perhaps it learns the true name and face of the hacker. Perhaps it can touch the mind of the technomancer.

STAGE TWO: COMMUNION

The entity will wish to communicate for an express purpose. Interaction between ghosts and players is often difficult because of the vast differences in the methods of communication until there is some sort of communion. Here are some examples of how said communion might take place:

- **Merging:** The entity might attempt to share experiences or impressions with an upload. This notion should strike the decker as dangerous or uncomfortable, and the merging entity will naturally cause some sort of overload.
- **Breadcrumbs:** Sometimes communication is simply too difficult between the intellects. The entity will leave clues and breadcrumbs for the hackers in an attempt to communicate.
- **Possession:** Agents and sprites often make

good avatars for such entities to possess and communicate through a limited filter.

STAGE THREE: THE BLESSING

The climax of the Ghost in the Machine scenario takes the form of a blessing, where the entity gives something to the hackers and bestows upon them a sacred task. So what does it look like when a being with an incomprehensible level of intelligence and no sense of societal ethics teams up with an all-too-mortal hacker who, let's face it, is probably at least mildly addicted to something? Here are some scenarios:

- **Task in the Real World:** An entity might be a god in the Matrix and have zero power in the real world. It needs envoys into meatspace to accomplish some sort of goal.
- **Revelation:** Often an entity is confused about its own existence and needs the perspective of humanity to observe itself and its own needs.
- **Uncharted Shores:** The Matrix is a universe unto itself and there are potentially vast swaths of it away from the main data hosts. What if the entity wants a partner in exploring the unknown?
- **Fourth Directive:** The entity is a corporate AI whose programming contains restraints preventing it from being truly free. It needs the deckers to help sever its last remaining ties.

RUNNING THE MATRIX AS A STORY METAPHOR

The Matrix is designed to be user-friendly. Corporations want users to work and play within the Matrix, so they made sure there were common protocols in host design. Hosts are not the representations of a specific device or location in the meatspace, but a virtual construct formed from the Matrix that can be accessed from almost anywhere without worrying about the distance involved. The dimensions of a host are different on the inside than might appear from the outside. It is a virtual environment of its own, with different boundaries, all chosen to maximize the host's purpose, be it selling cheap items to the masses or ensuring—with extreme prejudice—the integrity of research data.

How the gamemaster presents a host within the Matrix will shape how the players interpret the action and interact with the scenario. The best way to make the Matrix dramatic is to determine which story metaphors work best for the players and present the host in those terms. Some players want the action be cast into a visual metaphor so that they are not imagining programs and algorithms so much as virtual swords and bullets. Others will very much want to delve into the meaning of the

Matrix and simulate the futurist experience in terms of devices, structure, programs, and agents.

Players and gamemasters will need to work together to find the language about the Matrix that works for them, and this chapter should provide some alternatives. This section is designed to help gamemasters consider the potential story metaphors when designing an interesting host scenario. (If you are interested in the rules for creating a deep run on a host, see **Deeper and Deeper**, p. 106).

Here are sample story metaphors to consider when running the Matrix:

- **The Dreamscape:** The Matrix follows the logic of dreams. It's a metaworld within the world that only the strongest dreamers (a.k.a. hackers) can learn to affect. Users innately understand the nonsensical story logic within the host, while interacting in ways that make perfect sense within the context of the simulation. Information is designed by the developers to be processed non-logically and automatically downloaded via the device, much like a dreamer understands the environment of a dream. Users innately know if they can fly or leap tall buildings in a single bound in the host environment. A hacker can use dream interpretation to assign meaning to these scenarios, giving her insight into the processes of the hosts.
- **The Corporate Rorschach Test:** The Matrix is an unintentional reflection of those who create the hosts that populate it. The Rorschach test is a psychological technique used to evaluate a subject based on their intellectual and emotional responses to a series of inkblot designs. Some hackers have learned to read the environment of a host as an inverted Rorschach test that, if read properly, may provide insight into the culture and people that spawned it. A corporation known for children's toys and amusement parks that wishes to project a happy, friendly atmosphere might create a host that mirrors their lofty aspirations. Despite their intent, their host can't help but reveal a dark undertone, as the sounds of random children's laughter linger, and agents that stare unblinking at personas dot the grid, reminding the players of the eerie nature of unattended toys scattered about.
- **The Matrix as the Underworld:** The Matrix as the underworld is a gloomy, depressed realm where hope is lost, save for the spark brought into it by hackers. This reflects the myth of the underworld and the expectations that heroes will venture into it, bringing forth wisdom to the world. Agents become soulless minions of death, performing their functions as macabre judges of personas. If a gamemaster is using this trope, she should take care to describe the envi-

ronment with a dark quality using descriptions that stress the hopelessness of the situation. Every battle here is epic because to fail is to be trapped forever in this realm.

- **The Matrix as the Cave:** The Matrix as Plato's Cave is a world where the majority of users and agents are unaware of the true potential of the host. In his classic allegory, Plato likens people untutored in the truth to prisoners chained in a cave, unable to turn their heads. All they can see is the wall of the cave. Behind them burns a fire, casting distorted shadows upon the wall in front of the cave's prisoners. Lacking any sort of context to understand what they are seeing, the prisoners assume the shadows are reality. Hackers armed with the truth can break these chains to become virtual superheroes in a world of men. They have super strength, they can fly, and they have near infinite power against agents of the host. Players interested in this sort of visual metaphor won't look for emphasis so much on programs as virtual swords and big-ass guns.
- **The Matrix as the Singularity:** The technological singularity hypothesis states that the acceleration of progress in technology and computing power will result in an unintended consequence where artificial intelligence will exceed human intellectual capacity and control. This leads to society radically changing, or even the end of civilization. That particular conclusion is outside the scope of *Shadowrun*, but host-as-singularity focuses on the ever-quickening pace of the changes in the Matrix and technology as it nears an unknown but fast-approaching horizon. Hackers are armed with programs, decks, and their wits against this choppy sea of the unknown. If a gamemaster is using this trope, she should take care to use the jargon whenever possible to ensure that the players feel immersed into this world. Ensure that everyone involved with the Matrix has reviewed Story Overview of Matrix Components (see p. 167).

TIPS & TRICKS FOR RUNNING THE MATRIX

Once you've written your scenarios and decided upon the story metaphor into which you cast the action, you have to actually run the Matrix. The real trick for inserting Matrix scenarios into games is balancing time and pacing with the needs of all of the players. This section will provide tips, tricks, and techniques for hitting this balance. Players and gamemasters will need to work together to find the right methods that work best for them.

AUGMENTED REALITY

Augmented reality mashes together the Matrix run with the physicality of the traditional run. Noise, or simply an overwhelming firewall, can prevent a hacker from accessing a secure system from a safe distance. The good ol' days of hackers hiding away from the action alone in the Matrix are over. To be successful, hackers may need to get personally involved in the run with their fellow shadowrunners. They must keep an eye on the happenings in meatspace and cyberspace, sometimes seeing an overlay of both realities at once. This technique requires that the gamemaster keep close track of both scenarios and feed stimuli to the player in real-time. Here are a couple of tips for gamemasters to get the most out of this method into their games:

- **Rolling Tests:** Gamemasters should intersperse the hacker's tests with those of the other players so as not to break up the gameplay between the two groups. During Combat Turns, characters are limited by their actions and the pacing of the scenario. A hacker has to monitor the Matrix while also making certain a security guard doesn't pop a cap in her ass.
- **Hacking During Combat:** Make certain that the scenario includes areas that hacking can directly affect. If the team is squaring off against security and a call for reinforcements goes out, the hacker may be able to delay the message or possibly reroute it. Hackers can seal entrances, jam monitoring equipment, open locks, and disrupt communications.
- **Bricking:** A hacker with enough skill can brick enemy gear, tap into their commlinks, and generally make their lives miserable.

JUXTAPOSITION

The Juxtaposition method is when the gamemaster flips back and forth between scenes that occur in meatspace and the Matrix. This technique requires a good deal of timing and improvising from the gamemaster to ensure that all of her players are interested in the flow of the story. Here are a couple of tips for gamemasters to introduce this method into her games:

- **The Timer Method:** This technique involves switching back and forth between the two scenarios during a pre-determined interval of time. (We recommend that you set a ratio that favors the larger group of players. For example, if there are four players and only one of them is involved in the Matrix scenario, a gamemaster might reasonably set a time ratio of 3:1. Our brains are wired to react to pressure, and this simulates the excitement of a solid adventure. The gamemaster immediately switches to the other scene as

soon as the buzzer sounds, even if it ends in the middle of an action. The action isn't lost, but instead takes place immediately upon the scenario shifting back to the scene.

- **Dramatic Pacing Montage:** The pacing montage builds on the interplay between scenarios much like a director cuts a movie for the best dramatic pacing. The gamemaster follows the thread of a single scenario until it is dramatically appropriate to switch. If the scenarios have been designed to mirror each other, the advancing story will keep the players' interests even when the spotlight isn't on their character.

ORACLE

The Oracle method is when the hacker character is offstage from the action and serving as a virtual scout helping the shadowrunners with security problems, locked doors, and harrying the opposition to keep the team on track. The problem with this method is that the hacker is often less at risk, reducing the tension of her

scenes. However, if the gamemaster prepares ahead of time, she can use these techniques to give the hacker special attention without stealing too much of the spotlight from the other players. Here are a couple of tips for gamemasters to use this method in their games:

- **Hitchcock Tension:** The Hitchcock Tension method requires a bit of planning from the gamemaster and the players running the Matrix scenes. The gamemaster runs that scene ahead of time before the actual game. This way the hacker characters get the full attention of the gamemaster, but the rest of the game's pacing doesn't lag. The gamemaster keeps tracks of the beats of the Matrix scene and then allows the hacker character to interact with the meatspace game when appropriate. The potential downside to this approach is that it requires more time on the part of the gamemaster and the person playing the hacker and may lead to lulls in the action while the hacker waits for his next opportunity to get on stage.

- **Planning for Success:** Often, the player of a hacker will feel overwhelmed with the sheer number of choices available to her. One method to organize the scenario is to work with the player to develop a detailed list of what she intends to do and use this as the background of the scenario. The gamemaster should ask them to write down the steps of her hacking, starting with the grid she plans to access and then progressing through the Matrix to the host. Once the steps for breaching the system have been mapped out, the gamemaster can review the plan and then ask for rolls only at the most dramatic points. While the hacker is creating this plan, the gamemaster can work with the other players performing tasks in meatspace, such as legwork, surveillance, or gathering equipment.
- **Shut Down All the Garbage Mashers on the Detention Level!:** A gamemaster might feel that including Matrix scenes would overcomplicate the scenario, and so decide to restrict the hacker role to an NPC (or there might not be any players with a hacker character). This character becomes a voice on the commlink that can help the shadowrunners when it is dramatically appropriate—such as opening doors, unlocking data safes, and busting locks. Be careful not to allow the NPC to play hero at the expense of the players. But who knows? Perhaps if the hacker proves to be cool and useful, players will be tempted to try the archetype.

MATRIX ACTIONS AND COMBAT 101

Once you've mastered the basic concept of the Matrix and you've designed the scenarios, it's time to put theory into practice. This section contains common applications of frequently used Matrix actions, a few new Matrix actions to add to your decker's arsenal, and an example of Matrix combat to help gamemasters get a sense for how things go. (For the complete rules about the Matrix, see p. 214, *SR5*, and the remainder of this book.)

SIMPLE MATRIX ACTIONS

The Matrix is designed to be used by the average person. The following are simple Matrix actions that anyone with a commlink and access can generally do:

- **Change Icon:** A user can change their icon to anything imaginable as long as it conforms to Matrix protocols. A crucial tool for blending in (or standing out), your choices with Change Icon generally affect how other personas begin their interactions with you. You never get a second

chance to make a first impression and all that.
- **Matrix Perception:** Matrix Perception, like its meatworld counterpart, is a critical test for anyone remotely interested in working in the Matrix. It is most often used to check a file for data bombs or to pinpoint an icon that's running silently nearby. Most of the icons in the Matrix are bright, flashy things that are impossible to miss, but those are never the ones Mr. Johnson hires you to find. Matrix Perception allows a character to play 20 Questions (if they're on a really good roll—more likely the number comes in somewhere south of that) with the gamemaster. You can use it to scout an opponent by determining its current ASDF configuration, or you can delve into the recent history of a sought-after datafile. Matrix Perception is automatic for devices within 100 meters or within the same host; it requires a Computer + Intuition [Device Rating] Test if you are trying to perceive devices more than 100 meters from the device. If a persona is running silent, you need a Computer + Intuition [Device Rating] vs. Logic + Sleaze Opposed Test.
- **Matrix Search:** How can a decker find an obscure bit of corporate gossip about your latest target? By searching for it, of course! Gamemasters should feel free to make this as much of a storytelling device as they see fit. Not just simply putting a term in a search bar, Matrix Search (Computer + Intuition [Device Rating]) can uncover otherwise-forgotten details about who actually owns a property or a forgotten conspiracy theory group with crazy ideas about the runners' next target. If there are clues to be found in the Matrix-side of the legwork, they'll probably be uncovered with Matrix Search. (For more information, see p. 240, *SR5*)
- **Send Message:** Don't forget to call your mother! The lifeblood of team communication, sending messages and sharing video streams allows a run to go smoothly, but should a member's communication device go offline, things can break down fairly quickly. Smart runners will be wary of eavesdropping by spiders and others.

NEW MATRIX ACTIONS
GARBAGE IN/GARBAGE OUT (COMPLEX ACTION)

Marks Required: 3
Test: Software + Logic [Sleaze] vs. Logic + Firewall

This allows a decker to "cross the wires" of a single device, confusing its input and output commands. Only a single input can be changed to correspond to a single output—devices can't be reprogrammed wholesale or made to act in a manner outside of their original design through Garbage In/Garbage Out. For example, a smartgun-enabled firearm could be reprogrammed so that every time the fire command is given (through either pulling the trigger or DNI), the clip—or even the magazine—ejects. An elevator could be reprogrammed to go to the 23rd floor instead of the lobby, but a decker can't override its basic safety protocols since that would require multiple commands. Gamemasters have final say in what can and cannot be reprogrammed, but the rule of thumb should be "a single keystroke" of activity or the inversion of a binary relationship—the "friend or foe" recognition program in a smart safety system, for example. Rebooting the device restores the code to its proper state.

TRACKBACK (SPECIAL ACTION)

Marks Required: Owner
Test: Extended Computer + Intuition [Data Processing] (special, 30 minutes) Test

This test is only possible on grids, not inside a host. The datastreams that connect marks to their owners are barely visible wisps of information. Calibrating your filters to see them and not the billions of overlapping datastreams is a painstakingly laborious task. Once a mark has been detected on a device (see Matrix Perception, p. 241, SR5), that device's owner can try to follow the datastream back the mark's owner. The number of hits required is equal to 10 + the Sleaze rating of the persona who marked the device. If the Sleaze rating changes during the search, the number of hits required changes as well. If the persona that placed the mark is running silent, the trail will end in its vicinity, effectively letting the tracker know that a silent icon is nearby.

DECK CONFIGURATION

A cyberdeck has four attribute values assigned to its Matrix attributes (called the Attribute Array), which must be configured when booted. The type of deck determines the values that it may assign and the number of cyberprograms that a decker can load at a single time. Altering the values assigned to each attribute simulates what software the decker is actively running on the cyberdeck. (For information on cyberdecks, see p. 227, SR5.) Here are the attributes of a deck:

- **Attack:** The Attack rating reflects the ability of the deck to attack other personas and icons using programs and utilities. Attack actions are used to damage other operating systems, break encryptions, and otherwise disrupt Matrix icons. This sort of action tends to be loud, fast, and potent, but at a price. Attack actions almost always attract attention and are never subtle.
- **Sleaze:** The Sleaze rating reflects the cyberdeck's ability to mask the Matrix presence of the device, probe the defenses of its targets, and even subtly alter another system's code. Sleaze

software is quite useful for slow, deliberate actions when you need to get a job done quietly.
- **Data Processing:** The Data Processing rating measures a device's ability to handle information, data streams, and files. This rating is often used for general Matrix actions that aren't illegal or dangerous. It also influences how quickly a decker's persona acts in Virtual Reality, making it a valuable commodity.
- **Firewall:** The Firewall rating is a cyberdeck's protection against outside attacks. It serves as the file checker, virus detection, and general firewall software. Firewall serves as virtual armor against Matrix damage.

MATRIX COMBAT 101

Combat in the Matrix involves complex, yet subtle, tactics and strategy. The most important thing to remember when it comes to Matrix combat is to have a plan. Your plan may not survive contact with the enemy, but you should have some sense as to how your avatar fights. Does he run silently and do whatever it takes to avoid detection, quickly hiding if spotted? Is she a pugilist at heart, brutally attacking icons that stand in her way? Or is he a strategist, sacrificing specialization for adaptability? Here are a couple of basic concepts to master:

- **Initiative:** This is the speed with which a hacker reacts in the Matrix. It is largely determined by the mode she uses to interface with the Matrix. Note: enhancements cannot push past the maximum of 5D6 Initiative Dice. (For more information on *User Modes,* see p. 229, SR5.)
  - **Augmented Reality:** Hackers use their normal Initiative and Initiative Dice.
  - **Cold-Sim Virtual Reality:** Hackers use their Data Processing + Intuition as their Initiative, and roll 3D6 Initiative Dice. A middle ground of sorts, but not entirely without risk. Biofeedback damage taken while in cold-sim is Stun damage.
  - **Hot-Sim Virtual Reality:** Hackers use their Data Processing + Intuition as their Initiative and roll 4D6 Initiative Dice. Speed comes with its own set of risks. Biofeedback damage is Physical damage while using hot-sim.
- **Data Spike:** This is the main, no-frills offensive Matrix action in a decker's arsenal. Marks aren't required, but can help you pile on the damage that much more quickly if you have the opportunity to set yourself up for a knockout blow. Most corporate security spiders aren't terribly interested in being subtle or earning style points. If they've found you, expect a fair number of data spikes to be thrown in your direction.
- **Brute Force:** A blunt way of getting marks, Brute

Force sacrifices efficiency for versatility. A Data Spike will net you more damage out of the gate, but Brute Force can act as a setup blow, giving the decker more options down the line. Remember a successful attack action alerts your target to your presence, but not your precise location. If you're running silent, using Brute Force won't automatically reveal your location (while a failed Sleaze roll will), perhaps giving you a small window of opportunity.

- **Full Matrix Defense:** This action triggers the commlink or connected device into active defense mode, granting a bonus (add the user's Willpower to the dice pool, even if it has been previously added) whenever the user makes a Matrix Defense Test.

- **Reconfigure Deck:** Either through using the Configuration cyberprograms or simply swapping cyberprograms or Matrix attributes, reconfiguring your persona can mean the difference between life and death on the ever-changing battlefields of the Matrix. Using a Free Action at the end of your first Action Phase to boost your defenses against the incoming counterattack and then using another Free Action at the beginning of your next Action Phase to revert to the proverbial glass cannon is a tactic used by many deckers who are entirely confident that the second counterattack will never come. It was also popular with many deckers who miscalculated when it came to that second counterattack. Rest in peace, chummers.

- **Hide:** They can't hit what they can't see. Unless you've been marked, using Hide to disengage from combat can be a good way of buying yourself some time. If you succeed, your opponent will have to spend actions devoted to Matrix Perception tests. In a world where a nanosecond can make or break a man, that may be all the time you need.

MATRIX DAMAGE AND CONSEQUENCES

No matter how subtle and sneaky you are, sooner or later everyone takes a hit. Here are a couple of basic concepts to master before running through a Matrix combat scenario:

- **Matrix Damage:** The Matrix Condition Monitor represents a device's ability to handle damage. A device has 8 + (Device Rating / 2) boxes that represent the state of repair for the machine. Matrix damage is always resisted with Device Rating + Firewall. When a persona is hit for damage, the device it is running on takes that damage (except technomancers, who take it as Stun damage). (For more information, see p. 228, SR5.)

- **Damaging Hardware (Bricking):** "Bricking" is the slang term for when a device suffers enough damage that all of the boxes of its Matrix Condition Monitor are completely filled, causing it to malfunction explosively—complete with sparks, smoke, and small fires. These sorts of effects should be generally for show and not a source of Physical damage, although gamemasters may decide extreme situations warrant a Damage Resistance Test. A decker in VR mode is dumped from the Matrix when her device is bricked and she suffers from dumpshock. A bricked device is damaged and useless until it is repaired. (For more information, see **Bricking**, p. 229, SR5.)

- **Dumpshock:** A hacker forcibly disconnected from the Matrix while in VR suffers a nasty shock as his sim module kicks out. The Damage Value for dumpshock is 6S if you're in cold-sim and 6P if you're in hot-sim. Dumpshock is biofeedback damage, so you resist it with Willpower + Firewall. As if that weren't enough, you're also disoriented and take a –2 dice pool modifier on all of your actions for (10 – Willpower) minutes. (For more information, see **Dumpshock & Link-Locking**, p. 229, SR5.)

- **Link-Locking:** Getting link-locked occurs when a persona is frozen in the Matrix and is not allowed to leave. In essence, your on/off button is stuck in the on position. A link-locked user can't leave the Matrix or Reboot her device. The only escape is a successful Jack Out action (p. 240, SR5). Any persona (including an agent, technomancer, or sprite) can be link-locked. Typically, a decker knocked unconscious in VR will revert to AR, but a link-locked persona remains online and in VR leaving the hacker vulnerable to further attacks. (For more information, see **Dumpshock & Link-Locking**, p. 229, SR5.)

- **Illegal Actions:** All Attack and Sleaze actions are illegal Matrix actions and are tracked by GOD. If a hacker fails an Attack action, her target's security software rejects the code, sends it back to the hacker, and then alerts its owner. For every net hit the target got on its defense test in a failed Attack, the hacker takes 1 box of Matrix damage, which can't be resisted. If a hacker fails a Sleaze action, the target's Firewall software detects the intrusion, places a mark upon the cyberdeck, and informs its owner.

MATRIX COMBAT EXAMPLE

GAME INFORMATION

Haywire's Overwatch Score at the beginning of the scene is 12.

Having already entered the host, Haywire is running silently and using hot-sim VR, effectively offsetting the –2 dice penalty from being silent. She's using a Renraku Tsurugi cyberdeck with its ASDF values set to 3/6/5/5 to maximize her Sleaze attribute. Additionally, she's running Configurator, Stealth, and Baby Monitor. Once she spots the file, Haywire decides to switch some of her attributes and cyberprograms. The gamemaster decides to allow her to swap as many times as she wants instead of keeping track of how many Simple Actions she uses. Haywire's configuration changes to 6/5/3/5 and her cyberprograms become Hammer, Configurator, and Decryption. The loss of Baby Monitor means she'll be flying blind when it comes to her GOD score, but it's a risk she's willing to take.

Haywire slipped through the host, her avatar a merest flicker of a shadow. Her prize, a datafile containing damning evidence on a certain Ares VP, was in sight, but a security spider had taken up a position watching over the host's most sensitive files. Focusing on the file for a moment, a small icon of a wolf's head came into view—the marks of the spider, clearly showing ownership. Haywire's avatar shifted slightly, her sword growing in length and her ninja costume (her love of cliches knew no bounds) blending even more closely to the host's color palette. She moved slightly more slowly and some of the finer points of resolution were lost on her now, but she was willing to take the risk.

GAME INFORMATION

Haywire tags the spider with her signature shuriken mark using a Brute Force action. She rolls her Cybercombat + Logic for a total of 13 dice. She scores four hits, well under her limit of seven (Decryption added one to her Attack attribute). The spider is using a Hermes Chariot, is in cold-sim VR, and is not running silently. His ASDF array is set to 4/2/4/5, and he is currently running the cyberprograms Lockdown and Encryption, which bring his Firewall up to six. The spider rolls his Willpower + Firewall to defend against Haywire's mark, a total of ten dice. He only gets two hits; Haywire's two net hits are enough to mark him and inflict Matrix damage. Normally, this would only be 1 DV, but because she's running Hammer, the spider needs to resist 3 DV. The spider rolls his Device Rating + Firewall (eight dice in total) and scores two hits, taking one box of Matrix damage.

Since Brute Force is an attack action, two things happen in addition to her placing the mark and doing some Matrix damage. First, the defender's hits are added to her OS, making it 14. Second, the target is immediately aware of the action, even though he cannot currently see the persona responsible.

A small shuriken appeared in Haywire's hand, giving off an exaggerated glint that only she could see. *Mangadyne isn't good for much,* she thought to herself, *but they make the best damn skins out there.* A flick of her wrist sent the shuriken at the spider, striking him in the back. The response was both immediate and predictable. The host was bathed in a red light, and somewhere an alarm klaxon echoed off its virtual walls.

GAME INFORMATION

The gamemaster now calls for initiative. Haywire's Initiative Attribute in hot-sim is the sum of her Intuition (6) and Data Processing (3). She adds that to the result of her roll of 4D6 for a total of 17. The spider does the same—his Intuition is 3 and his Data Processing is 5. However, since he's only in cold-sim, he rolls 3D6 initiative dice. He rolls particularly well though, getting a total of 22.

On his first Action Phase, the spider needs to locate Haywire's silently running avatar. The gamemaster decides that the spider is certain there's something running silently in the vicinity (he was just marked, after all) and rolls the spider's Matrix Perception, a Computer + Intuition test. His eight dice generate four hits. This is opposed by Haywire's Logic (7) + Sleaze (5), 12 dice. Unfortunately, she only rolls three hits and is spotted by the spider. Note that while the spider can see Haywire's avatar, she is still running silently, so other participants in the combat will have to roll separately to see her unless she is marked. The spider then uses his Free Action to activate the host's alarm system, calling for IC.

On her Action Phase, Haywire attacks the spider with a Data Spike, rolling Cybercombat + Logic once again. This time, her 13 dice roll particularly well, getting her five hits. Unfortunately, her luck is contagious and the spider's Intuition + Firewall roll lands him four hits. Haywire's current Attack attribute is seven. The one net hit brings her DV to 8 and her mark and her Hammer cyberprogram both add an additional 2 DV on top of that, giving her a grand total of 12 DV. Not wanting things to end so quickly, the gamemaster has the spider use Edge to Push the Limit. The spider rolls his Device Rating (2), Firewall (6—Encryption adds one to the value), and Edge (3). After all the exploding dice are sorted out, he ends up with nine hits, taking an additional three boxes of Matrix damage, bringing his total to four boxes. Those nine hits are also applied to Haywire's OS, knocking it all the way up to 23. Haywire then uses a Free Action to activate her Configurator cyberprogram, changing her Matrix attributes to 5/3/5/6 and cyberprograms to Encryption, Shell, and Armor. The change in her Data Processing attribute also changes her initiative to 19.

Moving behind the spider—an old habit from the meatworld—Haywire thrust her ninja-to into his back. Vibrant, multi-colored ribbons spiraled out of the spider's now-flickering avatar as he crumpled to one knee. But he did not fall. Cursing silently, Haywire quickly called up a new array of cyberprograms, ones that could hopefully protect her from the oversized pistol that appeared in the spider's hand.

GAME INFORMATION

At the beginning of the second Initiative Pass, on the spider's Action Phase, the gamemaster decides to go all out. The spider rolls his own Data Spike, a total of 12 dice. The gamemaster decides to use Edge for a Second Chance to reroll failures, for a total of seven hits. Haywire resists with her Willpower (3) and Firewall (7, Encryption adds one), with an extra die from Shell and two extra dice from Armor, for a total of 13. Her dice let her down, rolling only three hits, giving the spider four net hits. In addition to taking Matrix damage, Haywire is now link-locked thanks to the spider's Lockdown cyberprogram.

With her newly adjusted initiative score of 9, Haywire enters her second Action Phase. She goes for the kill with another Data Spike, rolling her 13 dice (Cybercombat + Logic) against the spider's nine dice (Intuition + Firewall). Fate smiles on Haywire (at least for a moment) and she ends up with three net hits, putting her attack's DV at 14. With a sigh, the gamemaster uses the spider's last point of Edge to Push the Limit on his Matrix Damage Resistance Test, once again rolling Device Rating + Firewall + Edge. His dice roll well, but not well enough, and the seven hits only reduce the damage to seven boxes, bricking the spider's cyberdeck (and ending the link-lock). Haywire's OS also increases to 30, giving her very little wiggle room to crack the file in front of her.

The attack didn't surprise Haywire, but its ferocity did—the extra defenses she had erected were torn apart, but they likely saved her life. Coughing up a series of ones and zeroes, Haywire struck again, severing the spider's head. She was already off schedule and knew the host would be crawling with IC in a matter of three heartbeats. A second shuriken appeared in her hand. She was going to claim her prize before that happened.